SCHOOL OF ORIENTAL AND AFRICAN STUDIES
University of London

Please return this book on or before the last date shown

Long loans and One Week loans may be renewed up to 10 times
Short loans & CDs cannot be renewed
Fines are charged on all overdue items

Online: http://lib.soas.ac.uk/patroninfo
Phone: 020-7898 4197 (answerphone)

- 1 DEC 2003

1 9 JAN 2004

DISCONSOLATE EMPIRES

French, British and Belgian Military Involvement in Post-Colonial Sub-Saharan Africa

Alain Rouvez

with the assistance of:
Michael Coco
Jean-Paul Paddack

UNIVERSITY
PRESS OF
AMERICA

Lanham • New York • London

Copyright © 1994 by
University Press of America® Inc.
4720 Boston Way
Lanham, Maryland 20706

3 Henrietta Street
London WC2E 8LU England

Library of Congress Cataloging-in-Publication Data
Rouvez, Alain.
Disconsolate empires : French, British, and Belgian military
involvement in post-colonial Sub-Saharan Africa / Alain Rouvez
with the assistance of Michael Coco, Jean-Paul Paddack.
p.   cm.
Includes bibliographical references and index.
1. Africa, Sub-Saharan—Foreign relations—1960–   2. Africa,
Sub-Saharan—History—1960–   3. Africa, Sub-Saharan—
Relations—Europe. 4. Europe—Foreign relations—Africa, Sub-
Saharan. I. Coco, Michael. II. Paddack, Jean-Paul. III. Title.
DT353.5.E9R68   1994
327.44067'09'045—dc20   94–22104 CIP

ISBN 0–8191–9643–6 (cloth : alk. paper)

The paper used in this publication meets the minimum requirements of
American National Standard for Information Sciences—Permanence
of Paper for Printed Library Materials, ANSI Z39.48–1984.

La véritable tradition dans les grandes choses, ce n'est pas de refaire ce que les autres ont fait, c'est de retrouver l'esprit qui a fait les choses et qui en ferait faire de tout autres dans d'autres temps.

Paul Valéry

To my father,
for whom time was too short
to see the completion of this work.

Contents

Tables

Preface

The second half of the 20th century has witnessed the decline and dismantlement of many powerful colonial empires. They seemed to have outlived their historic role as the cost of keeping them exceeded the price that the "center" was ready to commit to preserve its hold over the "periphery." Rarely in the history of nations are the sovereign claims of the latter able to overrule the proprietary disposition of the former. When it happens, however, the transfer of power is sometimes not completed fast enough for all parties concerned. Or so it seems when analyzing the remarkable speed with which colonial empires disappeared, even considering the relatively longer agony of the Portuguese empire.

As the colonial order broke down, new governing principles in international affairs readily filled the power vacuum. Firstly, the period after World War II saw the emergence of a protracted Cold War, which divided many Third World nations into ideological blocs. Secondly, some of the former colonial powers seemed to suffer from persistent separation anxiety. France, and to a lesser extent Britain and Belgium, chose to retain some form of structured influence in their former colonial possessions, especially in sub-Saharan Africa. The structures they set up were a unique manifestation of a new, limited order in North-South relationships, deployed against the global constraints of the Cold War. The manner in which those structures were organized reflected the deeper aspects of the true national characters of France, Britain and Belgium. The detached pragmatism of Britain stands in contrast with the elaborate construction of France's relationships with parts of its former colonial realm, or with Belgium's frustrating efforts to preserve its interests in central Africa. Underscoring these attempts was the fact that the complex set of mutual dependency links created under the colonial empires failed to disappear overnight. Persuasion and diplomacy replaced direct domination in a world of sovereign, if unequal, states. Military might in the post-imperial era remained a source of influence, even though the rules of engagement had been radically altered.

After close to 35 years of experience, post-imperial relationships between metropoles and their former possessions continue to matter. The legacies of empire remain visible for decades, even though many transformations may have reconfigured the international order. The end of the Cold War did not suddenly change the zones and means of influence that France, Britain and Belgium were able to preserve in sub-Saharan Africa.

This work was initially proposed to the United States Institute of Peace, in Washington, D.C., as a contribution to the understanding of regional conflicts in the post-Cold War world. Did French, British and Belgium military involvement in sub-Saharan Africa help to regulate and reduce levels of conflict in this part of the Third World? The divergent experience among the three former colonial powers attests to the lack of a simple answer.

Acknowledgments

Writing a book, it turned out, is a somewhat laborious way to accumulate debts. The creditors - who should know better - are friends: some of them old and some of them met in the course of researching and writing this book. The currency is gratitude, never bestowed generously enough. Among those to whom I am immensely indebted figures W. Scott Thompson, whose unflinching faith in my ability to complete this work must have tested the limits of human patience. When research and editing are performed with the skills and intellectual grasp of Michael Coco, then the author should humbly acknowledge that his accomplishment has to be shared. Jean-Paul Paddack, before leaving for Madagascar, stood by during the exhilarating period of initial research and interviews. Jean Barrea provided his qualified advice on some key conceptual structures.

Indefatigable proofreader and stimulating reviewer, Gerry Landry never failed to accept the burden of my drafts and to share his knowledge and kindness. And there are those who shaped the book in its presentation, while crossing out my many offenses against the rules of the English language: Asta Zinbo, Geraldine Lampert, Dominique Paddack, Errol Vanderhorst, and Barbra Dorr.

Discretion demands that I not list the people whom I interviewed during my research in France, Britain, Belgium, Africa and the United

States. Their contribution was, as a rule, preceded by my statement that their comments would be off the record. Their anonymity does not detract from my deep appreciation of their assistance.

From its inception, this project has received the generous support of the United States Institute of Peace in Washington, D.C. On its behalf, David Smock, patient and full of warm encouragements, supervised the progress made. The Franco-American research center, U.S.-CREST, in Arlington, Virginia, hosted the research and editing team and supported a great share of the financial burden. This book would not have been possible without the understanding of its president, Jean-François Delpech. Finally, the Belgian company Leviers, my employer, funded the last stages of the work.

Needless to say, the shortcomings of this book are my own.

Alain Rouvez
Brussels
May 1994

Chapter 1

Post-Colonialism and International Regimes

To understand the creation and structure of an empire, it is necessary to seize its essence from the various ways imperial control has been enacted throughout history. Every age in the history of imperialism has had its own preoccupations. For centuries, it seemed that the imperial phenomenon was an inherent part of mankind's societal behavior. For better or worse, empires "shaped the political development of practically all the states of the modern world."[1] Against the inevitable drawback of thriving on the subordination of as large a domain as possible, empires have also, on the more positive side, been the main historic channel for linking or merging previously independent cultures and civilizations.

Imperial domination has expressed itself in an evolutionary way, surviving through many mutations in human history. The compelling, primeval drive to dominate produced structures of imperial control which adapted themselves to changing geographic and socio-cultural environments, as well as to historical experience. The rise and fall of Alexander the Great's Empire was different from the more systematic construction and the longer agony of the Roman Empire. The Chinese or Mongol Empires, the Inca Empire and the Holy Roman Empire shared the essence of imperialism, even though they were all embedded in their respective history and civilization. In a more recent era, the great colonial enterprises of Portugal, Spain, The Netherlands, Britain, France, Belgium and others were similar to earlier empires in their authoritarian expression, but differed strongly in their inspiration. Whatever their differences, all those empires were marked by the effective denial of the sovereign rights of the dominated populations, even though this was realized with varying levels of intensity.

By definition, empires are systems of control. The two basic elements of an empire, the center and the periphery, are engaged in an inherently unequal, interdependent and dialectic relationship. In the more polished words of Michael W. Doyle, empires are:

> system[s] of interaction between two political entities, one of which, the dominant metropole, exerts political control over the internal and external policy - the effective sovereignty - of the other, the subordinate periphery. To understand this interaction it is quite as necessary to explain the weakness of the periphery as it is to explain the strength and motives of the metropole.[2]

THE FALL OF COLONIALISM

In more modern times, imperialism has found a new life through European colonialism. The dynamics of colonial imperialism required the same trappings as traditional imperialism, but with a special twist. It still relied on an enormous disparity in power between the metropole and the subordinate periphery, but it was permeated by a doctrine of economic exploitation and mercantilism. Initially, the African colonies founded by European powers have for the most part been established for their economic utility to various interest groups within the metropole. Toward the end of the 19th century, the mercantilist phase of colonization was paralleled by a state-sponsored imperialist phase, involving new rationales for expansionism.[3] The competition between trading companies moved to the higher grounds of a contest between scrambling nations. Jules Ferry, French minister of foreign affairs from 1883-85, and an ardent believer in colonialism as a way to reinforce France's international prestige, stressed the new character of imperial colonialism: "Colonial policies are the international manifestation of the eternal laws of competitiveness."[4] Colonial power becomes a component of national prestige, and many industrial nations would succumb to its appeal. The British empire became by far the largest colonial construction, with 30 million square kilometers and 400 million inhabitants on the eve of World War I. France's empire came a distant second with 10 million square kilometers and 48 million inhabitants. Germany, Italy, Belgium, the United States, and Japan would equally follow suit even if for sometimes divergent motives. The Portuguese and Spanish empires were definitely on the decline by the time of Ferry's statement, having been diminished by the loss of all their possessions in Latin America. For those metropoles who conceived colonialism as a capitalist venture benefitting the metropole the results were not always matching the expectations. The "return on investment" of, for instance, France's formidable and costly effort to control the largest segment of the world's largest desert - the Sahara - cannot be justified in terms of capitalist logic. Other rationales have to be invoked, as national prestige, in France's case, or a way to enhance diplomatic leverage, as in the case of Bismarck's Germany.

Colonialism created the conditions of its own demise through the rise of destructive counter-forces whose spread it facilitated. Anti-colonialism took a whole range of expressions. There were mercantilist charges of unfairness by those foreign companies who did not benefit from the monopolies granted by the metropole to its own enterprises. More pernicious was the gradual appearance of nationalism among the colonized populations, awakened to the benefits of nationhood by the unsuspecting colonizers themselves. The years after World War II and before the early 1960s were marked by the tensions between the rising opposition to colonialism and the frantic efforts by all colonizers to preserve some kind of imperialist framework at a reasonable financial, political and moral cost. In 1947, India proved that colonialism was reversible, and by 1960 colonial imperialism was doomed. "Nothing in the history of the modern colonial empires," jested D.K. Fieldhouse, "was more remarkable than the speed with which they disappeared."[5] Decolonization did not mean the end of the economic or political preponderance of the former colonizers in some substantial parts of their ex-empires. Sub-Saharan Africa proved to be particularly vulnerable to this type of influence. To the puzzlement of die-hard colonialists, the loss of Europe's colonies in Africa made little difference to the wealth European countries derived from them, while the cost of colonial control was no longer borne by their authorities.

The end of colonialism was a historical development which the colonizers themselves helped to shape. Modern colonialism was born out of a power vacuum and Europe's technical ability to conquer, occupy and utilize new territories. As George Kennan observed in his BBC Lectures in England in 1957: "The establishment of the colonial relationship did not represent a moral action on somebody's part; it represented a natural and inevitable response to certain demands and stimuli of the age. It was simply a stage of history."[6]

Decolonization was truly revolutionary for the formerly subordinate periphery. New nations appeared on the international scene with all the formal trappings of sovereignty. There was a new reality and a new environment that had to be dealt with. Former colonizers had to interact by cajoling or coercing these new entities whenever their newly acquired sovereign rights clashed with the interests of the ex-colonizers. As Alastair Buchan described it:

> The fact that affects the structure of power in the modern world, [...] is the increase in the obstructive power of small countries - a phenomenon that is really quite new; the fact that we own the air space over our land space which creates the problem of air barriers; the steady pressure for the extension of seaward limits which is being gradually successful; the control by relatively small countries over vital straits and narrow waters.[7]

One should add to this the control over natural resources. Third World countries have at times sinned by self-indulging in their new political and economic leverage. They were courted, at least initially, by western buyers of raw materials and could subscribe to the capitalist or communist bloc partially based on which camp made the highest bid for access to natural resources. They could extract high economic or political prices from each camp for basing rights and access to military facilities, as Britain realized in its attempt to retain control over former naval bases. "Even the Russians," wrote Christopher Coker, a British scholar, "only gained access to Britain's old naval facilities by paying a price the British were not prepared to: aligning themselves with the regional postures of their host."[8]

The proliferation of many small Third World countries soon dissolved their combined leverage. The end of the Cold War struck a fatal blow to their ability to play one bloc against the other. Beyond their ideological orientations and differences, Third World countries all shared one common reality: poverty. For power and politics remain servants of economic strength; definitely a western attribute, not easily transferrable to those who joined the race too late.

For the ex-colonizers, the change brought about by decolonization was rather evolutionary, obliging them to face the loss of some considerable levers of direct political authority over their former colonies but sometimes with little effect on their economic preponderance. Still, in their eyes it was a tragedy of Darwinian proportion; but they would soon master the dynamics of adaptive change. The ex-colonizers learned to convert remnants of imperial liabilities into post-colonial assets. The success of this learning experience was unevenly shared among ex-metropoles. Either by political choice or as a result of impotence, some would eventually fail in retaining strong influence over all or segments of their former realms. In the process, some lessons of humility were learned and painful assessments made. In 1962, George T. Kimble from *The New York Times* expanded on some valuable, if idealistic, lessons from decolonization. These lessons were confirmed by future developments:

> Which brings me to what the colonial relationship has done for the colonizers. It has shown them that, in many respects, they were not so good as they thought they were; that they didn't always know what was best for others; and that, not infrequently, their best - including, as it did, parliamentary democracy, paper work and plumbing - held little appeal for others. [...] Again it has shown them - the British and the French, at any rate, and perhaps even the Belgians - that the only kind of power worth wielding is the one that decreases rather than grows with exercise. And it has encouraged them to believe that dying empires can be transferred into living commonwealth.[9]

The post-colonial tensions gravitated around the speed with which all partners succeeded in adapting to the new geo-strategic realities and responsibilities of the reformed political world order. New commonwealths and zones of influence would eventually emerge. The former metropoles were compelled to relinquish power, not out of philosophical considerations, but because a new world order had been imposed on them.

NATIONAL SOVEREIGNTY AND ZONES OF INFLUENCE

The combined shocks of decolonization and the demise of the Russian/Soviet empire in the second part of the twentieth century indicated that imperialism ceased to be a reality. The peculiarity of this era, unlike any other period in history, was the universalization of the principles of self-determination for any political entity which could claim to be a nation. Political ideals in the twentieth century have basically voided the operational reality of empires. The political price for denying this universal code of morality among nations has become high enough to deter imperial adventurism and to break up the remaining imperial structures. To collect a group of nations into one centrally governed entity has become so expensive politically as to become impractical for the conduct of foreign policy, even by the world's most powerful nations. The abandonment of imperialism on the international scene does not mean, however, that the management of international relations in the late twentieth century lacks any form of domination mechanism. The enduring presence of dominant power versus subordinate periphery has been reincarnated in the late twentieth century in "zones of influence." This concept amounts to much more than semantic finessing around the politically unacceptable notion of empire. It defines a new qualitative relationship between a center and its periphery, based on the at least formal respect of all instrumentalities of sovereignty. The concept of sphere of influence was introduced into international customs in 1885 in order to avoid complications between European powers which were partitioning Africa.[10] In that sense it predates even the Belgian colonial empire and the French and British scramble for Africa.

Imperial control over a subordinate nation is the strongest form of domination over a subordinate nation through complete denial of its sovereignty. On a scale of international control ranging from empires at one extreme to international systems composed of equally sovereign entities, zones of influence occupy somehow the middle ground. There is still a substantial foreign political constraint on the periphery, but compared to empires, it is far more restrained. The weakest form of domination and influence is among interdependent but truly sovereign entities.[11] The range of power available to the imperial metropole or the center of a zone of influence is defined as "the difference between the greatest possible reward and the worst possible punishment."[12] This range of power is understandably narrower for zones of influence than for empires. In the second part of the twentieth century, the range of influence, as Brian Barry argues, "includes the activation of commitments already made [..], persuasion, coercion (positive or negative - bribing, compelling, or deterring), and physical force."[13] It is important to note that physical force still lies within the instrumentalities of influence.

History teaches us that zones of influence in the second part of the twentieth century have been generated in two ways: either as the legacy of a colonial or imperial past, or through post-World War II diplomatic and military efforts to create them from scratch. France, Britain and, to a lesser degree, Belgium are the only countries as of 1994 which still belong to the first category. It is debatable whether Belgium should be considered as having a zone of influence. There is little explicit political consensus in Belgium to maintain one, but, *de facto*, Belgium has played the role of an occasional patron in central Africa, and it has never hidden that the region is still high on Brussels' political agenda.

In the second category, the United States and the former Soviet Union each figure prominently. Their respective zones of influence which they have built during the Cold War emphasized their global reach. Many other countries have joined this second category even if temporarily, but with more limited ambitions and only a regional reach. Australia, India, Libya, South Africa, Syria and even Tanzania have established or attempted to establish zones of influence in their immediate vicinity. The range of experiences gathered by those countries shows that a zone of influence can be organized with or without the consent of the member-nations of the targeted zone. A common denominator among the group of nations in the first and second categories is that their influence, whether a legacy from a colonial past or a new creation, has been backed by military force or the possibility of its use. Force can be applied either against the periphery or with the periphery's consent, depending on the type of influence that has been established: adversarial or consensual.

Modern history shows that economic and cultural forces can also grant a nation international influence without having to resort to military force or the threat of it. The economic might of Japan in East Asia, of Saudi Arabia in the Muslim world, and especially of Germany in the European Community or more recently in eastern Europe are examples of the use of economic power and pressure to gain political influence over other states. Spain and Portugal are still centers of cultural influence in their former colonies and they can sometimes convert this into some loose form of political influence, as in the case of Portugal's role in Angola and Mozambique. However, economic or cultural supremacy is not always sufficient to secure direct influence and there are limits to their reach. Analyzing the new world order in the early 1990s, *The Economist* conjectured that: "The fact that economic power has grown in relative importance compared with military power does not mean that it has displaced it as the *ultima ratio regnum*, the final arbiter."[14] Ultimately, enforcement capabilities are indispensable, and, according to the same source, "economic power could not have recaptured Kuwait; military power did."

The United States and the three former colonial powers which have retained a zone of political influence, namely France, the United Kingdom and Belgium, share a common approach to the way they have organized this influence. They used all levers available to them: economic, cultural and also, significantly, military. This latter dimension is what sets them apart from the purely economic influence exerted by countries like Germany or Saudi Arabia: in case of a serious crisis in their respective zones, the United States or the three ex-colonial powers have intervened unilaterally with military means to redress the situation which they thought could not be redressed otherwise. Other forms of influence are not precluded, but the directness of influence achieved through the use of military force or its threat provides a unique and extraordinary quality to the *rapport de force* between the center and its periphery.

With few exceptions, all nations belonging to the Third World were former colonies. Hence the suspicion that the economic exploitation that was at the core of colonialism remained the main rationale for the zones of influence established by former metropoles in the Third World. The fact that the new French, British and Belgian zones of influence covered segments or the entirety of their former colonial empires was viewed as additional proof that the suspicion was correct. The rationale was not always true for modern colonialism (i.e. roughly between 1870 and 1960) and does not suffice to describe comprehensively the subsequent zones of influence. Some have called the attempt by the metropoles to retain as much as possible of their influence "neo-colonialism" or "neo-imperialism." More appropriately, it should be called "post-colonialism," since the matrix of the new world order was directly inspired by the old order. The paradox was that neo-colonialism was in substance nothing new; economic dependence preceded decolonization. What was new was the metropoles' shift from politico-military tools of control to economic tools of influence. The latter had always been virtual tools, but were never activated as there was little need to do so in view of the existing colonial or imperial control mechanisms.

Neo-colonialism is a concept applicable to all capitalist countries which established an economic relationship with the independent countries of the Third World. Neo-colonialism occurred as an economic reality whenever the autonomy of a country was being reduced, mainly through one or several of the following four activities:[15] (i) when foreign companies maintained or reinforced their supremacy in the production capability of Third World countries; (ii) when the type of production reinforced the dependence of the Third World country on an industrialized state; (iii) when the terms of trade for Third World goods gradually deteriorated vis-a-vis goods of the industrial world; and (iv) when aid programs or financial assistance packages reinforced the economic influence of the donor country.

The term "neo-imperialism" as opposed to its synonym "neo-colonialism" seems to have been used more frequently for the United States than for any other western country, including former colonizers. The characteristics of the American neo-imperialism are the same as those defined earlier for neo-colonialism, but much more so. On the economic side, the United States emerged from World War II as the absolute superpower. The resentment against American economic preponderance in the Third World was generated by the vast overseas presence of American companies. This overseas production capability amounted to the second largest "economy" in the world after the American mainland economy.[16] Despite economic might which had no historic comparison, American neo-imperialism did not achieve the same level of political control over its sphere of influence (superpowers are entitled to spheres rather than zones) as the former European empires over their respective colonies. There has never been any American equivalent of British India. Lord Beloff offered the following comment on the distinctive features of the American hold on its sphere compared to colonial empires:

> If it is true that on the political side in the sense of a direct claim to or exercise of sovereignty, the American 'Empire' is much smaller than the European empires that have now all but disappeared, its informal empire, that is to say the propping up of states and regimes through advice and assistance and in the last resort military guarantees, is a considerable one. [...] The difference between the United States today and the old imperial powers [is that] the United States is clearly still reluctant to accept its imperial role as anything but an expedient resorted to in self-defence.[17]

This quote from Lord Beloff points to the dual nature of the United States' reach over its vast sphere of influence: economically, it was inspired by a principally non-political drive to gain markets and enhance production; strategically, it was pushed by expanding security commitments. Only when its security interests were at stake would the United States seek to establish political control or influence over sovereign entities. Later, security commitments and self-perceptions of its overseas credibility as a trustworthy ally would form the main justification to enhance its control over its sphere of influence. According to Raymond Aron, the originality of the American "Imperial Republic" during its post-war expansion years is a result of Nazi and Japanese aggression, and even more of the Soviet threat.[18] Edward Mortimer defends the view of a reluctant neo-empire: "The United States was drawn into imperialist behavior in spite of its Wilsonian ideology." But the initially inhibiting contradiction has been overcome by contemporary United States policy, "reflecting as it inevitably does the interests, appetites, and responsibilities that come with being a major world power," and engaged in a competition between itself and the Soviet Union.[19]

The interaction between the United States and the former European empires showed complementary preoccupations and interests. The Vietnam War and the United States' role in the Persian Gulf since the early 1970s clearly indicate a continuity in foreign patronage over these areas. The difference was that the American influence was not motivated by neo-colonialist economic considerations but by America's self-investiture as guardian of the free world. They were not completely alone in keeping Communism at bay in certain areas of the Third World. Once "the rigidities of the Cold War" had been established, the Americans were generally content with leaving the policing of some peripheral areas to their allies who were familiar with the terrain.[20]

THE ESSENTIAL POLITICO-MILITARY DIMENSION

I searched for what constituted the specificity of international or interstate relations and I thought that I found this specific character in the legitimate and legal resort to armed force by its actors.[21]

In a world where former imperial powers have seen their hold over their respective peripheries dwindle dramatically, new realities were shaping new concepts and tools of international affairs. The above quote, borrowed from Raymond Aron, stresses the quest for legitimacy in the use of force as a tool of international relations. This consideration strongly pervaded the structures of influence set up in post-colonial times. There are three main aspects which stand out when analyzing the strength of the politico-military dimension of a relationship of influence between a center and its periphery: (i) the formal commitments between the center and its periphery about the use of force, (ii) the center's military capability and the force available for interventions with its appropriate support structure, and (iii) the political resolve to engage those forces if need be.

The use of force within a consensual zone of influence can be formalized through an alliance or agreement. Robert E. Osgood, in an article on *The Nature of Alliances*, emphasized one of the essential functions of alliances beyond the creation of a collective protection against a common external threat. Osgood argues that alliances are also tools "to restrain and control allies [and] to limit an ally's freedom of action."[22] The implication of entering into an alliance is that allies cannot use force against each other. If the dominant ally wants to exert control over the minor, dependent allies, no direct military force can be used under the terms of the formal agreement to press the recalcitrant allies. Therefore, influence within an alliance is achieved by denying security to the rebellious ally. If the latter refuses to acknowledge the influence of the dominant ally, its security-umbrella against external threats is withdrawn. There are many variations on this rationale, but a military alliance among unequal allies puts the stronger ally in a position of security arbiter. Influence is exerted by some sort of built-in security blackmail that others implicitly accept. The weaker the ally, the greater its dependence. The influence of the principal ally will correlate to the intensity of the external threat at the origin of the collective protection system of the alliance. If the threat disappears, the center's influence over its allies will vanish. The network of alliances created by the United States to contain Soviet expansionism is a perfect illustration of Osgood's argument. *A contrario*, France's reluctance to join NATO's integrated military command structure provides an example of the suspicion generated by alliances even among allies. Finally, France's strong network of bilateral defense and military cooperation agreements with various African countries is a perfect example of the double-edged nature of alliances: to protect against external threats and to preserve control by the dominant ally.

Whether or not there is a legal framework regulating the use of military force by a center in its zone of influence, the center has to develop and maintain the necessary military tools to give credibility to the notion of such a zone. The military dimension defines the distinction between what is possible and what is desirable. The ultimate credibility test will rest on the amount of military force which can be brought to bear on the zone either to protect it against third parties or to crush any challenge from within. The center's military capabilities are at the core of this credibility test. Distance and geographic conditions mean that a center's military capability available for intervention must be highly specialized and mobile. In military jargon these forces form the power projection capability of a given center. The projection capability is often substantially enhanced by a center's overseas bases or basing rights. In addition to their value as power projection platforms, overseas bases are also an instrument of persuasion through the permanence of a real, even though limited, display of force within the zone or its immediate vicinity.

A center's credibility in the exercise of influence, even with the appropriate mix of military forces and overseas projection platforms, is also a function of its leadership's willingness to use force whenever challenged. Perceptions and anticipations are the only means to gauge, from a center's perspective or from that of the targeted zone, this highly political variable. The assessment of the center's determination to use force is a function of the center's internal political situation, its foreign policy priorities, its relationship with its zone of influence, and potential third party involvement.

Throughout this study, the concept of "zone of influence" refers to the ability to exercise political influence ultimately backed by military might. The military dimension is at the core of the concept as defined within the framework of this study. The military linkage to the political quest for influence may be subtle and never explicitly acknowledged, but it is understood as providing the backbone of the relationship. This selective definition of the concept of "zone of influence" does not presume that other forms of structuring such zones do not exist. It is important merely to distinguish the special role of military instrumentalities in the exercise of international political influence from the exclusive use of, for instance, economic and commercial might for the purpose of securing such political influence. The military dimension is not exclusive of any other dimensions, but it allows for higher levels of political control.

In observing the development of zones of influence by the United States and by European ex-colonizers, one is struck by the similarities in the type of influence which has been achieved by all. Despite great disparities in size, economic might and military means, the global environment in the late twentieth century has imposed convergent approaches to structure international influence. The former European colonizers were faced with a dramatic cutback in their control over ex-colonies, but the decline eventually stabilized around fairly well structured zones of influence. On the contrary, the United States, with only a minimal colonial past, created a zone of political influence after years of Wilsonian belief in the benefits of self-determination for other nations. The remarkable event was that the European deconstruction and the American construction produced analogous instrumentalities of international influence. For the nations concerned, the ultimate recourse to military force was an essential element of influence. Again, there is an important disparity in military means and in the motivations to assert international influence by force, but qualitatively there are striking similarities. The United States, France and Britain satisfy all of the following six criteria demonstrating a definite military dimension to their political grip over their zones of influence; only Belgium fails to satisfy criteria (1) and (2):

1. preserving a sufficient political consensus at home to sustain a zone of influence;
2. creating a network of alliances, defense agreements or political commonwealths to give a legal framework to the zone of influence;
3. operating overseas bases and naval facilities and securing overflight rights within potential theaters of intervention;
4. providing military cooperation assistance to member-nations of the respective zone of influence;
5. maintaining and updating a militarily significant power projection capability for potential use overseas; and,
6. not backing away from military intervention in the zone of influence whenever threatened from the inside or the outside.

The last criteria is the most relevant, because it constitutes effective proof of the center's willingness to include military force in its arsenal of means of influence.

The modalities of the expression of international power are constrained by the acceptable norms of specific eras. The second part of the twentieth century has produced new constraints resulting from a new world order and from new moral norms regulating the behavior among sovereign entities, whatever the disparities in strength. The advent of zones of influence after World War II demonstrates that dominant countries have to respect the order and its moral norms, at least symbolically. But it also demonstrates that "power expands until it meets its match."[23] Anytime there is a power vacuum over some areas in the world, either because of weakening international patronage, or because of a internal collapse of authority, a response by some other center of power is inevitable.

THE SPECIFICITY OF POST-INDEPENDENCE AFRICA

When the majority of sub-Saharan African nations attained independence in the early 1960s, three major colonial empires were dismantled simultaneously, in some cases peacefully, in others amidst violence and chaos. French, British, and Belgian possessions in sub-Saharan Africa were restored to the indigenous populations and a well-established system of control over huge geographic areas collapsed in a matter of years. New centers of power emerged, with many means of control in the hands of the Africans themselves, and others still in the hands of former colonial power-brokers. It was necessary for the transformation of the colonial power structure into a post-colonial order to respect the symbolism of sovereignty, rendered more important precisely because of the *de facto* dependency and fragility of emerging African states. The former colonizers sought to reorganize their old interests in the new environment while preserving as much of the colonial legacy as they considered useful. Remarkably, the whole transition from colonies to independent nations in sub-Saharan Africa has been relatively bloodless: France transformed its colonies into independent states through constitutional referenda; Britain, with a long pre-1960 history of granting independence, had learned the lesson of not yielding in time to nationalism; only Belgium, with no imperial tradition other than in Africa, faced a chaotic transition.

The complex set of colonial ties in the cultural, political, economic, commercial, and military spheres did not dissolve overnight. The dependency of sub-Saharan Africa on its former colonizers in all those areas was too encompassing to vanish so quickly. The colonial links were changed into contractual ones between sovereign entities. Agreements were signed in most fields with sometimes substantial assistance flowing from the European partner to the African partner in exchange for influence or privileged access to resources and markets. African countries were in great need of financial assistance and technical know-how, and willingly accepted those agreements. The most delicate agreements, because they touch on one of the most powerful symbols of sovereignty, were in the military domain. France, Britain, and Belgium have maintained some type of military involvement in Africa up to this day. This involvement has generally taken one of three forms: (i) assistance agreements, usually designed to help in formulating the military needs of the young nations and to train and equip their armed forces; (ii) defense agreements (signed only by France, except for the short-lived Anglo-Nigerian Defense Agreement), which give the African co-signatory some conditional protection against external, and sometimes even domestic threats; and (iii) direct military interventions by a European power, generally in support of the recognized local authorities, or as a primarily humanitarian operation with regime-stabilizing side effects.

The European military involvement in Africa is predicated on various factors, some inherent to Africa's post-colonial development, and others to European military capabilities. One of the most salient aspects of Africa's development has been the enduring weakness of African military forces in all former French, British and Belgian colonies. It is this endemic weakness which justifies the assistance and defense agreements with western or other powers, but it also is one of the enabling conditions for interventions by European powers. Regular armed forces in sub-Saharan Africa are often poorly equipped and insufficiently trained, and therefore unable to quell major internal rebellions or, in rarer instances, external aggression. European powers agree to intervene because these are low-intensity, low-risk operations for them, requiring often only light infantry troops with no heavy armor or little air protection. It is first and foremost the low threat environment in Africa which accounts for the overwhelming number of unilateral interventions by France, and to a lesser degree by Britain and Belgium in sub-Saharan Africa as compared to interventions in other, better armed regions of the world. The strength of these three powers is, to use a quote from Joseph Conrad, "just an accident arising from the weakness of others."[24] The virtual impunity and affordability of interventions in sub-Saharan Africa has been unambiguously stated by Louis de Guiringaud, foreign minister under French president Giscard d'Estaing, in an article in *L'Express* from December 1979: "Africa," he said, "is the only continent that is still to the measure of France, within its reach. It is the only one where it can still, with 500 men, change the course of history."[25]

Still, there are a few checks on Africa's impotence vis-a-vis Guiringaud's claim, mainly in the political and diplomatic arena. Interventions often need the approval of the recognized authorities in the country where they take place, but also in neighboring countries which are solicited for overflight, transit or basing rights. Belgian and British interventions have always been organized with the explicit approval of the country in crisis. France has intervened only twice against the authorities in place, in Gabon in 1964 and in the Central African Republic (CAR) in 1979. On both occasions, France had to defend its action against vehement African and international criticism.

From the European perspective, the feasibility of an intervention in Africa depends on two elements: military projection capabilities and the domestic political consensus which reflects the way "African interests" are defined. Traditionally, the political support for interventions has been high in France. Britain has had waning interests and felt less and less comfortable defending them *manu militari*. Belgium's political actors have been very much divided over the issue of interventions, especially in support of the regime of Zairian president Mobutu, and usually settle for the only common denominator, which is intervention for humanitarian purposes.

The next issue for intervening European powers is one of affordability and of combat-readiness. Can France, Britain or Belgium afford to assist or intervene in Africa? While military assistance programs require only a limited investment in training personnel and a modest contribution in equipment, the affordability of a direct military intervention is a wholly different matter. Interventions require specialized and combat-ready troops with adequate military transportation, which usually means air transport. In instances where no friendly local government can make staging facilities available, overseas possessions or naval power projection platforms are needed. Furthermore, the troops and support forces earmarked for interventions in Africa must be available at the time of the contingency. When French, British, or Belgian forces are involved in a war like the 1991

Gulf War, it would be stretching their logistical capabilities to expect them to be able to respond simultaneously to other exigencies in Africa, except for fairly limited ones.

Post-colonial intervention patterns have varied considerably in the three European countries under review according to (i) their perceived interests at stake on the African continent, (ii) the lead taken by their political authorities in acting with military means to secure their respective country's interests and commitments in Africa, and (iii) each country's respective military capabilities.

... ARISING FROM THE WEAKNESS OF OTHERS

The interaction between a center and its periphery does not depend only on the former's strength and motives but also, by definition, on the latter's weakness. The success of medium powers like France and Britain, or even a small power like Belgium, to invest parts of Africa and contend they represent their respective zones of influence can only be made possible either because the member-nations of the zones are willing to cooperate or because they are too weak to consider alternate options. Africa's military dependence was a function of the colonial legacy in military matters, but also of the military transfer processes between former metropoles and newly independent African states. In 1974, Chester A. Crocker, then Assistant Professor of International Relations at Georgetown University in Washington, D.C., and future U.S. Assistant Secretary of State for African Affairs, wrote a comprehensive analysis on the British and French post-colonial military legacy in Africa.[26] In the following excerpt, Dr. Crocker sets the stage of the whole power transfer issue:

> With hindsight, it is plausible to argue that the sweep of history was inexorable and unidimensional. African nationalist pressures and the decline in European power forced military decolonization to occur, the only variables being imperialist tenacity and the willingness of African to temporize. But the historical record obliges us to include other considerations. One of these is the partial autonomy of the military and political spheres. Military inter-dependence between metropole and colony could not be as rapidly and painlessly unravelled as could the formal political ties of external rule. The brutal but superficial rupture achieved by granting sovereignty to African territories could not have

been replicated in military terms without security consequences that neither side was willing to bear.[27]

There was no uniformity among ex-colonizers in the way the transfer of military power occurred. France's approach to entrench its influence in sub-Saharan Africa rested on propping up the African military rather than, for instance, putting the emphasis on building up democracy. The reason was simply a question of economy of means: the former was easier to implement and yielded larger direct influence than the latter. In an unusually candid statement on the political rationale behind the French training programs, a French officer explained that African armies:

> are the expression of new sovereignties over vast expanses of territories. It is important to bend the political orientation of those sovereign nations by playing a determinant role in the survival of the governments in place or in their eviction from power. Theses Lilliputian [military] organs discover therefore their essential political power in Black Africa, which must be kept under control.[28]

The paradoxical nature of African armies produced a doubly favorable circumstance to enhanced military dependence toward former colonizers: those armies were weak enough as to warrant declining European powers still a substantial role, but strong enough on their local domestic scene as to be a potent vehicle of political status.

Historically, the record of French, British and Belgian military decolonization varies largely. French Africa was a direct extension of the French mainland defense posture. French overseas possessions were a large reservoir of manpower, and the multi-racial *Troupes coloniales* were deployed worldwide. The officer corps was with few exceptions French, but the colonial troops were well integrated into the French Army. The Senegalese *tirailleurs* unit formed the prototype of French colonial troops in Africa. Starting in 1912, troops were being conscripted, even though on a selective basis through a lottery system. Service lasted 3 to 4 years, and conscripts often re-enlisted when their term expired, meaning that the bulk of French colonial troops were enlisted men. The *tirailleurs* regiment were genuine inter-African units, and typically made up of 44 percent Voltaic, 38 percent Senegalese, 12 percent Malian and 6 percent Guinean troops.[29] Geographical multi-purposefulness was the crux of the policy governing the utilization of these units. Sub-Saharan African soldiers fought in North Africa and in the Far East. Some 500,000 colonial troops, from all parts of the French empire participated in World War I on the French side. Twenty years later, and despite France's military defeat in Europe, 105,000 sub-Saharan troops participated in World War II on the side of de Gaulle's Free French forces.[30]

The British approach differed considerably from the French method until World War II. According to a celebrated statement, the British Empire was "pre-eminently a great Naval, Indian and Colonial Power."[31] The Royal Navy was the means to achieve imperial status, and India was the empire. Colonial possessions in Africa and elsewhere were often confined to a subsidiary role, merely staging post on the naval route to India. The Indian Army formed the core of the forces committed to imperial duties, of course in conjunction with the Royal Navy. The African security forces, "loose amalgams of local militia and constabulary forces, were not seen as a reservoir of imperial defence manpower, but as the guardians of a self-policing peripheral zone."[32] Britain's colonial recruitment policy in India, Africa and elsewhere had been influenced by its Indian experience, especially by the Sepoy mutiny of 1857 and its aftermath.

> A policy of racial equality and integration, which had begun to find favor in the Indian civil service just before the rebellion, was afterward forever considered out of the question by the army. Control was expected to be maintained by keeping units strictly segregated by ethnic and religious affiliations so that, in the words of one senior official of the time, 'Sikh might fire into Hindu [and] Goorka into either, without any scruple in the case of need.'[33]

Recruiting practices would favor certain tribes, usually more rural and nomadic tribes, over more educated and settled peoples so as to keep the latter out of military service and under the guns of their ethnic rivals.[34] Britain's African forces, like the West African Frontier Force and the King's African Rifles, played only a minimal role during World War I. Unlike France, it was not until 1939 that Britain began to draw substantially on its African colonies for troops. By the end of World War II, about 450,000 troops from British sub-Saharan Africa had joined the British war effort. It was only during World War II that a small number of Africans "became officers under Britain's slow and gradual process of developing indigenous officer cadres when political conditions permitted."[35]

Against the colonial philosophies of Britain and France, encouraging as much self-governance as possible in the case of the former and pursuing assimilationist doctrines in the case of the latter, Belgium's colonial philosophy was more mercantilist: minimal administrative costs for the greatest benefits. The result was that the colonial bureaucratic apparatus had to be financed from, and only from, the resources collected in the Congo. The self-financing applied also to the colonial military force, called the *Force publique*, and composed of local recruits and a Belgian officer corps mostly on temporary detachment from Belgium's regular forces. Both World Wars witnessed only a very marginal military contribution from Belgian colonial troops, and then only limited to operations on the African continent.

The post-World War II period saw an important reversal of trends: "Colonial empires in Africa and Asia became net importers of white manpower, and a significant drain on total metropolitan military power."[36] The reason for the reversal was partly self-imposed by the colonial powers for grand strategic and imperial designs, and partly the result of growing nationalist agitations in Africa and elsewhere. The heightened appreciation for the potential use of vast manpower was viewed as a way "to buttress a waning world power position."[37] But, by the mid-1950s, all colonial empires were on the defensive. For the first time in its colonial history, Belgium had to commit metropolitan forces in the Congo. France ended up deploying 60 percent of its metropolitan army in North Africa. The tide had turned.

The military legacy from the colonial powers to the newly emerging African nations was in accordance with their respective colonial philosophies and a direct product of it. One of the most distinctive characteristics of African armies is the way they are disconnected from the socio-political environment. In Africa, with only a few exceptions, the regular armed forces have not been associated with the political development leading toward independence. In fact, the armed forces were often used by the colonizers as a repressive tool against political dissent from pre-1960 independence activists. In all former French, British and Belgian possessions in sub-Saharan Africa, the only elements in society with military training were the former colonial troops, since virtually no armed resistance movements existed and none of these territories had gained independence through armed struggle. Many of the African soldiers "found themselves torn between their allegiance to the French Army and the loyalty demanded by the new leaders who represented groups and ideas against which they had been fighting."[38] Paradoxically, under the colonial administration, the army was one of the very few options available to the Africans for acquiring some social standing in their country. The military became a springboard for socio-political promotion. Such conceptions have been carried over to the post-colonial African armies, politicizing the military hierarchy. Post-independence recruitment methods and massive promotion to higher ranks under Africanization have destabilized military command structures and made them more fragile.

The French colonies would make the transition to nationhood without a national army. The multi-racial *Troupes coloniales* had been dispersed over the whole French empire, with little consideration to the origin of the soldiers. Colonial forces were an important reserve army of racially integrated troops with no systemic education. One difference in the French system compared to those of other colonial empires was in the treatment of African veterans.[39] Although lower paid and less educated than Africans in the service of Britain, the completion of military service in the French system procured voting privileges, otherwise virtually unobtainable. African veterans wound up with a preponderant voice in local politics. France derived important post-colonial benefits since French veterans in Africa were usually more pro-French than their British or Belgian counterparts were pro-British or pro-Belgian. At the time of independence, the integrated colonial army needed to be disbanded and its troops had to be reassigned, unit by unit or sometimes even on an individual basis, to their country of origin. The breakup of the approximately 61,000 African troops in the colonial army would produce some 14 national armies. The transfer of troops and the organization of national armed forces structures were, in most instances, subject to defense and military cooperation agreements between France and its former colonies.

British imperial and colonial forces lacked the cohesiveness of the French *Troupes coloniales*. Regional command centers respected territorial boundaries and control over military matters. British colonial troops were kept strictly segregated along ethnic lines. By favoring what they considered to be warrior tribes over others, the military in colonial Britain became dominated by selected ethnic groups. After independence, the British recruitment practices would have a lasting impact on the inability of new governments to use the armed forces as an instrument of national reconciliation. By denying their colonial veterans special political advantages, the former soldiers were less integrated in the new nation's home-rule efforts than their French counterparts. Starting in 1953, West African forces were organized according to localization policies, and the financial responsibilities for the local defense were also transferred to the West African territories. In East Africa, the Mau Mau insurgency in Kenya during the 1950s required a substantial (by African standards) commitment of British metropolitan forces which, at the peak of the insurgency, numbered five British battalions as well as several units of the Royal Air Force.[40] The devolution of authority and responsibilities was introduced in East and central Africa, but "with greater haste and less viable results."[41] Overall, military establishments in former British colonies in Africa were better prepared to face the challenges of independence: they enjoyed a greater degree of autonomy toward Britain than francophone African states toward France, and they had a longer history of localization within the territory of the eventual independent states.

The Belgian-installed military establishments in central Africa were marked by the dramatic disruption caused by the five-year long Congolese civil war which exploded right after independence day. The success of the hastily arranged transition process for the *Force publique* was predicated on the preservation of a Belgian officer corps for several years after independence. The local demands for a rapid Africanization of the officer corps were dismissed at first by Belgian authorities. The subsequent mutiny within the *Force publique* caused the panicky departure of all Belgian civil servants still active in the country after independence. The disruption was completed a few months later when the United Nations ordered all Belgian military personnel to evacuate the country. The ensuing military chaos made it difficult to establish continuity in the command structure and organization of Congolese military units before and after independence. The *Force publique* also covered the security of Rwanda and Burundi. At the time of the Congolese independence, a couple of battalions were assigned to those two countries and isolated from the Congolese agitation. Belgium would have an additional two years to prepare those two countries for independence. Belgian colonial troops were strictly mixed, even at platoon level where four tribes had to be represented in each platoon. By keeping men under arms for long periods of time and spreading the integrated units all over the Congolese territory, Belgian colonial authorities were able to break up the ethnic loyalty of their troops, replacing it with a strong loyalty to the *Force publique* itself.

The troops were mainly limited to a constabulary role, but little was done to enhance their political awareness or allegiance to non-military national institutions. At independence, Congolese troops resented and strongly distrusted political authorities, who returned the feeling with equally strong emotions.

The embryonic defense structures constituting the colonial legacy in military matters would have lasting security implications for sub-Saharan Africa. The entire sub-continent, with the exception of Portuguese possessions, counted no more than 325,000 troops in 1965. The 15 countries that were former French colonies accounted for only 64,000, or about one-fifth of this total. Guinea, with 9,000 troops, had the largest army, followed by Cameroon and Mali with 8,000 each. The average military establishment in former French territories was less than 4,500 men per independent country. Former British possessions, by then eleven independent countries not counting South Africa, accounted for 124,000 troops or roughly two-fifths. Nigeria, Africa's giant, retained a mere 25,000 troops, or about the same number as Ghana. The three former Belgian possessions in central Africa numbered 29,000 soldiers; Zaire (then the Congo) representing the lion's share with 25,000. African armies in the former three colonies exercised military and constabulary functions. The significantly lower average for troops in former French possessions indicates France's continued military role in those countries after independence.

In a remarkable book titled *Born Arming*, A.F.Mullins, Jr. explores how and why new nations in the Third World arm themselves. The study, which is 70 percent based on sub-Saharan African countries, compares the military build-ups in new nations with what is referred to as the "European Model."[42] This model postulates that Europe's century-long tumultuous international history was not without an intrinsic organizing principle. There was a close relationship between the elites' concern for security and the quest for development:

> In the European experience, elites had to make their [economies] work, not because of popular pressure to do so, but because if they failed they would be overthrown and conquered by someone who was better at nation-building than they were.[43]

In other words, international pressure was sanctioning elites for economic and political mismanagement. European authorities had to develop an effective army, which in turn required a healthy economic situation at home. There was an objective alliance between the ruling classes and the national economic players. The new nations in post-colonial Africa were not subjected to the same security-induced development scheme. Their elites have been shielded from the impetus to develop economic resources in order to pay for national security. The funding for security concerns came from powers abroad, who could either flood their African clients with weapons in quantities surpassing by far the latter's ability to pay for them, or directly engage troops from the metropole as a guarantee and shield. Sub-Saharan Africa was carved into various zones of influence, including a growing Soviet one. By shielding their clients from financing their own security concerns, ex-metropoles and superpowers offered protection but at the price of continued dependence from the periphery on its former or new patrons. Furthermore, one of the traditional engines of economic development in Europe, namely the elites' fear of military insecurity, was allegedly removed. Authorities in the peripheries saw their political freedom of movement not only being subordinated to the centers, but they had no incentive to change the *status quo* by favoring uncontrolled economic development which would produce economic elites capable of challenging them. The intimacy between the center and its periphery rested on elites which were captive to the *status quo*.

Chester Crocker points to two types of continuity between the new defense frameworks and the earlier, colonial order. The first continuity is functional. African security forces, with few exceptions, "have served to support the state structure and domestic order derived from Europe," including inherited boundaries.[44] The second continuity was formalized through defense and military cooperation agreement. France, through its unique network of bilateral defense agreements, gained a degree of intrusiveness into the domestic security responsibilities of its former colonies which was unparalleled by Britain and Belgium, or even by the United States in its Cold War sphere of influence. All three European ex-colonial powers signed military cooperation agreements with the new sub-Saharan states. While they aimed to provide technical and material assistance, these agreements provided a framework for continued interaction. The orientation of African security decisions could be influenced by playing the possibility of disrupting or increasing material and technical aid. The military interventions reasserted the African security dependence.

In conclusion, former French, British and Belgian colonies achieved sovereignty with weak defense apparatus, dependent to a large extent on continued support from the former metropoles, even though British territories had a greater margin of maneuver. Military impotence was compounded by economic dependence and poor development prospects. The implications for sub-Saharan Africa's position in the world have lasted for three decades and have confirmed the region's inability to change its external environment.

A DISTINCT INTERNATIONAL REGIME

Only three European colonial centers, France, Britain and Belgium, have tried, with varying success, to convert their direct imperial control into zones of influence or something which resembled, to some degree, such zones. They structured a new relationship which grew out of the colonial heritage. France, Britain and Belgium faced tough policy choices with far-reaching diplomatic and military consequences. Over more than thirty years, their foreign policy has consistently made room for shaping their political options and military forces in order to cater to their respective area of influence, even if only minimally. Their respective post-colonial governments have yearned to retain as much as possible of the former imperial structures of control, reformulated and readjusted through the prism of the post-colonial world order and morality. French, British and Belgian post-colonial governments are indeed the true disconsolate heirs of the former colonial metropoles. The difference is that history had moved to a new stage and some manifestations of international domination ceased to be feasible.

Their commonalties at three different levels make France, Britain and Belgium, together, a perfect subject for analysis: (i) they were former colonial empires, (ii) they have more or less successfully managed to secure a zone of influence exclusively or principally in sub-Saharan Africa, and (iii) they have all resorted several times to military force during the thirty years following decolonization. The occasional use or threat of military force to administer their relationship is what distinguishes those three countries from the Italian, Dutch, German, Spanish or Portuguese post-colonial experiences. The latter colonizers completely abdicated, by choice or by circumstance, the use of their military apparatus in faraway ventures involving former dependencies. There was a flurry of economic, commercial, cultural and other assistance programs and exchange agreements, but none that would even remotely imply any military interventionism or support role.

After more than thirty years, it is possible to evaluate the historical uniqueness of the French, British and Belgian post-colonial experiences. It was mainly in sub-Saharan Africa that they were able to convert their colonial empire into some post-colonial organized structure of influence and sometimes control. Each country decided in the early 1960s to preserve, as much as possible, their special status with some former colonies. Belgium, by the nature of its colonial possession, was limited to central Africa. France had disengaged itself from the Far East and North Africa by 1962. The remnants of France's empire in the Caribbean or in the Pacific regions are no longer considered colonies, but are French territory. Britain's overseas post-colonial role initially extended beyond sub-Saharan Africa to include the Middle East and the Far East. The momentous decision to withdraw all its forces east of Suez, completed in 1971, ended Britain's special influence in the concerned regions with the exception of Hong Kong or Brunei. For the sake of this study, only sub-Saharan Africa will be taken into consideration. It is in that region that the three European former metropoles have continued their military involvement in the pursuit of their interest and enhanced influence.

Conceptually, the interaction between the three European metropoles and their former colonies in sub-Saharan Africa can best be described by international regime theory. Stephen D. Krasner, a professor of political science at Stanford University, defined international regimes "as sets of implicit or explicit principles, norms, rules, and decision-making procedures around which actor's expectations converge in a given area of international relations."[45] In Krasner's view, regimes are characterized by the fact that they are more than temporary arrangements. "Since regimes encompass principles and norms, the utility function that is being maximized must embody some sense of general obligation."[46] One such principle is reciprocity, when participating actors within a given regime accept to sacrifice some interest with the expectation that others will reciprocate in the future, even if they are under no formal obligations to do so and the modalities of the future reciprocal benefits are unknown. An international regime among sovereign entities requires mutual trust and confidence.

A regime is far from static. Alterations in principles and norms cause changes in the regime itself, while changes in the rules and decision-making procedures represent merely an evolution within the regime. Finally, Krasner distinguishes the weakening of a regime from changes within or between regimes: "If the principles, norms, rules, and decision-making procedures of a regime become less coherent, or if actual practice is increasingly inconsistent with principles, norms, rules, and procedures, then a regime has weakened."[47]

The prevalence of self-interest and power among sovereign states means that regimes derive from voluntary agreements which respect these impulses. In the conventional international system, the actors are juridically equals, ultimately to rely only on themselves, and prepared to resort to force. Regimes are the product of a collective act of will. Additionally, in a community of self-centered entities, regimes need at least one of two basic ingredients to function: (i) a sense that coordination provides outcomes superior to uncoordinated individual actions, and/or (ii) an acceptable leader to provide a critical role in supplying the collective goods and services. Powerful actors in a system will inevitably constrain the choices of others. A regime may be imposed by dominant powers. The balance of power regime of the 19th century emphasized the role of major powers, for whom the regime was conceived. Smaller powers had no option but to follow.[48] Although covered by the regime, the weaker nations were not parties to the regime's balancing act. When weaker actors are not sovereign entities, as in colonialism, the regime's norms, principles, rules and procedures only apply to the interactions among colonial powers.

Donald J. Puchala and Raymond F. Hopkins, two American political scientists, demonstrated that colonialism qualified as a type of regime with a distinctive pattern of political and economic interactions. The regime only applied to the relationships among imperial powers.

> There was a pronounced competitiveness among metropoles as each country sought to establish, protect, and expand its colonial domain against rivals. Yet there was also a sense of limitation or constraint in major-power relations, a notion of imperial equity, evidenced in periodic diplomatic conferences summoned to sort out colonial issues by restraining the expansiveness of some and compensating others for their losses.[49]

The major colonial powers endorsed the subdivision of colonial territories, as well as the idea of their "civilizing missions." Colonial empires brought power, wealth and prestige, which collaborating local elites sometimes shared. The regime was geared to benefit the metropoles while simultaneously stabilizing intra-European politics. Colonies played an important part in maintaining the difficult balance of power in Europe. The legitimacy in colonization was founded upon consensus in six major norms, as listed by Puchala and Hopkins: the legitimacy of subjugating "uncivilized" nations; the acceptability of alien rule as opposed to self-determination; expansionism as a source of power; the necessity to stabilize the balance of power in Europe, which in turn justified colonial expansion; the right to economic exclusivity, at least before 1900; and noninterference in others' colonial administration.[50] The instruments of the colonizers included two powerful elements: the technological superiority of European arms and overwhelming economic might. The combination of colonial norms and means determined the parameters of international behavior for the members of the regime and shaped the expectations of outsiders.

The breakdown of the colonial regime was due to the gradual abandonment of two of its norms. Two World Wars nullified perhaps the most essential tenet from an international perspective, namely the European balance of power. Concurrently, the appearance of new anti-colonial powers and movements opened an ever-widening breach in the legitimacy of dominance-subordination schemes in the conduct of international relations. Sovereignty of new entities in the Third World embodied both the end of the former world order and the suppression of formal international subordination and alien rule. The stage was set for a new regime, where the new nations could participate as full actors in interactions that they helped to mold.

A central premise of this book is the notion that power abhors vacuum and is malleable to suit an infinite number of environments. In the early 1960s, the colonial empires had not been completely defeated in sub-Saharan Africa. They merely lost the more obvious and important levers of control. The temptation to continue to use the remaining instruments of influence in their hands was not a moral act. It was an inevitable response to existing stimuli, to paraphrase George Kennan's words. Sub-Saharan Africa was simply the only place, or one of the very few places, where French, British and Belgian appetites for influence went unsuppressed. The appetite grew with the eating. The old colonial regime gave way to chaos, indifference, or, as in the case of French, British and Belgian relations with sub-Saharan Africa, to a new international regime. Colonies were transformed into zones of influence, which entailed drastic changes in the norms and rules of international relations.

Three main factors define the successful transition of a colonizer into the center of a zone of influence: political support of the end-goal, adequate force projection capabilities, and the weight of past actions on the future. The first factor conditioned the way French, British and Belgian policy-makers defined their respective country's interests in Africa from 1960 to 1994. The attempts to play a political role in Africa relied on a conception which included the use of force. All three European powers were faced with hard choices over the allocation of resources and political capital to possible military operations abroad.

The next factor relates to the evaluation of the military option, which involves two main elements: power projection capabilities and a security framework facilitating the projection of forces. Each of the three countries under review have dedicated some of their respective military forces for potential, but not exclusive, use in the African theater of operations. Other existing military capabilities can, depending on circumstances, provide additional firepower and support. Most of the military units that have been or might be deployed in Africa need to be considered, as well as the major weapons systems in use for overseas force deployments. European military personnel is present in Africa, either under provisions of bilateral defense agreements (only in the case of France) or as part of military assistance programs. Both types of presence are a source of influence and information. They enable the European power to shape and supply local forces, and provide it with intelligence on the local operational conditions. In addition, France and Britain both benefit from national military bases on islands around Africa, which can considerably ease the logistical constraints of overseas interventions. Belgium does not have such overseas bases.

The last factor pertains to the lessons of past actions. On many occasions, France, Britain and Belgium have intervened militarily in sub-Saharan Africa. The historical record of these interventions constitutes the ultimate evidence of their political zones of influence. However, a closer look shows divergent patterns between the three intervening powers. The causes of the divergences are differences in political objectives and the distinct socio-political natures of their realms of influence in sub-Saharan Africa.

Chapter 2

French Political and
Military Involvement in Africa

France has intervened approximately thirty-five times in sub-Saharan Africa since the end of French colonialism. The interventions were politically successful in terms of securing French interests, usually requiring the preservation of stability and the *status quo*. These interventions were also militarily successful in terms of low casualty rates and of effectively achieving the immediate goals assigned to them. The conditions necessary to pursue such active military involvement have rested on a combination of political will power and military preparedness. Since de Gaulle, or because of him, France has given Africa a special place in its foreign policy. It was a reflection of the unique international role France sought to play, especially south of the Sahara, and the complex set of interests France was pursuing for itself through the special relationship with francophone Africa. At the military level, the virtual impunity of French interventions in sub-Saharan Africa and their low conflict intensity was illustrated by Louis de Guiringaud's claim that with 500 troops, France could change the course of history in Africa.[1] The effectiveness of those 500 men comes from an impressive array of French peacetime force deployments in francophone Africa. It also results from the French decision-making process, which all through the Fifth Republic has remained highly attentive to African affairs.

FRENCH DECISION-MAKING

Since the creation of the Fifth Republic in 1958, French executive power has been characterized by the pre-eminence of the president. The personality of the first president under this new constitution, Charles de Gaulle, served to reinforce the inherent authority that the office obtained following a 1962 constitutional amendment establishing presidential selection through popular vote. Constitutionally, most of the president's decisions have to be countersigned by both the prime minister and the competent minister. Other decisions can be made unilaterally, such as the nomination and dismissal of the prime minister, the call for a national referendum, and the dissolution of the National Assembly. In defense matters, the Constitution specifies that the president guarantees France's independence, ensures its respect for all treaties, and acts as commander-in-chief of the armed forces. In practice, these constitutional powers, strongly reinforced by a 1964 decree giving the president sole control over the launching of France's nuclear weapons, has led to presidential pre-eminence over defense and foreign policy decision-making. This pre-eminence has been particularly evident in the case of French policy toward Africa. It is an *ad hoc* development which resulted from the collapse of the French *Communauté* project with sub-Saharan francophone Africa in 1960. Since then, the definition of the main policy guidelines in African affairs have remained almost uninterruptedly the purview of the president and his advisory team.

Presidential power is far from absolute, however, even in the reserved areas of competence. Presidential decisions have to be implemented by bureaucracies which are not under the direct control of the presidency. As a separate administration, the presidency is a remarkably light machinery with only a small budget and no independent means of action. It can only intervene when the president decides to take up a specific issue. Everything then focuses on him, but he can only choose from the options presented to him.[2]

Crisis Management and Defense Policy-Making

When President Mitterrand first came to power, some of his close advisors suggested the creation of a French national security council, an idea that the president quickly rejected.[3] Instead, the president broadly defines security policy within the framework of several councils that he chairs. The Council of Ministers sets overall defense policy and provides the major orientations. The Defense Council makes decisions related to the general management of national defense. These councils also supervise the conduct of war. Finally, the Restricted Defense Committee (*Comité de Défense restreint*) meets more regularly and is responsible for the more practical military aspects of policy-making and policy implementation. The Defense Council, which consists of a core of six institutional members, although others may be invited to participate, meets roughly three times a year on an *ad hoc* basis. During the Gulf War, the Defense Council met for 41 consecutive days. The six permanent members of the council include the president, the prime minister, the minister of foreign affairs, the minister of defense, the minister of the interior, and the minister of economy and finance. The chairman of the joint chiefs of staff, the three military service chiefs, the secretary general for national defense, and the head of the armaments board (*Délégué général pour l'armement*) are generally present as well. The Restricted Defense Committee, chaired by the president or, in his absence, by the prime minister, is composed of the chiefs of the armed services, and assumes more direct military and technical responsibilities than the Defense Council.

There is no prescribed regulation regarding the composition of French crisis cabinets or the frequency of their meetings. When necessary, the president assembles a small advisory team, usually consisting of the minister of foreign affairs, the minister of defense, the Elysée military advisor and other presidential advisors, the chairman of the joint chiefs of staff, and the service chiefs. In the case of an African problem, the advisors for African affairs can be invited to participate. Such a team is not considered to be a permanent crisis council, but rather an extemporaneous assembly of advisors and experts.

Both the president and the prime minister have directive powers under the 1958 Constitution. In Samy Cohen's expression, they act as a "dyarchy":

> the president, because he is the commander-in-chief of the armed forces and guarantor of national independence, territorial integrity, Community accords and treaties; and the prime minister, because he is responsible for national defense and directs the action of the government, which

disposes of the armed forces and determines and implements all national policies.[4]

The ambiguity concerning who retains final authority over national security is lifted only in the case of the Air Force's strategic nuclear weapons, over which the president has exclusive powers. The prime minister defers to the president in matters of national security. Prime Minister Rocard only managed the domestic aspects of the 1991 Gulf War.[5] When the president and the prime minister are from different political parties, as was the case during the *cohabitation* in 1986-88 or after elections in 1993, an informal power sharing agreement has to be arranged. Prime Minister Chirac, during the first *cohabitation* period, never sought to create a double command mechanism over military operations.

The prime minister exercises his military responsibilities with the minister of defense. Both remain outside the operational command structures. Under the prime minister's authority, the Ministry of Defense is responsible for the execution of military policies, including mobilization policies, and for the organization and infrastructure of the armed forces. The minister of defense's attributions are therefore linked to the preparation of forces rather than their operational role.

Within the prime minister's office there is a very important crisis management organ for coordinating inter-ministry defense activities through a special secretariat, the General Secretariat for National Defense (SGDN). It is in charge of organizing the Defense Council meetings, synthesizing intelligence reports, and monitoring arms exports.[6] The SGDN is a deliberative forum which initiates proposals. It also coordinates and regulates the interaction between defense authorities and other national security actors. The SGDN operates as an inter-ministerial organ, with 665 personnel from various ministerial, academic or technical fields.[7] The SGDN is also responsible for crisis management in sub-Saharan Africa. The SGDN offers a permanent national security staff, but it does not have any of the policy-making attributes of a national security council.

At the military level, the execution of operations is usually supervised directly by the office of the chairman of the joint chiefs of staff (*Chef d'état-major des armées* or CEMA), who is directly responsible for the execution of military operations abroad, and is accountable to the president and the government. In crises, the operational command chain is limited to the president and the CEMA.

This enhances the authority of the president but makes him directly accountable for possible failures.[8] The CEMA will propose various action plans to deal with a given crisis, and will implement the decisions. The urgency and political sensitivity surrounding a French military reaction to a crisis in Africa, despite the modesty of the means engaged, often requires a command structure at the highest level. In other instances, a special operational command is set up with extensive authority to deal with the military solution to a crisis. In peacetime, a permanent staff under the inspector general for external forces is charged with monitoring the situation outside Europe and designing possible contingency plans.[9]

The president maintains a small military staff of advisors at the Elysée Palace called the *Etat-major particulier du Président de la République*. The commanding officer in charge of this small staff of three officers (one for each service) and administrative personnel acts as a liaison between the president and the security establishment. The position can be interpreted in a restrictive or liberal way, according to the president's desire.[10]

Policy-Making and African Affairs: the Institutional Actors

The President: The post-colonial political scene in France was dominated by only four presidents, who did not always share the same political background but exhibited remarkably concurrent views on France's general role in sub-Saharan Africa. De Gaulle was the originator of a policy which survived in its broad lines into the 1990s. The pre-eminence of the Elysée remained virtually unchallenged in implementing the Gaullist design of cooperative policies in sub-Saharan Africa. The application of the Constitution of the Fifth Republic formalized presidential predominance over foreign affairs.

> General de Gaulle made [foreign and especially African affairs] his, and his successors', reserved domain, expanding this domain and making sure never to lose control over it. Even today, foreign policy is defined at the Elysée; the [foreign] minister, who is chosen with care and whose position is on average more stable than that of his other ministerial colleagues, is one of the privileged interlocutors of the head of state.[11]

There also exists a small, special team of presidential advisors who help shape the general direction of French foreign policy, follow up on the presidential agenda, and act as intermediaries with advisors and

ministers of other heads of state. Africa, unlike any other region of the
world, has its own advisor(s) directly within the office of the French
president. The position of the Elysée advisor for African affairs
received its impetus and power from its first occupant: Jacques Foccart.
The de Gaulle-Foccart duo provided French African policy-making with
a visionary and an implementor, based on total trust by de Gaulle in
Foccart and on complete fidelity and discretion by the latter. French
policy-making toward sub-Saharan Africa has traditionally relied on
personalities more than institutions. It is only in more recent times that
the trend has been to incorporate institutional actors, such as the
Ministry of Foreign Affairs.

The role of the advisor has gradually shifted to reflect his position
as a special counsellor to the president and not as an executive officer.
The advisory staff at the Elysée has also been drastically reduced from
about 17 staff members[12] (not including dozens of support personnel)
under Foccart to two or three advisors (plus a few support personnel)
under the Mitterrand administration.

For 10 years, Jean-Christophe Mitterrand, the president's son and
a former journalist covering Africa, served as African advisor to his
father. Although accused of nepotism, the president's son served a
precise purpose. As one French official explained:

> his case may appear shocking as seen from France, but not as seen from
> Africa, where only the tribal chief or his kin are taken seriously. [...]
> He avoids getting personally involved in the issues, and keeps us, *grosso
> modo*, informed of his activities. We have no serious problems with
> him.[13]

He might have lacked policy-making experience, but he made "up
for it in that vital bureaucratic quality of access to the president."[14] The
nomination of his successors, all career diplomats, enforced the much
needed connection between the president's advisors and the Ministry of
Foreign Affairs, portending a greater role for the latter in the
management of African affairs.

At the Elysée, the coordinating body for African affairs holds a bi-
weekly meeting. Participants include the Elysée advisors, members
from the prime minister's office, the Ministries of Foreign Affairs,
Cooperation, Economy & Finance, and Defense, as well as a
representative of the Elysée Military Staff, of the Treasury, and of the
intelligence community. This group coordinates information on Africa,

acts as an advisory board and prepares decisions for submission to the president. In times of crisis, the "African" Elysée cabinet convenes on a weekly basis, or even more frequently, and is at times taken over by a higher, ministerial crisis cabinet.

Ministry of Cooperation: France's special relationship with sub-Saharan Africa is reflected in the creation of the Ministry of Cooperation and Development in 1961. This agency was formed solely to manage the agreements and accords between France and sub-Saharan (mainly francophone) Africa. Establishing a ministerial position for this task further illustrates the importance of the Franco-African relationship. With 58 percent of all French aid, including financial aid and loans, going to sub-Saharan Africa, France ranks first among donors to this region of the world.[15] The Ministry of Cooperation supervises about 30 percent of the overall French development budget to the Third World, or close to 6 billion French francs in 1988.[16] The peculiarity of the Ministry of Cooperation lies in its responsibility for both civilian and military aid programs. The Ministry maintains about 10,000 personnel in sub-Saharan Africa: 9,000 technicians, engineers, economists and trainers under the technical cooperation program, and 1,000 teachers.[17] Military cooperation personnel are also paid by the Ministry of Cooperation. During Mitterrand's presidency, half-a-dozen ministers of cooperation had succeeded each other by 1992. The first was the highly idealistic and ambitious Jean-Pierre Cot. He was to resign eighteen months later. The Ministry was then plagued by scandals of embezzlement which seriously threatened the whole government. The new conservative government which emerged from the March 1993 legislative elections entrusted the position of minister of cooperation to Michel Roussin, whose government career included four years as deputy chief of intelligence from 1977 to 1981.

Despite efforts under the early Mitterrand administration to integrate the Ministry of Cooperation and Development within the Ministry of Foreign Affairs, which would have ended the special policy focus on sub-Saharan Africa in French foreign policy, the merger was never realized.

Franc Zone and the Ministry of Finance: France's monetary cooperation program with 14 African countries[18] has transformed the French Treasury into a prominent force in sub-Saharan Africa. The Franc Zone has been dubbed "the first pillar on which France rested its neo-colonial structure."[19] By tying post-colonial currencies to its own, France has in return imposed a monetary discipline, coercive as it may appear, which resulted in keeping one step ahead of balance-of-payment difficulties. The corollary was that it relied often on rather demanding fiscal regulations. Still, the Franc Zone has been an effective control mechanism, admired for its overall success even if readjustments have often been advocated. It "is probably the most original of France's commitments in Africa," unparalleled by those of any other western country.[20]

The 14 participating countries can be grouped into two regions (West and central Africa), which, when one adds the Comoros, form the Franc Zone. The Franc Zone operates according to three principles: the absolute freedom to transfer funds; the unlimited convertibility at fixed parity between the currencies of the zone, called the Franc CFA[21] and the Comoran franc; and the centralization of African exchange reserves, 65 percent of which are with the French Treasury. From 1948 until 1994, the conversion rate remained at 50 CFA franc per French franc, despite chronic pressures to devaluate the CFA franc. The Franc Zone brings three important advantages to the participating African countries:[22] first, a basis for monetary stability and low inflation rates compared to the rest of Africa; second, open access to foreign exchange; and finally, strengthened regional solidarity through development of trade, facilitated by a common currency. The drawbacks were that the CFA franc became increasingly overvalued and that it contributed to the zone's trade deficit. The strain imposed by the unadjusted exchange rate also harmed the French budget. On January 11, 1994, in view of the cost to France as lender of last resort and under strong pressure from the International Monetary Fund (IMF) and the World Bank, the government of French Prime Minister Balladur agreed, in cooperation with the African partners, to a 50 percent devaluation of the CFA franc and a 33 percent devaluation of the Comoran franc. Without the devaluation, French aid funds would have been swallowed in helping CFA countries to service their growing foreign debts, and the IMF or the World Bank would not have extended fresh credits and loans.

France's control over the monetary policy of the Franc Zone, even after the humbling experience of the devaluation, will remain substantial. This monetary control and the French Ministry of Finance's role in the management of the francophone African debt are used to induce African countries to accept further economic reforms. In this respect, the Treasury has shown increasing receptivity, at times reluctantly, toward IMF and World Bank efforts to adjust economies and balance of payments. The more prudent approach of the financial community, eager to preserve stability and continuity, clashes regularly with the all too frequent policy changes at the Ministry of Cooperation. In view of their formidable leverage, the advocates of prudence often prevail. The Treasury plays another important role in the restructuring of Third World public debts since it hosts the Secretariat of the Paris Club. Since 1956, the Paris Club has regrouped representatives from the major industrialized nations, and reviews the government-to-government credit status and solvency of Third World debtor countries. Renegotiations and rescheduling of debt owed to official creditors or guaranteed by them is subject to an agreement by the debtor country with the IMF on an economic stabilization program.

Caisse Centrale de Coopération Economique (CCCE): A further means of France's financial involvement is the CCCE, whose role is to arrange for the financing of the productive sector and of the modernization of infrastructure. The CCCE provided 6-8 billion French francs per year in loans and grants to Third World countries between 1987-91; with FF 7.9 billion in 1991, of which FF 3 billion were grants.[23] A total of 34 countries in sub-Saharan Africa and the Indian Ocean received close to 90 percent of those loans and grants, with the remainder going to Maghreb countries and to 15 countries in the South Pacific. Côte d'Ivoire was the main recipient of CCCE funding in 1991 (FF 1.8 billion), followed by Cameroon (FF 1.1 billion), Angola (FF 714 million), and Gabon (FF 547 million). France has succeeded, either directly or through its influence within multilateral development organizations, in enhancing its financial leverage in Africa. France's use of its influence in multilateral organizations and meetings reflects an admission that the task of francophone Africa's development is too formidable to be undertaken by a single power. At the 1990 Franco-African summit in La Baule, President Mitterrand stressed the need for additional partners to tackle the Third World's (and Africa's in particular) financial crisis: "Aid to the Third World cannot rely only on the French contribution. France alone is not in a position to stop the current decline. What is needed is a worldwide effort."[24] France routinely uses its authority and leverage in the European Community, the G-7 meetings of the seven major industrial powers, the International Monetary Fund, and the World Bank to promote development schemes which favor its African partners.

Ministry of Foreign Affairs: Under the Fifth Republic, the Ministry of Foreign Affairs has often been relegated to a procedural, peripheral role with regard to foreign policy, especially policy on francophone sub-Saharan Africa.

> The institutionalization of the authority of the presidency of the Republic with the 1958 constitution, and the utilization of foreign policy as a major weapon in creating a more cohesive domestic situation, have considerably diminished the position of the Foreign Ministry in the area of policy formulation.[25]

With the Fifth Republic, foreign policy became the *domaine réservé* of the presidency. An alleged advantage of this *domaine réservé* is that the president's seven-year term provides a political continuity that the parliament or the government could not match.[26]

The Elysée staff, of forty to fifty people, deals with those areas that the president considers his own, and can, at times, rival or outstrip the influence of the Foreign Ministry. Nowhere is this more true than with regard to francophone Africa. The office of the advisor for African affairs at the Elysée and the Ministry of Cooperation and Development retain a tight control over their respective domains. Even if the Ministry of Foreign Affairs is less involved in the formulation of policies, especially with regard to sub-Saharan Africa, it remains an important actor in the execution of those policies. Of all the countries that France assists in sub-Saharan Africa, only one, anglophone Malawi, has a program managed directly by the Quai d'Orsay.[27] Normal diplomatic procedures were not applicable to former French colonies which retained close, sometimes even personal, ties with the presidency.

The enlargement of French influence in Africa to non-francophone countries under President Giscard d'Estaing has allowed the Quai d'Orsay to gain a greater say in African policy-making. With Roland Dumas as Mitterrand's minister of foreign affairs until 1993, power-sharing between the Elysée and the Quai d'Orsay had been problem-free. Dumas, a personal friend of Mitterrand for close to 40 years, could rely on the president's full confidence.[28] His nomination opened the door to a gradual shift of authority from the presidency to the government. This transfer is far from completed, but it marks the banalization of the formerly "special" relationship with African partners.

Prime Minister: The office of the prime minister is the only alternate maker of African policy beside the Elysée and the Ministry of

Cooperation and Development that has played a significant role, and then only during the periods of *cohabitation*. The office of the prime minister normally has an embryonic African staff. During the Mitterrand years, with the exception of the two *cohabitation* periods between the Socialist President Mitterrand and Conservative prime ministers, this staff was reduced to one advisor whose competence also covered other areas.

Cohabitation is an outcome of the intentional mismatch between the term of the president and that of the government in the bicephalous French system. It underscores the constitutional power of the prime minister in managing external affairs; this power is never exercised in sub-Saharan Africa when the president and the prime minister are of the same political party. The March 1986 legislative elections brought the right-of-center Jacques Chirac into office as prime minister until the next elections in 1988. The two leaders concluded an informal power-sharing arrangement, with Mitterrand in charge of France's general image and influence in Africa while Chirac focused on finances and concrete projects. The francophone African leaders "played the *cohabitation* game by cultivating both camps."[29] The March 1993 legislative elections gave an overwhelming victory to France's Conservatives, and Edouard Balladur became prime minister. This second *cohabitation* started on a less conflictual basis than the first.

The African Commercial Lobby: Of all the pre-conceived notions about the reasons for France's lasting political interest in Africa, one of the most tenacious is that France wants to preserve its privileged access to African resources and markets. The presence of an active African lobby in Paris feeds this perception by campaigning on the theme of Africa's economic importance to France. The defense agreements signed by France with some of its former African colonies often contained clauses guaranteeing France exclusive rights over the exploitation of strategic minerals. The combination of strategic and economic interests was deemed to be at the core of France's policy, aid programs and military agreements with African partners.

After thirty years of post-colonial influence in sub-Saharan Africa, much of this rationale has to be put in perspective. An interpretation which offered some credibility in the 1960s has almost completely lost its relevance in the 1990s. France's exports to Africa in 1991 were primarily with five northern African countries (54 percent) and with South Africa (7 percent). Sub-Saharan Africa, excluding South Africa, accounted for only 39 percent of the FF 75 billion (U.S. $12.5 billion)

French exports to the whole continent in 1991. Imports from the whole continent total FF 65 billion (U.S. $11 billion): 53 percent from northern Africa, 6 percent from South Africa, and 41 percent from sub-Saharan Africa.[30] France has been able to preserve a positive commercial balance with Africa since 1985, when the balance was close to zero. The commercial deficit with sub-Saharan Africa, excluding South Africa, was around FF 2.1 billion ($350 million). The breakdown by country in sub-Saharan Africa is given in Table 1.

With the exception of post-apartheid South Africa, French products have a difficult time penetrating non-francophone markets. French exports to South Africa increased by 73 percent compared to 1990 due to the new trade policy adopted after the dismantlement of apartheid.

There are around 1,200 small-to-medium sized French-owned companies in Africa, and approximately 1,800 subsidiaries of large French corporations, for a total of 245,000 employees out of a world-wide total of 1.75 million. French corporate investments in the Third World represent about FF 6 billion, only 5 percent of all French investments abroad.[31] Three important mutations have marked French commercial and industrial activities in francophone Africa: new Third World markets have been cornered, reducing the previous emphasis on francophone Africa; big industrial groups in Africa have abandoned most of the activities where they do not benefit from a monopolistic position; and African markets have contracted as local conditions have deteriorated. The times of easy profit under the protectionist umbrella of Franco-African agreements have passed. French companies failed to adapt to a more competitive environment, even in francophone Africa. The result was that by 1992, up to one-third of French subsidiaries in Africa had to close down and another third were in the midst of a deep restructuring.[32] The coziness of Franco-African trade will be further disrupted by political changes in Africa. The surge of new elites will break former ties and privileges, and French companies will have to reorganize their whole approach to doing business in the region.

The French trade surplus with sub-Saharan Africa in 1991, excluding South Africa which was not an aid recipient, was FF 2.1 billion, or roughly $350 million. This represents only 27 percent of the French civilian aid package. Military aid, in the form of French prepositioned forces, is not included in this aid package. France's trade surplus with sub-Saharan Africa does not justify in and of itself the extent and duration of French political and military cooperation. The assumption that French aid policy in sub-Saharan Africa is predicated

TABLE 1: French Trade with Sub-Saharan Africa, 1991

Country	Exports	Rank	%	Imports	Rank	%
South Africa	5,298	1	15.5	3,798	3	12.4
Côte d'Ivoire	3,589	2	10.5	3,217	5	10.5
Nigeria	3,566	3	10.4	3,837	2	12.5
Senegal	2,446	4	7.1	1,321	8	4.3
Cameroon	2,442	5	7.1	3,264	4	10.7
Gabon	2,256	6	6.6	4,968	1	16.2
Congo	1,519	7	4.4	904	10	3.0
Mauritius	1,084	8	3.2	1,388	7	4.5
Angola	992	9	2.9	1,957	6	6.4
Togo	932	10	2.7	148	22	0.5
Guinea	886	11	2.6	275	15	0.9
Burkina Faso	828	12	2.4	184	19	0.6
Madagascar	788	13	2.3	601	12	2.0
Mauritania	728	14	2.1	309	14	1.0
Benin	653	15	1.9	38	32	0.1
Mali	642	16	1.9	49	29	0.2
Zaire	622	17	1.8	275	17	0.9
Kenya	612	18	1.8	329	13	1.1
Niger	490	19	1.4	1,289	9	4.2
Chad	454	20	1.3	35	33	0.1
Total Top 20	30,827		89.9	28,186		92.1
TOTAL SSA	34,289		100	30,627		100

Source: "L'Afrique, un marché profitable," Jeune Afrique, 13-26 August 1992, 133-35.

on economic interests is thus put in perspective. The guaranteed access to strategic minerals is not as vital an issue as it may have appeared at the height of the Cold War, especially given the large use of substitute materials which have appeared on the market. Aid and trade policies do not correlate when considering French policies in sub-Saharan Africa.

HISTORIC OVERVIEW OF
PRESIDENTIAL POLICIES TOWARD AFRICA

Charles de Gaulle (1958-69)

Failing to find agreement among African colonies to create two large African federations in West and Equatorial Africa, de Gaulle offered a looser commonwealth type of association with France. The *Communauté*, or Community of former French colonies, was based on a common nationality, senate, and president. The president of the Community was the president of France, with substantial powers over such matters as common defense, external affairs, currency, economic policy and strategic minerals. The new member states of the Community enjoyed a large measure of internal powers. The project was submitted for ratification in all potential member states. Only in Guinea did voters reject the Community and, as a consequence, become precipitately independent on October 2, 1958. De Gaulle's first priority with regard to sub-Saharan Africa was to ensure the success of decolonization.[33] Whether de Gaulle saw the creation of the French Community as an instrumental step in bringing about the independence of francophone countries in sub-Saharan Africa or as an end in itself is still unclear. In an interview with Ambassador Francis Terry McNamara, former U.S. Ambassador to Gabon, Jacques Foccart contended that:

> General de Gaulle foresaw political independence in 1958. The General viewed the Community as a step in a process rather than an end in itself. De Gaulle, Foccart insisted, anticipated granting independence in 1965 or 1966; the fact that independence came only two years after the formation of the Community surprised the General.[34]

By 1960, all French colonies in sub-Saharan Africa, with the exception of Djibouti, had become independent. The Community had collapsed under the increasing pressure by member states to reach full independence. France sought to preserve its influence in the region by granting independence within the framework of strong bilateral cooperative links. President de Gaulle's immense political talent and his excellent image in sub-Saharan Africa, as well as his pragmatism and adaptability, made these links acceptable to African nations.[35] The preservation of strong ties between France and Africa also served as one of the cornerstones of de Gaulle's foreign policy.[36] This new cooperative relationship was formalized through a series of bilateral economic, cultural, judicial, and military agreements.

> At the military level, this went into effect in the Fifth Republic's endeavor to maintain France's tradition of a military presence in Africa. To a large extent this effort was successful, for, contrary to the situation of other colonial powers, French decolonization never meant the end of a military presence; rather, it meant an adjustment of such a presence.[37]

France organized its military presence in sub-Saharan Africa around two types of bilateral agreements: defense and military cooperation. These helped shape the legal basis of France's cooperative scheme which was to form a new, post-colonial "intimacy." John Chipman, in his book *French Power in Africa*, warns about French policy-makers' use of the word "cooperation" which, according to him, disguises:

> the practical effect of the agreements: continued development and other aid on the part of the former colonial power in return for continued loyalty and special favors on the part of the newly independent states of Black Africa. [...] The establishment of a policy of co-operation with independent Black Africa can therefore only be seen, both in its detail and in its general effect, as a successful assertion of power by France over the former colonial Empire.[38]

The success of de Gaulle's ingenious scheme to satisfy African demands for independence while maintaining France's position at the center of a free cooperative association with former African colonies is a tribute to his statesmanship. This "special relationship" is:

> a phenomenon which cannot be explained merely by observing economic, political, cultural or even military factors. It is more than the adding together of the benefits which can be gained in one field or another by the different countries [...]. There exists a certain mystery, an enigma, in the 'special relationship.'[39]

Dr. William Zartman, a well-known American specialist on Africa, identified four components behind France's unique and lasting commitment to cooperation with sub-Saharan Africa.[40] First, there is the cultural commitment and its corollary, the French *mission civilisatrice*, whereby France tries to convert the "accident of speaking a language together" into a cultural entity dominated by France. Much of the legitimacy of France's claim to world status comes from its cultural predominance over a francophone realm.

The second component is a moral commitment, impregnated with the Gaullist view that France owed its former colonies some support. It is a significant exhibition of genuine generosity induced partly by the role African colonies played during World War II,[41] a contribution which de Gaulle never forgot, and partly resulting from the sense "that France initially supported developing countries on the road to development and left before the job was complete."[42]

Third, there is the economic commitment to protect former areas of economic interest where French business, commerce and investments are still very predominant. Finally, the fourth element is the political commitment in the form of French support for a stable system of relationships with African countries. In return, there is an at least implicit African support for France's power position in the world merely by the existence of the large family of francophone countries. The United Nations is a forum for the manifestations of this support, where France's influence "guarantees [it] a dozen or so sympathetic voices in the United Nations General Assembly and helps justify [its] permanent seat on the Security Council."[43]

De Gaulle's early interest in Africa faded after the successful implementation of the cooperative plan. Jacques Foccart was granted considerable leeway by de Gaulle as a result of the French disengagement from Africa marked by the end of the Algerian war. The year 1963 denotes "the true beginning of de Gaulle's foreign policy,"[44] when he focused increasingly on Europe, NATO and France's place as an independent power. Foccart's initial title was modified after the collapse of the French Community from "Secretary General of the French Community," to "Secretary General in the Presidency of the Republic for the Community and for African and Malagasy Affairs." Foccart served without interruption under Presidents de Gaulle and Pompidou, except for a short absence in 1969 when the Interim President Alain Poher dismissed him after de Gaulle's resignation. Foccart had daily meetings with de Gaulle, and his

Secretariat was in charge of all policy problems related to sub-Saharan Africa. Foccart was also in charge of scheduling presidential visitors, including presidents of African countries.[45]

The close, personalized and informal network between French and African leaders has been sometimes dubbed "Franco-African intimacy," in which Foccart was the essential, unavoidable point of contact. Foccart, under de Gaulle only, had "also been given the immensely powerful task of overseeing the French secret services for the president."[46] Foccart has been called an "absolute king-maker on the continent,"[47] The accession to power of President Bongo in Gabon perfectly illustrated 's role. In discussing Foccart, one cannot help but mention his *réseau*, or network, a "loose web of well-placed friends and associates whom he could call upon to provide information or muscle as the situation required. The fact that this was not a tightly organized formal organization in no way detracted from its effectiveness."[48] Beyond the Foccart mystique remains the image of a discreet and highly knowledgeable advisor whose driving desire was to implement de Gaulle's African policy diligently. The prominence of his position and his influence is a reflection of the higher priority given to sub-Saharan Africa during the early years of independence.

The development of an independent nuclear arsenal under de Gaulle required a considerable budgetary effort at the expense of conventional forces, and overseas troops were the first to be reduced.[49] De Gaulle presided over the most significant military disengagement from Africa, made possible by defense agreements and the development in 1963-64 of an intervention force based in France. This redirection of France's defense policy led to a rapid decline in Africa's strategic importance for the defense of the metropole.[50] In 1962, there were some 70,000 French soldiers stationed in nearly 100 African garrisons; 1,800 troops on the Horn of Africa, 11,000 in 25 garrisons on and around the Malagasy Island, 12,000 in 25 garrisons dispersed over Equatorial Africa, and 45,000 in 45 garrisons in West Africa.[51] Over the subsequent years, the function of the bases would gradually change to mainly one of support to the home-based French intervention force. By 1964, French troops in Africa were down to 21,000, and by 1970 to only 6,500 men.[52]

Nevertheless, the reduction in military troops on the African continent did not signal an end to French military involvement. France was called repeatedly to intervene during the early years of independence in the new states, mainly in support of governments threatened by internal revolutionary movements. French forces were active in Cameroon, against the *Union des populations du Cameroun* movement in 1960-61, and in Mauritania in 1961. Less important interventions also took place in Gabon (1962), Congo-Brazzaville (1960 and 1962), Chad (between 1960 and 1963) and Niger (1963). The most publicized intervention took place in Gabon in February 1964 to support President M'ba. These efforts at regime stabilization were not conducted systematically, and there were some instances of internal rebellion (Togo, Congo-Brazzaville and Dahomey, all in 1963) that were not crushed by French troops. At this early stage in post-colonial history, however, France usually responded positively, both to preserve the viability of friendly regimes and to retain its own right to intervene. By 1964, de Gaulle assumed that the state of Franco-African solidarity was ensured and "his wish was merely to maintain the privileged and peaceful relationship between France and the African nations."[53] Subsequent internal troubles in 1965-66 in Dahomey, the CAR, and Upper-Volta came at a period of intervention fatigue in France, causing de Gaulle to caution African states on "the subordination of French aid to their ability of keeping order at home."[54] No French military action was taken in support of those latter crises, giving French armed forces a temporary respite of about three years. The last operations during de Gaulle's presidency took place in 1967 in the CAR and in Chad in 1968.

France's most controversial operation in sub-Saharan Africa under de Gaulle was the "covert" action in 1968 in Nigeria, which took the form of shipments of French arms to support the Biafran insurgency. This support stopped short of official recognition of the Biafran Ojukwu government, although it contradicted prior French policies of preserving the territorial integrity and political viability of newly independent states.

> President de Gaulle's private view (not necessarily shared by the Ministry of Foreign Affairs), was that the break-up of Nigeria, a potential African great power, was in the French interest. As a potential African regional power, a strong Nigeria could made France's policy in West Africa more difficult to implement.[55]

The Biafran secession, which was prolonged due to France's initial support, failed in January 1970, six months after de Gaulle's departure from power.

During de Gaulle's tenure as president, French action in Africa remained flexible and moderate in scope, not least because Africa had not yet become an arena for superpower rivalry. With the exception of the role played by France in the Biafran secession, French action was consistent with de Gaulle's cooperative policies and with the legal defense framework installed bilaterally with young African countries.

Georges Pompidou (1969-74)

President Pompidou might not have shared the same sentimental attachment to Africa as his predecessor, but he nevertheless pursued a policy heavily inspired by de Gaulle. The most visible sign of this continuity was the reinstatement of Foccart to his African responsibilities on June 26, 1969.[56] (The Interim President Alain Poher had dismissed Foccart less than two months earlier.) Four main developments marked Pompidou's policy toward Africa: the renegotiation of defense and cooperation agreements after continued French military disengagement from Africa, the spilling over of the superpower rivalry into Africa, the initiation of the Franco-African summit meetings, and the progressive expansion in the number of African countries supported by France. In many respects, the Pompidou presidency was a transition in African policy-making between the paternalism of de Gaulle and the more active policing of Africa under Giscard d'Estaing.

The most drastic overhaul of Franco-African relations since 1960 came with the July 1972 announcement by Niger to withdraw from its defense agreement with France. This move, which was followed by similar withdrawals or important revisions of defense agreements by Cameroon, Congo, Dahomey, Madagascar, and Togo, was indicative of a new mood in francophone Africa. Rather than belonging simply to a Franco-African or Euro-African entity, African states were beginning to see themselves as members of an emerging Third World.[57] The legal changes in the defense agreements did not upset France's military capabilities in Africa. Six countries maintained their defense agreements while others engaged in Technical Military Assistance Agreements, which do not require France to provide anything more than technical aid. The latter are not legally equivalent to regular defense agreements; nevertheless, France has felt compelled to intervene on several occasions in countries with only assistance agreements.[58]

The transition toward superpower rivalry in Africa was slowly gaining momentum during Pompidou's presidency. In the late 1950s and early 1960s, the Soviet Union had gained influence in Guinea, Mali and Ghana. With the possible exception of Soviet support to Ghana, Soviet activism was relatively benign and had only a limited impact on neighboring African countries. French strategists did not consider this Soviet presence as threatening, and little was done militarily to roll-back Soviet influence. The general trend in France until the early 1970s was to consider Africa as a "strategic extension" of Europe; in case of a general European war, Africa could serve as a hinterland from which a Soviet conquest of Europe could eventually be challenged.[59] The maintenance of a vast Euro-African strategic ensemble provided an additional rationale for strengthening military links between France and Africa. Until the mid-1970s, this view progressed to include new concerns such as the Soviet political infiltration into Africa through revolutionary wars and Soviet access to regional power platforms with new bases, mainly in the Horn of Africa. Soviet influence in Africa was not feared for its ability to deprive Europe of a safe withdrawal platform. Instead, it was considered a threat to European sea lanes, European access to African raw materials, and European security through the possible encirclement of Europe.

Even before Pompidou's death in 1974, France had come to recognize the potentially debilitating impact of the new Soviet gains in Africa, and the danger of an ideologically motivated superpower rivalry on the continent. France's position would be to contain the more aggressive aspects of the new Soviet policies while trying to insulate the francophone realm as much as possible from any superpower involvement. France wished to be viewed by its African partners as a third, less ideologically oriented force besides the two dominant world powers.

Another important development in French policy-making on Africa under Pompidou was the 1973 occurrence of the first post-colonial Franco-African summit in Paris, resulting from a request made by President Diori of Niger. It involved presidents or senior ministers from 10 African francophone countries and France.[60] The order of the day included discussion of the Franc Zone and of relations between Europe and Africa. This initial conference grew to be an annual event, which included 35 countries by the year 1990, and had become a major instrument of French policy-making on Africa.

A final contribution by Pompidou was his attempt to reach beyond the traditional francophone African partners, mainly with a view to extend France's economic activities.[61] Under his presidency, the circle of France's special partners in Africa was enlarged to include the former Belgian dependencies of Zaire, Rwanda, and Burundi. The practice of widening and, to some extent, diluting the French special relationship "has been resented and resisted by certain charter members of the francophone club."[62] The resistance arose from fear that their privileged status in Paris would be gradually eroded with the arrival of newcomers. France pursued this enlargement but continued to extend special treatment to the core members of the "old guard."

Valéry Giscard d'Estaing (1974-81)

Upon his arrival at the Elysée, President Giscard d'Estaing suppressed the "General Secretariat for the Community and for African and Malagasy Affairs," and did not reappoint Jacques Foccart. Instead he initially relied on René Journiac, a former assistant of Foccart, who did not benefit from the same power, influence, or staff as his predecessor. The president maintained closer contacts with the Ministries of Cooperation, Defense, and Foreign Affairs. The Quai d'Orsay saw its role increase in conjunction with the "globalization" of French influence in lusophone and anglophone Africa, requiring a broader approach than the prior African policy, which had focused exclusively on former colonies.[63] Journiac acted mainly as a presidential representative to African leaders and as a negotiator-at-large. His career was interrupted by his accidental death in February 1980. He was then replaced by his deputy, Martin Kirsch, until the end of Giscard's mandate a over a year later.

By the mid-1970s, the African environment had changed significantly from that which prevailed when de Gaulle shaped his vision of exclusive bilateralism. Events in Africa had overtaken some of the premises on which de Gaulle's approach rested, and France could no longer assume exclusivity in its dealings with former colonies. Soviet-Cuban penetration, already strong in the Horn of Africa, accelerated dramatically with the independence of the last Portuguese colonies in 1975. The immediate threat to the traditional French realm was limited, with the exception of Djibouti, due to its location in the Horn of Africa.[64] Still, France was extremely concerned by Soviet-Cuban moves and their "destabilizing" impact.

In the French view, the new Soviet influence exacerbated the structural weakness of the African continent and created a "climate of instability" affecting the historic "responsibilities" of France in Africa. [...] The French suddenly realized that their African clients, whom they had taken for granted for so long, were the prey of a rival great power. It was therefore essential that France reassure its African allies and reestablish a solid front against the Soviet threat - particularly since no other western nation was ready to enter the African struggle.[65]

In the mid-1970s, the U.S., which had previously considered the African continent as "secondary for their security interests,"[66] shared France's concerns about the increasing Soviet-Cuban presence on the continent. It would be incorrect, however, to view France's military activism in Africa at the time as subordinate to U.S. or NATO policies. France was not the *gendarme* of NATO, a comment often heard at the time of French participation in the two Shaba operations in Zaire. It would be an oversimplification to present France's agenda in Africa as subservient to a more general western agenda. France's interests in Africa were defined by its own compelling logic; they were different, though sometimes complementary, to western strategic concerns in the area. President Giscard d'Estaing was always very adamant in dispelling any sense of collusion between France and NATO.[67] While France avoided being seen as a superpower proxy, French military interventions objectively served overall western interests, although France alone bore their financial and political costs. The Gaullist case-by-case approach gave way to a more systematic, ideological pro-western approach. The Gaullists rejected the role of NATO-ization of France's African policies, and feared being dragged into some sort of African equivalent to Vietnam. In that concern, Gaullists paradoxically joined leftist attacks on Giscard's policy:

The paradox [...] lies in the fact that although it is basically faithful to Gaullist principles, it has been perceived as a departure - even a betrayal - of de Gaulle's heritage. [Through] resorting to a series of specific but simultaneous military actions, Giscard was trying to protect France's traditional sphere of influence in Africa, while also delineating France's role in a world still dominated by the superpowers. Because the African context itself had changed as a result of Soviet competition, there was an inescapable coincidence between France's own traditional interests and those of the West as a whole.[68]

Although a NATO patronage was clearly not acceptable to Giscard, he still tried to broaden the legitimacy of France's interventions by claiming to act on behalf of a Euro-African solidarity, which was much more politically acceptable in France. In his own words, Giscard clothed his action during the first Shaba crisis in 1977 under a European mantle: "Europe cannot disinterest itself from what happens on the African continent; it would be on its part the most guilty of all heedless attitudes. We wanted [during the Shaba I operation] to signal the solidarity between Europe and Africa."[69]

Not all European partners, however, were ready to grant France the right to act on their behalf, especially in a country with as controversial a regime as Mobutu's in Zaire.[70] France's failure to Europeanize support for and participation in military actions in Africa discredited the notion of any "inescapable coincidence" between its African policies and those of Europe in general, leaving France alone to do all the fighting.[71]

Never had the cumulative effect of contradictions in French policy-making toward Africa been so challenging as under Giscard. France wanted to be an autonomous military power offering a third option after the two superpowers, but it needed the active help of the U.S. to intervene militarily in Zaire and could not help but serve western interests. France wanted to act in Africa on behalf of a Franco-European solidarity movement, but was strongly rebuffed by some of its European partners for even suggesting the idea.[72] Under Giscard, France expanded its economic and political sphere of influence in Africa as a way to gain a larger hinterland and maintain its independence from the superpowers,[73] but was criticized for diluting the special relationship with older African partners[74] and antagonizing Belgian authorities.[75]

Whether successful or not, Giscard's African policy was marked by increased military activism and interventions. To that effect, France strengthened and modernized its military means of intervention. Toward the middle of his term, Giscard increased French military aid to Africa, which, more or less stagnant since 1960, jumped from $414 million in 1977 to $644 million in 1978, and has climbed ever since.[76] The number of French military bases and garrisons on the African continent decreased from about 100 at the end of the period of colonial hegemony to only six under Giscard.[77] At their reduced level in the mid-1970s, the bases served as staging points for a newly restructured intervention force. The legal framework of the bases was also revised, and the emphasis shifted toward rapidly deployable forces in France. Giscard advocated the strengthening of French forces "that would cope with the North-South threat."[78]

The restructuring of forces in France was carried out with virtually exclusive concern for French capabilities in Africa.[79] This took the form of adding the 31st *Demi Brigade* (3,500 men) with heavier armored firepower to the existing core of the *Force d'Intervention* consisting of the 11th Parachute Division and the 9th Marine Infantry Division. The total forces theoretically available for interventions overseas amounted to 26,100 troops. Taking into account logistics for rapid deployments and combat availability, the real number of troops available for immediate action in Africa was closer to 10,000.[80]

Acknowledging the threat of Soviet-Cuban penetration in Africa to French interests improved France's ability for military intervention, the necessity of which became evident. However, individual interventions had varying motivations. There were five main theaters of operation, all in francophone Africa: Mauritania (November 1977-June 1978, and 1979), Chad (June 1977-May 1980), Zaire (April 1977, and May-June 1978), Djibouti (1976 and 1977), and the Central African Republic (September 1979). All operations had a regime-stabilizing effect, although they were undertaken with various rationales ranging from humanitarian action (Zaire), to the deterrence of hostage- taking (Mauritania), the restoration of peace after violations of a cease- fire (Chad), and the removal of a head of state (CAR).[81] The last operation was one of Giscard's most controversial because it constituted direct interference in the internal matters of a sovereign entity against the ruling authority. With such an active record of keeping "his soldiers hopping,"[82] Giscard was criticized as "NATO's gendarme in Africa." François Mitterrand, then in the opposition, qualified France's role in Africa as that of the "Cuba of the West."[83]

A characteristic that appeared with increasing frequency in France's interventions under Giscard was the need to involve other African countries. Some of them had already expressed some tacit support for French actions by granting overflight rights, or by allowing French pre-positioned forces in their country to be used in another crisis area.[84] At the political level, there was often strong pressure from African leaders to invite France to act. The leaders of the Côte d'Ivoire and Senegal reportedly urged Giscard to take action against Emperor Bokassa I.[85] France increasingly advocated the creation of Inter-African forces to supplant its initial intervention. In some instances, as in the Shaba I crisis of 1977, France preferred to stay outside of the fighting by supporting the deployment of a Moroccan contingent in Zaire to deal with the rebels. During the Shaba II crisis of 1978, French and Belgian forces were eventually replaced by Senegalese, Ivorian, Central African, Togolese, and Gabonese contingents. France strongly encouraged such African multilateral actions, which were more successful than unilateral French action at gaining broad European support. The promotion of cooperative African involvement continued under the presidency of François Mitterrand, partly due to General Jeannou Lacaze, whose position as French chief of staff overlapped the end of Giscard's term and the beginning of Mitterrand's. Upon his retirement, Lacaze was named special advisor for African affairs to the minister of defense. He contended that France would could not act indefinitely in Africa on its own and should train Inter-African forces, headquartered in Togo, to deal with regional problems.[86]

The military operations in Djibouti in 1976 and 1977 were different in nature from other French involvements. In 1976, Djibouti was still a colony and Giscard, to his credit, no longer followed the Gaullist policy of relying on the Afar, an ethnic minority in power, to break the deadlock hindering the decolonization of France's last French colony on the continent.[87] Giscard also pursued Pompidou's policy of enlarging French influence in Africa, first by reintegrating Guinea-Conakry into the family circle through a memorable visit in 1978, and second by opening the Franco-African summits to lusophone, hispanic, and even anglophone African countries.

It would be wrong to view French activism under the presidency of Giscard d'Estaing as limited to anti-Soviet and military dimensions; it also rested on greater economic and cultural penetration. Giscard's general vision of Africa stressed long-term advantages for France and tried to act upon them:

> The president notices that Africa is fluid, vulnerable, but his thinking is concerned with the long term: that continent will be a major factor in international politics in the 21st century. Geographic proximity, and numerous links, among which often language, make it [France's] hinterland.[88]

The president shared the Gaullist view that "it was by reaffirming its commitment to Africa that France could regain its balance, and live the great Gaullist dream of a strong France, shouldered by the African continent it sought to awaken."[89] However, this priority in Africa required generous funding. Giscard launched some audacious and grand initiatives in favor of Africa in an effort to mobilize important resources from western nations and accelerate the development of the continent.[90] Giscard, who had been a minister of finance, understood that the source of African destabilization was economic in nature, and that military interventionism in itself would fail to address that issue.[91] Even in the economic field, however, he did not manage to gain the adherence of the major industrialized powers to this grand design.

Despite some policy setbacks, especially those involving the multilateralization of western military or economic support to Africa, and the abandonment of its dream of a Euro-African ensemble, France emerged from the Giscard presidency as the only reliable guardian and guarantor of political stability in francophone Africa. French military prestige, political influence, and economic impact in that region had been largely enhanced. The drawback was the frequent association of France with dictatorial regimes that had poor human rights records. Giscard's political career, and his capacity to win over European partners to some of his grand ideas for Africa, was undoubtedly damaged by the personal friendships he formed with two notoriously brutal and corrupt African leaders, Emperor Bokassa I of the Central African Empire and President Mobutu of Zaire.[92]

François Mitterrand (1981-)

The arrival of the Socialists at the Elysée sent shock waves throughout the francophone African community. African leaders feared the theoreticians of the French Socialist Party would mount efforts to end their cozy special relationship with Paris and destabilize their regimes. Before winning the presidential elections in 1981, the Socialists had indeed been extremely vocal about the necessity for France to stop supporting undemocratic and corrupt regimes that did not respect human rights. The reality of Socialist policy was quite different, even if it took several trials and painful policy re-evaluations for all involved before reaching a state of equilibrium in Franco-African relations.

President Mitterrand's policy toward Africa can be divided into five phases. The first is marked by a highly idealistic approach, with Jean-Pierre Cot, minister of cooperation, as its principal and flamboyant proponent. Cot's policy reflected pre-election Socialist aspirations and principles, which did not withstand the test of reality. This idealistic approach lasted for about eighteen months and ended with the resignation of Cot in December 1982. The second phase covers the years 1983 to 1986, a period marked by greater pragmatism and moderation in Franco-African affairs. The initial turbulence of the Socialists' arrival to power soon sparked a reaction back to the more traditional, Gaullist-inspired policies toward Africa. The third phase was that of *cohabitation*, the difficult marriage between a Socialist president and a Conservative-Gaullist prime minister. For the first time in the Fifth Republic's history, parts of African policy-making moved to the office of the prime minister, as is constitutionally decreed, despite the practice dating back to de Gaulle of keeping African policy-making within the strict confines of the Elysée. The two-year *cohabitation* interlude was followed by a period of rapid change in the world. The democratization of eastern Europe would prove contagious for the rest of the world, and Africa in particular. This contagion was paralleled by a massive retreat of the eastern European, Soviet, and Cuban presence in Africa. The combination of democratic reform and Soviet withdrawal has strengthened western influence and leverage over Africa. In France, the new policy trend was formally announced by the president at the June 1990 Franco-African summit of La Baule. The emphasis was on democratization of regimes in Africa, and France has made this an increasingly important condition of its aid policy. The fifth period covers the second *cohabitation* and coincided with a reassessment of the pace of democratization in Africa, and with Africa's increasing marginalization on the world scene.

New Principles, Old Realities: With François Mitterrand's arrival to power, African policy was intended to introduce a fresh start in France's relationship with the Third World. In various instances at the beginning of his first term, Mitterrand announced that "France [was] taking a stand favoring the creation of a new international economic order."[93] With regard to Africa, the new administration wanted to distance itself from the interventionist policies of President Giscard d'Estaing. France sought to introduce respect for human rights as a precondition for pursuing its own economic interests. Reflecting these priorities, Jean-Pierre Cot felt that France's aid policy needed to be "decolonized."[94] Nevertheless, these radical statements did not signify a complete break with the past, and military cooperation remained a tool of French policy in Africa. "Refusing military cooperation to our partners would be tantamount to forcing them to turn to others, in particular, to the two superpowers whose hegemony they fear. If not, it would expose them to the dangers of aggression and subversion."[95]

In the area of defense agreements, the new administration wanted its African partners to understand that the French guarantee to rescue them, especially from internal troubles, would not be as automatic as it was during Giscard's presidency. African states could no longer force France's hand in situations where France preferred to remain uninvolved.[96] In time, however, circumstances would compel the French government to review its initial policies and stress the need for continuity in French security commitments to Africa; the reality of French "permanent" strategic interests transcended the change of residents at the Elysée palace.[97] Continuity did not mean there was no room for policy change, but the Mitterrand administration's dilemma was how to bring about evolution without destabilization in Africa.

During the initial, idealistic phase, the Mitterrand administration faced its first crisis in Africa. Nigeria was alarmingly close to engaging in military action against Cameroon after border incidents between the two countries. Paris immediately supported Cameroon, and informed Lagos, via Washington, of French resolve to protect the territorial integrity of Cameroon against external aggression. Francophone African countries regarded this firmness favorably and felt it demonstrated the commitment of the new administration.[98] With regard to internal problems, however, Mitterrand had resolved not to get involved. French troops deployed in Africa were given clear instructions to that effect, a dramatic departure from Giscard's policies.[99] Thus, France did not intervene in September 1981 in the CAR when President Dacko was overthrown by General Kolingba. Making reference to Giscard's operation to remove Emperor Bokassa of the CAR in 1979, Mitterrand rejected the notion of being involved in a "*Barracuda* of the Left." The first phase of Mitterrand's African policy proved to be too challenging for both France and Africa. France could not reconcile a global Third World approach with its special relationship to francophone African states. The latter, in turn, were extremely wary of France's shrinking assistance funds. The diminishing French interest was also reflected in the reduced accessibility of African leaders to French authorities.

The Return to the Traditional Approach: France's enduring relationship with its "African cousins" prevailed over Cot's efforts to eliminate African preferential treatment compared to what France accorded other Third World countries. African leaders responded by bypassing Cot, addressing their concerns directly to the Elysée, and pointing out the benefits France derived from its special status with them. In December 1982, Cot resigned as he faced a growing difference of opinion with the president. This put an end to the "progressive" phase of Mitterrand's African policy. Cot's successor at the Ministry of Cooperation was Christian Nucci, "a reassuringly close and obedient presidential political ally"[100] whose career was later cut short by an embezzlement of public funds known as the *Carrefour* scandal. After Cot's departure, the Elysée became more entrenched than ever as the source of initiatives in African policy-making, where the affable advisor for African affairs, Guy Penne, teamed up with the president's son, Jean-Christophe Mitterrand. Penne, a former doctor and political associate of the president, lacked African experience, and spent much time trying to reverse Cot's decisions.[101] Jean-Christophe Mitterrand, a former journalist covering Africa, was put specifically in charge of contacts with African heads of state.

The first serious test of French willingness to participate militarily in Africa's defense came with the progression of Libyan support for the rebels in Chad in 1983. It took the dramatic fall of the Faya-Largeau oasis in northern Chad on June 24, 1983, for France to intervene on behalf of the Chadian government. French assistance came hesitantly, first through the provision of weapons accompanied by "instructors," then through the active participation of French troops in operation *Manta*, from August 9, 1983 to November 10, 1984. Mitterrand's reluctance to intervene resulted not only from his pledge not to get involved militarily in the Chadian conflict, but also from his appraisal that the local military forces were dangerously close to an open conflict with Libya.[102] The urgent appeal by prominent francophone African leaders (Mobutu and Houphouët-Boigny first among them) added weight to tip the balance in favor of intervention. The French engagement on the side of the Chadian government was far from unconditional. Mitterrand elaborated on the circumspection with which he viewed the Chadian conflict, stating: "Since France's presence is judged to be necessary, it must be realized that we shall not allow ourselves to be led anywhere we do not wish to go."[103] Nevertheless, operation *Manta* was costly and unpopular with the French public.

Despite the early reluctance, France again became militarily involved in Chad barely 15 months after *Manta*. This second operation, called *Epervier*, was launched in early 1986 and has endured ever since at a gradually reduced scale.[104] This intervention became unavoidable because of France's initial failure to acknowledge Libya's breach of the

September 1984 Franco-Libyan Agreement. This agreement ensured the non-interference of both parties in Chadian affairs, but the fact that France did not immediately cite Libya's violation of the agreement caused people to question the credibility of the French government. Subsequent Chadian victories with French support have blurred the earlier vision of a reluctant, bungling France. Nonetheless, doubt had been cast on the French image as a reliable, capable ally.[105]

The Military Program Law for 1984-88 brought about some important changes in the structure of French forces available for rapid deployment in Europe and overseas. The theory was that France needed a pool of forces that could rapidly intervene on Germany's behalf in the case of a general conflict in central Europe. Important helicopter airmobile capabilities were combined with highly mobile light armored divisions; a parachute division and an Alpine division were then added in a grand ensemble called the *Force d'Action Rapide*, or FAR.[106] One light armored and one parachute division were traditionally earmarked for overseas deployments, mainly in Africa. Their incorporation within the FAR made these two divisions dual-capable. They could be assigned in central Europe or overseas, thereby losing their specific designation for overseas operations. In practice however, the forces available for African crises remained largely unaffected by the creation of the FAR; they just had to prepare more thoroughly for an additional European mission, which would only affect African intervention capabilities in times of a major crisis in central Europe.

The First Cohabitation: President Mitterrand, who had been eager to exercise control over governmental activities,[107] after the legislative elections in March 1986 had to relinquish all direct control over domestic issues and share power with the conservatives on matters such as defense, foreign affairs, and cooperation and development. Except for these shared portfolios, the president forbade his advisors and staff "[from being] associated in any way to the slightest elaboration of government policies, or to their implementation."[108] Similarly, Prime Minister Jacques Chirac prohibited his ministers, except for those of defense, foreign affairs, and cooperation, to have any unauthorized contact with the president.[109]

This state of affairs meant that Matignon, the prime minister's office, became strongly involved in domains which previously had always remained under the direct authority of the Elysée, a novelty under the Fifth Republic. As noted by the press at the 1986 Franco-African Lomé Summit: "Africa, hitherto regarded as a presidential preserve, had become 'the scene of a contest for influence' between the president and prime minister."[110] Chirac's intent not to be outplayed by the Elysée in one of his strongholds, namely African Affairs, was demonstrated by his appointment of former Gaullist African advisor Jacques Foccart. High level African visitors to Paris would have to double all appointments in order to avoid antagonizing one of the poles of authority. One high-level French diplomat stated that, of all the African advisors at the Elysée and at Matignon, Foccart was the dominant personality and the center of decision-making.[111] With his personal network of contacts, Matignon became the focal point for African policy-making initiatives. However, both sides tried to avoid disputes, especially on African matters. In the words of Pierre Haski, this illustrated that "on the foremost issue in French African policy - relations with francophone states - there is very little difference between successive governments, except perhaps in style."[112] *Cohabitation* was no exception to this rule, despite tensions which tend to jeopardize long-term interests for short-term political gains.

> Thus, even under cohabitation, conflict was avoided, with only occasional "irritating differences of opinion." The most serious consequence of cohabitation, according to [a] well-informed official, was the blocking of some ambassadorial appointments. Under the Constitution the president is empowered to act on such nominations, but the prime minister must countersign the appointment.[113]

The *cohabitation* lasted through the reinforcement phase of operation *Epervier* in Chad. The "change of style" mentioned by Pierre Haski may have accelerated the French response, since Chirac appeared more eager to re-intervene in Chad than Mitterrand. Initiated under a Socialist government, this operation achieved impressive success in securing Chad from its ambitious northern neighbor. By February 1987, of all the territories previously under its control, Libya held only the Aozou strip. The French administration then made it clear to Chadian President Hissène Habré that under no circumstances should he count on French troops to recover the Aozou strip. For France, this issue had to be settled through a court of international jurisdiction.[114]

One of the only military interventions by France during Mitterrand's first term, with the exception of Chad, took place when France dispatched 200 paratroopers to Togo in September 1986. This force assisted the Togolese government in suppressing an internal uprising.

"This use of French force showed that France was still very interested in helping African leaders close to [it], and proved the political value of France's willingness to demonstrate its power in Africa."[115]

Mitterrand's Second Term: Following Mitterrand's reelection as president, he called new legislative elections, which brought a Socialist government to power. The new, moderate Socialist Prime Minister Michel Rocard reverted to the practice of deference to the Elysée in the conduct of relations with Africa. Mitterrand's second term has been marked by a more traditional and less erratic style of African policy-making. Gone were Cot's "Third-Worldism" and uncomfortable *cohabitation*. But, for the African states within France's zone of influence and beyond, far greater challenges and worries emerged from two completely different directions: the first is the gradual economic marginalization of Africa, reflected in increasing demands for assistance; the second relates to the new emphasis on democracy, the African equivalent of eastern Europe's democratic overhaul.

The first challenge to traditional French policies predated Mitterrand's arrival to power, but has become more acute during his two mandates. It results from the ever-increasing pauperization of Africa and the increasing burden African development assistance represents for donor countries, especially France. The privileged relationship which France maintains with francophone Africa has been denounced as excessively costly; a cost that France is less and less able (or willing) to bear on its own. Stéphane Hessel, author of a report on France's North-South policies, acknowledges that "today, the role of France should be more oriented toward the mobilization of other countries to assist [the African] continent."[116] The report was ordered by Prime Minister Rocard in an effort to evaluate whether France had done all it could for development in Africa.[117] The mere fact that such questions are the object of a general debate within France's political class is an indication of profound malaise in France's African policies. The purely economic/commercial dimension of the debate centers around a few hard facts. Gross sales by French companies in Africa are declining and they continue each year to lose market shares in sub-Saharan Africa to other industrialized or newly industrialized countries. Industrial leaders in France often encourage the government to redeploy French aid to other, economically more dynamic, Third World economies.[118] In addition, France's leverage is dwindling in view of the increasing role played by other donors, including multilateral organizations like the International Monetary Fund and the World

Bank.[118] Faced with this new international environment, France is trying to use its influence in international or European organizations to ensure complementarity between the various assistance programs.

The second new challenge for the Mitterrand administration in the late 1980s concerned how to support the impulses for democratic reform in Africa that have followed the democratization of eastern Europe, and how to transform them into lasting change without provoking short-term instability. In that respect, France's margin for action is limited. France finds it increasingly difficult to "support contested leaders, but hesitates backing opposition leaders whose goals, future behavior, and, above all, popular support are unknown."[119] At the La Baule Franco-African Summit in June 1990, Mitterrand elaborated the new trend in French "conditionality" for development aid:

> France will link its entire contribution to efforts made to move in the direction of greater freedom [...]. Aid will be more lukewarm toward regimes which conduct themselves in an authoritarian manner without accepting evolution toward democracy; it will be enthusiastic for those which take the step with courage.[120]

The French president acknowledged that democracy is a process, conditioned not only by cultural values but also by the level of economic welfare. In Mitterrand's words, "without development, democracy rapidly becomes an impossible exercise."[121] The president implicitly recognized the time required to install democracy in declaring that: "Everyone will, I am convinced, fix independently the appropriate modalities and the rhythm, as long as the direction is the right one."[122] The symbiotic relationship between development and democracy was supposed to result in a virtuous spiral. The early evolution has vindicated this approach.

> The pattern is remarkably similar throughout francophone Africa. Improvident dictators, under instruction from the IMF and (what matters more) from France, have been sacking civil servants - including teachers - and holding back the wages they owe. Unions go on strike. Hitherto clandestine opposition parties emerge and demonstrate. The protesters all come up with the same demand: a national conference.[123]

National conferences have been held throughout Africa, but with mixed results. In some instances, as in Benin and Mali, they have set in motion a transition process toward genuine democracy. In other cases, as in Côte d'Ivoire, Madagascar, and Cameroon, the jury is still out on whether the transition will occur and under what circumstances. In a third group of nations such as Gabon, Zaire, and Togo, the transition went awry. The upheaval caused by the strong injection of democratic ambitions in Africa yielded, not surprisingly, much violence. In some instances, France was called upon or forced to act, either to protect its citizens or to bring a minimum of order back to riot-torn countries. Mitterrand's second term until February 1994 has been marked by ten instances of military involvement. Operation *Epervier*, which continues at a low level, is not included in this total. The interventions took place in the Comoros (1989), after a mercenary coup d'état; in Gabon (1990); in Liberia (1990); in Rwanda (1990); in Djibouti (1991); in Zaire (1991); in Togo (1991); in Chad (1992); in Somalia (1992-93); and in Burundi (1993). (These actions are further analyzed in Chapter 5.) Except for the operation in the Comoros, all other interventions were linked to popular movements of discontent.

Mitterrand's decision-making process changed in response to the delineation of priorities. The inner Elysée cabinet was changed in 1988 to become a troika of advisors. The nomination of Jacques Pelletier as the fourth minister of cooperation and development under Mitterrand has been viewed as the admission of the Socialists' failure to propose and implement an alternative cooperation policy to the one in place for the last thirty years. Pelletier's profile as a consensualist, middle-of-the-road senator confirms the feeling in many African capitals that, with him, the "special relationship" is not endangered.[125] The profiles of the subsequent ministers of cooperation and development were in line with the new, more moderate approach. The image of the African policy-making community in France since the mid-1980s has been a more mature and polished one. However, no strong personality dominates Franco-African affairs anymore, leaving observers to wonder whether anyone is coordinating it all.[126]

Eighteen months after the La Baule speech, even the French president, at the occasion of the Fourth *Francophonie* summit in Paris in 1991, was increasingly diverted away from African affairs. Mitterrand adopted a new, more conciliatory tone regarding the slow speed and limited extent of democratic reform in Africa. He made it clear that each country must determine independently the modalities of democratic reform. This change has been interpreted as a sign of lassitude or disengagement from African affairs.[127] It was in vain that the proponents of democratic change in Togo (1991) asked French troops to intervene in favor of the Togolese prime minister, or asked those troops to stay, together with their Belgian colleagues, as in the evacuation operation in Zaire the same year (see Chapters 5 and 12 for more details). The waning French support of democracy in Africa stops well short of military action in favor of it. Expressing his views on Africa just before the European summit in Maastricht in December 1991, Mitterrand gave the impression that European concerns had overtaken his African policies.[128] Europe, East and West, dominated France's political agenda to the point where Paris no longer seemed to pay sufficient attention to its African partners. The 1992 Franco-African summit in Libreville confirmed the trend; the president had to be replaced by the prime minister to represent France, thereby deferring a responsibility which has traditionally been the center of the president's domain.

Cohabitation Revisited: In March 1993, legislative elections in France produced an overwhelming victory for a center/right coalition; they received 84 percent of the seats in the National Assembly. Expectations on the part of some conservatives that the president may resign were soon dispelled, despite the fact that he had to endure a second *cohabitation* with a rightist government, led by Prime Minister Edouard Balladur who succeeded Pierre Bérégovoy. Balladur seemed to accept the principle of *cohabitation*, and President Mitterrand confirmed his nomination without delay. The difference between the first and second *cohabitation* resides in the fact that the Socialist's popular mandate had declined dramatically. Still, Mitterrand was adamant about retaining all presidential powers over foreign policy and defense matters in what he called the "continuity" of French policy, especially with regard to the European integration.[129] Dominique Garraud, a journalist for the newspaper *Libération*, viewed that, with regard to defense policies, one likely point of friction between the Elysée and Matignon was with regard to France's military participation in foreign crises.[130] His remarks were directed to France's role in the former Yugoslavia. Strong disagreements and policy shifts were avoided with regard to African policy-making all through 1993. An encouraging sign was the fact that the existing team of African advisors at the Elysée, including newly appointed Delaye, "should have little difficulty in working in tandem with whatever Africanist a new, non-Socialist premier may bring in his entourage."[131]

The bureaucratic infights under Mitterrand's presidency notwithstanding, new, broad principles have been advanced, such as the necessity for democratization and the inclusion of other partners in the economic development of France's special domain. The principles seem to be accepted by most parties across France's political spectrum. The difficulty rests with the translation of principles into action. "[I]f France maybe knows what it wants, it does not know in any case how to go about it," remarked a French journalist.[132] Political changes should be prevented from generating too much instability, and forces in France and in Africa are still attempting to preserve the intimacy and the exclusivity of the special relationship, without allowing other western economic powers to challenge France's cozy predominance. A sign of French over-extension in Africa can be gathered from the halt brought to the addition of new members to Franco-African summits. France is much more cautious about expanding its influence, or its burden.

The Enduring Franco-African Bond

Despite claims that France has preserved much of the system put in place by de Gaulle for strong association with its former colonies, evolution since the 1960s has brought significant changes.

> In France as in Africa, the exclusive bilateralism implemented by President de Gaulle and Pompidou is no longer a standard policy. It appears that the implementation of Franco-African relations will be conducted in a multilateral approach tempered by the maintenance of privileged links within the framework of Franco-African summits.[133]

The end of exclusive bilateralism provides an opportunity and a challenge. The combined means of the various other actors involved, whether countries or international institutions, adds tremendous weight to their collective initiatives in Africa. This is obviously already the case in the various groups of industrialized nations discussing Africa's and other Third World countries' public or private debt (through the so-called Clubs of Paris or London). The drawback for a country with such a tradition of exclusive influence in Africa as France enjoyed over the decades following the end of colonialism is that it gradually reduces its control and margin for maneuver over shaping policy. A French political analyst, Jean-François Bayart, pointed in 1984 to the obvious limitations that French policy-makers will face in the future:

> one must agree with the fact that France's maneuverability in its African strategy has inexorably been reduced over time. Where French preponderance exists, it is being challenged by new actors [...]. Furthermore, the needs of Africa are too considerable for a country like France to satisfy them on its own, *a fortiori* if that country is itself in financial difficulty. [...] The management of a "grand African design" becomes an exercise in dealing with its constraints, which leaves a very narrow margin for action.[134]

The new democratization efforts supported by the Mitterrand administration may do more to dissolve the privileged intimacy between France and its African allies than the already dramatic effect of multilateralization. Democracy in Africa will erode the sometimes immense powers yielded by African heads of state, diluting their autocratic rule into a multipolar decision-making apparatus with various ministries, parliamentary actors, bureaucracies, and constituencies, which will all influence policies. The "normalization" of African politics will consequently mean that France will have to interact with all those new actors, at similar levels of power and competence. The African heads of state will no longer be the only partners.

France cannot disinterest itself from Africa for historical, cultural and geographic reasons. Although this special relationship implies certain responsibilities for France, it also enhances France's international standing. Having adopted the French language and many French cultural traits through history, francophone African nations share France's interest in preserving French stature and credibility in the world. The decline of France as a respected, medium-sized world power would have dramatic effects on francophone African countries. They would lose the prestige and respectability that their francophone affiliation confers on them in the eyes of other African states. Their common language would no longer be a symbol of power, but a mere convenience. Having adapted the French language, administrative traditions, and cultural traits, francophone sub-Saharan Africa needs a strong "metropolitan" center.

COLLECTIVE FRAMEWORKS

France never created a British-type Commonwealth after the demise of the *Communauté* in 1960. No organized structure existed to salvage some sense of congeniality from the defunct French colonial empire. It would take more than a decade after the end of colonialism for France to develop two separate forums which would reinstall some sense of collective solidarity between mainly African members of the former colonial empire and France. They do not match the British Commonwealth bureaucratic organization, but they represent a more flexible and dynamic framework to guarantee France a special zone of political, economic and cultural influence in the world. The two frameworks are the Franco-African summits and the *Francophonie* summits. Both are complementary, with strong overlapping membership, especially for francophone African countries.

Franco-African Summits

It was only in 1973 that France developed what would become a highly successful forum for Franco-African relations. The fall of de Gaulle's *Communauté* project was followed by the formation of strong bilateral ties between France and its individual former colonies, and by a series of attempts by the former colonies to shape their own regional or francophone associations. One of these associative efforts was the Afro-Malagasy and Mauritian Joint Organization (OCAMM under its French acronym). Membership has varied with time but remained under ten with participants including Benin, Côte d'Ivoire, the CAR, Upper-Volta (now Burkina Faso), Mauritius, Niger, Rwanda, Senegal, and Togo. De Gaulle was favorable to the creation of OCAM in February 1964 (with only one "M" since Mauritius was not yet independent) and, although not a member, France supported this regional organization.[135] OCAM, and after 1968 OCAMM, played only a minor role in African affairs and was undermined by internal divisions during the Biafran secession. By 1973, the vacuum left by OCAMM's inability to integrate francophone African states into some cohesive structure inspired President Diori of Niger to request a meeting of OCAMM's members, as well as France. It had become "evident that the role of this organization as a politico-diplomatic force was played out."[136] The Franco-African summits, inaugurated in Paris later the same year under the presidency of Georges Pompidou, came partly as a response to the tottering OCAMM.

This first post-colonial Franco-African summit involved presidents or senior ministers from 10 francophone African countries, as well as France. Since then, the roster of states at the summits has gradually expanded to include a range of lusophone and anglophone nations. From 1973 until 1988, the Franco-African summits have been held annually, with the venue alternating between France and Africa. The only exception was in 1974, when the meeting was canceled due to President Pompidou's death. In 1988, however, it was decided that the Franco-African summit would take place every other year, with a worldwide *Francophonie* summit in the intervening years.

The Franco-African summits are very informal gatherings of French and African heads of state or ministerial delegations. There are no formal invitations. There is no predetermined agenda, and the final communiqué avoids any confrontational statements. All parties attending the Franco-African summits know that their differences of opinion will be respected, and will not be publicized if they do not wish. This feature serves to facilitate the participation of otherwise antagonistic parties. The Franco-African summits have evolved into pragmatic occasions for Franco-African leaders to hold informal, private meetings on a bilateral basis, in small groups, and in full sessions. Franco-African summits last three days, with the first day devoted to French-speaking African leaders, joined by their French counterparts. Unlike the British Commonwealth, the Franco-African summits do not have a permanent secretariat. All administrative work for the organization of these meetings is handled by the African advisors at the Elysée and by the host government.

The increase in African participants every year illustrates the success of the Franco-African summits. Attendance at these summits has grown to the point where it actually rivals the participation in the Organization of African Unity conferences. In 1989, 22 heads of state attended the Franco-African summit, almost double the amount at the 1988 OAU meeting. This success has become almost a source of diplomatic embarrassment for French authorities, since the Franco-African summits has challenged the OAU as becoming one of the most influential forums for the discussion of African problems.[137]

The traditional means of evaluating the success of the summits has been the number of attendees. In terms of effective achievements, however, the record is slightly more blurred, partially as a result of the informal nature of the summits. At the 1989 Casablanca Summit, Omar Bongo, president of Gabon, summarized his frustration concerning the lack of tangible results of the meetings: "We talk, we talk, and then we go home. There is no follow-up. Nothing."[138] This statement fails to underscore the true purpose of the summits, which is primarily to benefit France. Attendance at Franco-African summits serves virtually as a requisite contribution by the African community to the enhancement of French status in the world, exhibiting France's unique links and influence in Africa. This contribution is later rewarded either through economic aid, or even military support.

From its performance to date, the Franco-African summitry stands out as both a sounding board for France's diplomatic initiatives in Africa and an assembly for legitimizing them. It is, more importantly, a forum for the enunciation of new French ideas on the African condition, a display that ultimately reinforces the image of France as a privileged spokesman between the West and the states of Africa.[139]

A Nigerian observer captured the feeling of French self-interest which permeates Franco-African summitry: "on balance...[the summit's] propaganda value far outstrips its concrete achievements."[140] African states often support this perception willingly, not only because they are dependent on French assistance programs, but also because it is in their own best interest that France continues to be perceived as a strong power broker on the continent. The demise of France as the primary African power could ultimately lead to greater destabilization in Africa.

The search for credibility and recognition as a true force in Africa may explain, more than anything else, France's eagerness to increase the number of African participants to the summits. After gaining the participation of most francophone African countries, the summit expanded to include lusophone and anglophone Africa. This augmentation did not go without some recrimination on the part of the old francophone guard, which became highly unsatisfied with the dilution of its ties to the former metropole. An aide to the Gabonese president once complained:

> If France extends its audience in Africa beyond the traditional realm, why could we not ask to do the same in Europe? If one does not want to return to the coherence of a community sharing a same Franco-African destiny, one could as well transform the forum in a gathering between Europe and Africa.[141]

Mitterrand strongly objected to including any other European power in the Franco-African summits,[142] and thus far has been able to avoid their disintegration.

There is no single, comprehensive theme to the continuous addition of participants to the summits, except for the enhancement of France's general standing on the continent, although some more circumstantial reasons may explain part of the expansion. There are basically five categories of participants. The first category includes those countries which belonged to France's former colonial empire in sub-Saharan Africa, and subsequently to the *Communauté*. This group of countries is often called the *pré carré*, or "square field." Although not considered as part of the *pré carré*, two North African countries, Morocco and Tunisia, have joined the summits. The second category includes those countries whose participation France actively sought because of a francophone link, namely Zaire, Rwanda and Burundi. The third category of countries is composed of the lusophone African countries, led by the leaders of the anti-Portuguese colonial struggle. Many of them had studied in France, and often led their liberation wars from the territories of friendly francophone states. The lusophone countries have always been very attracted to the francophone realm in Africa for its guaranteed access to French assistance, but also for the monetary and military stability which resulted from membership in that group. The fourth category includes the former Spanish colony of Equatorial Guinea, which is surrounded by francophone states, and Cameroon, which, surrounded by both anglophone and francophone states, asked to be included at the Franco-African summits. The last group of members which were welcomed to the summits included anglophone countries like Liberia, Sierra Leone, Sudan, and Uganda.

The sixteenth Franco-African summit, held June 19-21, 1990 at the French coastal resort of La Baule, was attended by 35 African delegations, 22 of which were led by heads of state. Table 2 provides a list of all participating delegations.[143] The informal agenda, "Debt and Political Evolution in Africa," acknowledged that the meeting was taking place amid a wave of "democratization" unrest directed at many of the participating governments. The French president's opening speech became a landmark in redefining French policy priorities with regard to Africa. It demonstrated how France effectively used the Franco-African summits to launch new policy initiatives and elicited support from the African participants partly through the international attention which the summits can draw. Subsequent developments in francophone Africa showed that the African summit members had clearly received the democratization message.

The 17th Franco-African summit, which was held in Libreville, Gabon, ended on October 7, 1992. The spirit of the La Baule Summit had receded dramatically, giving way to a much more pragmatic approach to political evolutions in Africa. The economic crisis was high on the agenda, as were regional conflicts on the continent with a special focus on Liberia. France was just recovering from the referendum on the European Union Treaty of Maastricht. In an unusual move, France was represented by the prime minister, Pierre Bérégovoy. After the very close call of the referendum on European Union (only 51 percent of French voters were in favor of the Maastricht Treaty) and personal health problems, the president remained absent.

TABLE 2: Attendance at the La Baule Summit

Delegations led by Heads of State	
Benin	Gambia
Burkina Faso	Guinea-Bissau
Burundi	Mali
Cape Verde	Morocco
Central African Republic	Mozambique
Chad	Niger
The Comoros	Rwanda
Congo	Sao Tome and Principe
Djibouti	Senegal
Equatorial Guinea	Togo
Gabon	Uganda
Delegations led by Heads of Government	
Tunisia	Zaire
Ministerial-Level Delegations	
Angola	Namibia
Cote d'Ivoire	Seychelles
Egypt	Sierra Leone
Guinea	Somalia
Mauritania	Sudan
Mauritius	

The French prime minister in Libreville emphasized the "essential link between security, democracy and development."[144] At first sight this statement may appear as a mere variation on President Mitterrand's formula in La Baule linking progress in democracy and in development. The addition of security indicates that democracy ceased to be the only priority, and that it had to be balanced against other vital interests. Bérégovoy insisted on the need for African partners to engage in more rigorous economic management, even though he denounced the excessive constraints imposed by the International Monetary Fund and the World Bank.[145] In the field of security, he established the criteria by which France will evaluate African defense policies:[146]

> The armed forces have to fully endorse their role as warrantor of the national institutions; they are not only the shield of the State, but also the protector of the citizens. Small, disciplined and law-abiding armed forces - this is the course for which you will always find France's support.

In one instance, namely Chad, future development aid had, since 1991, already been tied to a drastic demobilization and military restructuring programs of the armed forces. Economic considerations were in this case paralleled by domestic security threats posed by a large and loose military force. No other country in francophone Africa was engaged in a drastic reduction of its armed forces as of late 1993.

A View from Anglophone-Africa

Anglophone Africa has had mixed feelings about joining the Franco-African summits. Smaller countries, by nature more vulnerable, were the first ones to join the meetings by sending high-level delegations. Liberia, at the 1980 summit, was the first to do so. One of the most controversial cases was Nigeria, a competitor with France for influence on the continent. On the one hand, it was difficult for Nigeria to legitimize France's pre-eminent role in Africa by attending the meetings. On the other hand, the summit meetings have drawn such large and important participants that it was impossible for Nigeria to ignore them. Nigeria has found an intermediate solution by sending a delegation at ambassadorial level to the summits.

In March 1980, Liberian Foreign Minister Cecil Dennis was the star of the Franco-African summit in Paris. He was the embodiment of France's claim that the summits could reach beyond francophone and lusophone Africa, and that anglophone countries could also be part of France's zone of concern, and possibly, influence. For the Liberian foreign minister, there were obvious advantages to these summits. The following is an extract of his response to why Liberia wanted to join the club of France's protégés:

> And the French president. How many hours has he spent with the various African leaders of his country's former colonies? How many times has he listened to their complaints, requests, arguments?

> When I go to the United States, I am accorded thirty minutes with the secretary of state, and am given to understand that this is time taken off from more important matters. There is no question of small talk or personal exchange. Of course, we receive financial assistance and are questioned about the democratization of our regime. This is all right and proper. But nobody understands that it is not enough, that we are alone and lonely, that we want to belong. As I said - we are orphans.[147]

This statement is remarkable in many ways. First, it indicates that French power and influence in Africa are not solely the result of historic circumstances, but ensue from an impressive, ongoing effort. France has given priority to African affairs and is willing to pay the price in terms of the availability and time of high-ranking French officials, not to mention other political, military, and financial costs. Another remarkable element in this statement by Cecil Dennis is his longing to belong to a structured, almost protected, group of selected nations with close links to a strong western power. It also enhances the self-image of the African partners, who know that at any time they may solicit the attention, and possibly action, of their powerful European partner. The fact that African nations can affect French policy-making on Africa is a feature which distinguishes Franco-African summitry from the way Britain responds to attempts by its Commonwealth partners to affect British foreign policies. The isolation of the Thatcher government within the Commonwealth on policies toward South Africa is a typical example.[148]

Historically, Britain had been the first to understand the need to manage the post-imperial era by offering former colonies and dependencies some formal structure which would stress the attachment to a common, British past. The Commonwealth became the embodiment of the British imperial legacy. (The Commonwealth is analyzed in detail in Chapter 6.) France's efforts to formalize a multilateral, post-colonial association were far less successful. The Franco-African summits, emerging 13 years after decolonization, were partly an attempt to correct this lack of multilateral cohesion. They would be later reinforced and complemented by *Francophonie* summits (described later in this Chapter). Despite obvious links to a similar colonial past, Franco-African summits differ from the summits of the Commonwealth in at least three major ways.

First, the Franco-African summits are political in nature and are a manifestation of France's solidarity with its African partners.[149] They also aim to promote and gain support for French African policies among the African nations. The summit meetings help institutionalize France's role as a privileged partner with most of Africa. They are a French policy instrument which has a distinct place next to the Franc Zone monetary system and the military agreements between France and African countries. Together, these tools provide a unique combination of levers of influence, as well as certain obligations.

Second, France has extended African participation in the summits beyond the geographic limits of its former colonial empire, initially to other francophone states, but later also to lusophone and anglophone countries. Non-francophone countries have modified the nature of the summit meetings through their participation. Membership in the Commonwealth is restricted to countries of the former British empire. By opening its membership to new members, Franco-African summits gain flexibility and are more adaptive to changing political circumstances, transcending the often arbitrary borders of colonial times. Furthermore, by limiting the membership to African nations and not including former French colonies outside of Africa, France has inspired greater cohesion in the meetings than one could find in a more disparate group like the Commonwealth. Third, the informality and organizational simplicity of the annual Franco-African summits contrasts with the more formal biennial Commonwealth summit meetings and the 400-person staff at Commonwealth Headquarters.

Francophonie

Understanding France's view of the world requires underscoring the role of language as a foreign policy objective and a foreign policy tool. Sharing French as a common language creates links which, with adequate encouragements, open up to a sense of shared heritage. France's eagerness to spread the use of French as an international language has been fairly successful and has preserved the role of Paris as the world's francophone capital. Given the important gains of English as an international language, France has been even more concerned by the relative decline of French on the international scene.

France's lasting military presence in Rwanda after the 1990 rebel invasion illustrates the seriousness with which French authorities defend the use of French by foreign nations. The three-year presence of French troops on Rwandese territory cannot be justified by immediate security concerns, but must rather be viewed in the context of not letting a friendly francophone regime be replaced by an anglophone one. In June 1992, *The Economist* reported that:

> The rebels assert that the French are afraid that the victory of English-speaking Tutsis schooled in Uganda would erode a francophone sphere of influence. The previous round of peace talks in Paris in January collapsed when French officials rejected a rebel who spoke English, not French.[149]

According to this view, Rwanda has become the theater of a purely linguistic battle. Rejecting the linguistic dimension as a futile and senseless reaction by French authorities would miss a vital component of French foreign policy. Hence, France continues to provide ardent support to a vast diplomatic and cultural initiative aimed at reinforcing the cohesiveness of francophone population around the world while at the same time preserving France's role as cultural center of the francophone periphery.

Since 1970, francophone solidarity throughout the world has received embryonic organizational support from the *Agence de Coopération Culturelle et Technique* (ACCT). The ACCT would serve as secretariat and principal executive body to *Francophonie*, the assembly of all countries with French as the main language or as the language of a significant minority. The grand total of the world's French-speaking population is estimated at close to 134 million individuals.[150] Initially, the governing body of the ACCT was a council of ministers from participating countries. It was not until 1985 that member states agreed to upgrade the meetings to the summit level, to be held initially every year, and then every other year in alternation with the Franco-African summits. The location of the ACCT summits changes with each meeting. The move to elevate the level of participation to that of heads of state and government raised the international impact of this forum dramatically. From an obscure and ill-reported ministerial-level event, the *Francophonie* meetings after 1985 achieved a true international standing with large media coverage. The high visibility should not mask the low practical achievements of this group as such, although the summit meetings are often used to announce sweeping new policies by individual members.

Despite its participants' protestations to the contrary, *Francophonie* is essentially conceived as a counter-weight and alternative to the anglophone cultural predominance. The Secretary-General of the United Nations Boutros Boutros-Ghali finessed the issue at the 1993 summit: "I do not think that *Francophonie* wants to be a counter-weight to the great powers. It was, and still is, a subversive idea, a libertarian answer against imperialisms."[152]

The first summit meeting, held in Versailles in 1986, noted the evolution of the *Francophonie* movement toward a North-South dialogue which was more balanced than the Franco-African summits because the North was represented by France, Canada, Belgium, Switzerland, and Luxembourg. The North-South aspect of the meetings has raised the expectations of poorer participants that their needs would be recognized. The two subsequent meetings were marked by the Canadian and French announcement of the cancellation of their public loans to the members with the lowest income. The fourth summit, initially planned to take place in Kinshasa, was held in Paris in November 1991 due to Belgian and Canadian objections over Mobutu's human rights record. The 1991 summit assembled 47 countries, including a majority of 25 African nations. Other participants included former colonial French possessions such as Vietnam, Laos, and Cambodia, and countries with less obvious francophone connections like Egypt, Romania, and Bulgaria.[153] The 1993 summit in Mauritius regrouped 47 countries. The remarkable event at this summit was President Mitterrand's appeal to francophone solidarity in cultural matters in the General Agreement on Tariffs and Trade negotiations. France used the summit to demonstrate to the world that it was not alone in its opposition to parts of the proposed GATT agreements.

Programs implemented by the ACCT underscore *Francophonie*'s vocation to support development projects. The official summit language uses the word "solidarity" to describe efforts to channel funds contributed by the richer participants to the less privileged ones. Technical and scientific information is one of the sectors selected for assistance. The 1991 summit proposed the creation of a francophone television network directed primarily at Third World countries, as well as making environmental proposals.[154] Other francophone-specific sectors financed by the ACCT budget (about $58 million for 1990) have targeted agricultural research, child literacy, or various scholarship programs.[155]

Some critics of the francophone summitry regard it as a "Franco-African Summit - Bis" given the high overlap between the membership in both reunions, but also because they view it as duplicating the structure of a dependent South vis-a-vis a small group of donor countries from the north.[156] The fact that the two summit meetings alternate yearly reinforces the feeling of duplication, or at best complementarity. Another group of critics consider with increasing alarm the attempts by the ACCT summit to expand participation to non-traditional francophone partners. In fact, only 25 of the 47 member states use French as the principal language. The extension of the meetings to countries such as Bulgaria and Romania not only stretches the credibility and scope of *Francophonie* as an operational concept, but also represents the threat of the allocation of meager resources to East European members at the expense of Third World participants.[157]

France's Overlapping Networks

The Franco-African summitry has been a mutually beneficial system; an essential condition if it is to survive in the future. The returns to France and African countries are best evaluated in terms of access and influence. In the process, France has most adroitly made use of this forum to project itself as a privileged interlocutor between African states and the West on issues of mutual interest.[158] By showing that some issues are best solved within the club-like atmosphere of the Franco-African summits, the members gain additional leverage from their association. The same logic applies to a lesser extent to the *Francophonie* meetings.

In general, French post-colonial arrangements stressed francophone sub-Saharan Africa as a priority area of French policy. The Franco-African summits, together with the *Francophonie* meetings, salvaged some of France's colonial legacy by their organization into a very loose common structure. But this structure has been developed long after the end of the colonial period. The Franco-African summits started only in 1973, and the *Francophonie* summit reunions only in 1986. Both types of gatherings have reached well beyond the French colonial realm. It would therefore be incorrect to compare this dual French structure to the British Commonwealth, a pure product and the only formal legacy of the British Empire. The more dynamic and innovative approach of France has enabled it to preserve some of its colonial links, while incorporating other interests into a new French policy. In the words of scholars Dennis Austin and Keith Panter-Brick, the:

> initial lack of a post-colonial persona did not in the long run prove any great loss to France because it effectively cleared the way for a reformulation of France's overseas commitments. These have not simply been carried over from the past. There has been a redrawing of spheres of influence and a recasting of linkages and associations which, though they may appear analogous to the Commonwealth, are in fact *sui generis*.[159]

The British Commonwealth did not reinvent the place of Britain in the world. The Commonwealth, perhaps unimaginatively, was primarily geared to preserving a collection of links from the past. The dual French-sponsored summitry redrew the geo-political frontiers of French influence overseas, less constrained by the structures inherited from colonial times.

TABLE 3: Franco-African Summits[160]

Date (Place)	Principal Issues
1973 (Paris)	Problems of the Franc Zone, relations between Europe and Africa.
1974	No summit due to the death of President Pompidou.
1975 (Bangui, CAR)	Africa's economic problems.
1976 (Paris)	Africa's economic problems.
1977 (Dakar, Senegal)	Security problems of African countries.
1978 (Paris)	Destabilization in Africa (especially the 1977-78 cross border incursions by exiled dissidents into Zaire's Shaba region).
1979 (Kigali, Rwanda)	President Giscard d'Estaing's proposal for a "trialogue" of European, Arab and African countries.
1980 (Nice, France)	Senegalese President Senghor's call for creation of an "organic francophone community."
1981 (Paris)	Libya's intervention in Chad.
1982 (Kinshasa, Zaire)	President Mitterrand's plea for a North-South dialogue.
1983 (Vittel, France)	Chad.
1984 (Bujumbura, Burundi)	Chad, Africa's economic problems.
1985 (Paris)	Chad, Africa's foreign debt problem, South Africa/apartheid
1986 (Lomé, Togo)	Chad, Africa's economic problems.
1987 (Antibes, France)	Chad, Africa's foreign debt problem.
1988 (Casablanca, Morocco)	Impact of East-West detente on Africa, Africa's foreign debt problem, Chad.
1990 (La Baule, France)	Democratic trends in Africa.
1992 (Libreville, Gabon)	Reappraisal of Africa's security requirements and economic problems.

Chapter 3

French Armed Forces:
Power Projection and Cooperation

With the end of the Cold War and mounting budgetary pressures, the French government reviewed its defense policies, which had remained largely unchanged since 1966. The sanctity of the independent nuclear posture continued, even if weapons upgrades have been slowed down or revised. In conventional warfare, France has identified three zones of potential action: the first represents the defense of the homeland; the second includes all areas of concern to allied military operations; and the third corresponds to the NATO out-of-area zone, which includes the rest of the world, with special focus on the Mediterranean, Africa, and the Middle East.

In France's view, many out-of-area contingencies may be best pursued within a European framework, either through a strengthened role for the Western European Union (WEU) or through the creation of a Eurocorps with Belgium and Germany. The Eurocorps will be fully operational in 1995, although considerable ambiguities remain with regard to its rules of engagement in future conflicts and crises.

Despite the renewed interest in joint multinational forces for overseas assignments, France independently assumes many security commitments, as in sub-Saharan Africa or the Red Sea area. French military forces have been specifically tailored to these overseas responsibilities: the Army, with its rapid deployment force and overseas contingents; the Navy, with aircraft carriers, amphibious assault ships, and a worldwide presence; and the Air Force, mainly with airlift capabilities. A system of overseas deployment has been in place since the period of colonial empire, with a gradual shift of resources from overseas based troops to rapid deployment forces based at home. Nonetheless, France retains contingents overseas to facilitate reinforcements from France, or to police specific sub-regions. The system is characterized by pragmatism and economy of means. Forces are precisely tailored according to the specific threat within each region. This approach, often employing only minimal forces, has been extremely effective. It has enabled France to mount credible responses to local military crises while preserving the desired political climate.

Demands on French commitments within all three circles have put the defense budget under tremendous pressure. The nuclear component, which consumes one-third of the procurement budget, competes with diverse overseas commitments and other dimensions of conventional force funding. France, with a defense budget slightly larger than one-tenth of the U.S. defense budget, tries to achieve self-sufficiency in all areas while striving to maintain a global reach. France keeps roughly 30,000 troops overseas, about half of which are based in and around Africa. The pressure to scale down the worldwide deployment system is increasing as military budgets shrink and defense costs rise. The 1993 defense budget of FF 198 billion ($36 billion),[1] 3.1 percent of the gross domestic product, is second only to that of the United States among NATO countries.

Following the demise of the Soviet threat, the *Plan Armées 2000*, launched in August 1990, presented a radical restructuring of French armed forces and remains the basic framework for change. The Army has borne the brunt of manpower cuts. President Mitterrand announced in September 1990 that 50,000 French troops would be gradually withdrawn from Germany. Between 1991 and 1993, the strength of the armed forces dropped from 450,000 to almost 411,000 troops, divided between the Army (241,400), the Air Force (90,600), and the Navy (65,400).[2] Conscripts, the majority of which are in the Army, represent 47 percent of the armed forces. In 1992 the length of service for conscripts was cut from 12 to 10 months. The reorganization of the French armed forces is characterized by an intense debate over the future of conscription.

The French experience during the Gulf War led to reinforcement of inter-service staffs between the Army, Navy and Air Force. The emphasis was on creating joint planning structures and integrating operations to allow for greater interoperability among the three services. Interoperability became the new leitmotif of French defense planners. Two such inter-service command structures were announced in 1991 for interventions inside and outside Europe. In April 1992, the Defense Ministry announced a third command structure for French special forces, thereby regrouping diverse commandos with elite parachutist units, other commandos from the Army and the Air Force, and the special intervention group of the gendarmerie.[3]

The armed forces chief of staff will head the joint services operational headquarters to supervise the operational aspects of troop deployments abroad. The two new command structures will not be fully functional before 1994. The headquarters for overseas operations will initially be located at Maisons-Laffitte, and its early development will be monitored by the officers of the French rapid deployment forces (see below). Eventually, both foreign operations headquarters will be regrouped at the military base of Creil, together with the headquarters of French Special Forces and that of military intelligence (*Direction des renseignements militaires*).[4]

The arrival of a conservative prime minister in March 1993 may change some fundamental aspects of French defense policy. The decline of defense spending initiated under Socialist governments was denounced as too fast by the right wing parties. The role and rules of engagement for French forces abroad may be viewed differently by the president and the government, which complicates potential interventions or participation in international peace-keeping operations.

POWER PROJECTION: THE ARMY

The most important structural modifications under *Plan Armées 2000* concern the Army. The plan eliminates one Army Corps and reinforces the other two.[5] By 1997, the Army may be reduced to 225,000 troops, down from 288,500 in 1991. When restructuring is complete, the French Army will consist of one corps based in France for European operations; a rapid reaction force of five divisions for out-of-area operations; and the French contribution to the 42,000 troop Eurocorps, consisting of one French division and the Franco-German brigade.[6]

The French rapid reaction force (*Force d'Action Rapide* or FAR) is separate from the continental defense structure, although it could be integrated with it in time of war. The FAR is one of the major units (*grand commandement*) of the French Army, occupying a special place at the same command level as the traditional Army Corps. From its inception, the FAR has had a double vocation: first and foremost, it was a response to German concerns about French willingness to participate in the forward defense of West Germany; and second, it provided a command and control structure under which to group designated forces for possible power projection, although not all its forces are meant to be deployable overseas. The FAR has not been fundamentally affected by the changes proposed in the *Plan Armées 2000*; on the contrary, the result may be to render its troops more effective and to modernize its equipment, especially the helicopters.[7] Future plans may provide the FAR with clearer missions and rules of engagement, maintaining its flexibility while significantly increasing its firepower.

Politically, the motive behind the creation of the FAR was to tell Germany that France would be on its side should any hostilities break out on the central European front. In June 1983, the French president approved the new armed forces structure, including the creation of the five FAR divisions. Grouping an airmobile and light armored divisions together in combat formations under a single tactical command and control headquarters enhanced the long range projection of a light but hard hitting and flexible force, ready to be employed against any potential invader in central Germany. The planning effort for the FAR was paralleled by a reappraisal of the role of the *Force d'Intervention*. This force was designed to intervene outside Europe, in an unstable yet heavily armed Third World. To better face potential threats in this new international environment, France decided to include the *Force d'Intervention* in the FAR. A parachute division and a marine infantry division added versatility and mobility to the European role of the FAR; the airmobile and light armored units of the FAR brought more firepower to its out-of-area role. Finally, the subsequent addition of a fifth division for Alpine combat appeared less satisfactory in view of the FAR's dual employment doctrine; its usefulness in the FAR was questionable, despite its considerable array of anti-tank guided missiles. Adding all five divisions, the FAR's total peacetime strength is about 50,000, climbing to 63,000 in wartime.[8]

Many African and French observers were skeptical of the way the *Force d'Intervention* became diluted in the FAR and considered it "a sideward step into Europe, further decolonizing the French Army."[9] Other critics claim that by creating this polyvalent pool of resources, the FAR did not add any new forces to the French Army, but simply restructured existing forces under the command of a new General Staff (which they insist is the only new element of the FAR).

In fact, the FAR is no more than a pool of individual military units available to decision-makers for rapid deployment. The FAR is not an independent Army Corps. Due to its multiple roles and logistical requirements, the FAR was not conceived to counter an enemy at France's borders.[10] The FAR has no exclusive front to hold, but can be active on various fronts with only part of its total forces. Outside Europe, the FAR's role is to assist friendly nations in crisis or conflict and to protect French citizens and interests abroad.[11]

All units in the FAR share one common denominator: speed of deployment. Consequently, the forces of the FAR are relatively light, but incapable of sustained or high-intensity missions. They lack adequate logistics capability, equipment, and material to conduct extensive field operations. Air mobility depends primarily on *Transall* aircraft with relatively limited payloads. Sealift is slow and not always useful in places such as central Africa. Dependence on American logistical support is politically risky and strategically tenuous. European assistance is difficult to secure except for humanitarian efforts. Hence, only specialized units of the FAR are likely to be used.

Composition of the FAR

COMFAR: The role of the FAR's General Staff, *Commandement de la FAR* (COMFAR), with headquarters at Maisons-Laffitte, near Paris, focuses on the four following tasks: (i) providing an operational General Staff; (ii) acting as a center for innovation; (iii) planning future engagements by the FAR, and providing options to the joint chiefs of staff or the head of state; and (iv), controlling operational preparations, including follow-up and logistics.[12] In times of overseas crises involving FAR units, "each intervention, wherever it occurs, has important political implications and must therefore be directed by the head of the joint chiefs of staff himself, in close liaison with the president of the republic."[13]

The 1991 Gulf War was the COMFAR's first real operational test. About 8,800 men from the Army, mainly from the FAR, were deployed in the French *Daguet* Division.[14] The FAR forces came from the two light armored divisions and the airmobile division.[15] Among the other practical achievements of the COMFAR is the creation of mobile command and control organizations. These "contingency headquarters" are totally transportable by air, and some portions can be airdropped.

4th Airmobile Division: With its 240 helicopters and 7,500 troops based in Nancy, this division is primarily designed for rapid anti-armor operations up to 350 km away from its bases.[16] The division is equipped with 90 *Gazelle* helicopters carrying four anti-tank missiles, as well as with other helicopters for reconnaissance, command and control, and logistics support. The 4th Airmobile Division is not self-deployable overseas, as the range of its helicopters is too restrictive. Helicopters could theoretically be ferried to North Africa, but only with refueling stops in Corsica or southern Italy, and on a pre-positioned aircraft carrier in the southern Mediterranean. Sealift of helicopter squadrons to sub-Saharan Africa would take a minimum of two to three weeks, thereby defeating the purpose of rapid deployment. Airmobile divisions are not as mobile as is commonly believed; while their component regiments can move rapidly anywhere within helicopter range, the transport of a whole division is more difficult than the transport of an infantry division.[17]

6th Light Armored Division: This division is able to project itself more than 800 km over roads without refueling. It is "the ideal partner to support the action of the Airmobile Division,"[18] due to its mobility and anti-armor capability. The extensive use of wheeled armored vehicles is considered "the French Army's most distinctive feature."[19] The 6th Light Armored Division was primarily integrated into the FAR for its potential utility in central Europe. The Division has a personnel strength of 8,300-men and is equipped with 72 AMX-10RC wheeled armored fighting vehicles, 24 wheeled armored vehicles mounting *HOT* anti-tank missiles, 24 self-propelled tracked 155-mm artillery pieces, and 48 *Milan* man-portable anti-tank weapon systems. The AMX-10RC weighs 16 tons and requires airlift capabilities unavailable to the French military. Elements of five different regiments of the 6th Light Armored Division were attached to the *Daguet* Division in the Gulf War, providing six squadrons of twelve AMX-10RCs each.[20]

Three units of the famous Foreign Legion are assigned to the 6th Light Armored Division: the 2nd Foreign Legion Infantry Regiment, the 1st Foreign Legion Cavalry Regiment, and the 6th Foreign Legion Combat Engineer Regiment.

9th Marine Infantry Division: Like the 6th Light Armored Division, the 9th Marine Infantry Division is a light armored unit, although it is significantly lighter than the 6th, since its main wheeled fighting vehicle, the ERC-90-SAGAIE (with an over-road range of 800 km), weighs only eight tons. The Division's wartime strength is 8,200 troops. The 9th Division has only eighteen 155-mm artillery pieces, but it has been equipped with 96 *Milan* man-portable anti-tank weapon systems. All of this material is air-transportable, but French airlift capability is not sufficient to move it all at once. In addition to its lighter weight, the 9th Division also differs from the 6th Division in its specific amphibious capabilities and training. Although it is a full part of the Army, it must rely on the Navy for its assault and landing ships, making the 9th Division a close equivalent to the U.S. Marines. Together with the 11th Parachute Division, it is perfectly suited for rapid overseas operations.

11th Parachute Division: With 15,000 troops at wartime levels, the 11th Parachute Division is the largest of all FAR divisions in terms of manpower. It is equipped with 36 lightly armored ERC-90-SAGAIE wheeled fighting vehicles with 168 *Milan* man-portable anti-tank missile launchers. To accomplish long-range deployment and airborne assault missions, the 11th Division has seven parachute infantry regiments, one light armored cavalry regiment, one engineer regiment, one artillery regiment, and one command-and-support regiment. Among the parachute infantry regiments is the Foreign Legion's 2nd Parachute Regiment, considered to be one of the most skilled airborne units in Europe. The regiment's four companies are all highly specialized: one in night movements and heliborne operations, another in mountain warfare, a third in amphibious landing and reconnaissance, and a fourth in sniping and demolition. Based in Corsica, the Foreign Legion's 2nd Parachute Regiment is also among the best prepared for deployment overseas.

27th Alpine Division: This unit has 10,000 men in wartime, the majority of them conscripts, trained to fight in mountainous, wooded, or urban terrain. It is equipped with 96 *Milan* man-portable anti-tank missile launchers, and its fire support includes thirty 120-mm mortars, and twenty-four 105-mm guns.

Professionalization and Combat Readiness

The level of professionalization of French forces within the FAR is higher than in most other units. The 4th Airmobile Division, the 6th Light Armored Division, and the 9th Marine Infantry Division are composed of a minimum of 80 percent career soldiers. The 11th

Parachute Division is only 66 percent professional, and the 27th Alpine Division much less. To accommodate the growing requirements for professional manpower in the out-of-area commitments, draftees since 1983 have the option of serving 12 months beyond the period of regular military service in exchange for higher pay.[21] Professionalization is important for units which must be deployed on very short notice because French law constrains the armed forces from sending drafted soldiers into combat without a prior vote in the Senate. This vote would deprive military planners of surprise and secrecy, and would limit the French president's power to send an expeditionary force overseas without a lengthy parliamentary debate.

The theoretical level of readiness of the FAR is impressive. The FAR's General Staff claims that it can make 70 percent of its wartime personnel and 80 percent of its material available within 24 hours. In 48 hours, 100 percent of the personnel with 95 percent of the equipment can be combat-ready.[22] For immediate alerts, the FAR permanently maintains between one and three companies ready within two hours. The rest of the regiment can be ready within six hours.

The FAR also rotates units between France and overseas bases, foreign bases, and/or foreign engagements. There are about a dozen such rotating companies, including those present in Chad. The period of rotation is about four months. Beside their value as training vehicles, the unit rotation system also enhances morale and esprit-de-corps. Some units of the FAR also participate in joint exercises abroad, either in Africa or Germany. The two main units engaged in sub-Saharan actions are the 11th Parachute Division and the 9th Marine Infantry Division.

Mobility will remain the key feature of the FAR. The forces of the FAR for engagement in the Third World (mainly sub-Saharan Africa) "will have less as their objective to defend permanent French interests, but will rather be used to unblock promptly [...] a situation which would run against those interests in a sudden and serious way."[23]

France is unlikely to engage more than 3,000 men from the FAR in Africa for a single operation. Extreme circumstances might push the number to the equivalent of a small French division (6,000-7,000 men) as the maximum required to meet the political and military needs imposed in a sub-Saharan context. Most actions would require only one or two companies, or a regiment at most. Critics assert that there was no need to create the FAR for such limited engagements.

French Army Forces Deployed Overseas

The FAR was not created with African interests in mind. In fact, the FAR did not add to or change any of the resources previously committed for African operations. Nevertheless, the French rapid deployment force is a cornerstone of the military apparatus available for overseas commitments. French bases in West and central Africa, the Indian Ocean or elsewhere could not be maintained if reinforcements could not be deployed to them quickly. The FAR gives cohesion to these bases and forward-deployed forces. Although some of these overseas forces can bring militarily significant firepower to bear on local crises, they gain their credibility from the fact that the FAR is the ultimate guarantor of French overseas interests.

Beside the forces available in France for power projection overseas, other units of the French Army are more or less permanently deployed abroad, or rotate frequently on overseas tours of duty. The troops of the Marine Infantry and the Foreign Legion figure prominently among Army units abroad. The Marine Infantry are the successors to the colonial troops, by definition deployed overseas and often reinforced with locally recruited men. Today, formations of the twelve Marine Infantry regiments can be found in almost all French overseas territories and foreign bases. Deployments include French Guiana and the Antilles, La Réunion, New Caledonia, Polynesia, and the foreign bases and temporary facilities in Africa.

Overseas deployments of the Foreign Legion are mainly restricted to the protection of the space center in French Guiana, the Pacific nuclear test center, and Mayotte. The Foreign Legion also participates in the defense of Djibouti with a half brigade. Some regiments of the Foreign Legion have been integrated within the FAR. The total strength of the Foreign Legion is about 8,500 men, divided into eight regiments. These eight regiments include one parachute regiment, one armored regiment, four infantry regiments, and one engineer regiment.[24]

POWER PROJECTION: THE NAVY

Pursuant to its desire to retain a global reach, France maintains a very versatile navy. Overseas responsibilities dictate widespread and multi-functional French naval deployment in order to protect commercial sea lanes, meet geo-strategic requirements, and provide for nuclear deterrence. In terms of naval versatility, France must have militarily significant capability in all areas of naval power: submarines, aircraft carriers, anti-air ships, anti-submarine ships, amphibious forces, frigate escorts, surveillance, mine-hunting and mine-clearing, together with repair, support, and logistical vessels and the supporting land-based infrastructure. The nuclear dimension adds a supplementary burden to this diversified panoply, with more than 90 percent of all French nuclear warheads deployed aboard six nuclear submarines.

The Navy is manned by 65,400 military personnel, 19,500 of which are conscripts. Current policies emphasize the nuclear element, which consumes 37.6 percent of the Navy procurement budget.[25] One-hundred nineteen combat and support ships are earmarked for conventional warfare. According to projections by the French Navy, this number will drop to 111 by 1995. Current forces include 14 attack submarines, two aircraft carriers, one helicopter carrier, five anti-air ships, 12 anti-submarine ships, 24 frigates and light frigates, 19 patrol boats, 22 anti-mine ships, 13 logistics ships, and seven transport ships.[26] Naval aviation will remain stable with 143 aircraft in 1995 against 142 in 1990.

These forces are articulated around four main plans of action. The first is to protect the permanently deployed strategic submarines with intelligence and mine-hunting forces. A second plan provides for one task force consisting of two aircraft carriers and anti-air ships. A third objective is to maintain a power-projection force of amphibious ships and frigate escorts. Finally, light surveillance frigates patrol overseas possessions to reaffirm French presence in distant regions.[27]

To protect its widespread interests, the French Navy has divided the world seas into four operational zones in which it maintains forces: the Atlantic, with French naval headquarters in Brest; the Mediterranean, with headquarters in Toulon; the Indian Ocean, with sea-going headquarters aboard the *Marne* command ship; and the South Pacific, with headquarters in Papeete, Tahiti. The Atlantic zone includes three sub-zones: the Channel and the North Sea; the Caribbean, with its command base at Fort-de-France; and the South Atlantic, with its command base at Dakar/Cap-Vert.[28] The French Navy forces permanently deployed overseas include five ships in the Antilles and Guiana, 11 ships in the Indian Ocean, six ships in Nouméa, seven ships in Papeete, and six ships at the nuclear Experimentation Center of the Pacific. Together with two training ships and two in reserve, the total number of French ships based overseas is 39.[29]

Combat Ships

Aircraft Carriers: Carriers compensate for diminishing access to foreign bases and overflight rights, and are invaluable in policing operations and in promoting regional stability. Their mobility is impressive, up to 1,000 km in 24 hours, and their movement is readily responsive to national command authority. With aircraft aboard, the strike radius extends up to 500 km from the carrier. Research and surveillance aircraft can monitor vast zones around the battle group. Aircraft and on-board systems provide electronic and signal intelligence. The simple act of deploying an aircraft battle group overseas is sometimes sufficient to deter hostilities.

France operates two medium-sized aircraft carriers, the *Clemenceau* and the *Foch*. The operation of two carriers is barely sufficient to keep at least one of them at sea at all times while the other is being serviced.[30] They each have a full load displacement of 32,780 tons and a crew of 1,700 men. A French carrier battle group represents a force of eight to eleven ships and 38-40 aircraft. The maximum speed of the *Clemenceau*-class carrier is 32 knots (59 km/h). France operates the largest carriers in Europe and is the only western European country to operate carriers with aircraft catapult propulsion systems.

Nonetheless, aircraft carriers are not always an ideal tool for power projection, often requiring several weeks to reach their theater of operations. Deep inland enclaves are inaccessible to the aircraft from a carrier battle group, although such areas are often the focus of crises where France intervenes, as in Chad or Zaire. Many deployments in Africa require quick action to smother a nascent crisis or rescue civilian populations. Carriers are not equipped to fight civil disorder, jungle wars or protracted internal crises. Nor do French aircraft carriers have the ability to launch troops or commandos ashore. The main power projection tools on French carriers are the 15 *Super Etendard* strike aircraft, which, even armed with smart bombs, are not always the best way to deal with delicate low-intensity crises or violent civil disorder. Finally, maintaining an aircraft carrier battle group in a state of alert along the African shore for an extended period of time is a very expensive way to deal with a limited crisis, given the cost of maintenance and repairs.[31] For France, an aircraft carrier battle group is a limited resource which cannot be committed to any one region for long periods of time.

Aircraft carrier groups can provide useful assistance in those African conflicts or contingencies which permit longer preparation and deployment schedules. The transition to independence of Djibouti in 1977 benefitted from the support of a naval Task Force headed first by the *Clemenceau* and then by the *Foch*. Another instance of French carrier deployment in support of a sub-Saharan military involvement came in 1984 during the withdrawal phase of the *Manta* operation in Chad. A *Foch* carrier group was deployed in the Gulf of Sirta, north of Libya, for two months in order to deter Libyan action aimed at disrupting the withdrawal.[32] In 1977, President Giscard d'Estaing wanted to deploy a carrier off the shore of Mauritania, but none were available. The subsequent French military intervention against the *Polisario* was undertaken by *Jaguars* based in Dakar, but because of the distance involved, the planes were not able to deliver as much ordnance as carrier-based aircraft might have done.[33] Nevertheless, these few operations in a sub-Saharan African context do not alone justify the acquisition of aircraft carriers by the French Navy. If France were to lose its bases and landing rights in sub-Saharan Africa, aircraft carriers would have an enhanced role. Such a scenario is hardly realistic, however, because it would imply that France would not have any base-access agreements with African nations. Were this the case, French commitments would be downgraded and interventions rendered less likely, except for humanitarian purposes.

Over the medium term, France will have to replace its two aging aircraft carriers. The new ships will offer an increased capacity in several respects: a full load displacement of 36,600 tons (against more than 90,000 tons for a U.S. carrier of the *Nimitz* class), 35-40 fixed-wing aircraft, a larger flight deck, and a catapult powerful enough to handle aircraft of up to 22 tons.[34] The first of these new carriers, the *Charles de Gaulle*, will be launched by 1996 and be operational by 1998.[35] Unlike Britain, France does not have small aircraft carriers for short take-off and vertical landing planes like the *Harrier*, which is not used by the French armed forces.

Helicopter Carrier: The French Navy still maintains a 1961 vintage helicopter carrier, the *Jeanne d'Arc*, to use for training officer cadets in peacetime. It is convertible to a wartime role as a commando ship, helicopter carrier, or transport for one battalion. Eight *Lynx* or *Alouette* helicopters can be accommodated in the wartime configuration, against four in peacetime.[36] French aircraft carriers also have the ability to adapt to helicopter operations, the *Clemenceau* having transported 42 helicopters during the 1990-91 deployment to the Persian Gulf.

Amphibious Assault Forces: The French Navy has nine ships for amphibious operations. The new 8,000-ton *Foudre*-class ships were designed to embark a mechanized regiment of the FAR and also to act as logistic support ships. Each carries four *Super Puma* helicopters, 470 troops (up to 1,600 in emergency), two Landing Craft/Tanks (LCT) or 10 Landing Craft/Material (LCM). Two 6,000-ton Landing Platform/Dock (LPD) ships of the 1960s-era *Ouragan*-class, deployed in the Atlantic, have the capacity to transport 320 troops, 10 tanks, 21 wheeled vehicles, two *Super Frelon* helicopters, two *Puma* helicopters, and five landing craft. A Landing Ship/Dock (LSD), the *Bougainville*, was assigned to support the nuclear test center in the South Pacific. It can transport 500 troops, six tanks, and two *Super Puma* helicopters, and can dock a 400-ton ship. This panoply is further complemented by five *Champlain* medium landing ships (LSM) with a capacity of 140 troops and seven tanks. There are an additional eight LCTs, and 20 LCMs. The *Champlain*-class ships are deployed mainly in the Indian Ocean, the Antilles/Guiana zone, Papeete, and New Caledonia.[37] Other French amphibious ships are deployed around the world.

The FAR's 9th Marine Infantry Division, an Army unit, provides the bulk of France's amphibious ground forces. The Navy has 2,600 troops under the rubric *fusiliers-marins*, of which 600 are organized in five commandos of 120 men each, with the remaining 2,000 troops deployed as naval base security forces. The five commandos are highly trained in a variety of specialized combat skills and are roughly comparable to the U.S. Navy's Sea-Air-Land (SEALS) forces.

Frigates: The frigates and destroyers that make up the bulk of European fleets are the ships best suited for out-of-area operations because of their small size, relatively heavy firepower and low manning requirements. For France, the number of frigates will increase from 22 to 26 between 1990 and 1995 as obsolete *aviso-escorteur* escort ships are replaced. The new light frigates and surveillance frigates each carry one helicopter and represent an important increase in surveillance capability over the *aviso-escorteur*. By 1995, France will start deploying the first of six *Lafayette*-class light frigates, which will be ready to respond to crises overseas. They are armed with advanced surface-to-surface missile and anti-air defense systems, and are designed "to participate in a strategy of action in tense crises, but which do not require the dispatch of an aircraft carrier battle group."[38]

The *Floréal*-class surveillance frigates are lightly armed and built to simpler commercial shipbuilding standards. The surveillance frigates are the direct result of budgetary constraints and cost only a fraction of the *Lafayette*-class frigates. The *Floréal* class contains none of the stealth features, advanced protection, sophisticated sensors, electronics, or weapons that are found on light frigates. They also have limited armament, with only a single 100-mm gun, surface-to-surface missiles, two close air-defense systems, and one eight-ton helicopter. The ship has a long range of 9,000 miles at 15 knots.[39] *Floréal* frigates do not carry armor and are not intended for combat. The *Floréal*-class ships have been specifically designed for operations to "show-the-flag" and maintain order in France's scattered overseas possessions, around important economic zones, and along commercial routes. By 1995, the six surveillance frigates will be deployed in regions of low risk where France wishes to assert its sovereignty.

Submarines: Few operations in a sub-Saharan context require the use of submarines. In low-intensity crises, attack submarines can conduct special operations in addition to their anti-submarine and anti-ship functions. These operations can include mine laying, insertion of special operations forces,[40] blockades, and attacks on commercial shipping. There is no indication that France has ever used its attack submarines in those roles during interventions in sub-Saharan Africa.

Naval Aviation

The aviation capabilities of the French Navy consists of a rather aging fleet of aircraft in the following categories. Four types of aircraft are 25-years or older: the *Etendard IV P*, the *Crusader*, the *Alizé*, and the *Atlantic*. The coming decade will be critical for French naval aviation as these aircraft will be replaced. After 1998, the naval version of the *Rafale* fighter will replace the *Etendards* and the *Crusaders*.

Currently, the *Super Etendard* tactical strike fighter and interceptor represents the only strike capability available on French aircraft carriers. The plane can fly at supersonic speeds and has a theoretical radius of 850 km with a standard load of one *Exocet AM.39* missile and an external fuel tank.[41] The strike capability with a carrier launch is approximately 500 km. The *Crusader* aircraft is equipped with a radar warning receiver and air-to-air *Sidewinder* and *Magic* missiles, but is also capable of delivering bombs and ground attack missiles. It is supersonic and has a maximum combat radius of 850 km.[42] The 24 *Alizé* carrier-based maritime patrol planes will be retained in land- and sea-based service until the year 2000. The *Alizé* has a combat radius of 1,200 km and can be equipped with torpedoes, bombs, and rockets.

The French Navy operates 38 *Atlantic* patrol aircraft, 10 of which are in storage. These aircraft cannot operate from French aircraft carriers. They are due for replacement by the *Atlantique 2* version, which has far superior sensors and advanced integrated navigation and communications electronics.[43] The first two *Atlantique 2* were delivered in 1989, but 40 more deliveries have been scheduled through 2002. Both the old and new versions can carry one air-to-surface missile and two anti-submarine torpedoes; their main wartime task is to locate and destroy enemy submarines, but they can also lay mines. They were designed to patrol 500 nautical miles from their base for eight hours or 1000 nautical miles from their base for three hours.[44] This exceptional range explains why France has deployed one *Atlantic* each in Dakar and Chad, respectively, for search and rescue missions or intelligence and surveillance tasks. These planes are also ideally suited to serve as navigational aids to strike aircraft or bombers.

The Navy's helicopters also suffer from old age. The 17 operational *Super Frelons* are used for assault transport, anti-submarine warfare, and search-and-rescue missions. They are scheduled to be phased out of service gradually, beginning in 1995. The 36 *Lynx* will be replaced by 2010. The Navy also operates 44 light *Alouette III* helicopters as training or utility aircraft.[45]

POWER PROJECTION: THE AIR FORCE

The Air Force is the second largest service in the French armed forces with 90,100 men, 32,700 of whom are conscripts. The French Air Force is divided into seven commands: strategic, tactical, air defense, air transport, communications, training and engineering. The Air Force has a history of active participation in overseas military operations, contributing airlift capabilities, tactical fighters, reconnaissance aircraft, air defense, and air refueling. In the early 1990s, two new roles have been added: electronic intelligence and battlefield monitoring with the new *Gabriel* and AWACS aircraft. The most sophisticated Air Force operations in sub-Saharan Africa were linked to the 1983-84 *Manta* and 1986 *Epervier* interventions in Chad. The air-defense system developed in Chad during the *Epervier* intervention has been in use for several years to defend Chadian airspace and airfields.

Military Air Transport

The *Commandement du Transport Aérien Militaire* (COTAM) is responsible for French military airlift. The French Air Force is ill-equipped for long-range, heavy air transport, and the majority of its air transport fleet is aged. After the 1991 Gulf War, the WEU reported that: "The European members of the coalition force found there were serious deficiencies [in airlift capabilities]. France flew 3,200 hours to transport 5,500 troops and 2,500 tons of freight, mainly with *Transall* C-160s and aged DC-8s."[46] Allotting a generous 20 hours per round-trip flight to the Gulf, this represents about 160 flights. American C-5 *Galaxies*, with a maximum payload 132 tons or 340 passengers,[47] could have performed the same job with approximately one-fourth the flights. During operation *Manta* no less than 133 flights were required to transport 3,000 men and 3,500 tons of freight from France to Chad between August and September 1983 using civilian Boeing 747s and DC-10s, in addition to military transport aircraft.[48] Modern low-intensity conflicts in a theater like Africa require, according to General Henri Paris, a ratio of one-to-five tons of equipment and material per soldier. Rapid logistics, therefore, becomes the crucial factor to the success of a military operation overseas.[49]

"In theory, COTAM should be able to quickly ferry 1,500 metric tons over a distance of 1,000 kilometers, or 750 metric tons over 7,000 kilometers."[50] Such deployments would require a fleet of 100 transport aircraft, each with a 20 to 25 metric ton payload. Except for some very small planes, COTAM had, in 1990, a fleet of 88 transport planes at its disposal. This fleet included 70 C-160 *Transalls*, 12 C-130H *Hercules*, and six DC-8s.[51]

Second-generation models have all been equipped with flight refueling probes. Ten of the latest aircraft ordered by France were equipped as hose and drogue tankers, and five more were modified for rapid conversion to tankers. A C-160 can air-drop 62 to 88 paratroopers, depending on their equipment. In the airlift role, later generation C-160s can carry up to 8.5 tons over a distance of 5,000 km. These planes have a cruise speed of 260 knots and a ceiling of

26,000 feet; they can operate from a 700-meter landing strip. The Air Force has expressed the desire for a new type of transport plane, the European Future Large Aircraft, which was still in the research stage in late 1993. In order to relieve some of the burden of the *Transall* fleet, and thereby stretch its lifetime, the Air Force bought the American C-130 *Hercules* planes and the smaller Spanish CN-235.[52]

It was a highly unusual, and overdue, step for France to decide on the acquisition of the C-130, given French propensity to buy aircraft from French producers. The C-130 entered the French Air Force when a long-range air transport plane became necessary, especially for African commitments. The two versions of the *Hercules* bought by the French Air Force in 1987 are the C-130H and the C-130H-30. The C-130H can air-drop 64 paratroopers. The C-130H-30 is a "stretch" version with a lengthened cargo compartment. It has a range of 2,100 nautical miles and can airdrop up to 92 paratroopers.[53]

The French Air Force has acquired six CN-235 transport planes, which are ideally suited for regular air links between French bases in sub-Saharan Africa.[54] This high-wing, short take-off and landing plane can carry up to 41 paratroopers or 48 fully-equipped infantrymen. Like the *Transall* and *Hercules*, it features a tail loading ramp for rapid airdrop of paratroopers or cargo. In its military version, it has a payload of five tons and can carry lightweight vehicles.[55] The acquisition of the CN-235 was motivated by concerns that the *Transall* and *Hercules* transporters were wearing out too fast under the stress of constantly supplying French troops and bases abroad, in addition to training parachute units. More often than not, the *Transall* and *Hercules* were flying at a less than full cargo load. Substituting the CN-235 on some of these missions allowed for a more optimal use of cargo space.

COTAM is entitled to requisition commercial transport when necessary. It has never done so, however; instead, COTAM has made agreements with commercial airlines. Air France and UTA have both signed conventions to make a pool of six to ten of their airliners available to COTAM as little as six to twelve hours after the request has been issued.[56] These agreements do not bear on specific planes, but rather on an overall transport capability. DC-10s or Boeing 747s are often used for this type of operation.

There are several problems with using commercial airplanes in military operations. One shortcoming is their reliability in times of crisis. The 1944 Chicago Convention provides a legal framework for the participation of commercial airlines in military-related operations, allowing for the transportation of men and non-lethal material, including fuel.[57] In addition, commercial airliners do not offer the short take-off and landing capabilities, rapid delivery ramps, or adaptability to difficult terrains which military aircraft provide.

French interventions in sub-Saharan Africa have benefitted from in-flight refueling capabilities in three situations: first, in deploying tactical aircraft to distant theaters without landing *en route*, although it is necessary to plan flight routes which minimize problems of overflight of third countries; second, in maintaining airplanes in a prolonged state of in-flight alert; and third, in permitting tactical or strike aircraft to make long-distance raids. The latter two roles were mainly reserved for the Chadian operations. The French Air Force owns eleven C-135-FR *Transall* aerial tankers. In addition to performing their primary in-flight refueling mission, the C-135-Fs can also carry cargo, which is needed during deployments of tactical aircraft for aircraft spares and ground crew. Given their lower flight ceiling (6,000 meters) and slower speed compared to jet-powered aircraft, the C-160 *Transalls* equipped for in-flight refueling must operate in relatively safe environments protected from air-to-air and ground-to-air threats.[58]

Tactical Aircraft, Air Defense and Airborne Intelligence

The missions of the *Force aérienne tactique* (FATAC), or tactical air force, are aerial reconnaissance, neutralization of enemy air power or air defenses on the ground, and air cover to protect ground operations. FATAC participated extensively in the *Manta* and *Epervier* operations in Chad. Its participation was facilitated by air-to-air refueling capabilities. FATAC flies *Jaguar*, *Mirage* III-E, *Mirage* IV-F, *Mirage* F1-CR, and *Mirage* 2000-N aircraft. Only the *Jaguar* and the *Mirage* F1-CR are deployed frequently in sub-Saharan Africa.

The *Jaguar* is a Franco-British tactical support aircraft with a range of 400 to 700 km. Some of them have in-flight refueling systems. Developed as a fighter-bomber, the *Jaguar* can carry up to four tons of armaments from an assortment including air-surface weapons, nuclear weapons, laser guided bombs and missiles, anti-radar missiles, area attack weapons, and runway cratering/airfield denial weapons.[59] The *Jaguar* is primarily a day fighter because it lacks radar and modern navigation systems. The *Mirage*-F1 has a combat radius of between 425 km and 1,390 km. For attack missions the F1 can carry a variety of underwing stores, including various types of bombs, missiles and rockets. The *Mirage*-F1-CR's main mission is aerial reconnaissance, and it can be refueled in flight. It has a maximum combat radius of 1,390 km and combat air patrol endurance of over two hours. It is equipped with an infra-red reconnaissance system, and collected data can be transmitted in real-time to air-portable ground stations. In addition, in its secondary ground attack role it can be armed with a variety of both air-to-surface and air-to-air weapon systems. With its highly accurate navigation and delivery systems, the F1-CR is one of the French Air Force's more capable combat aircraft.[60]

The deployment of *Jaguars* and *Mirage*-F1s to Libreville and N'Djamena are routine operations requiring 10 hours of flight with one stopover in Dakar and in-flight refueling two or three times over a total distance of about 8,000 km. These flights are usually done by groups of two or four airplanes supported by C-135-Fs or C-135-FRs. In 1984, during the absence of French aircraft carriers in the eastern Mediterranean, France sent four France-based *Jaguars* on a reconnaissance mission to the former French sector in southern Beirut. This operation illustrates the FATAC range of action.[61]

French air defense aircraft include the *Mirage*-F1 and the *Mirage* 2000-DA. In the African sub-Saharan theater, air defense is accomplished in the air mainly with the *Mirage*-F1 and on the ground with *Crotale* low-altitude air-defense missile systems and SATCP short-range portable air-defense missiles. The heavier, medium-range U.S.-made *Hawk* air-defense missile system was deployed in Chad in 1986, and was credited with shooting down a Libyan bomber.[62]

Configured for electronic warfare the *Transall* C-160G is known as the *Gabriel*. It performs electronic communications and intelligence gathering missions. During the Gulf War, one *Gabriel* was deployed to Saudi Arabia.[63] The *Gabriels*, however, are intended primarily for use in Europe and are rarely deployed to Africa.

In 1991, the French Air Force took delivery of its four Boeing E-3F Airborne Warning And Control System (AWACS).[64] The AWACS is effectively a mobile, flexible, and jamming-resistant high capacity radar station as well as a command, control and communications center. Its on-station endurance is six hours at 1,610 km from its base. French AWACS are also equipped with a probe for in-flight refueling. Operating at 30,000 feet, AWACS radar can scan a surface of 312,000 km². Each aircraft has a crew of 22 men. France organized its four AWACS into the 36th Airborne Detection Wing at the Avord air base.

Outside Europe, French AWACS can perform several important roles: providing aerial surveillance and monitoring against low and high flying threats; guiding fighters to intercept airborne attackers; substituting for ground-based radar stations; acting as command, control, communications and intelligence platforms; and participating in general crisis management as a force multiplier. Overall, AWACS are a "deterrent and a strong signal to any potential aggressor."[65]

When operating from friendly countries, AWACS are under a relatively low risk and produce much useful surveillance intelligence. Their mobility allows them to be rapidly deployed where they are most needed, and then be gradually phased out when ground based radar systems are introduced to the crisis area. In the early stages of the French operation *Epervier* in Chad, the ground radar cover was insufficient. Had France then possessed AWACS planes, one of them could have covered the airspace until ground-based radars were erected. AWACS aircraft will revolutionize French ability to monitor distant events and to organize protective cover for possible operations. Integrated in the armed forces, the AWACS are a useful tool for pre-crisis and crisis management.

Military Use of Space

France's military space programs have been very modest in comparison to those of the two superpowers. In 1984 and 1985, two French civilian telecommunications satellites were sent into orbit with added equipment allowing for secure and independent military communications. This was the *Syracuse I* system. By late 1994, a follow-up system, *Syracuse II*, will piggy-back into orbit on civilian telecommunication satellites. Due to restrictions inherent in the use of the civilian telecommunications space platforms, *Syracuse I* and *II* will not cover the Pacific and Indian Ocean region. Europe, Africa, and the Middle East, however, will remain in the satellites' footprint.[66] Future French military space programs include the launching of a joint French-Italian-Spanish military reconnaissance satellite system called *Hélios*, which involves the development of two satellites, the first of which is scheduled to enter into service in 1994, and the second a year later. The satellite's resolution is one meter.

The virtually global reach of the *Hélios* and *Syracuse* systems will reinforce the status of France as an international power. Studies on a radar-equipped *Osiris* satellite have started as well, which would give France an all-weather surveillance capability by the beginning of the next century. In 1992, Pierre Joxe, then minister of defense, strongly advocated the development of military space assets.

> Without them, no nation can seriously entertain worldwide ambitions. The stakes in space go beyond the strict definition of defense. [...] They are national. Not to possess this capacity would affect the very status of the nation.[67]

Joxe added that the French government should attach the same importance to the military space programs in the 1990s as it did to the independent nuclear capability in the 1960s.[68] The space programs form a cornerstone of the ability of the French Army, Navy and Air Force to project power overseas. By monitoring overseas activities from space, France has taken a necessary step in maintaining its future military role beyond Europe.

The preceding sections have demonstrated that France will commit the necessary resources, within existing budget constraints, to obtain the weapons systems necessary for preserving a versatile military power projection capability. This effort includes the troops deployed in Africa and the upgrading of their equipment. Africa will retain its special status in France's global defense posture in the foreseeable future.

DEFENSE AGREEMENTS AND MILITARY COOPERATION

French deployments in Africa are governed by bilateral military agreements with its African partners, a scheme devised by de Gaulle to preserve France's privileged links with its former colonies. The extent and number of such agreements form the cornerstone of France's military edifice in Africa and provide the legal basis for one of Africa's most extensive and lasting security alliances with a foreign power.

With regard to military relations, France offered to sign one of two types of military agreements with African nations: defense agreements or military cooperation agreements. While defense agreements principally govern the use of French military power in Africa, military cooperation agreements attempt to restructure African military power. The two types of agreements are complementary and are presented as the legal embodiment of France's commitment to protect young African nations. Their value as tools of French influence should not be underestimated, although the cooperative agreements infringe less on the sovereign rights of the African party than the defense agreements. John Chipman argued that, with those agreements, "the principal aim of the French government was to maintain its influence in Africa while preserving its ultimate freedom of action."[69] With some variance, these security arrangements are still in place thirty years later.

Defense Agreements

Between 1960 and 1963, eleven defense agreements were signed between France and the newly independent francophone countries in sub-Saharan Africa, including: the Central African Republic, Chad, Congo, Côte d'Ivoire, Dahomey, Gabon, Madagascar, Mali, Niger, Senegal, and Togo. The early refusals came from Guinea (evident from its decision not to join the *Communauté* in 1958), Upper-Volta, and Cameroon. The latter two "would not sign such agreements for fear of the deleterious effects of an overwhelming French presence, and decided to 'satisfy' themselves with technical assistance agreements."[70] By 1993, eight countries still maintained defense agreements with France, including five original signatories and three later adherents. These countries are: Cameroon (1974); Central African Republic (1960); Comoros (1978); Côte d'Ivoire (1961); Djibouti (1977); Gabon (1960); Senegal (1974 - renewed); and Togo (1963).

Mauritania does not have a formal defense agreement with France, but the military intervention in 1977-78 through operation *Lamentin* indicated that at least a *de facto* arrangement existed between the two countries. All agreements with Mauritania have always been secret.[71] Other countries like Niger and Burkina Faso have signed more limited Logistical Support Conventions. These conventions enable France to mobilize some useful logistical support points when engaged in regional operations. Logistical Support Conventions also provide France with overflight, staging and transit rights.

The conceptual framework behind the defense agreements was broadly defined in the early 1960s and has not fundamentally changed since then. Internal security is handled by the local authorities although, upon request, France could provide some additional assistance. French forces have a mission to guarantee overall defense and provide technical cooperation, and can complement local forces in case of aggression or subversion.[72] The specific conditions and stipulations concerning interventions are usually confidential, although they are based on two main elements: (i) a system of bases, staging points and overflight rights accorded to French forces; and (ii) light and mobile French forces in the host country. France is responsible for keeping its command, communications and intelligence centers in a state of readiness.

The most visible and controversial clauses of some of the defense agreements relate to the presence of French troops. Over time, France has gradually reduced the number of bases and troops deployed in Africa, while restructuring and reinforcing home-based forces which are made available for overseas interventions. In December 1993, France maintained troops in seven countries, not counting military advisors: the CAR, Chad, Côte d'Ivoire, Djibouti, Gabon, Rwanda (in their final month), and Senegal. Troops are permanently deployed in Côte d'Ivoire, Djibouti, Gabon and Senegal; semi-permanently in Chad and the CAR; and had been on a short-term, though prolonged, assignment in Rwanda.

Annexes to defense agreements include special clauses relating to raw materials. Many African states which have these agreements give France privileged access to strategic materials and minerals, including uranium. French privileges include not only the acquisition of these materials, but also participation in informational exchanges to define their research, exploitation, and trade.[73] Other annexes give France a virtual monopoly to supply and maintain military equipment to these African signatories.

This system of bilateral defense agreements "saved face" for all signatories. It enabled France to dismantle the least essential parts of its costly colonial network of bases and staging posts in Africa without losing its influence and the prerogative to send additional forces if necessary. Likewise, African countries received the guarantee of a legal framework for French support without having to compromise excessively their newly acquired independence. France was undoubtedly the stronger power in these agreements, and French action was not automatic. The French president retained the privilege to intervene or abstain from involvement in African internal and external conflicts.[74]

In spite of France's apparent autonomy in deciding whether or not to become involved, there have been actions which have partly challenged this privilege. *De jure*, the privilege was never questioned, but *de facto* the French government has, at times, been dragged into African crises by a combination of pressure from old allies in Africa and France's self-imposed burden of preserving its credibility by never wanting to give the appearance of shirking its commitments. The results were a series of actions which, although not automatic, were undertaken regardless of France's professed rules of engagement. This lack of consistency, which is more obvious when comparing French administrations, can even be found within a given administration. In 1990, France intervened in Gabon but refused to lend open military support to Côte d'Ivoire. Both countries had a defense agreement with France and were experiencing domestic troubles, although the challenge to their political stability was interpreted differently. Despite criticism for the lack of consistency, France has more often than not been vindicated in its use of a flexible, *ad hoc* approach to each country in order to ensure stability. It is difficult to set general policy guidelines because each situation is country-specific. French troops intervened in Rwanda, with which no defense agreement had been signed, but not in Côte d'Ivoire, which has a longstanding defense agreement with France and whose president requested military assistance. It may be more correct to analyze the probability of a French intervention in terms of a pragmatic evaluation of potential destabilizing consequences, rather than in legal terms. Persistent African military weaknesses, along with France's perennial concern about maintaining influence in the world arena, are the two basic motivating factors behind any given intervention. Stability in francophone sub-Saharan Africa is the way French policy-makers promote French influence. This leaves all parties with little room to maneuver, and makes policy evolution slow and difficult. The only condition common to all thirty French interventions in sub-Saharan Africa, barring recent actions in Nigeria (1968-69), Liberia (1990), and Somalia (1992-94), is that they all occurred in francophone countries.

Despite the weak correlation between countries with defense agreements and countries where France has intervened over the last three decades, the agreements are not irrelevant. On the contrary, they are one of the conditions which enable interventions to take place,[75] even though action may be conducted in another country that is not necessarily the signatory to an agreement. Within the framework of these defense agreements, five countries continue to maintain prepositioned French forces: the CAR, Côte d'Ivoire, Djibouti, Gabon and Senegal. Restrictions, sometimes more theoretical than practical, can be imposed by the African countries on the deployment and mobility of French prepositioned troops. For example, unless provisions in the defense agreement stipulate otherwise, those troops can only be deployed in other crisis areas with the permission of the local African authorities. When French military authorities contemplated removing some of their troops from Djibouti to assign them to Chad during operation *Manta*, the Djibouti government strongly opposed the move, claiming that it was not covered by its 1977 defense agreement with France.[76] African countries have been increasingly reluctant to see French military facilities on their territory used as a base for action in other countries, unless the local government can exercise some control in authorizing their use.

Military Cooperation Agreements

Defense agreements and cooperation agreements are part of a single, comprehensive military strategy. Military cooperation, deployment of forces, and the direct intervention of French home-based forces form the three levels of French military assistance to African countries. The ultimate goal was to endow African partners with "armed forces which could efficiently defend themselves in order to maintain a *status quo* favorable to the former metropole."[77]

Initially conceived as a vehicle to assist the formation of new African armies, military cooperation subsequently became more permanent. It evolved into an on-going cooperation framework, with African officers and non-commissioned officers educated either in France or at French-sponsored military schools in Africa. French military cooperation today is a vast network involving almost 35 countries, 23 of which are in sub-Saharan Africa. French military assistance involves a large numbers of personnel, including about 1,000 technical experts and instructors overseas. Table 4 presents an overview of the 23 sub-Saharan African countries which have military cooperation agreements with France. The scope and gradual enlargement of French military assistance programs reflect the importance French authorities confer on them for furthering their policies over the medium-to-long term. The increase in beneficiaries in the mid-1970s corresponded both to Giscard's drive to enhance France's presence on the African continent and to the wave of independence granted to a series of micro-states.

The organization of military cooperation is based on ordinances and decrees dating back to 1959. At the governmental level, the Inter-ministerial Group for Cooperation and Military Assistance (GICAM), within the General Secretariat for National Defense (SGDN), coordinates ministerial decisions and follows any activity undertaken. The Ministry of Cooperation, which was created to manage all accords between France and African states, is responsible for executing the policy of military assistance not only for francophone and, more recently, lusophone countries in Africa, but also for Indian Ocean and Caribbean states. The military cooperation office within the Ministry of Cooperation is headed by a two-star general of the French armed forces. He is assisted in Paris by a team of about thirty military officers. In 1991, about FF 910 million (U.S. $170 million), just under 20 percent of the entire Ministry of Cooperation budget, was allotted to the military programs.[78] The number of African countries that receive some form of military assistance from France has roughly doubled over the years, although the resources available for each country have declined on average.[79]

Other Ministries are also involved in this cooperative structure. For example, the Foreign Ministry is responsible for military cooperation with Malawi, the only anglophone sub-Saharan African country with which France has a cooperation agreement.[80] The Ministry of Defense provides the manpower, equipment, and military facilities. It also supervises the distribution of military aid. The General Staff of the Armed Forces and the Armament Board are closely associated in defining and monitoring the assistance programs. It is therefore necessary to add the considerable, but hidden, expenses of the Ministry of Defense, and the lesser responsibilities of the Ministry of Foreign Affairs, to the budget of the Military Cooperation Mission in order to evaluate the total cost of French military assistance.[81]

French military cooperation is divided into three main fields: (i) dispatching French military cadres to advise and train African military personnel, or to direct specialized programs for which there are not enough African specialists; (ii) hosting African military trainees at French military schools, or sponsoring African training centers; and (iii) assisting African armies by directly furnishing equipment.

TABLE 4: Military Cooperation Agreements

COUNTRY	DATE	DESCRIPTION
Benin	7 Feb. 1975	Technical-military cooperation
Burkina Faso	24 Apr. 1961 24 July 1965	Technical assistance Logistical support
Burundi	7 Oct. 1969	Special agreement regarding entry examination of military personnel.
Cameroon	21 Feb 1974	Logistical support and military cooperation
CAR	3 Aug. 1960 5 Aug. 1960 8 Oct. 1965	Technical-military cooperation Special agreements Technical-military cooperation
Chad	6 Mar. 1976 5 Apr. 1978	Technical-military cooperation (effective 1 Mar. 1979) Employment agreement governing helicopter teams.
Comoros	10 Nov. 1978 4 Aug. 1979	Examination of personnel French technical-military examination for training purposes
Congo	1 Jan. 1974	Technical cooperation: training and equipment
Côte d'Ivoire	24 April 1961 8 April 1965 26 Jan. 1978 19 Mar. 1980	Technical-military assistance French examination for logistical support personnel Special agreements for cooperation in armament and pilot training
Eq. Guinea	9 Mar. 1985	Military cooperation
Gabon	17 June 1960	Agreement and convention
Guinea	17 Apr. 1985	Technical-military cooperation

Djibouti	27 June 1977	Provisional protocol on the stationing on French troops
	15 Dec. 1977	Logistical and sanitary support
	23 Apr. 1978	Personnel examinations (effective 31 Oct. 1982)
	23 Apr. 1978	Air force cooperation
	3 Sept. 1979	Creation and operation of a military post office
	14 Feb. 1980	Protocol on the powers of military police regarding crimes
	12 Feb. 1985	Operation of a military post office
Madagascar	4 June 1973	Military affairs and technical assistance
	29 Dec. 1978	Military hospital
Mali	6 May 1985	Technical-military cooperation Technical cooperation: training of administrative personnel
Mauritania	27 Apr. 1985	Technical-military cooperation
	27 Apr. 1986	Technical-military cooperation
Mauritius	25 May 1979	Special military cooperation
Niger	19 Feb. 1977	Technical-military cooperation
Rwanda	18 July 1975	Special military assistance
Senegal	29 Mar. 1974	Defense cooperation
	29 Mar. 1974	Protocol regarding the flight safety of military aircraft.
	29 Mar. 1974	Development of the *Direction des Constructions et Armes Navales*
	26 Oct. 1979	DCAN transfer methods
Seychelles	5 Jan. 1979	Special navy agreement
Togo	23 Mar. 1976	Technical-military cooperation
Zaire	22 May 1974	Technical military cooperation
	9 July 1976	Technical military cooperation

*Source: "Les accords de défense et de coopération militaire technique"
Marchés Tropicaux, 29 December 1989, 3871.*

Three Forms of Military Technical Assistance

The largest French program for sending military aid to Africa is the *Assistance Militaire Technique* (AMT). Allotted a budget of about FF 598 million in 1991 (60 percent of the military assistance budget) from the Ministry of Cooperation, this program sends *coopérants* to furnish technical aid to African countries. Except for particular instances, however, these military assistants do not replace African officers in commanding national armies. Some French military *coopérants* advise ministers or high government officials. Through them, France gains intelligence on the status of armed forces in francophone Africa.

The number of AMT technical advisors and instructors is high because of the demand for their services in the field, although in the late 1980s their presence was decreasing. There were about 3,000 AMT *coopérants* in the early 1960s after the independence of many African states, but by 1991 their numbers had dropped to 902. All of the French armed services are represented among the *coopérants*: about 57 percent come from the Army, specifically the *Troupes de Marine*. Table 5 breaks down their presence in Africa in 1991.

AMT assistants are integrated into the forces of the host country, and even wear the uniform of that country. The uniform is perceived by the African officers as a sign of trust. The AMTs report to an African commanding officer, but "are equally responsible to the head of the military cooperation mission in the local French embassy."[82] The latter is directly responsible to the ambassador, the minister of defense, foreign affairs or cooperation.[83]

French training of African military personnel can also be completed through the use of the *détachement d'assistance militaire d'instruction* (DAMI). Members of the DAMI remain in Africa for periods of three to six months and provide a cooperative form of training. DAMI is a less costly form of cooperation than the AMT program because the shorter periods of service do not require that France relocate the families of the servicemen.

A second means of French cooperation with African countries consists of instructional programs for officers, which are carried out in both France and Africa. Since 1962, France has received close to 33,000 interns from African armies for training at officer schools. The military training effort in 1991 commits about FF 114.2 million, or approximately 14 percent, of the Cooperation Ministry's financial resources. In 1991, 1,800 interns arrived in France from sub-Saharan

Africa to participate in the program, which can last from a few months to several years, depending on the field. Sub-Saharan Africa represents the bulk of the worldwide total of 4,000 trainees. Côte d'Ivoire is the largest beneficiary with 269 trainees in 1988, followed by Gabon (197), Cameroon (169), Congo (158), Togo (144), Mauritania (129), Benin (123) and Senegal (109).[84] Due to budgetary constraints and the limited capacity of its military schools, however, France is unable to

TABLE 5: French Military Advisors in Sub-Saharan Africa

Country	Number of AMT
Gabon	98
Zaire	95*
Djibouti	81
Togo	75
CAR	71
Côte d'Ivoire	68
Cameroon	62
Mauritania	57
Niger	51
Chad	43
Comoros	39
Senegal	29
Guinea	28
Burundi	22
Rwanda	21
Burkina Faso	12
Congo	12
Madagascar	11
Benin	10
Mali	10
Equatorial Guinea	4
Mauritius	3
Total:	**902**

* All cooperation personnel in Zaire left the country in October 1991.

Source: Mission Militaire de Coopération, Ministère de la Coopération et du Développement.

meet the entire demand from African countries that wish to have many more of their officers trained. The prestige attached to graduating from a French military school sometimes conceals the ill-adapted training African candidate-officers receive in France, which is geared mainly to combat on the European theater.

In order to develop a more Africa-specific training program and solve the financial and capacity limitations at French military schools, France relies on small, regional training schools for African soldiers from an increasing number of countries. There are four such facilities which are financed, organized, and co-administered by France. In 1991 the schools were filled with about 230 trainee-officers. Trainees enter by competitive examination.

The Inter-African *Ecole militaire d'administration* in Lomé, Togo, opened its doors in September 1986. Soldiers who attend this small school receive nine months of training, which improves their administrative and management skills. An instruction center for armored troops has existed in M'Banza N'Gungu, Zaire, since 1969. Following an important purchase of *Panhard* light armored vehicles, the first French military *coopérants* arrived in 1976 to assist in the technical training of the Zairian military cadres. The center passed from Zairian to French control in 1979 under the auspices of the French Military Cooperation Mission and was renamed the Training and Application School for Armored Forces (*Ecole de Formation et d'Application des Troupes Blindées*). The school can host approximately 70 trainees. Ten African countries have sent their soldiers to this center. The *Division d'application des transmissions*, or Applied Transmission Center, was opened in 1983 in Bouaké, Côte d'Ivoire. Each training program can accept a maximum of 15 trainees at a time. The Inter-African Infantry Administration Division or *Division d'Application d'Infanterie* (DAI) in Thiès, Senegal was created in 1987. It is the final stage in training officers to command infantry units in an African context. About 30 interns from 16 francophone African countries attend classes.

The third aspect of French military cooperation with the countries of Africa is the direct provision of material aid. The level of French military aid that was delivered to Africa increased during the 1980s, but has stabilized since then. The 1991 budget for such assistance was FF 198 million ($35 million).[85] Despite the modest amount France has furnished, this assistance represents a large portion of the actual military equipment available to francophone African states.[86] The chief of the Mission of Military Cooperation and the Ministry of Cooperation have virtual autonomy in determining which of the francophone African countries will receive aid, as well as the extent of the assistance. The arms and equipment are distributed according to certain priorities, with the countries sharing both defense and cooperation treaties with France generally receiving a larger share of materials. The budget does not allow France to fulfill the needs of all 23 contracting countries, but is intended to complement their own national efforts. In general, Chad and Senegal receive roughly 25 percent of the aid budget.[87] Rwanda received a 75 percent increase in its equipment aid after the 1990 rebel invasion. Chad has also received some exceptional credits directly from the Defense Ministry's budget.

Aid fluctuates according to France's evaluation of a country's needs and prevailing circumstances at any particular time. France has always been careful not to over-endow African armies with advanced equipment or encourage arms races. The whole military aid program has shown a remarkable ability to regulate carefully the dissemination of French arms. "The Ministry attempts to satisfy the maximum possible demands within the budget and thus implicitly manages regional balances of power in francophone Africa."[88]

The equipment aid consists mainly of light combat vehicles, transportation vehicles, transmission equipment, and other materials which often have civilian utility. An Interministerial Commission for Weapons Exportation approves the donations or grants, following the advice of the Ministry of Cooperation. Arms exports are not supervised by that ministry and are purchased with funds beyond its purview.

Although arms sales are not part of the French cooperation programs, they have an impact on foreign policy. France's armament policy throughout the Fifth Republic has been to achieve self-sufficiency in weapons production. Given the limited size of the French armed forces market, French arms manufacturers have had to rely on export markets to augment their sales and maintain low prices. France developed its export markets throughout the 1980s, exporting $36.6 billion in arms, thereby becoming the third largest arms exporter in the world, with a market share of 7.5 percent.[89] Exports amounted to $6.1 billion in 1991, and to $8.9 billion in 1992. Sub-Saharan Africa never represented a major market for French arms manufacturers, despite the sometimes exclusive reliance of some francophone African countries on French weapons and equipment. The relatively small African defense procurement budgets, as well as France's close monitoring of potentially destabilizing arms races on the African continent, have kept exports within relatively confined limits. In the 1980s, France delivered over $5 billion worth of arms to all of Africa, almost on par with the U.S., but far behind the former Soviet Union (France sold the equivalent of only 11 percent of Soviet sales to Africa).[90] French arms deliveries to sub-Saharan Africa vary between 2.5 percent and 4 percent of France's worldwide arms sales. The French government must approve all arms exports.

Evaluation of the Military Cooperation Framework

Since the 1960s France has sought to increase the number of African military cadres trained in France, expand its training capabilities through the development of inter-African schools, and increase the number of military advisors in Africa. Since the 1980s, however, each of these figures has declined or has leveled off.[91] No dramatic cuts occurred in any given country; rather, the reductions affected almost all beneficiaries. With the gradual increase in the number of African partners, there has been a reduction in the average amount of French cooperation with individual countries.

Because of France's domestic budgetary constraints and the increased number of countries that seek to receive a portion of limited available resources, the days in which France, by itself, can maintain all aspects of its military assistance programs may be limited. It is unclear whether France will be able to convince other western powers to assume part of its military assistance burden. John Chipman recognized the rationale for this burden-sharing:

> Specifically in the economic, but also eventually in the military spheres, France will wish to see the engagement of other western actors. [...] Military assistance to francophone Africa will remain an important French priority, and the desire to have others take on the responsibilities will grow, but the needs of the weaker francophone African states are so overwhelming in the economic sphere, that all western powers will wish to ensure, with France, balanced policies of military and broader economic assistance.[92]

The willingness of western powers to assist France is generally weak. France and Belgium maintained complementary military assistance programs in Zaire. Belgium terminated them in 1990, and

France followed in 1991. France, Britain, and Portugal are attempting to work together in Angola to redefine the role of the Angolan armed forces and assist in their restructuring. The U.S. is supportive of France's assistance programs in Chad and has sent aid to Chadian authorities. Elsewhere in francophone Africa, France operates independently.

Chapter 4

French Overseas Military Facilities

France's worldwide military facilities can be divided into two major categories: geo-strategic outposts and techno-strategic assets. Geo-strategic outposts at places such as Dakar, La Réunion and Djibouti derive their value from their location, but also from the legal and military environment that France has developed for their use. They are part of the French policy of monitoring and influencing the evolution of events abroad, checking the actions of others in overseas regions, and maintaining open sea lanes. Techno-strategic assets enable technological progress to increase the strategic reach of France. There are two main overseas assets of such value: the nuclear experimentation center in the Pacific and the space launch site in French Guiana. Both facilities provide France with independent means to pursue important military and technological activities, and, respectively, allow France to keep its place as a nuclear power and retain access to outer space.

In the African context, there are only geo-strategic assets to consider. Some, like La Réunion and Mayotte, are French possessions, and therefore part of France. Their military use is unconstrained. The other overseas assets, including all bases on the African continent, are the result of legal agreements between the host state and France. The use of foreign military bases is delicate and is integrated within a legal framework. General Revol, commenting on the role of French bases in Africa, stated that the bases are necessary "firstly to help those of our African partners who may be experiencing difficulties, and secondly to hold our place in the world."[1]

African nations hosting French forces are keen to emphasize that French forces are deployed in their countries only at their invitation. In an address to the Ivorian National Assembly in 1962, President Houphouët-Boigny argued that:

> It is important to remember that France no longer has any strategic interests in Abidjan; the French troops are stationed here at our request; there can be no doubts that France will be greatly relieved when she is asked to withdraw her troops.[2]

Houphouët-Boigny's statement indicates how the political risk of the French military presence was shared with the host countries, no doubt because there were more important political benefits to share as well. French bases in Africa are the direct product of agreements. For the African states, the presence of French garrisons on their soil demonstrates "the true signature of the defense agreements."[3]

Foreign bases have a value to French authorities which transcends the terms of the defense agreements. Pascal Chaigneau, a leading French analyst of France's role in Africa, noted that France has always considered the African bases as "the cornerstone of its world-wide strategic system."[4] They are, he adds, "the formal tools of France's world-wide military presence."[5]

The bases in Africa perform a variety of functions in the framework of an African and global strategy. First, French overseas bases, in and of themselves, can deter aggression against the host state. They are the local symbol of French resolve. Second, a significant amount of force can emanate from the bases and be actively engaged on the side of the host government. Third, the bases are instrumental in the power projection capabilities of France, complementing French military airlift and aircraft carriers. For French military planners:

> What is important, [is] not the positions themselves, but the force which can come out of them and lean on them. Therefore these positions are really interesting only insofar as they contribute to the operations of the mobile forces and insofar as they facilitate it.[6]

It is the actual presence of a few pre-positioned forces which makes intervention by larger metropolitan forces possible. Even the expansion of the French military airlift capabilities could not substitute for overseas bases. It would imply a different force configuration with drastically different operational consequences. The French approach to the military use of its bases is gradual, with three tiers of active deployment options. At the first level, involving troubles within an African state, French local forces would only be called in after the local police and armed forces had failed to control the situation. At a second level, in case of a more severe crisis with possible repercussions outside the territory, specialized forces stationed in reinforced bases or in France might intervene. At the third level, in case of a serious or external threat, forces based in France would stage the intervention.[7]

TYPOLOGY OF OVERSEAS MILITARY FACILITIES

In Pascal Chaigneau's words, "behind the single concept of 'base' there are different realities."[8] French overseas military facilities can be categorized according to different criteria. In legal terms there are three different types of overseas military facilities. The first type are the sovereign overseas bases, and French forces deployed on such overseas facilities are called permanent forces (*forces permanentes*). In and around sub-Saharan Africa, only La Réunion, Mayotte and the Iles Eparses have permanent forces. The second type includes the deployment of forces on a foreign base made available to the French military under a bilateral agreement. These *forces de présence* serve as a reminder of the immediacy of a French reaction in case of trouble. Such forces are based at several sites, all of which are in Africa, including Djibouti; Dakar, Senegal; Port-Bouet, Côte d'Ivoire; and Libreville, Gabon. The bases at all four sites have been occupied uninterruptedly since the end of the colonial empire. A last legal form of French military role in overseas territories are the temporary forces (*forces temporaires*). These forces have been dispatched with the approval of a foreign government. They perform specific actions over a limited time frame. French forces in Chad belong to this category, after Chad requested the complete evacuation of French bases on September 27, 1975.[9] Subsequent deployments of French forces were designed for specific tasks. French forces in Bangui and Bouar (Central African Republic) are also temporary, since the French bases were ceded to the Central African authorities on July 5, 1971. These types of forces are sometimes composed of or reinforced by rotating units (*compagnies tournantes*) of 150-180 men each.

A functional typology of military facilities includes the following categories: (i) principal bases and facilities, which are the strategically located logistical pillars of the French intervention forces; (ii) security garrisons in sensitive areas; and, (iii) ports of call and logistical support on air supply routes.[10] One military facility can have different functions. For example, La Réunion, Dakar and Djibouti are typically principal facilities, although the latter two also have security forces. Port-Bouet and Libreville are security garrisons for region-stabilization, but often serve as relay stations and ports of call for intervention elsewhere. Bangui, and especially Bouar, serve as security garrisons and provide logistical support for operations in Chad.

FRENCH OVERSEAS POSSESSIONS AROUND AFRICA

France's overseas territories are divided into five *Départements d'outre-mer* (DOM), four *Territoires d'outre-mer* (TOM), and two *collectivités territoriales*. Guadeloupe, French Guiana, Martinique, and La Réunion belong to the first category; French Polynesia, New Caledonia, Wallis-et-Futuna, and the *Terres australes et antarctiques françaises* (TAAF) belong to the second category. The islands of Mayotte and Saint-Pierre-et-Miquelon have a third status as territorial collectivities, rather than DOMs. The laws passed by the French Parliament apply automatically in the DOMs, but not in the TOMs, unless a local Territorial Assembly has approved them. The DOMs are part of the European Union, while the TOMs have only an associative link with it.[11] The *collectivités territoriales* have an even weaker legal link to France. French possessions also include the Iles Eparses, a group of five islands in the southwestern corner of the Indian Ocean.

These overseas possessions are national territory, and their citizens are French citizens. They are more closely associated with the homeland than residents of the British overseas dependent territories are with Britain. For example, Hong Kong citizens are not automatically British subjects. Most territories, with the exception of New Caledonia, appear closely anchored to France, although islands with an indigenous population have at least one separatist political party, which generally represents a rather small minority of the population. The territories without a real indigenous population, such as the Iles Eparses, are also subject to forces urging secession from France. These claims come from two neighboring countries: Madagascar and Mauritius. Domestic or international separatist claims do not necessarily threaten French authority, but they are a constant annoyance which can flare up dangerously if unchecked.

Only the French overseas possessions in the vicinity of Africa will be analyzed in this study, namely La Réunion, the Iles Eparses, Mayotte, and the islands of Kerguelen and St-Paul. They are all on the eastern coast of Africa. Only La Réunion and Mayotte have military installations useful for power projection capabilities. The latter two French possessions must be considered in conjunction with the French foreign base at Djibouti. Together, they form a strategic ensemble to monitor French interests in a vast area stretching from the Red Sea to the upper Antarctic region. La Réunion is also France's maritime key to the South Pacific.

La Réunion

French Vice-Admiral Jean-Jacques Schweitzer emphasized the pivotal role of La Réunion for French policy in the Indian Ocean. "If La Réunion were to leave the French orbit, our other possessions would not deserve our keeping them. France would not be a 'border nation' [of the Indian Ocean] and could as well withdraw to the West of Corsica."[12] The island of La Réunion is not a foreign base; it is a *Département* of the French Republic. In La Réunion, base rights, naval facilities, and troop stations are not subject to delicate negotiations with local authorities. Few people in La Réunion advocate full independence from France, although certain political parties there strive for greater autonomy within the French government. The island is relatively small and roughly oval in shape. It is about 65 km long and 50 km wide, with an estimated population of 580,000 in 1989.[13] La Réunion also administers the five territories of the Iles Eparses.

France heavily developed La Réunion after its June 1975 withdrawal from the naval facilities of Diego Suarez (now Antsiranana) in Madagascar, with which it had had a defense agreement since June 27, 1960. France never fully regained the same capability for repair and maintenance of ships in the Indian Ocean. The Malagasy authorities have expressed a willingness to reopen the Antsiranana harbor to the French Navy for repair and resupplies, but the infrastructure of the harbor needs serious renovation.[14] The capacity of the Pointe des Galets harbor in La Réunion was expanded in 1986 with new piers in the Baie de la Possession capable of receiving 50,000-ton ships, compared to only 15,000 tons for the previous facilities.

Since 1973, La Réunion has been the headquarters of French military forces in the Indian Ocean. French forces (both permanent and rotating) in La Réunion total approximately 3,300 troops, including those on the Iles Eparses and Mayotte.[15] This amount does not include about 500 gendarmes. The Army maintains one Marine Paratrooper Infantry Regiment (2 RPIMa), one Foreign Legion company, and one support battalion (53 BCS), which is equipped with 327 vehicles. The permanent contingent includes 1,116 troops. An additional Regiment of locally recruited troops of *Service Militaire Adapté* (4 RSMA) is integrated within the Marine Infantry troops. Finally, La Réunion occasionally receives three-to-four month visits from rotating regiments, mostly parachutists. The Air Force operates a small flotilla of two *Transall* and two *Alouette* helicopters, but no fighter aircraft, although the existing infrastructure was planned for them. At 2,400 meters in length, the airfield is slightly too short for the C-135 tanker planes. Plans exists to increase the length of the runway to 3,000 meters. There are no ground-to-air defense systems on La Réunion. The Air Force contingent varies between 200 and 300 personnel. The Navy presence specifically earmarked for La Réunion, and therefore independent from the Indian Ocean fleet, consists of three patrol boats, one light transport ship, and one police patrol boat. The Navy personnel numbers between 60-70. La Réunion also hosts a Franco-American *Omega* navigation base in the small port of Saint-Paul.[16]

The troops are not deployed in a defensive posture, but are gathered on La Réunion for possible action elsewhere. The Army can align up to 1,000 combat troops for fast deployment, either by air with rotations of the *Transalls*, or by sea with the amphibious transport ships of the Indian Ocean fleet. La Réunion is capable of receiving reinforcements or pre-positioned supplies and equipment. Potential contingencies in the vicinity of La Réunion would be of low intensity, however, and the current French force structure there could cope with them. Mauritius and the Seychelles have occasionally required outside assistance, but either France or Britain have been able to quell revolts with limited displays of power. The French relationship with Madagascar was difficult when the latter was supported by the USSR, but there has never been any serious threat to French possessions of the Iles Eparses.

Iles Eparses

The Iles Eparses are composed of five islands: Les Glorieuses, Bassas da India, Europa, Juan de Nova and Tromelin. They are placed under the direct authority of the prefect of La Réunion. Their status as part of France is vague since they are not categorized as a DOM or a TOM. Madagascar, around which the islands are scattered, claims the first four. Mauritius claims the island of Tromelin. During a visit to Madagascar in June 1990, President Mitterrand proposed the creation of a working group of international lawyers to review the contending claims.[17] France maintains a continuous but symbolic presence on the islands, sometimes of only one gendarme and 10-15 parachutists.[18] The 200-mile Exclusive Economic Zone (EEZ) around each atoll and the potential military uses of these islands by other major powers contribute to the various claims over the Iles Eparses.[19] France has not developed the infrastructure on the islands, disproving fears that France would use them for its own military aggrandizement.

> The thesis that France is building a massive military and naval presence in the Indian Ocean cannot really be substantiated in the face of obvious lack of any modern installations in the Mozambique area or of any policy to develop these French territories in ways that would make them significant in an Indian Ocean war.[20]

Juan de Nova disposes of a small airfield. Tromelin, an island of about 700 meters by 1.5 km, contains a meteorological station. It occasionally disappears underwater during heavy storms. Bassas da India is extremely small and would possibly not qualify for an EEZ, although the other four islands might.

Mayotte

Mayotte, with a population of 40,000 on 350 km² of land, is one of the four islands constituting the area known as the Comoros and is attached to France with a special status of *collectivité territoriale*. The three other islands, the Grande Comore, Anjouan, and Moheli, became independent in July 1975 through a unilateral declaration under the name Comoros, which France recognized in December 1975. A referendum in February 1976 reaffirmed Mayotte's commitment to remain attached to France with a majority of 99.4 percent.[21] Demands by Mayotte inhabitants to become a French *département* have not received a favorable response from French authorities.

Mayotte has a superb lagoon which protects rather modest harbor facilities. In 1987, France approved a long-term plan for the construction of a deep-water port at Longoni and an airport to accommodate larger aircraft.[22] Until the completion of this project, the Grande Comore remains the only island in the Comoros with an airport accessible to all types of aircraft. The demand for French assistance, even of a military nature, in Comoros is great, as a 1989 mercenaries' coup demonstrated.

The military value of Mayotte lies in its key geographic position at one end of the Strait of Madagascar, its lagoon, and its proximity to the African mainland, to which it is much closer than is La Réunion. Its value is merely potential since "French warships visiting Mayotte still have to anchor offshore and use lighters."[23] French naval repair ships make occasional use of Mayotte's calm and protected waters. The power projection capability will remain undeveloped as long as the airport capacity is not increased. The airstrip has a length of 800 meters and might be extended to 1,500 meters, long enough for fighter planes but still too short for tanker aircraft.

France keeps a small detachment (*forces permanentes*) of 112 troops from the Foreign Legion garrisoned on the island. A single rotating company, usually drawn from units of the Foreign Legion, covers Mayotte continuously and is replaced every three months. Given Mayotte's status as territorial collectivity, it can also mobilize some troops for a *Service Militaire Adapté*, namely the equivalent of one section. The Navy presence attached to Mayotte is limited to one patrol boat.[24] With the end of the Soviet threat and the improved relations with Madagascar, France has fewer incentives to develop the military potential of the island.

Iles Australes

Some 2,600 to 3,000 miles southeast of La Réunion, the Iles Australes (Kerguelen, Saint-Paul and Crozet) are administratively independent. France maintains only a scientific mission on these islands but no military presence. France, however, has always been keen to exclude the Iles Australes from any treaty concerning the demilitarization of the Antarctic. This objective could be more than just a diplomatic desire to keep French options open; there seemd to be some indication that Kerguelen might be a future site for French nuclear experiments, once Mururoa and Fangataufa in the Pacific are "exhausted."[25] Kerguelen offers the potential for a submarine facility, but is much less adaptable to accommodate an airport for regular use. Meteorology, combined with poor geographic conditions, make the airport project costly and dangerous both to install and to use.

FRENCH FOREIGN BASES IN AFRICA

In sub-Saharan Africa, France operates bases in Dakar, Senegal; Port-Bouet, Cote d'Ivoire; Libreville, Gabon; and Djibouti under bilateral defense agreements. Troops deployed in those four countries are called *forces de présence*, accentuating the immediacy and durability of their engagement on the side of these four host countries. French forces in Chad and the Central African Republic have a different legal status and are called *forces temporaires*. Their role is theoretically limited in time, even if their stay is routinely extended. France has no formal basing agreement with Chad or the CAR, but its troops are dispatched as a military support to those countries. Forces in Chad and the CAR are composed of rotating regiments. These rotations are often timed to provide a permanent contingent, as an arriving unit will immediately replace a departing unit.

Djibouti
The Republic of Djibouti became independent from France on June 27, 1977. With an area of 23,000 km² and a population estimated at 483,000 people in 1987[26] (200,000 of which are in the city of Djibouti alone), Djibouti remains highly vulnerable to outside influence. Its very poor economy makes it totally dependent on foreign trade and assistance. Two of Djibouti's more powerful neighbors, Ethiopia and Somalia, have had a tense relationship which culminated in the Ogaden War in 1977-78. Somalia historically wanted to annex Djibouti on ethnic grounds. Instability is common to Djibouti, which is marked by "a contested and repressive government, held in contempt by the majority of the population; a war-seasoned opposition [...]; and a threatening regional environment."[27]

After independence, the new government of Djibouti signed seven cooperation agreements, one friendship treaty and one military protocol allowing France to maintain a military presence in the country. The language of the 1977 military protocol specifically prohibits French troops from participating in internal operations to reinstall order or using the territory of Djibouti as a staging point for action against third countries unless approved by Djibouti's authorities.[28] This French presence was oriented toward the double strategic goal of (i) controlling the Bab el Mandeb Strait, a choke point in front of former Soviet bases in South Yemen and the island of Socotra; and (ii) peace-keeping in the Horn of Africa, mainly by guaranteeing Djibouti's sovereignty. The strategic value of Djibouti is invaluable since it is the only western window on the Red Sea.[29] The Tadjourah Bay can accept up to 2,000 ships at one nautical mile from each other.[30] The harbor is equipped with limited maintenance and repair facilities. There is a modern airport capable of landing large jet-engine aircraft. Djibouti is not only a naval and air base, but it is also an observation post and a regional bridgehead. Military analysts stress the primary role of Djibouti as an observation post over all other functions.[31]

French forces in Djibouti are called *forces de présence*, as opposed to temporary forces, to highlight their role under a general defense agreement between the two countries. Djibouti has the largest deployment if compared to other countries that have defense agreements with France. The potential risk to French troops is significant, and the responsibilities coupled with the French presence are extremely heavy. The French forces total about 3,850 troops, with the addition of rotating units from France.[32]

The Army contingent has the largest presence, with a command and support battalion, the 10th BCS (*bataillon de commandement et de soutien*); an interservice regiment, the 5th RIAOM (*Régiment interarmes d'outre-mer*); and a half-brigade from the Foreign Legion, the 13th DBLE (*demi-brigade de la Légion étrangère*). In 1992, this represented a total of 2,605 men, equipped with 12 AMX-13 tanks, 12 *Sagaie* wheeled tanks, one battery of 105-mm howitzers and 155-mm guns, 12 *Milan* missile systems, anti-tank artillery guns, one battery of ground-to-air guns, and 466 vehicles. The Army light aviation deployed five SA-330 *Puma* helicopters. The heavy Army presence indicates the primary commitment of France to back Djibouti's sovereignty. The Air Force, with 906 troops, also plays a defensive role against neighboring threats with its squadron of 11 *Mirage F1-C* ground-attack fighters, one C-160 *Transall* transport plane, and three *Alouette* light helicopters.

There is only a modest French Navy presence in Djibouti consisting of a Marine Commando and logistics staff, for a total of only 243 troops. French naval forces in the Indian Ocean are not attached to a specific harbor in the region; their headquarters are afloat. It is undeniable, however, that Djibouti is the most important support harbor for this fleet.[33] This situation allows France to use the fleet as it sees fit, unconstrained by any defense agreement while benefitting greatly from the protection and facilities of the harbor of Djibouti.

The French presence in Djibouti has gained wide regional acceptance. French troops are insufficient to protect the whole territory of Djibouti effectively, but they act as trip-wire for a larger French intervention. "A radical destabilization would doubtlessly occur if France withdrew its troops."[34]

Djibouti has played a very active role in resupplying French and other vessels that were engaged in the allied mine-clearing and sea-traffic protection operations in the Persian Gulf in 1987-88. In the 1990-91 Gulf War, France initially benefitted from the support of Djibouti, although this became less necessary as soon as the well-equipped Saudi facilities became available. A similar situation occurred for the French contingent of the U.N. operation in Somalia.

Naval Indian Ocean Command

The headquarters of the eleven ships of the French Indian Ocean fleet is aboard the *Marne*, a 17,800-ton tanker which allows for mobil refueling and carries a maritime zone staff. It accommodates a 45-man commando unit and can transport 250 troops. One on-board helicopter and the *Syracuse* satellite communications systems add to the command capabilities of the on-board headquarters. The usual ports of call for the fleet are Djibouti, La Réunion, and Mayotte. The Indian Ocean fleet includes 11 vessels: four light frigates, two patrol combatants, one light transporter ship, one infantry and tank disembarkment ship, one petrol supply boat, one support ship, and one repair ship.[35]

This permanent structure for the Indian Ocean has only minimal Navy air support, with one *Alouette III* helicopter and one land-based *Atlantic* patrol aircraft. The Indian Ocean fleet is shaped to support long-distance actions, with three support and supply ships for six light combat units. The range is a priority over heavy armor, especially with the future introduction of the *Floréal*-class frigates. The amphibious capability is modest, with a *Batral*-type light transport and landing ship. All of this demonstrates the policing, rather than combat, vocation of the Indian Ocean fleet. It is a naval *force de présence*. Additional firepower is available through naval aircraft battle groups. French aircraft carriers and other units are often deployed in the region.

Other powers also patrol the western shore of the Indian Ocean. The United States is present with a leased naval base at Diego Garcia (part of the British Indian Ocean Territories), and enjoys access to naval facilities in several border nations. Britain has virtually abandoned the Indian Ocean despite ownership of the British Indian Ocean Territories. The Soviet Union had a strong naval presence due to treaties with Madagascar, Mozambique, Ethiopia, South Yemen, and India. Only France offers the unique combination of sovereign territory and a large naval presence in the Indian Ocean - the second largest in the region since the demise of the Soviet Union.

Dakar

Dakar is the largest harbor in West Africa, ideally located as a maritime and air transit point between Europe and Latin America, the Gulf of Guinea, and southern Africa. Dakar is one of the most important French overseas communications and logistics centers that allows France to monitor the sea lanes in the mid-Atlantic region. France disposed of a military, tri-service base under the Defense Agreement of June 22, 1960 with the then Federation of Mali. The base initially consisted of a harbor, an arsenal, three airstrips, one transmission station, and several military camps spread over an area 30 km long and 15 km wide.[36] The defense agreement was renewed on March 29, 1974 and French facilities were reduced to one base, the main camp of Bel-Air, with a small access to the harbor but no independent airstrip. The facilities were manned by a contingent which was gradually reduced from 10,000 men in 1960 to 1,200 since 1974.

For French military operations, Dakar has the dual vocation of being a port of call for naval operations in the South Atlantic and a forward base for projecting French power in West and central Africa, especially when Algeria denies overflight. The airport facilities and harbor of Dakar have been used by other allied powers. The airport was used extensively by Britain during the Falklands War after the French and Senegalese governments gave their authorization.[37] Belgian planes used the facilities during the Shaba II events in 1978, in which U.S. crews were also dispatched to assist in the American airlift.[38]

Total French forces in Dakar, also classified as *forces de présence*, numbered about 1,160 troops in 1992 divided among the three services, not including 100 military advisors and medical personnel.[39] The Army maintains a 516-man battalion of Marine Infantry (23 BIMA) with 97 vehicles including 10 AML light armored vehicles. The Air Force deploys 386 troops and possesses one *Transall* aircraft and two *Ecureuil* helicopters. France does not maintain major naval forces in Dakar. In fact, it has only one airplane permanently assigned to Dakar, an *Atlantic*, together with two tug boats and a small disembarkment unit, and around 260 troops. In times of a serious crisis, French ground forces could simultaneously defend the national airport and stocks of pre-positioned equipment until reinforcements arrive from France. They could also protect French citizens at selected gathering points. Additional defense tasks in a major crisis have to be undertaken by metropolitan reinforcements since the local contingent would be spread too thin. In regional crises of lesser intensity, a company could be partly airlifted and deployed elsewhere, which is the extent of the radiation power of forces based in Dakar. There are no rotating French units that regularly visit the Dakar base. French and Senegalese forces participate in annual battalion-sized exercises, and once every three years a major exercise is organized with additional troops from France and Côte d'Ivoire.

Libreville

Gabon has signed two security agreements with France. One of these is a defense agreement, signed on August 17, 1960, granting exceptional facilities to French forces and access to the air base at Libreville; the second is a special agreement for maintaining internal order, signed on March 11, 1961. A former U.S. Ambassador to Gabon described one of the roles of the French force in Libreville:

> To illustrate how quickly the French military can react, the troops at Camp de Gaulle on the outskirts of Libreville, in Gabon, are said to be under standing orders to have a platoon of fully armed troops at the presidential palace, five miles from their camp, within 30 minutes of an order from the local French ambassador.[40]

Libreville, a forward air base with a very limited French presence, is principally a staging post for French metropolitan forces operating in sub-Saharan Africa. These forces also prevent destabilization of the local government. Gabonese bases have been used extensively by France during interventions in central Africa. Belgian forces detached a small contingent at Libreville during the Franco-Belgian evacuation at the time of the Zairian armed forces mutiny in 1991.

French *forces de présence* in Libreville number slightly under 500 troops. These troops are mainly from the Army, with a battalion of Marine Infantry, the 6 BIMA, and two rotating companies, one of which is always a parachutist unit, and 71 vehicles. The Air Force maintains only one *Alouette* helicopter.[41] The air base can host a C-160 *Transall* plane.

Port-Bouet

Port-Bouet, a small base a few miles southeast of Abidjan in Côte d'Ivoire, is a testimony to the special relationship between France and the late Ivorian President Houphouët-Boigny. This force has had a passive role since Ivoirian independence, but has served as a deterrent to both outside forces and internal challengers to President Houphouët-Boigny's power. The role of French troops in Port-Bouet is very similar to that of French troops in Libreville: implicit regime-stabilization and technical support for metropolitan interventions by securing the air base and pre-positioned stocks. The base is also used as a staging point for air transport and long distance flights of tactical aircraft.

The *force de présence* in Port-Bouet consists of 481 men, 475 of which are from the Army, with troops from Marine Infantry (43 BIMA) and one rotating section. The Army equipment includes 10 AMC light armored vehicles, five AMX-13 tanks, and 15 vehicles. The Air Force is present with only one *Ecureuil* helicopter and a two man team.[42] The French Air Force has landing rights at Abidjan and at Bouaké, a city in the center of the country.

Central African Republic

In 1971, French authorities turned the base at Bangui over to the Central African authorities. The deployment of French troops in the Central African Republic has been directly linked to developments in Chad. After the 1975 loss of the French Chadian base in N'Djamena, France partially transferred these units to the garrison at Bouar, close to the Chadian border, and to Bangui because of the presence of an important airport there. These garrisons are not considered principal bases as in Dakar or Djibouti, and troops deployed in the CAR are only temporary rotating forces. In 1981, the *Eléménts français d'assistance opérationnelle* (EFAO), the French temporary forces, were established in the CAR, following the Chadian operations *Barracuda* and *Tacaud*. The EFAO forces come mainly from the 11th Parachutist Division and the 9th Marine Infantry Division of the FAR.

The roles of the EFAO in the CAR are: (i) to intervene outside the borders of the CAR; (ii) to protect French citizens in the CAR; (iii) to protect the airport of Bangui, which was vital to the Chadian operations; and (iv) to assist the CAR in air transport with French *Transall* planes, which is often the only link between distant parts of the country. When the *Epervier* defense system in Chad is withdrawn, it is presumed that some of the French forces in the CAR will also leave. During the earlier *Manta* operation, French Boeing 707s and DC-10s landed at the Bangui airport because the airport at N'Djamena was then unable to accommodate large planes. In addition to their role in the Chadian theater of operation, there is no doubt that the French presence contributes to the internal military stability of the CAR, whose armed forces count only 4,000 troops for a surface of 238,000 square miles.

French *forces temporaires* in the CAR are spread between the bases of Bangui and Bouar, with roughly one-third of the forces for the former and two-thirds for the latter. In Bangui, the French forces consist of one Army light aviation detachment with helicopters, one Infantry company, and one platoon of light armored vehicles; and in Bouar, of one infantry transport unit, one squadron of light armored vehicles, and one battery of artillery. These Army forces number 1,057 men. The Air Force presence includes about 100 personnel in charge of four *Jaguar* aircraft and two *Transall*. The data on forces and equipment available in the CAR is not fixed. The high mobility and flexibility of the French forces in the CAR make it difficult to give a precise account of the troops involved. Rotating units move in and out of the country, and their numbers vary with the changing security situation in Chad. This primarily concerns the forces in Bouar, which at times have numbered as many as 1,100 troops. The forces in Bouar, together with the two *Transall* transport planes, are distinct from other French forces in Senegal, Gabon or Côte d'Ivoire in that they constitute a dynamic operational ensemble which can intervene autonomously without having to wait for the arrival of metropolitan reinforcements.

Chad

During World War II, the base of N'Djamena was the transit point for all air transports between the Atlantic and Indian Oceans. It later served as a transit point between France and its East and central African colonies. French military facilities in N'Djamena were considered one of the principal bases. It counted about 2,300 men who were evacuated in one month after the Chadian government requested their departure on September 27, 1975. Under the technical cooperation agreement of March 6, 1976, France retained transit rights over Chad and refueling facilities in N'Djamena. In 1977, the base was reoccupied by roughly 1,100 French troops, only to be abandoned in May 1980 during the civil war. In more recent times, French forces deployed in Chad are part of specific operations (*Manta* and *Epervier*) and are technically only temporary forces. Their presence can, however, last for as long as five years, but they do not benefit from base agreements. The forces are deployed in a deterrent rather than a combat mode. Given the geography of Chad, airports are the key to controlling the country, and their protection is of paramount importance. France has extended the airstrip of N'Djamena, and in 1990-91 the airstrip in Faya-Largeau was reconstructed with funds from the French Ministry of Cooperation.

French *forces temporaires* under the *Epervier* defense system in Chad are spread over the whole territory. The Army has versatile capabilities and maintains roughly 750 men mainly from the Marine Infantry, but also from the Foreign Legion and other units. The bulk of French forces are in N'Djamena and Abéché, although the latter post is gradually being evacuated. There are Army training detachments (10 officers and 20 NCOs each) dispersed in southern Chad at locations with an airport or airfield, including N'Djamena, Mongo, and Sarh. The Army also operates a *Hawk* short-range air defense battery, very short-range air-to-surface missiles called SATCP, and an *Oeil Noir* radar system. A small detachment with four helicopters (*hélicoptères de manoeuvre*) of Army Light Aviation completes the Army deployment. The Air Force has impressive abilities with eight *Mirage* F1-C combat aircraft, two *Mirage* F1-CR reconnaissance aircraft, one C-135 tanker aircraft, and four *Transall* transport aircraft. The emphasis of operation *Epervier*, through its deployments in Chad, but also in Bouar and Bangui, was on Air Force defense and strike power. This is indicative of the sort of retaliation France conducts in case of a Libyan aggression. The French Navy contributes one *Atlantic* aircraft. It may appear odd to discover a French Navy unit in the middle of the African continent, but experience has proven that the Navy pilots on the *Atlantic* aircraft were extremely competent for reconnaissance and rescue missions in the desert, which resemble rescue missions at sea in terms of the vast, empty area to be covered.

Cameroon

Although there are no French bases or garrisons in Cameroon, France maintains about 60 men there. Cameroon has been an important asset for France during the various Chadian crises. Without it, the operations would have been much more difficult if not impossible, and certainly more costly. In fact, Cameroon is the necessary supply route for heavy and non-urgent equipment to Chad. Cargo is delivered in the port of Douala and then carried by rail for 525 miles northeast to Ngaoundéré. It is then transported by truck for the remaining 470 miles to N'Djamena. This process is rather long and logistically difficult. The transfer is inefficient in terms of time and damage, but it is the only route available apart from airlift. The transportation of equipment from France to N'Djamena takes about one-and-a-half to two months.

AN INTEGRATED NETWORK OF MILITARY BASES

The total cost of French pre-positioned garrisons in the CAR, Côte d'Ivoire, Djibouti, Gabon, and Senegal was estimated at FF 2.3 billion in 1989 (U.S. $400 million), with Djibouti accounting for more than three quarters of it.[43] The cost of the military operations in Chad are not included. At the height of French military deployment in Chad, these types of operation could impose an additional charge of up to U.S. $1 million per day.

From a military perspective, the military facilities in and around Africa fulfill two main roles. One is linked to France's maritime strategy of preserving open sea lanes with regions in the world which are vital for the French economy. Key facilities with regard to this maritime strategy are in the triangle joining Dakar, La Réunion, and Djibouti. The second role of the African facilities is to help fulfill French obligations under various defense and cooperation agreements with sub-Saharan countries. The primary goals of the French commitment are to preserve a friendly francophone realm, to respond to political demands by African states, and at times to ensure France's access to raw materials. Strategically, the land mass stretching from Senegal to Zaire is indivisible. As events in Chad illustrated, friendly African countries put considerable pressure on France to intervene. France's failure to respond would have shaken the confidence of other francophone countries in France's military power. The African forward basing and access facilities are an integral part of France's regional defense posture and can be complemented but not replaced or dislodged by technological developments in the fields of communications, remote sensing, or long-range strike capabilities.

Bases, military facilities, and French overseas possessions also fulfill roles with implications extending far beyond their immediate vicinity. The African bases and the French Indian Ocean possessions provide services that are integrated in the worldwide network of French possessions, including those in the Pacific, the Caribbean, and the North Atlantic. They often act as telecommunication relays, navigation intelligence collection platforms, or as other elements for electronic and signal intelligence gathering. Guiana, located close to the equator and on the sea, offers optimal conditions for space launches. Other French overseas possessions contribute supportive space tracking and data relay systems. Finally, France could not have continued to upgrade its nuclear weapons without its Pacific experimentation center.

France's dependence on its overseas territories and bases is paralleled by the host countries' dependence on French military, economic, and cultural assistance. The French military presence is generally well accepted by the local population, although sporadic opposition movements may appear. French troops therefore are under instruction to keep as low a profile as possible.

Chapter 5

French Interventions
in Sub-Saharan Africa

As the western European power which has undertaken the most interventions overseas, France has learned better than others the benefits and constraints of using military power in distant theaters of operation. France has also learned that steadfast intervention policies, though costly, can be rewarding if maintained over a sufficient period of time. These interventions are a dramatic demonstration of France's commitment to an original and highly effective system of collective security which it has underwritten, often implicitly, with numerous African nations.[1] According to Pierre Dabezies, former French Ambassador to Gabon, three formal conditions are necessary, in theory, for French action abroad: "The existence of a defense agreement between France and the country involved; an explicit demand by the latter; and freedom of decision for the French government, which, in no instance, could be committed automatically." In practice, Dabezies adds: "French interventions depend less on precise criteria than on circumstances."[2] Indeed, there have been exceptions to each of the three formal conditions for intervention. The 1978 operation in Kolwezi, Zaire, took place even though no formal defense agreement with France existed. The support given to Biafra against the Nigerian Federal Government, or Emperor Bokassa's eviction from power in the Central African Republic in 1979, could hardly be considered as having been performed at the request of the recognized authorities. Finally, France's arm was strongly twisted by some of its staunchest African allies when operation *Epervier* in Chad was launched in 1986. While France has the ability to influence events in certain well-defined zones in sub-Saharan Africa, it is also subjected to pressure from its African partners. It is the quality of the African country's bilateral relations with France, its perceived strategic value, and the ideological orientation of the African entity requesting assistance which are the primary factors that influence the decision to launch a military intervention. France's conception of itself as a reliable ally also provides some self-imposed incentive to intervene.

A common thread that emerges from France's military involvement in Africa is that, more often than not, the political *status quo* in the African nation has been supported. France appears to be averse to revolutionary enterprises, even in the context of the recent drive for democratization in Africa. Priority has been given to reducing tension through negotiation and political settlement, avoiding abrupt ideological overhauls. Another remarkable aspect of French interventions is that France's record is untarnished by defeat, and French casualties have remained low during over thirty years of intervention.

The success of the post-independence French military operations in Africa has been based on setting reasonable goals and the preparedness of French troops. France's relatively modest military means available for power projection has invited a corresponding modesty in the military objectives it advanced. By the nature of the operations, by chance, or by political will, the overseas actions have never exceeded a certain level, either in volume or intensity.[3] The notion of a "certain level" is fairly flexible. Some operations involved over 3,000 French troops, while others were carried out by less than 30. Some actions saw French ground troops in direct combat, while others were mere policing operations or evacuation missions. The "enemy" ranged from rioting mobs to well-trained and well-equipped Libyan troops. The golden rule observed by French policy-makers has been to assess the feasibility of an operation realistically and avoid being engaged in any situation that France cannot influence. Rather than shy away from using force altogether whenever the risks are too high, French authorities prefer to display some force, but with weak conviction that difficulties will be favorably resolved.

To face the wide spectrum of African contingencies and crises, French military authorities have adopted a flexible strategy based on a combination of home-based and Africa-based forces. The French forces are deployed in a security system which allows for appropriate, fast and graduated responses depending on the crisis' intensity. The ability to modulate and fine-tune military responses is a key element in an environment where most interventions take place below the level of open combat. Nonetheless, the political exploitation of forces as an effective military tool has sometimes produced fiascos, as with weapons deliveries to Biafra in 1968-69, or controversial results, as with the withdrawal of French troops from Chad after operation *Manta* in 1984.

The final major component of French success in overseas military interventions is public support at home. The relatively smooth implementation of overseas interventionist policies and the very low casualties incurred by French troops abroad partially explain the French public's support, or at least its benign indifference.[4] The support for multi-faceted military activism in Africa is also linked to the general public's perception of France's role in the world as a power that still retains the potential to influence events abroad. In that respect, sub-Saharan Africa is an ideal environment where French influence can be exerted over huge geographic areas at relatively low cost and with low risks. It is also a place where history and links of political, cultural, and commercial solidarity join to reinforce France's longing to radiate beyond Europe.

Historically, France's actions in sub-Saharan Africa can be divided into five broad phases:

1. a period in the early 1960s, which can be labelled as "family consolidation" under de Gaulle, when post-independence Franco-African links had to be redefined;
2. the Biafran fiasco, which occurred when France ventured outside its traditional zone of influence;
3. the Chadian quagmire, which has dragged on for more than 30 years with only short periods of respite;
4. a crusade to fend off ideological destabilization in Africa under Giscard; and,
5. the Mitterrand years, going from an idealistic approach to the Third World to dealing with pre-democracy chaos.

FAMILY CONSOLIDATION

The early Gaullist years (1958-1964) were marked by the emancipation of francophone Africa from its metropole, but also by the various attempts by France to avoid the complete dilution of its Franco-African "family." Through diplomatic agreements and a series of military interventions to beleaguered friendly regimes in Africa, General de Gaulle managed to consolidate the Franco-African links and bring a new dynamic and a new sense of cohesion to this relationship. De Gaulle viewed it as almost a moral obligation for France to continue to lead its former colonies toward economic prosperity and political stability. There was no pattern in the way French authorities dealt with various caballing factions, frustrated military officers, and other coup instigators in the early 1960s. During this period the French still had local garrisons in place that were capable of quelling local trouble without any additional influx of metropolitan forces. Some of these early interventions so closely resembled colonial policing operations that, for French troops in the field, there were few differences. Sometimes, the same French troops, before and after independence, fought the same rebels while pursuing similar tactics. These operations went largely unnoticed in the western media. In many instances, France's actions were given less publicity than its conspicuous inactions. This was the case during the Togolese coup in 1963 and subsequent coups in Congo-Brazzaville, Dahomey, Senegal and Niger.

France's interventions in the early 1960s were followed in short order by a relative hands-off period for the next two years. There seems to have been a pendulum swing of de Gaulle's African intervention policy defined against the background of the Algerian civil war. At first, France had eagerly assisted its former colonies in managing internal order. Then, with the war in Algeria raging and with centers of instability in Africa burgeoning everywhere, there appeared to be a general fatigue, albeit temporary, with conducting military interventions. Eventually, the pendulum made a short but vigorous swing toward greater involvement, with the intervention following the 1964 coup in Gabon to topple President M'Ba. This event roughly marked the end of the "family consolidation" period.

During the early years of francophone Africa's independence, de Gaulle authorized the intervention of French troops in almost a dozen instances.[5] Most of these interventions were performed in accordance with defense agreements signed right after independence. The vast majority of these actions were aimed at restoring domestic order. Except for the 1964 intervention in Gabon, all of the early French actions were made at the request of the local authorities.

France did not respond to every request made by its African partners. On three significant occasions, no French military action was forthcoming: when Léopold Sédar Senghor was almost overthrown by his Prime Minister Mamadou Dia in Senegal; when then Colonel Etienne (Gnassingbe) Eyadema headed a triumvirate of military officers which assassinated Togolese president Sylvanus Olympio; and when Hubert Maga was replaced by General Soglo in Dahomey. French caution and restraint could be partially attributed to the Algerian War and the resulting trauma. Still, France continued to monitor events in Africa closely, lest the whole edifice be destroyed.

Several crises in Africa may have been diffused simply by the sudden reinforcement of a French garrison or by an appropriately organized military exercise. On the basis of overlapping personnel and structures, the French have been able to use their military force as "counter-insurrectionary instruments in the most important centers of potential anti-government action, viz. the local army camps."[6]

The pattern of French military involvement during the de Gaulle years shows a definite correlation between military support and key pro-Gaullist African regimes, as in Côte d'Ivoire, Cameroon, and Gabon. Leaders of less important African nations, according to Richard Joseph, "have been expendable, and no-nonsense, military regimes allowed to replace them."[7] From the chaos in the early 1960s emerged a new set of priorities for evaluating the need for French military involvement based on the additional need for France to appear credible as self-proclaimed guarantor of stability in francophone Africa. In general, the family consolidation period was fairly successful in its implicit objective of preserving strong links between the former metropole and the new African partners. Guinea dropped out, but four years after the wave of independence in French Africa, the outlines of a reliable French zone of influence in Africa had been clearly drawn. Military interventions were instrumental in bringing about this development and they underscore the special links between Gaullist authorities and African regimes, which recognized their dependence on France for all important security matters.

Cameroon (1957-62)

Toward the end of French colonial rule, Cameroon had to deal with a powerful insurgent movement, organized in 1948 by trade unionists known as the *Union des populations camerounaises* (UPC). After a failed revolt in May 1955 to gain power, the French administration banned the movement. The UPC went underground and waged guerrilla actions. It is estimated that between 1957 and 1962, 10,000 to 20,000 people died as a result of the insurgents and the heavy-handed counter-insurgency. At first, the repression was organized by the French administration. After Cameroon's independence on January 1, 1960, the counter-insurgency was organized by the newly elected Cameroonian government led by President Ahmadou Ahidjo.[8] Immediately after independence, President Ahidjo asked France for assistance in controlling the UPC rebellion, and de Gaulle agreed to send an expeditionary force. The French forces consisted of five battalions, one armored squadron and one squadron of fighter-bombers under the authority of General Max Briant.[9] French troops formed the spearhead of the repressive forces, with the Cameroonian administration following and implementing the Ahidjo government's policies. The "pacification" effort, a rather violent repression, lasted until late 1962, when the last French forces left the country. A French witness at the time reported that the Cameroonian authorities "had not been the least eager to request forceful methods. And the French government did not want to prolong this faraway intervention in which it wanted to maintain a maximum of discretion."[10]

An initially reluctant General Charles de Gaulle had to be convinced by his African affairs advisors, headed by Jacques Foccart, of the necessity for a French operation, even if it had to take place only shortly after granting independence to Cameroon. France and Cameroon succeeded in quelling the UPC rebellion with very little adverse reaction from French or world public opinion. At the time, France was engaged in the bloodiest period of the Algerian war of independence, which distracted most of the attention of potential opposition parties in France and abroad. The French intervention in 1960 against the UPC exemplified a continuation of colonial policy. France's military action against the UPC movement was almost uninterrupted from the mid-1950s until 1962.

Mauritania (1958-63)

In the late 1950s, as Mauritania moved toward independence, the Moroccan government stated its claim to all Mauritanian territory with growing insistence. Armed raids by rebel forces from Morocco entered Mauritania through the Spanish Sahara or southwestern Algeria. The attacks were repulsed by French troops, who organized a combined operation with the Spanish military. Code-named *Ouragan*, the operation took place in February 1958. In a brief war, it destroyed the raiders, regrouped in a "Liberation Army," in all its operational zones, both in Mauritania and in Spanish Sahara, except at Ifni, which was then in Moroccan hands. The Moroccans maintained their claim to Mauritania, thereby eliciting renewed French military vigilance in the region. At the diplomatic level, the French government hurried Mauritanian independence in its anxiety to safeguard its position in the region.[11] Mauritanian independence came on November 28, 1960, with French forces still operating in the country. French troops stayed in the newly-independent Mauritania to maintain peace until cooperation agreements had been signed. As one observer of Mauritania described it in 1963: "Without French financial aid and technical assistance, without French diplomatic support and even military protection, it is difficult to see how independent Mauritania would survive at all."[12]

On March 29, 1962, a bomb attack against a Mauritanian Army officer's mess killed three French officers.[13] Findings pointed toward Moroccan support to the attackers.[14] Rebels, also backed by Morocco, launched a raid aimed at destabilizing the government. With the help of French troops, this Moroccan-sponsored takeover attempt failed. The Mauritanian government needed the deployment of French forces once again in order to stay in power, "even if this aroused old fears and resentments and lent force to the argument that Mauritania was just a French puppet."[15] France was solicited by Mauritania to intervene on numerous occasions, namely in the Hodh region, in the Adrar, in Port-Etienne, and finally in the capital itself, Nouakchott. Morocco would eventually recognize Mauritania in late 1969. In 1972, Mauritania asked for a revision of the agreements signed with France after independence. No new open military agreements were concluded.

Minor Policing Operations (1960-63)

On February 28, 1964, the French daily *Le Monde* published an article listing some of the French interventions in Africa between 1960 and 1964.[16] It was a rare occasion when French authorities officially recognized the role they had taken in supporting young governments in francophone Africa. These actions had often gone unreported by the press, either because of the priority given to the Algerian war, or because Jacques Foccart's renowned proclivity for secrecy may have concealed these events from public scrutiny. This predilection was likely shared by the African leaders in the countries concerned.

Some of the minor policing operations performed by France in the early post-colonial years had little or no political impact. One such incident was the settlement of an ethnic dispute between the Ballalis and the Mbochis in Congo-Brazzaville in 1960. During the same year, smaller-scale interventions also occurred in Gabon to repress local riots. Alain Peyrefitte, then minister of information, reported that French troops intervened several times in Chad between 1960 and 1963. The French Army was still quite powerful in Chad and oversaw administration in the northern regions of the country. French troops were moved toward the Ghana-Togo border in December 1962 during tensions between the two countries.[17] Another example of French power occurred when French troops were briefly deployed in Congo-Brazzaville in September 1962 to maintain internal order following anti-Gabonese demonstrations. The origin of this action was a disputed decision by the referee of a soccer match between Congo-Brazzaville and Gabon that led to rioting in the two countries. In Gabon, thousands of Gabonese soccer fans took to the streets and hunted down all Congolese residents. The latter were officially expelled from Gabon by a presidential decree. Subsequently, anti-Gabonese demonstration broke out in Congo-Brazzaville and the Gabonese population took refuge in an Army camp. The incidents in Brazzaville were not followed by official expulsions. French troops participated in calming down the excited mobs.

Senegal (1960)

After unsuccessful attempts to maintain some cohesive confederate structure in western Africa, and shortly before the disintegration of the *Communauté*, Senegal and the French Sudan, later to become Mali, regrouped in the short-lived Mali Federation from April 1959 until its collapse in August 1960. The Mali Federation was ruled jointly by Léopold Sédar Senghor from Senegal and Modibo Keita from French Sudan. The formation of the Federation was based more on the aspirations of the political elites than on historic, economic, geographic, or cultural grounds. The point of contention was the control over political institutions. Sudanese radicals led by Keita aimed at setting up a unified state under their control, while the Senegalese political leadership believed that "the continued existence of the Federation threatened their domestic political base."[18]

On August 16, 1960, Sudanese armed forces chief of staff, Colonel Soumaré, ordered the French commander of the gendarmerie to place a few platoons of gendarmes, exclusively of Sudanese origin, on stand-by to move to Dakar on short notice. The order was given to prepare for the upcoming August 27 presidential elections. The Senegalese defense minister voided the order. French officers serving with the gendarmerie sided with the more moderate Senegalese leaders. They would help arrest Colonel Soumaré and assist the Senegalese in outmaneuvering Keita and his friends by deploying Senegalese gendarme units to strategic points in Dakar. The French High Commissioner, representing the French *Communauté* of which the Mali Federation was a member, was responsible for the use of French forces still based in the Federation. He, too, sympathized with the Senegalese position, and his action reflected at least a benevolent neutrality in their favor. When Keita realized that he had lost control over the gendarmerie, he called on the French High Commissioner to demand the intervention of French troops. The latter refused to honor Keita's request on the grounds that this was a purely domestic matter, thereby limiting Keita's chances of achieving Sudanese control of the whole Federation. Keita and Senghor quickly moved to divide the Federation into two separate countries.

While the French military role was confined to non-intervention by French troops, it was clear that French military authorities, both those within the High Commissioner's office and the French officers serving in the gendarmerie, played a crucial role. France was initially not opposed to the idea of the Mali Federation, but "once the break-up seemed inevitable, there was no question as to which side [they] would choose. Certainly, a Federation without Senghor's strong moderating influence would not serve France's purpose."[19]

Congo-Brazzaville (1963)

The situation in Congo-Brazzaville had deteriorated markedly in August 1963, three years after independence, when Abbé Fulbert

Youlou, the Congolese president, proposed to create a one-party system and to make restive trade unions more compliant. Between August 13 and August 15, shortly after several labor union leaders had been arrested, a general strike degenerated into threatening demonstrations and mutinies against the government. Youlou felt the mounting pressure and asked de Gaulle for assistance. The latter assigned General Kergaravat, commander of all French troops in the CAR, Chad, Congo, and Gabon, to protect President Youlou. The 500-men French garrison, stationed at the country's main harbor of Pointe-Noire, was reinforced by troops airlifted from Bouar, in the CAR, and Dakar, Senegal.[20] French armored vehicles patrolled the streets of the capital on August 14 and were deployed around the presidential palace.[21] Kergaravat had close to 2,000 French troops at his disposal in the country.[22]

A major cabinet reshuffle did not suffice to calm the demonstrators. Faced with an increasingly hostile crowd, Youlou initially summoned Kergaravat to order his troops to open fire. The Congolese president was troubled by the extent of his unpopularity and the violence of the mob's reaction against him.[23] In a psychologically perplexing move, probably inspired by a phone conversation with de Gaulle,[24] the Congolese president relinquished the use of force to quell the demonstrations and decided to sign a letter of resignation. The crowd rushed into the palace and took the president prisoner while French troops observed neutrally. De Gaulle authorized Foccart to do everything possible to save Youlou from execution by the Congolese provisional government. Many months later, the French succeeded in getting Youlou out of the country.[25]

The French role in the 1963 crisis in Congo-Brazzaville would significantly affect de Gaulle's future outlook on similar uproars in other countries. First, in terms of political control, France lost considerable influence over its former colony. Youlou's regime might have been unpopular and corrupt, but he was an enthusiastic and devoted admirer of de Gaulle and France. His successor, Alphonse Massamba-Débat took radical steps toward revolution, and a year later established a one-party Marxist-Leninist state. The second change which affected French authorities after the overthrow of Youlou was that other African states began to question France's attitude, perceived as lax and overly motivated by French self-interest.

France's inaction in January 1963, after the assassination of the Togolese president Sylvanus Olympio, combined with Youlou's removal from power, evoked strong doubt among other African leaders about France's commitment to assist them in difficult political situations. African anxieties were further enhanced when President Maga of Dahomey was deposed by a military coup in October 1963, which led to lasting unrest and instability in that country. Youlou's demise had an important impact on young post-colonial African nations. He represented the first example of African leadership, and direct heir of colonization, who was rejected by popular protest based on purely political considerations rather than tribal or economic discontent.[26]

Niger (1963)

After its independence in August 1960, Niger remained closely bonded to France. "French management was maintained at pre-independence levels in both administrative and commercial affairs, and a French military garrison was maintained in Niamey."[27] Hamani Diori, the first president, was a staunch supporter of France. In December 1963, a brief mutiny took place when a company opposed the reassignment of their commander. The mutiny was quelled with the assistance of French troops in Niamey, and 80 people were arrested. The whole incident was without political impact. A few weeks later, tension between Niger and neighboring Dahomey peaked because of a border dispute over a small island on the Niger river. Niger sent troops along the border and announced the imminent expulsion of the sizeable Dahomeyan community in Niger. The true reason may have been that President Diori of Niger did not trust the new authorities in Porto-Novo under Colonel Christophe Soglo and feared the potential spread of revolutionary fervor to Niger. The authorities in Niamey, fearing domestic subversion and concerned after a recent, though unrelated, mutiny, "were tempted to take severe preventive security measures against foreigners."[28] However, no further intercession by French troops was reported during the tension between Dahomey and Niger, despite an intervention at the inception of disturbances.

Gabon (1964)

The 1964 bloodless military coup attempt against Gabonese president Léon M'Ba by one of his rivals, Senator Jean-Hilaire Aubame, triggered the most widely publicized intervention or security operation carried out by France in its former colonies since the dawn of African independence.[29] For the first time, French troops put a head of state back into power after he had already been overthrown.

The coup against M'Ba took place during the night of February 17-18, 1964, when elements of the Gabonese army opposed to the president seized the main buildings in the small capital of Libreville. M'Ba and the president of the National Assembly were arrested in the presidential palace that night. On the morning of the 18th, a message by the putschists was aired on the radio asking for non-interference of French aid personnel - military and civilian - in the internal affairs of Gabon. In the afternoon, President M'Ba read a communiqué on national radio announcing his resignation. The putschists then drove him away to Lambaréné, a provincial center, far from the capital where an intervention by French troops was feared. Martial law was decreed during the night of February 18th. The next day, just as the revolutionary committee was announcing the constitution of a new provisional government headed by the leading opposition figure Jean-Hilaire Aubame, local French troops cleared the airport. Minutes later two French companies were flown from Dakar and Brazzaville to Libreville to occupy the strategic points in the capital. They rushed to the radio station and took control of it by 2:00 p.m., then continued their advance on the capital and surrounded the palace. By 6:00 p.m. on February 19th the insurgents surrendered and the old government was put back in place. According to the French-censured news reports not a shot was fired, yet this left an unexplained 16 to 25 people dead, including 1 or 2 French soldiers.[30] M'Ba, after less than 18 hours out of office, was reinstated as president of Gabon.

France's actions were officially justified by its defense agreement with Gabon, "which implicitly provided for the personal protection of the Gabonese president."[31] In effect, the treaty provided for an intervention by French troops if the government of Gabon, menaced by subversion, solicited their aid. French authorities confirmed that they had received a call for help by the M'Ba government in the first hours after the mutiny, but it was only after the return of order to Libreville that the Gabonese vice-president claimed that he had requested French assistance, leaving a strong suspicion that the call had been made *ex post*.[32] The fact that President de Gaulle had been out-paced by the rhythm of coups in other former French colonies may have prompted him to act decisively in Gabon. Alain Peyrefitte explained the French government's broad interpretation of the defense agreement, whereby

France intervened to save a particular regime rather than to protect a state against an external aggression:

> It is not possible that a few gunmen be left free to capture at any time any presidential palace, and it is precisely because such a menace was foreseen that the new African states have concluded with France agreements to protect themselves against such risks.[33]

Gabon was a special case. It is questionable whether de Gaulle would have been equally provoked had the coup occurred in Mali or in any of the other countries which had previously suffered coups without any military response from France. The underlying causes for the French action were linked to Gabon's economic importance and its vast natural resources, including large oil reserves, compounded by a favorable environment for foreign investment. Other reasons complemented France's interest in Gabon's political stability. By some accounts, Jean-Hilaire Aubame was considered as a candidate with U.S. backing, which might have made him undesirable for Gaullist authorities.[34] The editor-in-chief of the magazine *Jeune Afrique*, Béchir Ben Yamed, suggested that the French intervention may have been encouraged by the intervention of British troops in East Africa:

> There is little doubt that the counter-coup d'état by the French paratroopers was facilitated by the recent British incursions in Tanganyika, in Kenya, and in Uganda. It is, however, important to point out that, in the case of these three countries, the situation was quite different; their call for a foreign force was an act emanating from the supreme authority, a choice made in the exercise of governmental responsibilities by presidents, whose respective authority the mutineers themselves did not seek to put into question.[35]

Finally, de Gaulle's gratitude to long-time African allies for their enthusiastic support of his *Communauté* project expands on other explanations for the intervention by adding an emotional element of trust and responsibility.

Although the putschists did not benefit from widespread public support,[36] the strong international rejection of the French intervention in Africa, especially among non-aligned nations, meant that "France consequently reduced the visibility and increased the selectivity of such military actions."[37] In subsequent years, de Gaulle would not forget the damage the intervention in Gabon had done to French prestige in the

Third World.[38] Except for one overt intervention in the Central African Republic, and the special case of Chad, no military interventions took place under de Gaulle. This is as much a testimony to French caution after unfavorable international publicity of the Gabonese events as it is evidence of the circumspection with which potential African coup leaders viewed France.

Central African Republic (1967)

On November 10, 1967, a company of 80 men from the 11th Parachute Division was sent from France to Bangui, the capital of the CAR. This newly formed division had been created as a core intervention force after the 1964 events in Gabon. The reasons for the French deployment in the CAR were unclear. At the time, *Le Monde* speculated about the motives for this action.[39] It attributed the French military intervention to either the troubles in neighboring Congo-Kinshasa - formerly Leopoldville - or to internal dissatisfaction with the CAR's military regime under President Bokassa, who had staged a coup in January 1966 to come to power. From June through November 1967, Belgian and French mercenaries in Congo-Kinshasa attempted to seize control of the Katanga and Kivu provinces. Lack of local support and prompt counter-action by President Mobutu, supported by American pilots, resulted in the collapse of the revolt. On November 5, 1967, the mercenaries in the Kivu province fled to neighboring Rwanda. They never seriously threatened to move into the CAR.

The second explanation for French action, internal dissatisfaction with Bokassa's military regime, seems more likely. The Bokassa regime had been criticized for its inability to improve standards of living and its refusal to grant amnesty to political prisoners. Bokassa had also launched an austerity program intended to curb corruption and reduce the salaries of the prestigious civil servants.[40] *Le Monde* reported that a tract circulated by the *Front de libération nationale de la République Centrafricaine* had condemned President Bokassa to death. As noted by a close observer of the CAR: "By September 1967 Bokassa was so obsessed by the fear of plots that he made a trip to Paris to ask the French government to grant him the protection of French troops."[41] The number of French troops in the CAR subsequently grew until they represented 20 percent of the 1,100-strong military force in the country by 1969.[42] At the time, the threat to Bokassa's regime appeared equivocal. The French military move to dispatch a company to the CAR, viewed in this context, was more a pre-emptive manifestation of support through a limited display of force than it was a true intervention.

THE BIAFRAN BLUNDER

The French role in the Biafran secession deserves a special review because it is so atypical of France's prior approach to sub-Saharan Africa. Firstly, it concerned a country outside the traditional French zone of influence. Secondly, French policy was geared toward the break-up of a country and a redefinition of colonial borders. Thirdly, it put two allies, France and Britain, in opposing camps during the entire conflict, from 1967 to 1970.

On July 6, 1967, the hostilities of the Nigerian civil war broke out when the Federal Government of Nigeria under General Gowon used military force to put an end to the secession of the Biafran province in eastern Nigeria. The Biafran leader, General Ojukwu, had declared Biafra's independence a few days earlier on May 30, 1967. The Ibos, the majority of whom were Catholics, were by far the dominant ethnic group in Biafra, which contains most of the country's oil resources, as well as a thriving agricultural sector. The war was one of the bloodiest in African history, with over one million lives lost, mainly Biafran civilians who starved to death.[43]

Outside support was essential for both factions, and it enabled them to continue the fighting. An initial arms embargo by a number of western nations, including France and the U.S., on all parties involved proved insufficient to end the conflict. Britain and the Soviet Union did not subscribe to the embargo. Estimates of British military equipment supplied to the Gowon regime vary between 15 percent and 45 percent of all the equipment acquired by the Federal Government.[44] (See Chapter 9 for more details on the British participation in the Nigerian civil war.) The Soviet Union provided fighter and bomber aircraft to the Nigerian Federal government, of the type that Britain would later refuse to send after Biafran lobbies in Europe conducted emotional campaigns to prove that civilian populations would be the first victims of air raids. French aid to Biafra paled in comparison. It was only in August 1968 that de Gaulle reversed his decision to maintain the embargo on Biafra.

De Gaulle was not displeased by the prospect of weakening Nigeria. Historically, the relations between France and Africa's giant nation had been antagonistic. Nigeria resented the predominance of a non-African nation, especially in what Nigeria perceived as its natural zone of influence, namely West Africa. Furthermore, Franco-Nigerian diplomatic relations had reached a low on January 5, 1961, after France exploded its third nuclear bomb in the Algerian Sahara on December 27, 1960. Nigeria viewed this as an opportunity to challenge French influence and decided to castigate France by breaking diplomatic relations and giving the French ambassador 48 hours to leave. Despite its popularity in Nigeria, "as a diplomatic move, however, the gesture appears to have been a serious mistake. [...] Nigeria's rebuke failed to stop the atomic tests and did not encourage other African governments to sever relations with Paris."[45] Diplomatic relations were not restored until May 1966, after French president Charles de Gaulle, who felt the affront could not be so easily forgiven, turned down repeated Nigerian requests to reopen relations.

Initially, French involvement in the Biafran secession was limited and covert. To anyone close to the scene it was clear that France was "meticulously careful not only to avoid being drawn into the conflict but to discourage the buildup of arms and armaments in any part of Nigeria."[46] Under pressure from public opinion at home, and at the ardent request of francophone African allies, de Gaulle eventually supported Biafra despite his prior approval of a total arms embargo. In a landmark pronouncement on July 31, 1968, the French Council of Ministers issued a statement explaining why France supported the cause of the Ibos:

> The Government considers that the bloodshed and suffering endured for over a year by the population of Biafra demonstrate their will to assert themselves as a people. Faithful to its principles, the French Government therefore considers that the present conflict should be solved on the basis of the right of peoples to self-determination and should include the setting in motion of appropriate international procedures.[47]

Supporting secessionist forces was an incredible challenge to the OAU's ruling on the inviolability of colonial borders. France, however, would stop short of officially recognizing the Biafran Republic. Five Third World countries recognized the "state" of Biafra: Côte d'Ivoire,

Gabon, Haiti, Tanzania, and Zambia. The war dragged on over a long period of time. The Biafran troops were outnumbered and became increasingly under-equipped due to long and difficult supply lines. The Biafran-controlled enclave shrunk steadily under the assaults from Federal Nigerian troops. France started to distance itself from the Biafran secessionists after President de Gaulle stepped down in 1969, and its support was severely reduced. On January 8, 1970, General Ojukwu fled the country and his successor asked for peace.

Although it is difficult to assess the priority of the reasons for French support of the Biafrans, they can be broadly enumerated as follows: the latent competition with anglophone Nigeria for hegemony in western and central Africa; the fact that the Ibos were Catholic; the appeal of friendly African countries;[48] defiance against Britain, which supported the Lagos authorities; and last - and probably least - token commitment to the right to national self-determination for the Ibos. De Gaulle's argument for supporting the Biafrans was never intended to go as far as complete independence. In *The International Politics of the Nigerian Civil War 1967-1970*, John Stremlau claims that de Gaulle:

> appears to have been more inclined to the argument that France's long-term interests and those of her former West African colonies would be best served if Biafra were allowed to sustain a war of attrition long enough to force a political settlement. Such a compromise solution would, conceivably, reduce the likelihood that the new Nigeria would enjoy the internal strength necessary if she wished to dominate West Africa.[49]

The indirect support was not organized through the official channels at the Ministry of Foreign Affairs or the Ministry of Cooperation, but through the more nebulous services of Jacques Foccart. French action in the region involved three types of activities: forwarding weapons to the Biafrans, covertly funding mercenaries to transport supplies to the Biafrans (especially much needed pilots) or to fight on their side, and organizing a highly visible naval maneuver in support of Gabon.

The first aspect, the provision of weapons, was the most essential part of France's involvement. Although the French embargo on Nigeria was never formally lifted, French arms comprised 10 to 50 percent of all foreign weapons received by the Biafrans, reaching a total of $5 million.[50] Substantial deliveries started in September 1968. French arms and ammunition deliveries to Biafra were estimated at ten to thirty tons a day; British sources tended to quote the higher figure.[51]

The second element of French involvement on the side of Biafra was the provision of manpower, first mercenaries, and later observers, who were literally checking whether or not the Biafrans were wasting French equipment.[52] The exact role of the French government in arming and dispatching mercenaries to help the Biafran armed forces was murky at best. French mercenaries were already active in Biafra before the decision by de Gaulle to support the secession. French mercenary pilots participated in the supply of arms because French military deliveries, transiting through Gabon and Côte d'Ivoire, had to be airlifted after the capture of the Biafran harbors of Port Harcourt and Calabar.[53] Most of this mercenary activity was linked to the French presidential advisor for African affairs, Jacques Foccart.[54]

Militarily, French troops never became directly involved in the Nigerian civil war. In a unique instance of the indirect use of French forces, the passage of a French Navy task force in Gabon was exploited to stress France's diplomatic position in this explosive regional context. In November 1968, a French aircraft carrier battle group showed the flag off the coast of Gabon and stopped at Libreville and Port-Gentil to mark French backing of Gabonese sovereignty, which was threatened by Nigeria.[55] The Nigerian Federal authorities had reason to threaten Gabon because the latter offered important staging facilities for the resupply of the Biafran forces.

French involvement in Nigeria has been viewed as not only insufficient to sustain the secessionist forces, but outright counterproductive. In an interview with author John J. Stremlau concerning the French role, Biafra's chief of staff, Major General Philip Effiong, snapped: "[they] did more harm than good by raising false hopes and by providing the British with an excuse to reinforce Nigeria."[56] While the British motivations for becoming the Federal Nigerian government's supplier predate French involvement, the other part of Effiong's argument has some validity. The whole war would have been much shorter without foreign interference, simply as a result of the exhaustion of military supplies. The Biafrans also failed to achieve de Gaulle's less ambitious plan to help them reach a favorable political settlement, even within some form of confederation. By January 1970, the secession had failed, and so did the French attempt at weakening the Nigerian Federation. It is the only instance where French policy in sub-Saharan Africa failed to such a complete and irreversible extent.

THE CHADIAN QUAGMIRE

Chad is a French colonial creation. It was France's goal to construct one continuous African empire - with Chad linking Algeria, western and equatorial French Africa - and to check British and German advances in the region. Since the beginning, that strategic interest prevailed over considerations of economic benefits.[57] This was amply reaffirmed by France's post-colonial policy in Chad. The policy needs to be examined as a continuous effort spanning over thirty years and four French presidents. After early efforts before 1969 to police the country and to bring about an illusory "national reconciliation," France's objectives shifted toward the containment of Libyan expansionism. That strategy was vastly complicated by the volatility of Chad's domestic political situation. France has been in a state of semi-permanent intervention in Chad since the late 1960s. Chad became a test-case for France's credibility in Africa and its ability to stabilize its African *protégés*. With the threats of Libyan involvement in Chadian affairs, France faced the challenge of trying by all means to avoid the domino effect on neighboring African nations, which President Mitterrand acknowledged on various occasions. "What counts," he explained in 1981, "is Chad's integrity. Otherwise all African borders will be shattered."[58] In 1983, he told U.S. Ambassador Vernon Walters that by intervening in Chad, France was concerned about territories further south: "it is Black Africa, Cameroon and Niger that we have to protect."[59]

Toubou Revolts (1968)

With Chadian independence on August 11, 1960, François Tombalbaye, a native from the agrarian south, became president and installed a government dominated by southerners. He consolidated his power in a single-party regime and repressed all forms of opposition. Despite Chadian independence, the unstable northern prefecture of Borkou-Ennedi-Tibesti, with a nomadic population, remained under French military administration until 1965. Afterwards, the abuses of the government were especially harsh in the north, and enhanced the volatility of the political situation. By 1968, with the revolt of the Toubous in the Tibesti region, Chadian authorities lost control and asked France for assistance. This request set in motion a long series of

French interventions, which were never able to end Chad's tenacious and violent factionalism.

Tombalbaye asked France for help in rescuing a contingent of Chadian gendarmerie that had been trapped by rebellious Toubou guards at Aozou. On August 28, 1968, one battalion of French paratroopers was airlifted to assist the Chadian government in putting down the rebellion, reinforcing the 1,000 French troops already stationed in Fort Lamy under the defense agreement.[60] The French Air Force assisted the government in transporting the Chadian reinforcement troops.

The timing and circumstances of the French intervention have left some observers wondering about the hidden motives of both the French authorities and President Tombalbaye. The Tibesti region was not the only trouble spot in Chad. *Jeune Afrique* alluded at the time to important minerals in the Tibesti mountains which might have triggered the French reaction.[61] The same source also argues that Tombalbaye viewed with great alarm the expansion of the Toubou rebellion throughout the northern region to join forces with the *Front de libération nationale du Tchad* (FROLINAT) rebels, then operating in the northeastern part of the country. The French intervention successfully protected Tombalbaye's regime but could not restore Chad to normalcy. The regime was "further discredited by being openly seen as a puppet of France."[62]

Pacification of the North (1969-1975)

The initial Toubou revolts in northern Chad were more spontaneous uprisings than organized rebellions against the Chadian central authorities. With the creation of the FROLINAT in 1966, Toubou discontent received a political structure and acquired a certain cohesiveness and ideology. FROLINAT's support was regional, Muslim and ethnic, even though it never advocated the secession of the north. The movement was usually fraught with internal rifts, and the political and military leadership were often disunited.[63]

In early 1969, the government had lost control over large areas above the 16th Parallel, also referred as the Borku-Ennedi-Tibesti region. Only the main settlements in these three zones remained in the central government's hands. Again, Tombalbaye reluctantly called for French assistance under the Franco-Chadian Defense Agreement. President de Gaulle, shortly before his resignation, authorized a French military intervention. In April 1969 a French expeditionary force of about 1,500 men, composed of five companies of the 2nd Foreign Parachute Regiment and one company of the 2nd Foreign Infantry Regiment, was sent to Chad. By early 1970, additional reinforcements of 1,000 *Troupes de Marine* and 1,000 Air Force personnel brought the total number of French forces in Chad to more than 3,500 men.[64] The French forces drove the rebels back into the Tibesti desert, while suffering only eight killed and 90 wounded. The pacification of the north was achieved through small units, organized ambushes, and attacks on enemy positions with ample heliborne support. These operations were directly inspired by French tactics in the Algerian war. "But while the French achieved a military victory, they failed to conduct civic action programs or take steps to ensure political stability. The problems which had led to the insurgency still existed."[65] The French expeditionary force was reduced by June 1971 and removed in August 1972. This withdrawal did not affect French garrisons in Fort-Lamy and Fort-Archambault, which continued to operate under the defense agreements.

Tombalbaye was killed by members of the armed forces in a coup d'état on April 13, 1975. French forces stationed in N'Djamena did not intervene. Because some Chadian units, which had joined the putschists, had been on the move for two consecutive days before arriving in N'Djamena to overthrow the president, it is likely that the French military intelligence in Chad had some advanced warning.[66] After the coup, General Félix Malloum became president of a Chadian supreme military council.

Operation Tacaud (1978-81)

A major stumbling block between France and the Malloum regime was the hostage taking of Mrs. Claustre, a French sociologist, by the rebel leader Hissène Habré. Unable to settle the matter through the good offices of the Chadian government, France started direct negotiations with Habré. Enraged by this initiative, which bypassed him altogether, President Malloum ordered the complete withdrawal of all remaining French troops from Chad by September 27, 1975, and the return of the bases to the Chadian authorities. This move, completed by October 1975, was followed by a partial restoration of the French military role in Chad. In March 1976, the Malloum government signed an agreement with France "under which Chad received substantial civil and military aid, and, in return, allowed stopover facilities for French aircraft at N'Djamena."[67]

The rebellion under the leadership of Goukouni Oueddeï and Hissène Habré exploited the weakness of the Malloum regime. The French withdrawal had in effect cleared the way for them on their march to the capital. By insisting on the withdrawal of French troops and guns in 1975, Malloum sealed his fate.[68] In April 1978, FROLINAT's forces were within 250 km of the capital N'Djamena. President Giscard d'Estaing, waiting after the first round of legislative elections in France, finally dispatched the whole of the 2nd Foreign Parachute Regiment, two companies of the 2nd Foreign Infantry Regiment, a company of Marine Infantry, and several squadrons of supporting tactical aircraft and air bombers. Operation *Tacaud* had started. A total of 2,500 French troops were deployed in Chad at the time.[69] FROLINAT's advance was halted in two important battles, at Ati on May 19 and at Djeddah on June 2. France's help had been decisive.

The French objective in the intervention was not to destroy the Chadian opposition completely, but to salvage Malloum's regime while trying to achieve a lasting peace. France urged all parties in Chad to agree to power-sharing arrangements through a national reconciliation policy.[70] Diplomatically, France demanded that Libya reduce its support of the FROLINAT movement. A power-struggle ensued between Malloum, Habré, and Goukouni, with France acting as umpire between them, never allowing any of the parties to be completely defeated and trying to co-opt them in a national balancing act. France ultimately failed to arrive at a national reconciliation, despite the high hopes raised by the creation in March 1979 of the *Gouvernement d'union nationale de transition* (GUNT) under the presidency of Goukouni, which regrouped the three main factions in Chad. Malloum was completely marginalized. Goukouni's faction eventually assumed the GUNT acronym. Habré's faction, and its better armed and disciplined military branch called the *Forces armées du nord* (FAN), would be engaged in a bitter contest for power against GUNT. France took sides in the dispute and, despite Habré's role in the Claustre hostage-taking, favored him because he seemed to be the more moderate, and therefore more acceptable, Muslim leader. The French supplied Habré's forces with modern weapons.[71] Eventually, Habré was ousted by Goukouni and fled to Algeria. The French troops, still in Chad, found themselves in an awkward position. They were now acting as protectors of Goukouni, the man they had come to fight under the Malloum regime, against Habré, the man whom they had come to view as a potentially acceptable leader. Goukouni's close ties with Libya were a further cause of contention between him and France. Shortly after Habré's dismissal, France drew the only practical conclusion; French troops left Chad completely by May 16, 1980. The heavy cost of keeping troops in Chad was barely justifiable in such a transient environment. An OAU peace-keeping mission allowed France to withdraw without losing face. France's Chadian policy was in shambles, with no viable alternative in sight.

In June 1980, Libya and the GUNT signed a treaty of friendship and cooperation, allowing Libya to intervene if Chad's internal security was threatened. The occasion for Libyan intervention was given on October 7, 1980 during an offensive attack by Habré's forces. Libyan aircraft bombed Faya and N'Djamena. By mid-December, Libyan forces occupied the capital and Abéché in eastern Chad. In a politically suicidal move, Goukouni signed an agreement in Tripoli on January 6, 1981, paving the way for a gradual union of Libya and Chad. The strong reaction of rejection, both internally and internationally, discredited Goukouni's leadership and gave rise to a collusion of forces that eventually deprived him of power and drove him out of Chad. The southerners, who had not been consulted about the union agreement, were antagonized further. France strongly denounced the proposed merger and reinforced its military personnel in the CAR.

Operation Manta (1983-84)

France was not in a favorable position in Chad during the first year of Mitterrand's term. The Libyans had a massive 10,000 troops in Chad. Nevertheless, the new French administration, following the general trend within the OAU, would recognize the GUNT's hold on power and reverse the previous administration's policy of favoritism granted to Habré's movement. France's diplomacy then aimed at replacing the Libyans with an Inter-African force. Under pressure at home and abroad, President Goukouni requested the withdrawal of Libyan troops in October 1981. In a surprising move, Colonel Qaddafi complied with Goukouni's demand, probably because he was expected to be elected as OAU chairman for the following year.

Paris had little to gloat about after this unexpected and easy diplomatic victory. One Chadian observer confided to the French news agency AFP that: "By evacuating Chad, Libya thumbed its nose at

France. It cannot escape its responsibilities."[72] Nothing was further removed from Mitterrand's initial intentions than to have the role of Chadian domestic peace-maker thrust upon him, especially if this involved the deployment of French troops. The GUNT soon appeared unable to control the country after the Libyans had left. Habré re-emerged and launched devastating attacks from his Sudanese sanctuaries. The 4,800-man Inter-African force remained completely passive and did not fire a single shot. Habré reached N'Djamena on June 7, 1982. From 1978 to 1982, French diplomacy had run a full circle from Habré to Goukouni and back to Habré. Mitterrand recognized the new Habré regime in N'Djamena on June 9, 1982, and agreed to participate in the reconstruction of the capital, although military aid was not immediately forthcoming.

In a typical Chadian fashion, where enemies are ousted but never completely disappear, Goukouni was preparing his revenge with Libyan assistance. Heavily armed with Libyan supplied equipment, Goukouni proceeded to occupy the entire Borkou-Ennedi-Tibesti region, and captured Abéché on July 8, 1983. Habré launched an appeal for aid, to which Zaire responded generously by sending a contingent of paratroopers. Habré's appeal also prompted the U.S. to sign a military assistance agreement and deliver arms to Chad. President Ronald Reagan corresponded directly with Mitterrand to urge him to intervene. In a diplomatically embarrassing move for France, President Reagan publicly offered to France the use of AWACS surveillance planes based in Sudan. The publicity surrounding his offer forced Mitterrand to refuse it lest France appear as an American proxy. An appeal launched by France's moderate African partners, who were disturbed by Qaddafi's "green imperialism," was more effective. They probably tipped the balance in favor of a French intervention. For François Mitterrand, who had wanted to distance himself as much as possible from Giscard's image as Africa's gendarme, it was an extremely difficult and painful decision. The French newspaper *Le Matin* estimated that it was a question of French authority in Africa and in the world. "For François Mitterrand today, as yesterday for Valéry Giscard d'Estaing or Georges Pompidou, one evidence prevails: without its network of friends and its exceptional relations in Africa, France is mutilated on the international scene, ceasing to exist as a world power."[73] While France was bickering about the necessity of intervention, the U.S. had taken small steps to upgrade its military support to the Habré regime. A small group of American instructors was dispatched to Chad to assist the Habré forces in the use of the *Redeye* missile. For *Le Monde*, for the first time France was "losing ground" in its traditional zone of influence.[74] Beyond the issue of influence - mainly a problem to France - the two countries differed on policy choices. The U.S. sought in vain to destabilize the political authority of Qaddafi. The French did not seek the Libyan leader's downfall, but rather tried to check his advance into Chad and to relaunch the negotiation process. France's interest in keeping the Americans at a distance was consistent with Libya's concern about increased American backing of Habré should France have refused to play its part.[75]

An intensive Libyan bombing raid, allegedly involving up to 50 bombers and support aircraft, of Habré's forces in early August 1983 eventually triggered France's reaction.[76] On August 9, after long deliberation, Mitterrand decided to send French troops to Chad. The first troops arrived in N'Djamena the next day. The chief objective of operation *Manta*, the biggest French operation overseas since the Algerian war 20 years earlier, was to deter Libya without engaging in actual combat. In order to appear credible, France took a firm stand on a position easily conceded by Libya: Libyan forces were not to cross a "red line" running more or less along the 15th Parallel in the middle of the country. South of this line, French troops might engage any Libyan units in combat. Libya reacted to the French intervention "with surprising moderation, wishing to avoid open confrontation with France."[77] With regard to the internal situation in Chad, the goals of the French policy were two-fold: to separate warring factions, and to open negotiations to end the civil war.

Up to 3,300 French troops and advisors provided Habré with air support along the 15th Parallel and formed a 225-mile long security line crossing the whole country.[78] The *Manta* deployment involved 2,700 troops (some levied from French forces in the CAR) and 700 vehicles from the Army; 550 men, 25 planes, and four radar stations from the Air Force; and even 50 men and two surveillance planes from the Navy.[79] The *Manta* system was deployed over three countries, the bulk of it in Chad, but with other positions in Bangui and Bouar in the CAR, and Libreville in Gabon. The latter two positions were mainly rear bases for the Air Force. Air transport was used to an extent never achieved before by France in sub-Saharan Africa. The first batch of troops required 133 transport plane sorties, including civilian B-747s. These planes could land only in Bangui, Libreville and Douala until the airstrip in N'Djamena was enlarged to accommodate them. Many heavy supplies and armaments were subsequently routed by train and road through Cameroon. The Air Force was heavily involved in the operation, as *Manta* was launched primarily in response to the significant Libyan air threat. The pre-crisis Air Force presence in the area included four *Jaguar* aircraft with one C-135 tanker in Libreville. In 1983, two units of four *Jaguars,* plus a tanker, were sent to N'Djamena and Bangui, and four reconnaissance *Mirage* F1s, plus a tanker, were sent to N'Djamena. Fighter aircraft in Chad had to be based in N'Djamena, which was the only airstrip which could host them. Eight additional airfields in Chad were open for the fleet of medium-sized French C-160 air transport planes.

The operation met one of its principal goals by early 1984: stopping Goukouni's forces and their Libyan allies from extending further south. The French intervention forces were reduced to a patrolling role along the 15th Parallel. France and Libya acted with caution and refrained their respective allies. With regard to the political objective of national reconciliation, their failure was complete despite several attempts at bringing all Chadian factions to the round table. Breaking the fragile truce, Goukouni's forces attacked the post of Zigueï on January 24, 1984, about 200 miles north of N'Djamena and below the 15th Parallel. The retaliation came the next day when French fighter aircraft attacked the retreating forces. A *Jaguar* fighter jet was shot down. This action prompted Mitterrand to extend the limit of the exclusion zone further north to the 16th Parallel. A stalemate ensued, as the Libyan-backed rebels were not strong enough "to attempt a breakthrough of the French *cordon sanitaire*, and Habré's forces could not dislodge them from the north of the Red Line."[80]

By moving his troops northwards, Mitterrand broke the spirit of the initial approach, which was to block further Libyan penetration. The new message was telling the Libyans to get out.[81] Mitterrand was under heavy pressure to bring the French troops home. Through secret negotiations,[82] Libya and France reached an agreement on September 17, 1984 calling for the simultaneous and complete withdrawal of French and Libyan troops from Chad. France complied by November 9, fifteen months after the first elements had arrived in Chad. The pull back was code-named operation *Silure*.[83] During the withdrawal of the *Manta* defense system, the French Navy dispatched a task force in the Gulf of Sirte in operation *Mirmillon*. The two-month deployment of the naval task force was meant to deter Libya from launching any action in Chad that could compromise the ongoing French departure. The task force in the Gulf of Sirte included the aircraft carrier *Foch*, a cruiser, three frigates, and two submarines.[84]

It is unclear what France expected to gain from the September agreement. The primary goal of containing Libya and Libyan-supported advances was attained at a high budgetary cost and with substantial French force deployment. Libya had gained a strong, unchallenged foothold in northern Chad, forcing France to admit implicitly the *de facto* partition of the country. After an unsuccessful meeting between Qaddafi and Mitterrand on November 15, 1984 at Elounda on Crete, the French president was forced to admit that he had been duped by his Libyan counterpart. Libyan deceit, which had started right after the September 1984 agreement, would completely void the positive effects of operation *Manta*.

Operation Epervier (1986 -)

The next intervention, called *Epervier*, in addition to its anti-Libyan dimension, also facilitated the gradual consolidation of Habré's grasp on power throughout the country. His regime grew stronger with the inclusion of a growing number of defections from, and alliances with, other factions throughout the country. By late 1985, some French troops had been held on standby in the neighboring CAR, and French planes had resumed reconnaissance flights from the CAR to check Libya's force build-up in Chad.[85] Far from disengaging, the Libyans were building up their presence in northern Chad, bringing the estimated total to 4,000 troops and advisors in November 1985. By February 1986, they were ready to support an important offensive by the GUNT forces across the 16th Parallel against three different localities. Habré's forces repelled the attack and appealed to France for assistance. The French president, having always made it clear that France would not accept any Libyan transgression of the Red Line, retaliated by ordering an air raid against the Libyan-held airstrip at Ouadi Doum in northern Chad. This runway commanded the Libyan logistical resupply and support of the GUNT troops further south and was a major platform for launching air raids across the 16th Parallel. The French attack temporarily disabled this base, but more importantly, signaled French resolve to hit Libyan military assets if need be.

Operation *Epervier* started on February 14, 1986, when the French Air Force offensive deployment in the region had been strengthened to four *Mirage* F-1Cs, twelve *Jaguars*, three C-135Fs, six *Transalls*, and two *Atlantic* aircraft. The attack on February 16 was carried out by *Jaguar* fighter-bomber aircraft based in Bangui, assisted by a *Mirage* F-1C stationed in Chad, and C-135F tanker airplanes.[86] The *Jaguar* strike was particularly remarkable because the planes operated 1,500 km from their base. Two *Atlantic* aircraft from the French Navy participated in the mission, providing surveillance and battle management capabilities. By temporarily incapacitating the airstrip, France was able to secure reinforcements of manpower and equipment to N'Djamena and to other spots closer to the 16th Parallel. The next day, in response to the French air raid, Libya sent a TU-22 on a long-range bombing mission over N'Djamena, but the strike did no serious damage. The operation involved all three French armed services, but with a heavy preponderance of the Air Force. Their assignment was to reinforce the deterrence capabilities of the Chadian government under the 16th Parallel and to prevent Libyan air superiority in southern Chad. French military missions were both defensive and offensive.

The main aspects of the initial deployment were completed by February 25, when the air defense system was declared operational. The installment of a radar belt surrounding N'Djamena was a priority objective. Specialized equipment for electronic warfare and intelligence collection were dispatched to Chad, including a DC-8 *Sarigue* and a *Gabriel*.[87] The U.S. made four Lockheed C-5A *Galaxies* available to the French Air Force for the transportation of French *Hawk* high-altitude air defense batteries. The latter were too large to be carried by French military transport planes.

Total forces under operation *Epervier* reached 2,300 troops, including elements of the 2nd Foreign Regiment of Infantry and the 22nd Marine Infantry Regiment. French ground troops were "tasked with training the Chadians in tactics and in the use of French-supplied hardware, maintaining equipment, providing intelligence and immediate fire support and protecting French bases."[88] The force configuration for air strikes and air support changed frequently over time, but was maintained at levels sufficient to carry out deep strike operations if called upon to do so. By July 1986, the air component of *Epervier* comprised six *Mirage* F-1Cs and two F-1CRs, sixteen *Jaguars*, six *Transalls*, four C-135s, and one *Atlantic*.[89]

Chad's internal situation evolved dramatically in the next few years. The political consolidation of Habré's domestic position was paralleled by one of the most stunning victories ever achieved by a sub-Saharan African army against a well-armed, Soviet-instructed force. In a series of highly successful campaigns, Habré's forces defeated a Libyan force estimated at 15,000 men and ousted them from Chad except for along the northern Aozou strip. The success of Habré's forces rested on his use of highly mobile, lightly armed columns against heavily armed Libyan formations. The first campaign achieved the reconquest of the strategically important palm plantation of Fada. Libya allegedly suffered 700 deaths (against 20 for Habré's forces) and lost 100 armored vehicles, including 30 tanks.[90] Libya retaliated by bombing the town of Arada, south of the Red Line. France responded on January 7, 1987 with a new air raid against the Ouadi Doum radar installations, "blinding" the Libyan Air Force. The objectives were limited to the radar installations.[91] The attack was carried out with fourteen planes, including *Mirage* and *Jaguar* strike aircraft.

The Chadian forces continued their rapid advance, capturing the positions of Zouar, and then, in a stunning 90-minute raid, the air base of Ouadi Doum, killing 1,200 Libyans.[92] Faya-Largeau, impossible to defend without air support from Ouadi Doum, was evacuated by the Libyans in April 1987. France and the U.S. closely monitored Habré's advance, supported him with logistical assistance, and shared regularly updated intelligence with his forces. French support had been transformed by the Chadian successes, as Mitterrand announced that: "There will be no French military intervention, but there will undoubtedly be support from France to allow Chad to dispose of the means to recover its dignity."[93] On December 16, 1986, French planes had parachuted arms and provisions to besieged Chadian forces in a move which was described as "exceptional."[94] In a further display of its support to the authorities in N'Djamena, France supplied heavy weapons material to the Chadians. Habré could rely on a solid rear base. Emboldened by their success, Chadian forces moved to take the city of Aozou, but failed to do so. They took their revenge on September 5, when they neutralized the air base of Maaten es Sara, located 65 miles inside Libyan territory, and destroyed or captured much equipment, including 22 military planes. Qaddafi responded with a triple air raid against Chadian positions. The French Army shot down one Libyan TU-22 above N'Djamena. A second TU-22 harmlessly dropped bombs at Abéché, and a third fled.[95] On September 11, Libya and Chad entered into a cease-fire agreement. In July 1989, Habré and Qaddafi met for the first time, in Mali, and Libya subsequently accepted recourse to the International Court of Justice for a peaceful settlement of the dispute over the Aozou strip.

After Habré's successful campaign resulting in the September 1987 cease-fire, the strength of *Epervier* has been gradually reduced from its 1987 peak of 2,700 troops. It was down to 1,500 troops by January 1989, and to 1,150 troops by January 1992. Some radar systems were dismantled, the *Transall* transport planes were no longer stationed permanently in Biltine, and the *Jaguar* strike aircraft were withdrawn to Bangui, although they paid occasional visits to Abéché. Even the French Navy pulled its *Atlantic* patrol plane back to its normal base in Dakar. In December 1989, the dismantling of the Abéché air defense system deprived *Epervier* of another 300 men.[96] The Air Force maintained only eight *Mirage* F-1Cs and two reconnaissance *Mirage* F-1CRs in N'Djamena and Abéché.[97] The defense system could be reinforced quickly from Bangui. One strategically important achievement of the French cooperation was to upgrade the airstrip in Faya-Largeau, which opened northern Chad and facilitated the resupplying of Chadian forces close to Libyan-held territory.

Habré's Fall and Déby's Problems

Just before Habré met with Qaddafi, Habré's brilliant former commander-in-chief, Idriss Déby, formed a new opposition party. Capitalizing on growing discontent with Habré's domestic policies, Déby could build a small force with which he would harass Habré's troops from bases in Sudan. An attack was repelled in March 1990, thanks in part to the French passive reinforcement of the Abéché bases, 135 km away from the Sudanese border. France dispatched two combat companies and a unit of the third Marine Infantry regiment based in N'Djamena, but none of these units saw combat. There have been reports that other French units, based in the CAR, went into Chad secretly and engaged Déby's forces in combat at Am-Guéréda on April 10, 1990.[98] Seven months later, the rebels based in Sudan launched an attack on border positions in Chad. France reinforced its garrison in Abéché, close to the zone of combat. In an effort to pre-empt the possibility of a French intervention, Déby formally announced to the French that he would not challenge the *Epervier* defense system.[99] France at that time was actively engaged in the military build-up in the

Gulf War and did not view the diversion of spare logistical capabilities to a new Chadian intervention favorably. Idriss Déby was eager to underline the domestic nature of the conflict, thereby attempting to defuse any perception of collusion with Libyan interests. On November 25-26, Déby achieved a series of significant victories over the governmental forces led by Habré, who narrowly escaped capture. The French spokesman at the Ministry of Foreign Affairs declared on November 27 that: "France is not involved and will not intervene in combats which are internal to Chad."[100] On December 2, 1990, Defense Minister Chevènement reminded the press that France refused to consider the attacks by Déby as an outside aggression, "purposely disregarding the massive deliveries of weapons by Libya to the rebel forces as a proof, however patent, of such an aggression."[101]

As a precaution, France dispatched a company of the 2nd Foreign Parachute Regiment from its base in Corsica to N'Djamena, with the stated objective of "ensuring the security of French citizens," a real concern in times of power vacuums in the Chadian capital.[102] A key town, Abéché, fell without combat on November 29, opening the way for the rebels to move to N'Djamena. French forces in Abéché did not move during the takeover. Two days later, Habré was reported to have fled the capital, while French forces in N'Djamena occupied strategic positions in the city.[103] With French tactical air support, the outcome of the conflict for Habré might have been radically different, but France denied him such assistance. Meanwhile, more French forces converged on N'Djamena, with reinforcements coming from Bouar in the CAR, and from Abéché, bringing the total in N'Djamena to 1,500. Roughly 950 expatriates were evacuated, and French troops protected one of the main Chadian military camps in town from being pillaged.[104] When Déby finally arrived in N'Djamena, his entry was low-key and bloodless.

The French political circles never fully trusted Habré, who was responsible for the continued detention of Claustre, a French aid worker, in April 1974. Habré's difficult character and his growing unpopularity made his departure an event which French authorities did not view with complete displeasure. The French military also had reason to distrust Habré after April 1975 when he tortured and executed Commandant Galopin, a French officer who had tried to negotiate the release of Claustre. There is little wonder why Idriss Déby, educated at French military academies and much admired for his military prowess and bravery, was the unacknowledged but preferred candidate of the French, even at the cost of temporarily renewed trouble in Chad. France neither created nor tried to inspire Déby's rebellion, but once he appeared victorious French authorities did nothing to stop him. They trusted that Déby would not let himself be manipulated by the Libyans, despite his *de facto* alliance and impressive arms deliveries from them.

The new Chadian authorities, under the leadership of Déby, asked France to maintain the reduced *Epervier* system in place with the same assignment of protecting Chad against external aggression. In December 1991, rebels supporting ousted President Habré, then still in exile in Senegal, threatened the government of Idriss Déby. Their vanguard was reported to be as close as 65 miles from the capital.[105] France quickly responded and dispatched 450 paratroopers to reinforce the 1,150-strong *Epervier* garrison already in Chad. Four *Jaguar* fighter-bombers were also added to the seven *Mirage*-F1s that the French Air Force had deployed in Chad. Reinforcements were flown in from French bases in Gabon, the CAR, and from Toulouse in France.[106] By securing key points in the capital, French troops allowed the Chadian president to send more of his troops to the front. The situation there rapidly evolved to favor government forces. One regiment of French paratroopers was repatriated on January 7, 1992. "France's quick response was widely interpreted as a warning to Habré that French troops would intervene to prevent the overthrow of the Déby government."[107] As an African advisor at the Elysée confided to *Libération*: "France could not let Déby down; even though he is no true head of state, he does what we advise him to do."[108]

GISCARD'S LONELY STRUGGLE AGAINST DESTABILIZATION

The Gaullist presumption of a lasting coziness in the military relationship between France and many of its African allies was shattered in the mid-1970s. In the name of non-alignment and greater independence from the former colonial ruler, several francophone African nations, led by President Diori of Niger, renegotiated or canceled their defense agreements with France. This came when greater Soviet assertiveness on the African continent opened a credible alternative to dependence on western patrons, or at least provided African countries with a strategic blackmail option to raise the stakes.

By the mid-1970s, Soviet-Cuban penetration in Africa received a dramatic impetus with the independence of the Portuguese colonies, which followed Soviet gains on the Horn of Africa. France woke up to the new reality that its African partners, whom had been taken for granted for so long, could suddenly become the prey of a new rival power. President Giscard d'Estaing took the lead among western nations in what French analysts perceived as a "battle against destabilization."[109] In this perspective, the most dramatic interventions were two French operations in Zaire's southern Shaba province in 1977 and 1978. Giscard also pursued an active policy on the Horn of Africa which resulted in two military operations in Djibouti in 1976 and 1977, when the Soviet Union was heavily consolidating its influence in that region. Contact between Emperor Bokassa and the Libyans triggered Giscard's controversial order to remove the emperor of the CAR, an operation which French troops executed without bloodshed.[110] Elsewhere, French aircraft launched a bombing strike in Mauritania against advancing columns of the Polisario Front on November 1977; French troops remained involved in Mauritania until May 1978 and intervened again in 1979. Giscard took advantage of an unstable situation in Africa, where Soviet penetration seemed more dangerous than ever before or since, to enhance France's position as the only true guarantor of stability on the continent.

Djibouti (1976-77)

During the 1970s, France had to protect Djibouti from Somali and Ethiopian annexation ambitions. On September 28, 1974, right after the fall of the emperor of Ethiopia and when Djibouti was still under French control, the French Navy dispatched a task force, code-named *Saphir*, which included the *Clemenceau* aircraft carrier with four escort and support ships. Somalia was prevented from taking advantage of Ethiopia's domestic weakness to annex Djibouti. The mission lasted six months and achieved its goal of marking French resolve to protect Djibouti while major changes were occurring in neighboring countries.

In the following years, France moved toward granting independence to Djibouti, a delicate process given the historic antagonism between the two leading ethnic groups in the country, the Afars and the Issas. Independence, on June 27, 1977, came amidst an explosive regional background marked by the Ogaden War between Somalia and Ethiopia. France's concern with Soviet expansionism in the region compounded its concern with the ethnic tensions inside and outside Djibouti's border. On April 16, 1977, a new naval task force, baptized *Saphir II*, was sent to Djibouti to thwart attempts at destabilizing the country during the independence transition process and to protect the new republic from its neighbors' irredentist claims. The means available to the task force were impressive: at first, the *Clemenceau* was dispatched with an escort and a supply ship; she was relieved by the *Foch* just before the independence date so that the two aircraft carriers would be present at the most critical time.[111] The *Foch* remained offshore from Djibouti until November 30, 1977. It was not a coincidence that the *Foch*'s withdrawal occurred only two weeks after the expulsion of the 6,000 Soviet advisors from Somalia, which ended the Soviet's overwhelming predominance in the region. The Soviet switch of alliance in favor of Ethiopia, combined with widespread international recognition of Djibouti's independence, made it possible for France to withdraw its costly naval task force.

French forces where not involved in actual combat during either of the two *Saphir* operations. This did not preclude them from pursuing a forceful policy of high visibility. Air sorties launched from the aircraft carriers reached 2,300 during the six-month operation of *Saphir I*, and the sortie rate reached 4,300 during the eight months of *Saphir II*.[112] The offshore positioning of the aircraft carriers was deemed indispensable despite the French Air Force presence at the Ambouli air base in Djibouti. Given the proximity of the Somali border, the aircraft stationed in Ambouli had only a one-minute warning. The aircraft carriers were able to position themselves at a safer distance.[113]

The highly specialized anti-terrorist unit of the French gendarmerie performed another action in the region at the time of Djibouti's independence. Since 1974-75, a banned liberation group called the *Front de libération de la Côte des Somalis* had organized violent demonstrations in the French colony of Djibouti. This group benefitted from the active support of Mogadishu. In one instance in 1976, the group took a school bus of Djibouti children hostage along the Somali border at Loyada. France responded by sending elements of its police unit, the GIGN (*Groupement d'intervention de la gendarmerie nationale*). The police unit was flown over from France, and soon rescued the thirty captive children; unfortunately, two of them had been killed and several others wounded.[114]

Mauritania (1977-80)

In 1973, the *Frente Popular para la Liberación de Sakiet el Hamra y Río de Oro*, better known as the Polisario Front, was created with the objective of achieving the self-determination of the Western Sahara. Algeria and Libya were its principal backers. The Front soon brought the armed struggle into Mauritania, which in December 1975 had annexed one-third of the Western Sahara, while Morocco had annexed the other two-thirds. The Polisario Front mounted guerrilla attacks against Mauritanian interests in the Western Sahara and in Mauritania itself; it also harassed French interests in the region. An attack on Nouakchott by the Front in June 1976, although militarily unsuccessful, was a major shock to Mauritanian morale. The Mauritanian government signed new military agreements with France soon afterwards.

In 1977, French assistance to Mauritania was stepped up under operation *Lamentin*, directed out of the French base in Dakar and out of Nouakchott. Its primary objective was to stop the Polisario advances and the destruction of economic targets by Polisario commandos.[115] The operation was also a response to the abduction of eight French citizens by Polisario guerrillas during an attack on Zouérate in May 1977. Zouérate, a town in northeast Mauritania, is the center of an important mineral extraction complex and is vital to the Mauritanian economy. France initially provided assistance to build up the Mauritanian forces from 3,000 to more than 15,000 troops.[116] The French Air Force dispatched about ten *Jaguar* aircraft with tanker-transport planes in November 1977. Moroccan troops were airlifted by the French Air Force to assist the Mauritanians in the fight.   French strike planes first raided Polisario columns on December 12-13, 1977 after a Mauritanian train transporting iron ore from Zouérate to the port of Nouadhibou was attacked. Following the offensive the Polisario regrouped its forces to provide concentrated air cover during the withdrawal phase. In coordination with Moroccan artillery and reconnaissance planes, and with Mauritanian ground forces, four French *Jaguars* dealt a decisive blow to the retreating Polisario columns, destroying up to 150 vehicles as well as stocks of fuel and ammunition.[117] Although the Polisario claimed to have hit several airplanes, French authorities denied any losses. On December 18 and 19, 1977, French airplanes raided a second time in retaliation against a Polisario attack on the Mauritanian garrison in Tmeimichat, a position a few miles from the border with Western Sahara and on the railroad linking Zouérate to the harbor of Nouadhibou. Given the limited range of the *Jaguar* airplanes and the modest number of tanker planes available, the raids were logistically difficult to carry out and required precise intelligence on the whereabouts of the Polisario columns. The aircraft, based in Dakar, were only equipped with guns; the distance did not allow for either heavy bombing loads or a prolonged presence.[118] This time, the Moroccan Force participated in the attacks on fleeing Polisario columns. Less than a week later, on December 23, 1977, the Polisario released eight French hostages in Algiers.

The French Navy was present offshore Mauritania in December 1977. Although this naval deployment had been planned well before the crisis as part of a routine exercise, the Western Saharan conflict gave it a special significance. President Giscard d'Estaing had envisioned sending an aircraft carrier, but none were available in December 1977. An aircraft carrier would have been able to launch an air attack from much closer to the combat zone than was the case with the *Jaguars* in Dakar.[119] The Navy also operated five *Atlantic* long-range reconnaissance planes to monitor the movement of the Polisario.

In another instance of French air support to Mauritanian ground forces, in May 1978, *Jaguar* aircraft raided Polisario columns in the vicinity of Zouérate. Although French authorities denied that French planes had operated above the Western Saharan airspace, conflicting reports placed the French attack squarely outside Mauritanian borders.[120] In the course of the same month, French air cover under operation *Lamentin* was officially terminated.[121]

The French Tactical Air Force executed one of the most spectacular aspects of this operation, but the Navy also undertook many monitoring and other supportive actions and the Army sent special forces to Dakar, as well as 105 military instructors who were "more or less running the Mauritanian Army."[122] French military support was complemented by assistance from Kuwait, Morocco and Saudi Arabia. Despite their combined efforts, Mauritania proved to be very vulnerable to Polisario attacks. It was some time before Mauritania could extricate itself completely from the conflict because of the inertia of a peace process in which other countries such as Morocco (which maintained 9,000 troops in Mauritania), Algeria, France, Libya and others were also involved. An agreement between Mauritania and the Polisario Front was eventually reached in August 1979, whereby Mauritania relinquished all claims on the Western Sahara. In turn, France ended its direct and overt role in the conflict on Mauritania's side.

After the July 1978 coup, French military personnel in Mauritania decreased rapidly. In August 1979, following the peace agreement, France agreed to provide Mauritania with up to 200 advisors and technical personnel to run a training program at Nouadhibou and to continue running a French military air communication center at Lamentin, near Nouakchott. Out of Dakar, the French Air Force continued its reconnaissance flights over Mauritania.[123] By May 1980, the Mauritanian government had expelled the 200 French advisors.

Zaire (1977)

In the spring of 1977, a group of insurgents, heirs to the Katangese secessionist gendarmes of the early 1960s, reappeared in Zaire after twelve years of exile in Angola. They belonged to the Lunda ethnic group, which was spread over an area comprising the Zairian Shaba province (formerly Katanga), northern Zambia, and part of eastern Angola. In the early 1960s, after the secessionist adventure with Tschombé, Katangese gendarmes took refuge in Angola. When the *Movimento Popular de Libertaçào de Angola* (MPLA) of Agosthino Neto took power in Luanda, the Katangese were courted by the MPLA in the latter's war against rival contenders for power. The rapprochement between the MPLA and the Katangese was not a mere alliance of interest; it involved modifying the ideological orientation of Katangese refugees, and, more relevantly, providing them with weapons and training. In 1968, Nathanael Mbumba, former police commissioner of Kolwezi under Tschombé, founded the Katangese political movement called the *Front de libération nationale du Congo* (FLNC). The ranks of the former Katangese gendarmes were enlarged and rejuvenated by successive waves of Lunda sympathizers, family-members and refugees. Mbumba allegedly visited Cuba and East Germany in July and September 1976 to negotiate aid. Cuba provided advisors and training, and East Germany contributed weapons.[124]

The Katangese Lunda's attempted to take over the Shaba region, possibly pre-empting the imminent normalization of relations between Angola and Zaire. The act implied the political and military neutralization of all Zairian organized dissidence in Angola and assumed the weakening of the Mobutu regime by internal discontent in Zaire. Shaba was the major source of wealth for Zaire, and its loss would render the central government more vulnerable. On March 8, 1977, 2,500 men of the FLNC entered Zaire. Disorganized and unprepared for the attack, units in the border region of the 33,400-member Zairian Army fled or collapsed altogether with very little fighting.[125] The rebels advanced 80 km inside Zairian territory and took control of several localities.

The popularity of the FLNC in Shaba was more than the result of ethnic links; it was also the expression of serious discontent with the behavior of the Zairian authorities and the brutality of the armed forces, particularly in Shaba. Avoiding any references to a Katangese connection, President Mobutu denounced the event as an international aggression carried out by mercenaries from Angola with Soviet, Eastern German and Cuban support. He then called on his western backers, mainly France and the U.S., for military assistance.

At first, the American administration under Carter responded timidly to these events, but soon embraced the Zairian cause with more ardor and sent C-130s, ammunition, parachutes, and other equipment. The Belgian government was in the midst of a crisis, a rather frequent occurrence in the 1970s, when the government had just offered its resignation. The Belgians extended some cautious help, mainly in the form of accelerated weapons delivery. Belgian political forces were split over what sort of attitude to take. Some parties saw the Katangese invasion as an opportunity to abolish the Mobutu regime, not wishing to compromise current and future political relations by offering the perhaps tottering regime too ardent support. Belgium abstained from any form of direct military intervention.

France was much more supportive. At the request of Zairian president Mobutu, France intervened indirectly and in a measured way. Many French citizens worked in the Shaba region, and France was eager to keep the mineral resources there away from superpower rivalry.[126] Giscard d'Estaing had favored a drastic improvement in Franco-Zairian relations and wanted to signal to Mobutu that French authorities supported him during times of instability. France, under President Pompidou, had signed a General Agreement of Technical Military Cooperation. This agreement included the dispatchment to Kinshasa of a French military advisor. France sold 35 *Puma* and *Alouette* helicopters, 17 *Mirage*-5s, and 290 light armored vehicles.[127] France's interest in Zaire was motivated by commercial considerations and Zaire's tremendous reservoir of minerals, but also by the shared language. France could not allow Soviet proxies destabilize its newly consolidated interests.

An open French intervention was not deemed appropriate, and France developed a scheme whereby one battalion of Moroccan troops would be sent on 10 French *Transall* planes and one DC-8. An appeal by Mobutu to the OAU requesting assistance against an external aggressor provided the justification for this Moroccan operation. Operation *Verveine*, as the French would call it, began on April 6. France's role was limited to air transportation of the Moroccan forces, 125 vehicles, and 50 tons of ammunition. It involved 25 air crews, comprised of 125 individuals plus a ground crew of 25.[128] In his memoirs, President Giscard d'Estaing would later admit that a few French troops had participated in the ground operations: "General Méry had taken the initiative to send a team of a dozen parachutists to mark our presence and to collect intelligence."[129]

The 1,256 Moroccan soldiers were transported to the operation zone which extended 70 km west of Kolwezi. The rebels were soon defeated and left the country completely during the second half of May. Towns and villages were often reconquered from the FLNC without fighting. The rebel attack caused 247 casualties, eight missing in action, and 343 wounded on the Zairian side, plus 29 military men condemned to death.[130] After May 20, the Moroccans decided that their presence was no longer necessary and ceased their military operations, marking the end of the first Shaba crisis.

The Carter Administration approved of the French operation, which was only criticized by progressive African countries. Moroccan troops did all of the actual fighting. The Egyptian government of Saddat also provided a team of pilots and ground-crews totalling 50 persons and put *Antonov* transport planes at the disposal of the intervention force. In Belgium, the French master-minded operation was seen as a French supplantation of Belgian power in Belgium's former colony.[131] The Belgian foreign minister bitterly remarked that: "The French have not asked us for our advice on their Zairian policy. I have insisted on receiving continuous and precise information from them [...] but one cannot really consider that there were consultations or meetings."[132] The Belgian resentment lingered until the second Shaba crisis in 1978 and affected the way France and Belgium would implement their respective interventions.

Zaire (1978)

Both France and Belgian launched simultaneous, although barely coordinated, interventions during the second attempt by ex-Katangese rebels to destabilize the Shaba region in southern Zaire. The French operation *Bonite*, in May-June 1978, involved 600 Foreign Legion agents in an effort to rescue Kolwezi and protect expatriates. These interventions, with U.S. assistance, are described in Chapter 12.

Central African Republic (1979)

Operation *Barracuda*, by which French troops removed Emperor Bokassa I of the Central African Empire on the night of September 20, 1979, was one of the most controversial military interventions carried out by France. It became a landmark against which other interventions would be evaluated. Soon after his election, President Mitterrand vowed never to authorize any *Barracuda*-type operations. An acceptable rationale for intervention to remove the emperor was built around Bokassa's increasingly barbarous and megalomaniacal rule. His excesses had become intolerable, and "conducive in the long-run to the worst anarchy."[133] The scandal of *Barracuda* was that it was such a blatant interference in the internal affairs of a foreign country against the recognized authorities. The shock was exacerbated by the fact that, after giving France his virtually unconditional support (Bokassa had insisted on keeping his French nationality), he was deposed once he ceased to be useful to his patrons.

Colonel Jean-Bédel Bokassa started his despotic reign with a coup d'état in December 1965. His relationship with France was initially marked by mutual suspicion and distrust. The situation changed with the March 1975 visit of President Giscard d'Estaing, which opened an era of more cordial relations. President Bokassa's consolidation of power culminated in his Napoleonic coronation in December 1977. During student demonstrations and riots in January and April 1979, the Army killed between 150 and 200 protesters and took 100 adolescents to prison, where they were beaten and tortured to death. These later massacres brought considerable embarrassment to French authorities. France encouraged the creation of an international African Mission of Inquiry which, on August 16, 1979, concluded with "quasi-certainty" that the emperor had personally participated in the prison massacres.[134] France in vain advised Bokassa to step down before the findings of the Mission of Inquiry were made public. A meeting between Giscard's

African advisor, René Journiac, and the emperor was arranged by President Bongo in Franceville, Gabon. Journiac reiterated the French advice. Bokassa allegedly responded by hitting Journiac with his cane.[135] On August 17, France ceased all assistance to the country, except for essential education, food and health support. The token military assistance had been suspended in May.

Bokassa then turned toward Libya for aid and went to see Qaddafi on September 20. This visit was a major concern to France, which at the time was engaged militarily against Libyan-sponsored insurgents in Chad. Bokassa had already accepted to be converted to Islam during a previous visit to Tripoli in September 1976. No doubt Qaddafi would have obtained major concessions from the desperate emperor. Libya had already dispatched a team of 37 police advisors. French authorities were fed up with the erratic and brutal behavior of their former protégé and wanted to prevent any form of alliance between Libya and the Central African Empire. The night the emperor was in Tripoli, an estimated 1,000 French troops were flown in from Chad and Gabon and moved to the strategic points in Bangui.[136] They had come to re-establish the republic. Around 11:30 pm, one hour after the arrival of the first French units, David Dacko, a former ruler of the country, disembarked from a French *Transall*. Dacko had been informed in advance of the French plan and had been waiting in N'Djamena for a French plane. He announced the end of the empire and was installed as president. Bokassa, meanwhile was refused asylum in France and took refuge in Côte d'Ivoire. French troops reactivated the military base at Douar and in the following months maintained a visible presence in the newly rechristened the Central African Republic.

Operation *Barracuda* is still remembered as "the most shameful intervention by France in the internal affairs of an African government."[137] What had gone wrong in the political exploitation of the otherwise smoothly run operation? A distinguished African panel accused Bokassa of almost certain participation in a serious crime. His style and eccentricities were a source of embarrassment to many African governments. The French intervention had been approved by four African presidents: Houphouët-Boigny of Côte d'Ivoire, Senghor of Senegal, Mobutu of Zaire, and Bongo of Gabon, although they could not agree on a successor to Bokassa.[138] A crowd of 200,000 people in Bangui had cheered the fall of the emperor with chants of: "*Vive la France!*"[139] The fact was that after the early euphoria, there was a feeling of humiliation among Africans. The French president was the manipulator, the "Super-Foccart,[140]" installing a hand-picked candidate, by force of arms, without any consultation with other political personalities in the country. The anger at France was compounded by the fact that the removal of the emperor was partly the result of Giscard's own miscalculations after supporting him so eagerly. Giscard had rid Africa of a brutal dictator, but in a clumsy and arrogant way. It would be Giscard's last military intervention, and, during the French presidential campaign in 1980-81, his handling of Bokassa's removal would often be criticized by his opponents.

MONITORING EMERGING POLITICAL FORCES

Coinciding with the arrival of François Mitterrand at the Elysée in the early 1980s, strong political forces have been reshaping many African nations. From tiny, exposed island states to giants like Zaire, popular movements or special interest groups have, with weapons in hand, expressed their political discontent. France has been involved in a variety of these confrontations, and often the mere appearance of French troops would suffice to calm the antagonists in a given crisis. By the early 1990s, however, the frequency and intensity of the confrontations had increased, and some situations were spinning out of control. Africa's awakening to democratic reforms presented France with an unusual challenge: how to encourage those necessary reforms without destabilizing the continent and without overstretching France's patience and military commitment.

Seychelles (1981)

Small island states like Seychelles and the Comoros have been particularly vulnerable to coups d'état, many of them carried out by mercenaries. In November 1981, more than five years after its independence from Britain in June 1976, Seychelles was subjected to a third coup attempt. A group of 50 men, mainly South African mercenaries, attempted to overthrow the government of Albert René. Government forces detected them upon their arrival at the airport and captured six of them after fierce fighting. The other 44 mercenaries hijacked a plane and flew back to South Africa, where they were arrested and later tried. Allegedly, South African defense officials inspired or at least knew about the coup.[141]

Tanzania dispatched 400 troops to restore order. France sent a warship and followed up with a team of military experts. Hindsight suggests that both countries may have overestimated the threat of the events in the Seychelles and overreacted. President Réné had requested French intervention. Part of France's rationale for sending a warship also stemmed from a desire not to leave the initiative to the Soviet Union, which at the time was trying to gain additional footholds in the Indian Ocean region as support points for its Navy.[142]

Cameroon (1981)

Border disputes between Nigeria and Cameroon have always been latent, waiting for a pretext to flare up. Territorial waters were the subject of a particularly violent episode on May 16, 1981. A shooting incident occurred between the Cameroonian Coast Guard and its Nigerian counterparts in the Rio del Rey area, which is in Cameroonian territory. As a result, seven members of the Nigerian Coast Guard were killed, with no Cameroonian losses. The fact that these coastal waters of the contested area were covering oil fields made the ensuing diplomatic and military escalation even more difficult to calm. Both countries were at the verge of severing all relations, and there was risk of war. The next day, authorities in Lagos organized a televised public relations campaign, inflating the incident out of proportion and trying to enhance anti-Cameroonian resentment. The government began to speak openly of its intention to launch a retaliatory action.[143] The tension continued to build during the next few weeks. The Nigerian Federal Government conspicuously moved *Mig* fighter aircraft closer to the border, and Nigerian military planes were in frequent violation of Cameroonian airspace. At the end of May, the Nigerian foreign minister notified the French chargé d'affaires that Nigeria was ready to take "corrective" measure against Cameroon and threatened to freeze French interests in Nigeria if France meddled in the dispute.[144]

For President Mitterrand, elected a week before the incident, the crisis became the first test of his approach to African security affairs. Paris at first reassured Yaoundé of its unconditional support. Then, in collaboration with the United States, the French informed the Nigerian authorities that France would not stand by passively, but would intervene on the side of the Cameroonians. Mr. Ahidjo, then president of Cameroon, was promised immediate intervention in the form of French *Jaguars* based in Libreville and airborne troops stationed in

Bangui.[145] At the request of the Cameroonian government, France approved weapons deliveries "to face a possible worsening of the border tension with Nigeria," but also because Cameroon was a valuable asset for French operations in Chad. Strong French support eventually deterred Nigeria from its military enterprise, and the dispute was later resolved through OAU mediation.

Gambia (1981)

On July 30, 1981, civilian conspirators attempted a coup against the regime of the Gambian president, Sir Dawda Jawara. He was in London at the time and requested the assistance of Senegal. Nearly 3,000 Senegalese troops entered Gambia from different directions, and within a week had routed the rebel forces. The operation was successful, albeit at heavy cost in Gambian lives, and the Senegalese forces were asked to stay.[146] Paris gave its green light and supported the Senegalese action, while the British government sent a special force team to free hostages, including the president's first wife, who had been taken by the rebels.[147] Senegal had signed a mutual defense pact with Gambia in 1966 and revised it in 1980. The bulk of the Senegalese intervention was carried out by Senegalese para-commandos who had been airlifted in two successive waves to the airport close to the Gambian capital. If all Senegalese aircraft had been operational, the Senegalese Air Force could have accomplished the airlift on its own with its six *Dakotas* from the 1940s and its six *Fokker* F-27s, although it has been suggested that French logistical support and possibly air transport capabilities were made available to the Senegalese.[148]

This action is illustrative of an indirect intervention; France was not acting in Gambia through a Senegalese proxy, but rather supported a regional action by a close ally. France's interests in Gambia are quite limited, but because Gambia is surrounded by Senegalese territory, Senegal has good reason to promote Gambian stability. The extreme leftist political convictions of the Gambian coup leader, Kukli Samba Sanyang, may have contributed to the Franco-Senegalese perception of a threat to regional stability. The Gambian military dependency on its neighbor led to the creation of the Confederation of Senegambia in December 1981 to cover defense and security issues, foreign policy, communications and transport. The Confederation was dissolved in September 1989 due to divergences in the extent of integration necessary between the two countries.

Togo (1986)

On the night of September 23-24, 1986, a squad of at least 70 armed men, who, according to the Togolese authorities, had come from Ghana, crossed the border into Togo and started occupying strategic points in Lomé, the capital. The attackers moved to occupy the military barracks in Lomé where President Gnassingbé Eyadema's resided, the radio station, and the headquarters of Togo's sole political party. The invaders intended to kill President Eyadema and establish a provisional government under Captain Francisco Lawson, an exiled army officer, and Gilchrist Olympio, the son of Togo's first president. President Olympio had been assassinated in 1963 by an army group led by Eyadema. The two insurgent leaders were enjoying asylum in Ghana at the time and were known to have tried to rally opponents of the Eyadema regime.

The fighting between the Togolese armed forces and the attackers officially left about 20 dead, although unofficial sources put the total closer to 80. During heavy street fighting, 40 attackers were arrested,[149] two of whom were said to have had Ghanaian identification papers. Six civilians were also killed, among them a French and a German national. While there was no doubt that the insurgents had launched their attack from Ghana, Togolese authorities most likely exaggerated the extent of Ghanaian involvement. For Eyadema, the foreign involvement allowed him to turn public attention away from domestic security problems, which were the real source of his troubles.[150] Alleged foreign involvement also placed the attack within the scope of the defense agreements with France.

On September 25, France dispatched 180 soldiers[151] to Lomé to prop up Eyadema's regime and quell insurgent moves before the Franco-African summit was held there in mid-November. These troops did not move out of their assigned camp in Lomé. President François Mitterrand ordered the military intervention after a telephone call from the Togolese leader. The French Ministry of Defense announced that the Togolese president had invoked the 1963 defense agreement between the two countries and requested military aid. The French troops were backed by four *Jaguar* fighter-bombers flying for days over Lomé in a show of support to President Eyadema. In a further display of force, the French Navy sent the mine hunter *Croix du Sud* on a "routine visit" to Lomé during the same month.[152] On September 26, three days after the coup attempt, Zairian president Mobutu placed

350 troops "at the disposal of the Togo government," with no time limit on the duration of their stay.[153] The mere presence of the French military was sufficient to calm the insurrectionists. No fighting was reported, and France withdrew its troops after a fortnight.

The rapid French reaction was partly due to France's domestic political situation. During the period of *cohabitation* in France, President François Mitterrand and Prime Minister Jacques Chirac were engaged in competition to show the extent of their solidarity with their African friends at a time France was being heavily criticized for failing to check Qaddafi's advance in Chad.[154] The show of international solidarity with African friends was meant to symbolize French strength and determination to act as a responsible partner in Africa.

Congo (1987)

The Congolese Army attacked a village called Owando in northern Congo on September 6, 1987. The village had been barricaded by family and supporters of Pierre Anga, an opposition figure to the Congolese president Denis Sassou-Nguesso. The Army had earlier on come to arrest Anga on suspicion of participating in a July 1987 coup plot against the president. Anga refused to go quietly, and an officer and several soldiers of the arresting force were killed.[155] An assault force, which included some Cuban paratroopers, was later dispatched on a French military transport plane.[156] The attack left four dead by the official estimate, although opposition groups claimed much higher (and probably exaggerated) casualty figures.[157] Anga escaped, but he did not have the popular support to stage another successful coup or present a serious threat to the government.

France's military role in quelling the Owando rebellion was very limited; what made it remarkable was that the French response had been elaborated and implemented by the French prime minister, Jacques Chirac, and not by the president. A year earlier, "Sassou-Nguesso dropped his official anti-imperialist and anti-Zionist line and improved relations with France, and notably Prime Minister Jacques Chirac."[158] Sassou-Nguesso reactivated the military cooperation agreement which had remained frozen for 23 years. When the Owando rebellion started, the Congolese president requested one military transport plane. He addressed his demand directly to the prime minister's office. Jacques Chirac immediately acceded to this request without informing the Elysée.[159] Mitterrand had to remind Chirac that decisions involving the dispatch of French troops overseas were the constitutional responsibility of the president.[160]

Comoros (1989)

The Comoros unilaterally declared independence on July 6, 1975. It signed a defense agreement with France three years later, which allowed for "mutual assistance" in case of external aggression.[161] It also included French technical military aid to train the 1,000-strong Comoro army. At the occasion of a widely contested constitutional referendum, violent protestors accused President Ahmed Abdallah of electoral fraud. Abdallah, who had staged and endured coup attempts, was assassinated on the night of November 26-27, 1989 by members of the presidential guard. Witnesses later testified that Bob Denard, Africa's most infamous soldier of fortune, was personally involved in the murder, although there are conflicting versions of the events.[162] Immediately following the assassination, Denard staged a violent coup against the constitutionally designated interim president, leaving 27 policemen dead and 200 people under arrest.[163] Denard apparently led 500 presidential guardsmen and 30 French and Belgian mercenaries in a rocket attack on the police headquarters and army barracks at Moroni on the night of November 28.

In the months following the death of Abdallah, Denard found himself facing increased isolation and domestic unrest as South Africa and France made diplomatic efforts to rid the Comoros of the mercenaries. A Comoro opposition leader, Mr. Mouni Madi, asked the French government to intervene on the grounds that the mercenaries were holding the people of Comoros hostage.[164] France's response to the crisis emphasized at first using diplomatic channels in cooperation with South Africa and flexing French naval muscle around the island of Grande Comore. South Africa, which had heavily subsidized the Comoro presidential guard for years, offered asylum to the mercenaries in exchange for their peaceful withdrawal. While Denard's presidential guard was fortifying positions around the capital and recruiting reinforcements in Paris, France put an 800-man task force on alert on the French island of Mayotte, some 120 miles southeast of Grande Comore.[165] It included the 250 French troops garrisoned on Mayotte and 300 Foreign Légionnaires. Marine Commandos were also flown in, and four French warships anchored off the island.[166]

France adopted a strategy of pressuring Denard by a show of force. The use of French troops in an intervention maneuver had been firmly ruled out in a joint statement released by President Mitterrand and Prime Minister Michel Rocard on December 13, 1989. After a negotiated settlement of the crisis, 50 French paratroopers flew on board five *Puma* helicopters to the islands' capital for a brief ceremonial hand-over of power on December 15, during which the French commander refused to talk directly to Denard. Denard and 25 French and Belgian acolytes left for Johannesburg on board a South African military aircraft the same day.[167] The South Africans played a key role in the negotiations that led to the mercenaries' agreement to leave without a fight. South Africa had been out-maneuvered by the French each step of the way during the negotiations. "The result is that while South Africa has been left holding Denard and his band of thugs, the French have been left holding the Comoros."[168] Under a two-year assistance program approved by the new provisional government, the French police assumed control of the Comoro police, French military officers took control of the Comoro army, and French paratroopers took over the presidential guard.[169]

Gabon (1990)

On May 22, 1990, the National Assembly and the single political party in power in Gabon approved the adoption of a constitutional reform program that would open the country to a multi-party political system. The next day, riots erupted in Libreville and Port-Gentil when Joseph Rendjambe, leader of the main opposition party, the PGP (*Parti gabonais du progrès*), was found dead in a Libreville hotel room. PGP supporters accused the government of having killed him. On May 24, the PGP staged large demonstrations in the main Gabonese cities, and order collapsed in Port-Gentil. The population, unhappy about declining revenues due to the drop in oil prices, went on a rampage. Similar rioting occurred in Lambaréné and other cities. An irate mob took the French vice-consul in Port-Gentil hostage, but released him soon afterwards. Eight French citizens working in the petroleum sector in Port-Gentil were also held hostage and released after a few hours. Meanwhile, President Omar Bongo had ordered his elite presidential guard to position tanks around the presidential palace in Libreville.

Although there were few anti-French manifestations, hundreds of the 20,000 French citizens living in Gabon felt sufficiently threatened to want to leave the country.[170] With the breakdown of the Gabonese armed forces, which were unable to cope with the rioters, President Mitterrand sent two companies to Gabon, one from the 2nd Foreign Parachute Division based at Calvi and one from the 2nd Foreign Infantry Division regiment based at Nîmes. Roughly 300 men in total, these troops supplemented the 500 French troops of the 6 BIMA normally stationed in the country. The operation was code-named *Requin*. The Quai d'Orsay announced that the intervention was only for the protection and repatriation of expatriates, and that the French troops had no mandate to intervene in Gabon's internal affairs.[171] The 1960 Security Accords between France and Gabon included secret provisions for assistance in the case of domestic disorder, but this agreement was not invoked in the 1990 intervention. On May 25, Port-Gentil appeared to be calm and the oil fields out of danger. The city had suffered a great deal of destruction from the rioting, and PGP supporters continued to hold demonstrations for the resignation of President Bongo. In Libreville, all had returned to normal by Sunday, May 27. Elf-Gabon resumed offshore oil production by May 29.

The PGP opposition, having claimed to be pro-French with no intention of harming French citizens in Gabon, was disappointed by the French reaction.[172] The French forces assumed the delicate role of gendarme without trying to repress the emergence of a genuine democracy. They took position at sensitive points, patrolled the streets of Port-Gentil, and closely monitored the situation throughout the country. They did not actively participate in restoring public order. Arguably, both sides benefitted from the French military presence. For the government, the advantages appeared obvious: "By reinforcing - even temporarily - the contingent stationed for thirty years in Gabon, Paris provided a serious support to the beleaguered regime of President Omar Bongo."[173] For the opposition, it is likely that the French intervention moderated the repression by the authorities, granting them some international audience and national standing after rather hastily organized political demonstrations.

By the first of June, French Foreign Minister Roland Dumas was sufficiently satisfied with the restoration of peace to Port-Gentil that he reduced the French forces.[174] The intervention was considered an overall success, executed with great smoothness and a minimum of casualties. The official totals were three Gabonese nationals killed and six to twelve wounded. The French suffered no casualties. After the events, President Bongo heeded some of the demands of the opposition and agreed to share the executive power with a prime minister.

Liberia (1990)

In December 1989, Liberian rebel leader Charles Taylor launched an uprising that engulfed Liberia in a devastating civil war. Taylor led a small group of 200 to 300 rebels across the border from Côte d'Ivoire into Liberia. Local recruitment rapidly swelled the numbers of the insurgents, while at the same time reducing discipline. President Samuel Doe and his U.S.-equipped army put up a fierce resistance. Taylor was further prevented from taking the capital by division within his own ranks. By early June, the battles and massacres taking place around the capital forced the United States, and to a lesser degree France and Britain, to prepare contingency evacuation plans and send naval tasks forces to the area.

The U.S. Navy dispatched a Marine Expeditionary Unit under operation *Sharp Edge*. The first elements of the U.S. task force arrived off Monrovia on June 2, 1990. The force, which included the amphibious assault ship *Saipan*, remained on stand-by for two months. On August 6, following a threat by one of the rebel leaders to take U.S. hostages, about 250 Marines landed within the U.S. embassy compound and over two weeks evacuated 1,600 foreign nationals.[175]

Meanwhile, the French government sent the naval landing ship *Ouragan* to the region to assist in the evacuation of French expatriates. Leaving the port of Toulon on May 29, the ship stopped first in Dakar and remained available for possible further action.[176] After the successful U.S. operation, French forces were not called upon to intervene in Liberia. The rebels killed the Liberian president on September 9, 1990, after capturing him inside the headquarters of a five-nation West African force (ECOWAS Monitoring Group or ECOMOG) established to bring peace to Liberia.

Rwanda (1990-91)

See Chapter 12 for a detailed description of the joint Franco-Belgian intervention in Rwanda in late Fall of 1990.

Djibouti (1991)

In May 1991, about 40,000 Ethiopian refugees, most of them from the Ethiopian armed forces, crossed the border into Djibouti during the collapse of President Mengistu's regime. The massive inflow of heavily armed military refugees was particularly threatening for Djibouti's 4,100 man armed forces, as the Ethiopians moved with tanks and other heavy military equipment. Politically, the Ethiopians could tip the delicate ethnic balance between the Afars and the Issa, the two core groups in Djibouti. President Mitterrand authorized French troops stationed in the country to assist Djibouti's forces in coping with the refugees, first disarming and then deporting them.[177] This mission, code-named operation *Godoria*, was perfectly compatible with the 1977 defense agreement, as it was considered a French response to an external threat to Djibouti. In parallel with this operation, France launched a second operation called *Totem*, providing emergency medical support in Ethiopia between May 25 and 27. Only one *Transall* airplane was involved to transport the medical team and a few vehicles. *Totem* was exclusively a humanitarian operation, unlike *Godoria*.

Only months later, President Hassan Gouled Aptidon of Djibouti faced a domestic uprising, which resulted in violent clashes between Afars guerrillas and government troops. President Gouled requested France's assistance under the 1977 defense agreement.[178] His claim that Djibouti was the victim of external aggression, however, was not accepted by France as justifying anything more than providing mediation between the contending factions.

Zaire (1991)

See Chapter 12 for a detailed description of the joint French, Belgian, and U.S. evacuation operation in Zaire during late 1991 following mutinies within the Zairian armed forces.

Togo (1991)

On November 28, 1991, troops loyal to President Gnassingbé Eyadema surrounded Prime Minister Joseph Koffigoh's official residence with tanks and demanded the restoration of Eyadema's powers. The soldiers behind the coup were members of the 2,000-man presidential guard, recruited from the same tribe as Eyadema. The prime minister wanted to dissolve this powerful guard, which maintained its allegiance with the president. A few months earlier, during a national conference of the country's prominent representatives advocating democracy, the president had been stripped of all but ceremonial powers. A few days before the coup d'état, the prime minister had banned the president's political power base, the *Rassemblement du peuple togolais* (RPT). The fighting around the prime minister's residence killed at least 23 people and probably closer to 50.[179] The fighting stopped on November 30 when Eyadema asked the troops to return to their barracks after the arrival of 300 French troops to Cotonou in neighboring Benin, only 93 miles from Lomé. The French troops did not cross the border. In theory, the prime minister was still at the helm, but the deadlock with the armed forces remained and he would have to grant concessions to hard-liners from the former ruling party. On Tuesday, December 3, the president and the prime minister appeared on state television to announce the formation of a new transitional government, but no date was set for elections. This transitional government would have to share power with the RPT and the military, a major concession on the part of Koffigoh.

The prime minister and Togolese pro-democracy campaigners in Paris called for a French military intervention to preserve the newly acquired political reforms, but French authorities would not intervene directly.[180] In an ironic twist, the Togolese opposition invited the former colonial power to settle domestic problems. The dilemma for France was compounded by the fact that "anti-French feeling ran high as many Togolese criticized the former colonial power for not sending Koffigoh military support."[181] Nevertheless, French troops in Benin remained on stand-by with the official mission of protecting the 3,000 French citizens in Togo and monitoring the democratic process. Thirty French soldiers were dispatched to the French embassy in Lomé to reinforce security.[182] These thirty men were the extent of the French military intervention in Togo.

The mixed French reaction is symptomatic of the absence of a new approach to the support France should provide to emerging democracies in sub-Saharan Africa. Caution is the key concern when intervening on behalf of democratic reform. When the lives of French expatriates are not endangered, as in the case of Togo, there are few incentives to take drastic action. The military risk in responding to Koffigoh's appeal was not negligible. The challenge of the Togolese armed forces, and especially of the presidential guard, to a French intervention should not be disregarded. "Contrary to the armed forces in other African countries, [the Togolese forces] are powerful and well-structured," commented Jacques Isnard from *Le Monde*, and the competence and cohesion of these forces are "precisely the main obstacles in the assumption of a French action which would go beyond the protection of its 3,000 citizens."[183] The putschists also had discretely passed the message to the French that Koffigoh would be executed if French forces intervened.[184] To justify its reluctance to engage in a second *Barracuda*-type operation, France hid behind a legal technicality. The Franco-Togolese Defense Agreement stipulates that a request for French military intervention in Togo's internal affairs should be made by the Togolese head of state, and not the head of government.

Zaire (1993)

In late January 1993, French and Belgian troops were dispatched to central Africa to rescue European expatriates who were again endangered by mutinies and riots in Kinshasa. The operation is described and analyzed in detail in Chapter 12.

Somalia (1992-93)

The U.N. Security Council adopted Resolution 794 on December 3, 1993, thereby authorizing the U.S.-sponsored operation *Restore Hope* in Somalia. U.S. troops numbered up to 25,000 at their peak. On December 7, 1992, France decided to participate with a contingent which would reach 2,450, compared to 900 for the Belgian contingent. French forces in Somalia included two battalions from French forces in Djibouti (one from the 5 RIOM and one from Foreign Legion's 13 DBLE), as well as one detachment of transport helicopters and twelve anti-tank *Gazelle* helicopters from the 4th Airmobile Division of the *Force d'Action Rapide* and logistics units. The French Navy assisted with four vessels, including one frigate, one light transportation ship, one assault ship and a command ship.[185] Belgian ground forces included mainly Para-Commandos as well as logistics and communications units. The Belgian Navy was present with one command and supply ship.[186] Contingents from France, Belgium or other participating countries were assigned specific sectors: France to the northeast of Mogadishu, and Belgium in the southern region of Kismayo. Their tasks included patrolling streets, protecting humanitarian aid and food distribution, and controlling local airports.

The fact that the operational command was in the hands of an American was a new development. Acting with the specific authorization of a U.N. resolution was also a radical departure from other military interventions undertaken by either France or Belgium in sub-Saharan Africa. Neither country had prior colonial or military experience in Somalia, although France was present in neighboring Djibouti. Operation *Restore Hope* was atypical and the French and Belgian participation was not motivated by considerations linked to policing or maintaining a zone of influence. Britain did not participate in the military deployment in the region. In the second phase of the intervention in Somalia, called UNOSOM II and executed under U.N. military command, France's contribution gradually dropped to 1,100 troops, while Belgium's fell to 250 by the end of 1993.

Rwanda (1993 and 1994)

On February 20, 1993, President Mitterrand sent 240 troops to Rwanda, in addition to the roughly 250 troops still present after the 1990-91 intervention, "to protect French nationals."[187] The remaining 400 French citizens in Rwanda were guarded by roughly 500 French soldiers. Less than two weeks earlier, fighting had resumed between the 1,500 rebels from the *Front patriotique rwandais* (FPR) and government troops. Some 100,000 refugees left the combat zone. They were wandering in the streets of Kigali, the capital, as rebels approached. Although French authorities adamantly stressed the humanitarian role of their military presence, sources within the FPR and the OAU cease-fire monitors pointed to the direct participation of French troops in the fighting on the government's side.[188]

The Belgians remained absent during this additional tumultuous episode in their former colony, despite their earlier intervention in 1990 alongside the French. Perceptions about the limited real danger to the expatriate population in Rwanda partly inspired this restraint, especially in view of the semi-permanent French deployment already in the country. Belgium wanted also to distance itself from the regime of President Habyarimana, which was accused of involvement in ethnic massacres causing 300 deaths in the northwestern part of the country. Following the report of an international commission to investigate the killings, Belgium was reviewing its entire cooperation policy with the Rwandese authorities.[189] The fighting stopped on February 21, 1993, when a cease-fire was reinstalled on the basis of the previous cease-fire signed in July 1992 between the government and the rebels. French troops left only in December 1993, when a U.N. peace-keeping force was deployed in Rwanda. Four months later, French paratoopers were back in Rwanda to help evacuate the expatriate community, in conjunction with half-a-dozen other western nations (see Chapter 12).

Burundi (1993)

A bloody coup on October 21, 1993 murdered Burundi's first democratically elected president, Melchior Ndadaye, and three senior members of his government after only 100 days in office. Parts of the armed forces had wanted to pre-empt the government's plan to dilute the former ruling Tutsi tribe's control of the security apparatus by bringing in more Hutus. The remaining members of the government took refuge in the French embassy. Several days after carrying it out, the paratroopers who had usurped the presidency found their coup falling apart. The putschists met with opposition from all sides, including from senior officers who guaranteed the government's security. The arrival on November 5 of fifteen French military specialists for the protection of VIPs enabled the government to leave the embassy compound and reassert control.[190] Meanwhile, ethnic violence had spread all over the country, killing several thousand people and creating hundreds of thousands of refugees.

International condemnation of the coup was unanimous. France was forced by circumstances to take an active role in solving the crisis. Significantly, the government-in-hiding did not consider taking refuge in the Belgian embassy, clearly indicating which of the two European powers exercised a dominant influence in Burundi.

Cameroon (1994)

In a replay of the 1981 border dispute between Nigeria and Cameroon, a swampy peninsula at Nigeria's southeastern edge, called Bakassi, became the theater of clashes between soldiers of the two countries. In the first week of March 1994, France dispatched thirty paratroopers and two helicopters to Cameroon to mark its solidarity under the Franco-Cameroonian defense agreement. This firm action outraged Nigeria, but avoided any escalation in the oil-rich region.

FLEXIBLE RESPONSES

Motives for Intervention

The foundation for French military actions in sub-Saharan Africa rests on a combination of four main sources of motivation. In decreasing order of international acceptability, these incentives include: (i) supporting the territorial integrity of African partners and retaliating against external aggression; (ii) participating in maintaining internal order and re-establishing control on behalf of the legal authorities in power; (iii) intervening for humanitarian reasons; (iv) issuing pronunciamentos of new regimes more or less favorable to Paris.

The first two categories refer to responsibilities conferred to France through traditional defense agreements, codifying the use of French forces, or at the urgent request of the head of state of a country threatened by external or internal destabilization efforts. Both categories are considered internationally acceptable foundations for intervention. However, an external aggression or serious domestic destabilization threats in themselves are not sufficient to trigger a French intervention automatically. The French government always retains the right to ultimately decide on whether or not an intervention is an appropriate response. In reality, French interventions depend less on precise criteria or legal commitments than on circumstances. France makes its own *ad hoc* assessments of the danger to stability, the potential menace to its citizens, and the threat to its credibility as peace-guarantor in Africa.

The French president's freedom of action is far from absolute. Friendly African heads of state have often exerted informal pressure to "twist the president's arm." In the past, they have succeeded in convincing the president to take military measures by invoking either a direct regional threat or by insisting on the necessity of an intervention for France to maintain its status as a reliable ally. One positive aspect of this pressure for France is that it implies African endorsement of French intervention.

French actions to restore internal order at the invitation of an African government are among the most contentious and are subject to vehement opposition from voices in both France and the beneficiary state. Speaking after the Gabon intervention in 1990, President Mitterrand strongly denied that the goal was to restore internal order: "never, under my authority, has France engaged in that kind of intervention."[191] The French presence in Chad was justified as a protection against external aggression. In Rwanda, the danger to French expatriates has led to a situation where French troops outnumber French expatriates. Officially, little reference is made to the need to preserve order against the destabilization efforts of anglophone rebels - not a laughing matter in the capital of *Francophonie*. In the case of Rwanda, and many other previous interventions, the line between a purely humanitarian operation and a regime-supporting action seems to have been crossed; France, for better or worse, directly interfered with political developments in the country.

Interventions on humanitarian grounds involve primarily the rescue or protection of French citizens abroad. The French participation in the U.N. operation in Somalia is an exception; the humanitarian relief was destined for the local population and not for the expatriate community. A plausible argument for humanitarian intervention is often found under international law. The international acceptability of a humanitarian operation is a function of four main criteria: the attitude of the recognized authorities in the country of intervention; the limited duration of the operation; the absence of interference in the domestic affairs of the country of intervention; and the political context in which the action takes place, with special attention to the civil or international cause of the disorder triggering the humanitarian action.[192] France has always been adamant in obtaining formal approval from the legal local authorities, and this has at times been facilitated by referring to an external threat. The limited duration principle has frequently been discreetly overlooked, often despite highly publicized early claims that a given operation would be short-term. The criterion of non-interference in domestic matters has been the most widely evoked principle prior to an intervention, and the most consistently violated on the ground. Although the principle of non-interference was never intended to be respected in some cases, in other instances its violation was a sort of inevitable by-product. Whether intended or not, military interventions for humanitarian purposes by a western power such as France are inevitably a partisan act against the party that endangers French expatriates. The enormous disparity between French military capabilities and those of any armed African antagonist is often sufficient to tilt the balance against the latter. Africa has been the main theater of French humanitarian military interventions. This reflects the large French expatriate community in Africa, the low military threat, and the excellent familiarity French troops have gained with the sub-Saharan theater. French expatriates in Africa are frequently subject to instability, but they remain in a volatile area because they know that France will intervene if their lives are endangered.

Two additional motives for French interventions are conceivable, although they have not been confirmed. One would be to provide military protection where emerging African democracies face a serious domestic threat, and the other would be to dispatch a monitoring force during eruptions of violence in local crises. The forceful non-intervention to rescue the democratization process in Togo in 1991 illustrated the difficulty of suddenly being entrusted with the role of godfathering democratic reform. France did not feel compelled to shelter the nascent Togolese democracy to the point of actually engaging French troops in combat. The second role is inspired by France's 1990 intervention in Gabon, which assembled many ingredients of a peace-monitoring task force, with the additional preoccupation of protecting French expatriates and interests in the country. Remarkably, during the rebellion in Gabon neither the insurgents nor the Gabonese government requested the departure of French troops.[193] The passive French presence acted as a powerful restraining factor on violence levels, and French mediation efforts gained a lot in credibility due to the presence of French troops. Though it was not their primary task, French troops performed a *de facto* peace-monitoring role with success. They have an important advantage over U.N. peace-monitoring forces in terms of deployment flexibility, pre-positioned troops and material, military credibility, and an international legal framework pre-existent to the crisis. Officially, France has not yet integrated democracy-supporting and peace-keeping objectives into its African intervention policy, and might very well deny that it is even considering such tasks. It remains, however, that such tasks are well within the capabilities of French forces stationed in Africa. The answer could well be found in the three "basic of rules intervention" identified by *The Economist* in an article dated September 28, 1991. The three rules commend western powers in future contingencies:[194] (i) to be sure, when possible, that "the people on whose behalf the intervention is contemplated really want it;" (ii) to be certain that the intervener can win; and (iii) not to engage in an intervention unless "it also serves a clear and demonstrable self-interest." The third condition might be the most difficult for France to fulfill in the future; as the demand for its role as Africa's policeman may increase, the marginal returns for French interests will diminish.

Typology of Military Actions

French military involvement in pursuing the traditional or new objectives can vary in intensity, from mere gesticulation to deployment in actual combat. Whatever the intensity of action chosen, timeliness has been the key in avoiding escalation. French interventions in Africa are based on the propitious arrival of a small but appropriate force within a crisis region. Such an action is far more likely to be viewed as a tangible and earnest display of political intent than a promise of much larger forces. To guarantee rapid a overseas military response, France has relied primarily on forces permanently stationed in certain foreign countries or in French overseas dependencies. Such units can respond in a few hours in the case of a local crisis, or in less than 24 hours in the case of a regional crisis. Supplies and reinforcements are flown in from France soon afterwards. France will remain dependent on pre-positioned overseas forces as long as it does not possess sufficient long-range airlift capabilities. There has been a growing tendency for intervention forces to rely on large amounts of sophisticated equipment, a trend which will continue as potential adversaries obtain more advanced hardware.[195]

At the lowest intensity of involvement, options utilizing military means include the provision of technical assistance, training and instruction, construction of military infrastructure, and the acceleration of arms sales and new arms credits. A higher degree of involvement would consist of dispatching pre-combat units or intelligence collection platforms. AWACS surveillance aircraft can operate from safe distances and signal France's commitment to take action. The presence of monitoring aircraft also signals that any element of surprise is lost to the aggressor. Air transport assistance, logistics teams, and communications specialists further reinforce an intervening country's military presence in a crisis area. When appropriate, the transition from passive to more active engagement can be made through naval task forces. An aircraft carrier is a multi-capable platform that offers options ranging from passive support all the way to active combat.

Active military support is achieved with the deployment of actual intervention forces. For instance, a squadron of *Jaguars* together with tanker aircraft and reconnaissance planes could open an active suasion campaign. The arrival of visible ground troops would serve the same purpose, although troops can undertake more versatile assignments. Pre-combat strategies routinely involve the protection of the embassy compounds and key points along a possible evacuation route for expatriates, including the airports. Still closer to the combat threshold are security patrols by French troops. Once French troops are deployed, even in a non-combat role, their moves are paralleled by various diplomatic maneuvers signaling French political resolve to take appropriate action. The effectiveness of deterrence relies on the ability to determine the pertinent allocation of force and diplomatic pressure, but also on a realistic appraisal of overall objectives. The protection of Chad below the 16th Parallel is a perfect example of how to balance a firm commitment with a credible objective.

Finally, when all else fails to deter an aggressor, or when an immediate response is deemed preferable to a long, drawn out deterrence effort, force is used more aggressively. At the lower end of the spectrum, special forces can covertly execute reconnaissance, attack or sabotage missions, or any other type of exceptional swift action. If properly executed, clandestine operations offer the advantage of sometimes being publicly deniable while leaving no doubt to the enemy as to who commandeered them. Actual open, direct combat by French troops in sub-Saharan Africa has been very rare; fighting has been limited in duration and scope.

What is ahead?

The main point of contention concerning the French military role in sub-Saharan Africa is not the availability or pre-positioning of troops, but the future modalities and conditions for their use. During the period when the first democratic aspirations surfaced in Africa, the French military has generally avoided becoming entangled in the inevitable conflicts. At the same time, it has successfully protected French expatriates and has even been called upon to calm local violence.

More than ever before, France realizes that military intervention has only limited significance unless it is conducted in conjunction with economic and diplomatic efforts. As democratic reforms in Africa become more effective, it is likely that the French military role will come under closer scrutiny from African and French political forces; however, it is unclear whether new democratic governments would reconsider France's military position and ask the forces deployed on the continent to withdraw. Contrary examples exist, as in Senegal, where a long-standing democracy has accommodated itself to the presence of a French garrison. From the French perspective, the military forces stationed in Africa and the ability to deploy additional forces to the continent rapidly are, with the Franco-African summits and the Franc Zone, the only true manifestations of France's unique relationship with francophone Africa. Of the bilateral arrangements which de Gaulle put in place in the early 1960s, the military role may be the last to go. Its disappearance would be the unmistakable and irreversible sign of a new era in Franco-African relations.

Chapter 6

British Political and
Military Involvement in Africa

The British assumption of total impotence in influencing sub-Saharan African states was "a pendulum which had swung too far." Thus wrote Roger Martin, a former British deputy high commissioner in Zimbabwe, in the late 1980s. He added that:

> Most British diplomats do not believe it is possible, and hence do not in practice try, to determine events in Africa. A dramatic decline of British confidence in the ability of any outsiders to influence decisively African behavior took place in the years just before and after the dissolution of Britain's African empire. [...] The nadir of perceived impotence was Rhodesian UDI [Unilateral Declaration of Independence] in 1965. If the British could not even influence the British rulers of a British colony, what hope was there of influencing black sovereign states? Without guns, such other levers of influence, words and money did not confer power.[1]

British assumptions of impotence have not yet been reversed as a matter of policy. When viewed in light of developments outside of Africa, mainly the whole region east of Suez, the decline of Britain's ability to influence events overseas is even more dramatic. The decline was perceptible in all manifestations and instrumentalities of influence in Africa, particularly through the loss of colonial possessions, base rights, bilateral defense agreements, and power projection capabilities.

British authorities chose two avenues to regain some of the influence lost on the world scene and curb what seemed an inexorable path toward decline. The first option, resting on a premise dating back to Churchill, is aptly described as "influence by association." Her Majesty's government regarded it as its purpose to make use of Britain's special transatlantic relationship to "help steer this great unwieldy barge, the United States of America, into the right harbor."[2] The extent of Britain's success is a matter of debate. In Europe, it has achieved an undeniable impact. In Africa, three decades after the end of colonialism, the convenience of this approach was by definition limited to the scope and direction of American involvement in African affairs. America's policy of anti-colonialism in the 1960s was followed in the next decade by one of containment of Soviet expansion. Britain felt comfortable in neither of the two roles. Influence by association failed to stop Britain's relentless loss of influence in Africa. Under the premiership of Mrs. Thatcher, British and U.S. policies were rigorously at odds even over the applications of sanctions toward South Africa. Britain's second option to retain some say over African affairs involved the invitation of the new African states to membership in the Commonwealth. This post-imperial construction eventually failed to provide Britain with a tool to enhance its influence overseas.

The most visible manifestation of British retrenchment from overseas commitments was in the military cuts following the dramatic decision to withdraw from all countries east of the Suez Canal. Cold War considerations and Britain's assigned role within NATO subtracted from the British capacity to play an active military role in its post-imperial zone of influence. Residual capacities were maintained and put to use in sub-Saharan Africa. The end of the Cold War may trigger a reversal of British absence in the Third World. Military disengagement from Europe has already liberated forces and financial resources to reinforce a more active military role overseas. The urge to cash in on the post-Cold War peace dividend has tempered overly optimistic expectations with regard to this role. Beyond the issue of resources, however, the main concern remains generating enough political will and consensus for a more active British role, whether east of Suez or in Africa.

BRITISH DECISION-MAKING

In the traditional view, the ultimate decision-making body in the British executive branch is the cabinet under the chairmanship of the prime minister. The cabinet operates under the convention of collective responsibility to the parliament.[3] The full cabinet, speaking with one voice, embodies the collective identity of the government. All ministers must at all times support cabinet decisions. "A minister may, of course, oppose a decision during discussion in cabinet, but he must not, after the decision has been made, reveal that he disagreed with the majority, or that he has any reservations about the government's policy."[4] With practice, the cabinet has been transformed from "an executive body into a reporting and reviewing body."[5] Most issues presented at the weekly meeting of the cabinet at 10 Downing Street are already settled. The complexity of modern government encourages the delegation of decision-making from the full cabinet to smaller groups of ministers, the committees, with the occasional addition of non-cabinet members of the executive branch. The prime minister chairs the committees or selects a minister to do so. "The moment that any cabinet committee's decision is recorded, it has the same validity as a cabinet decision - unless it has been challenged in committee and the issue accepted by the prime minister as the one to be decided by cabinet."[6] Committees, therefore, hold considerable power within their own areas of competence.

The powers of the prime minister include the ability to appoint and dismiss both cabinet and non-cabinet ministers. Under Margaret Thatcher's premiership, committees were established as "*ad hoc* groups of hand-picked ministers to push through decisions."[7] John Major has halted the trend and relies on more formal, publicly announced, committees with fixed membership of senior departmental ministers. Much of the strength which the prime minister enjoys in relation to his cabinet, and to parliament, flows from the support which he or she enjoys from his party and its strength in the House of Commons. Conversely, if he or she "loses support in his party [...] then his [or her] days as prime minister are probably numbered."[8]

In British government, constitutional and practical considerations highlight the central role of ministerial departments, which "capture all but the most powerful ministers, and send them forth into Whitehall" to represent their interests.[9] Ministers are individually responsible and accountable to parliament for all decisions of their departments.

British Policy-Making and Military Interventions

Defense policy decision-making is, in theory, supervised at the highest level by the full cabinet. Routine defense issues are not submitted to the full cabinet, but are reviewed by the Defence and Overseas Policy Committee.[10] The daily management and execution of defense policy is the task of the Defence Council. In times of war or serious security crises an *ad hoc* war cabinet assumes responsibility under the chairmanship of the prime minister. Its membership can vary according to the type of emergency. On April 1, 1964, during the Wilson premiership, a Defence Council was established under the chairmanship of the secretary of state for defense. Vested in the Defence Council are the functions of commanding and administering the armed forces. The Defence Council membership includes the secretary of state for defense, two ministers of state, the chief of the Defence Staff, the three single service chiefs of staff, the procurement chief, and the scientific advisor, among others.

Military interventions in out-of-area regions are initially considered by the full cabinet. The *ad hoc* war cabinet then takes over the day-to-day management of a war or intervention, dividing its time between "running the war effort and worrying about its portrayal in the news media."[11] During the 1991 Gulf War, for example, the war cabinet contained the foreign secretary, the defense secretary, the chancellor, the chief of the Defence Staff, the prime minister's foreign policy and security advisor, and his private secretary. The Gulf War cabinet was further complemented by the attorney general for advice on international law, and by the energy secretary, who was also the government's publicity coordinator. John Major's Gulf War cabinet has been called "more collective than any for a generation."[12]

Once the full cabinet or the war cabinet has made the political decision to engage in some sort of military action overseas, it directs the chief of staff to produce a plan with the mix of force needed for action. A joint headquarters is charged with general military supervision. In peacetime, low-intensity conflicts abroad usually do not require further intermediate headquarters. The intervening force is then tailored to the specific needs of the mission.

Britain established a permanent joint command structure after the Falklands War. In peacetime, it remains embryonic, with a skeletal permanent staff and a three-star commander assigned to direct the Joint Task Force Headquarters. The role of the command structure increases greatly during British military operations; in the 1991 Gulf War against Iraq, the commander took the staff directly to the crisis area.

British Post-Colonial Priorities in African Affairs

Britain's approach to policy-making on Africa has been marked by pragmatism rather than ideology, concentrating on the protection of British interests rather than on actively trying to shape events.[13] Policy toward sub-Saharan Africa is, in practice, the domain of permanent officials at the Foreign and Commonwealth Office. In the FCO hierarchy, the secretary of state for foreign and commonwealth affairs and a few other junior ministers are the only political appointees connected to the African portfolio. The structure of career officials includes a permanent under-secretary, a deputy secretary for Africa and Asia, an under-secretary for sub-Saharan Africa, and geographical departments for West, East, central and southern Africa. The junior ministers often merely approve recommendations of career officials on African affairs. "Since most of Africa is a low-priority area, relatively few submissions are passed by a junior minister to the secretary of state, and very few to the prime minister's office."[14] Southern Africa, especially the sanctions issue and military deployments, are exceptions to non-interference from the prime minister.

Civilian aid programs, headed by a House of Commons minister, are remarkably stable. Bureaucratic inertia and the perception that "the existence of an aid program gives access and some influence, that would be lost if there were a cutoff,"[15] explain why little change occurs, even when ministers feel inclined to cut or reduce some aid programs out of exasperation with some African governments. Parliamentary criticism of aid programs is very limited, and the annual financial bills go through parliament virtually unamended.

In 1987, a British analyst of African affairs identified nine fields of British interests in Africa. These areas, which remain applicable today, are, in rough order of priority:

1. promoting trade;
2. increasing British investment;
3. safeguarding the resident British community;
4. securing access to the strategic mineral supply;
5. managing the African debt crisis;
6. developing aid programs;
7. maintaining strategic links;
8. supporting friendly and stable governments; and
9. obtaining desirable economic policies.[16]

Trade and investments in sub-Saharan Africa have declined in relative terms, although not absolutely. The British community is also decreasing as a consequence of trade and investment practices; southern Africa, and in particular the Republic of South Africa, where Britain has over £3 billion of investments, is a significant exception. Africa's debt is an increasing source of concern. Aid programs have reached a plateau but are resilient to reduced funding levels. With decreased tensions in East-West relations, Africa's strategic importance is declining. Given the rapid turnover in leadership and drastic changes in some African states, the good relationship with specific governments *per se* has become less of a coveted objective for British diplomacy. Economic and commercial policies have moved to the top of the priority list, aiming at loosening the propensity of Third World countries to centralize their economies. Since the time the above list of British priorities was established, a new 'ideological' criteria has gradually emerged from current international developments, particularly the democratization of political processes in Africa. Democracy and market-oriented economies have thus become part of the definition of British interests in Africa.

Only safeguarding British communities and supporting friendly governments have been evoked as rationales for single-handed British military action in independent sub-Saharan Africa. It is unlikely that any other of the above interests would prompt a military intervention if not mingled with some danger to British expatriates or to legitimate governments. Democratization is, therefore, an important factor, increasing the international legitimacy of a government that might request British military assistance.

OVERVIEW OF BRITAIN'S AFRICAN POLICIES

The French president's direct involvement and control over African affairs has no equivalent in British government. British heads of government have at times directly influenced African policy-making, although their interference was limited to special situations and crises. Ongoing relationships with Africa were managed for the most part at lower echelons of the government. Of the eight prime ministers who have governed since the late 1950s, several have taken an active role in African affairs, often less out of interest or choice than because of compelling circumstances. The governments which have shaped Britain's African policy-making are mainly those of Harold Macmillan, Sir Alec Douglas-Home, Harold Wilson, and Margaret Thatcher. Barring a major crisis elsewhere, the first years of John Major's premiership and its impact on African affairs will probably be assessed in the light of Britain's reaction to the end of apartheid in South Africa.

Harold Macmillan (1957-63)

One of Harold Macmillan's first tasks when he became prime minister was to repair the damage of the 1956 Suez intervention. As Randolph Churchill observed in *The Rise and Fall of Anthony Eden*: "Among the most serious consequences of the Suez debacle was that it nearly destroyed the Anglo-American alliance. It was one of Mr. Harold Macmillan's greatest acts of statesmanship that he was able to heal the breach so very soon after he became prime minister."[17]

Following Britain's resignation to the fact that it could no longer, for political and economic reasons, afford the luxury of an empire, Macmillan's premiership was highlighted by the move toward independence of all British colonies in continental sub-Saharan Africa, with the exception of Rhodesia. The independence of Ghana came on March 6, 1957, after which African affairs remained a low priority for Britain until 1959. One event which brought British rule in Africa back into the spotlight was the brutal treatment of some detainees from the suppressed Mau Mau revolt in Kenya. The brutality culminated in a massacre of eleven detainees during a riot at the Hola detention camp. Beyond the political scandal it caused to his government, the prime minister considered the brutality a "bloody reminder that white minority government could only continue in Kenya by the use of deadly force."[18]

Despite the colonial administration's victory over the Mau Mau rebellion, "in the end it lost them Kenya."

Another factor which influenced Macmillan's approach to African affairs was the French attitude toward Africa. "De Gaulle's African policy was to be profoundly influential upon the Macmillan government - and vice versa."[19] On one occasion, de Gaulle's prime minister, Michel Debré, had observed that in Africa, "either the French and the British - as the two principal colonial powers - had to decide jointly to stay, or both to clear out."[20] In February 1962, one month before de Gaulle signed the Evian Accords granting Algeria's independence, Macmillan lectured Sir Roy Welensky, the Rhodesian irredentist, on the dangers of using force against nationalist aspirations in Africa:

> In Algeria the French have a million men under arms, and they have now suffered a humiliating defeat. It is too simple a reading of history to think that you can exercise control simply by the use of power. Indeed, I cannot guarantee that British troops would undertake the kind of duties that would be necessary.[21]

For Britain, the French experience was a restraining influence on the use of the military option in Africa. While it was left to Harold Wilson to define later the withdrawal east of Suez, Macmillan had already set the stage - including the political prerequisites - for a British military disengagement from Africa.[22] From similar challenges to their respective authority and influence in Africa, Britain and France drew opposite policy conclusions. Unlike their French counterparts, British policy-makers embraced all too eagerly a non-interference policy, which paralleled their view that enhanced interference was not an efficient way of dealing with Africa's troubles.

The culmination of Macmillan's view on sub-Saharan Africa was his famous 'Wind of Change' speech given before the South African Parliament in Cape Town on February 3, 1960. The most famous quote from his speech stated that: "The wind of change is blowing through this continent, and, whether we like it or not, this growth of national consciousness is a political fact. We must all accept it as a fact, and our national policies must take account of it."[23]

In retrospect, it might be hard to appreciate the power of this speech, the point of which is now taken for granted. Macmillan's idea was not new at the time, either, and other colonial powers, including France and Belgium, had come to similar conclusions about the inevitability of national consciousness in Africa. What was truly new in this speech was the acceptance of these new forces by the prime minister of the world's first colonial power. "Certainly, after February 3, 1960, nobody in the West looked at Africa in the same way, and the storms followed with mounting rapidity - and violence."[24]

Three additional issues marked Macmillan's role in African affairs. Firstly, the Central African Federation, a grouping of the territories of Northern and Southern Rhodesia, as well as Nyasaland (now Zambia, Zimbabwe and Malawi, respectively), was a source of concern for Macmillan's government until the end of his term. The Federation dissolved on December 31, 1963, less than three months after Macmillan had left office. Secondly, the withdrawal of South Africa from the Commonwealth came as another blow to British attempts at maintaining some kind of structure with their former colonies. Macmillan announced the withdrawal to the Commons on March 14, 1961. He had taken the whole issue very personally and, when the rupture was unavoidable, felt "weighed down by a sense of grief and foreboding, almost a sense of despair."[25] Thirdly, the concurrent developments in the Congo also created some difficulties for Macmillan. His concern, which he shared with President Kennedy, was focused on the necessity of avoiding Soviet penetration in Africa as a result of the Congolese disturbances. "Although in spirit (and moved by right-wing Tory pressures), Macmillan was with Katanga over its struggle for independence, he continued to pay lip service to the U.N."[26] As evidence of his engagement on the side of the U.N., he unexpectedly and reluctantly agreed to a request from the Indian Air Force, which was part of the U.N. contingent, for twenty-four 1000-pound bombs to be used against airfields in Katanga. This ambiguous attitude caused some upheaval in Britain and a crisis in parliament. In 1963, Macmillan removed any ambiguity by endorsing the U.N. military operations, which Britain and France had previously criticized.

Although Britain remained militarily present in sub-Saharan Africa during Macmillan's premiership, no major military action took place, even at the time of the disagreements over the dissolution of the Central African Federation. Macmillan had inaugurated the political framework for approaching the transition from colonialism to independence in Africa. It was based more on a realistic evaluation of the costs to Britain of trying to keep control than on the belief that British colonies in sub-Saharan Africa were ready for independence.[27]

Sir Alec Douglas-Home (1963-64)

Sir Alec Douglas-Home's tenure as prime minister lasted only one year, during which time his government had to deal with the East African mutinies. The forceful and timely action of the British troops was as much the result of a genuine desire to avoid a proliferation of Congolese-type mutinies as it was of accident. The Royal Navy units in the region at the time of the mutinies were in fact heading for Malaya and had initially been diverted to East Africa to deal with the coup in Zanzibar. (See Chapter 9 for more details.) The action was the only post-colonial fighting mission British troops have undertaken in sub-Saharan Africa. Other troops would be dispatched during various crises, but they were never engaged in actual combat. The British intervention in East Africa did not herald a new era for British military activism in Africa; it was a final colonial enterprise in which Britain assisted the young East African republics at their own request. It marked the end of British military rule in Africa. Subsequent military involvement was often conducted under Commonwealth or U.N. supervision, or as part of very small prevention forces.

Harold Wilson (1964-70)

Harold Wilson's first tenure as prime minister was marked by bold diplomatic and military policies, some of which had lasting consequences. Having inherited the legacy of reduced colonial activity from previous governments, Wilson initiated the removal of British troops from east of Suez as the continuation of a process that had begun with the independence of India. As part of this landmark decision, which was based on the general reorientation of British foreign policy, Wilson simultaneously reduced funding for large military expenditures, including a large aircraft carrier.

In sub-Saharan Africa, two major events marked the Wilson administration: the Rhodesian Unilateral Declaration of Independence (UDI) trauma and the Biafran secession. In the case of the Rhodesian UDI, the main challenge was how Britain was going to respond. Rhodesia was, at least nominally, still under the authority of the British governor. Wilson had rejected the use of force against the Smith regime despite strong pressure from the U.N. and the Commonwealth for Britain to intervene. As Wilson confided in his memoirs: "The foreign secretary was having the roughest possible ride at the United Nations, where almost every 'non-aligned' nation, headed by the

Africans and supported by the Soviet bloc, was pressing for immediate action."[28] Within the Commonwealth, two African nations, Tanzania and Ghana, did break diplomatic relations with Britain over the refusal to intervene with force. Failure to find an appropriate response to the challenge of UDI could result in driving:

> one Commonwealth country after another into greater dependence on the Russians or, worse, to force them to choose between the Soviet Union and China, in what was rapidly becoming a major enterprise in African penetration. That was why it was not an exaggeration to say that the speed and direction of policy on UDI was part of 'a battle for the soul of Africa.'[29]

Under pressure to act, the Wilson government launched the Beira patrol to sanction Rhodesia by cutting its main oil supply line. Rhodesia retaliated with counter-sanctions against Zambian oil supplies crossing through Rhodesia and forced Britain to arrange an air-lift of oil supplies to Zambia. Circumvented from South Africa and Portuguese Mozambique, the Beira embargo was unsuccessful in achieving its stated objective of bringing the Rhodesian economy "to a halt."[30]

In the late 1960s, Nigeria became Britain's main preoccupation overseas.[31] Britain, a longtime arms supplier, continued to deliver weapons to the Federal Nigerian Government. For Wilson, "a refusal would have meant not a lurch into neutrality, but a hostile act against a fellow Commonwealth country" whose integrity Britain supported.[32] Moreover, the Soviets were in the wings ready to supply everything Nigeria needed. The role of arms supplier to the Federal Nigerian Government was not without political cost to Britain because the Biafran lobby all through the western world proved very effective at defending Biafran secession. Britain tried to hold a very thin line between supporting a fellow Commonwealth country and avoiding the appearance of increasing Biafran suffering. Britain abstained from delivering aircraft and aerial bombs, only to realize that the Russians provided to the Nigerians that which Britain had refused.[33]

Since the 1960s, British decision-making on Africa has been fairly impervious to the growing influence of the Soviet Union and China in sub-Saharan Africa. Africa's declining importance in British overseas interests and a pragmatic appraisal of the sometimes superficial ideological alignment of African states explain the low profile of British policy-makers on the issue of communist penetration in Africa.

The subsequent governments of Edward Heath, Harold Wilson (2nd term), and James Callaghan were marked by greater avoidance of direct participation in sub-Saharan crises. British military involvement did not go much further than military assistance programs. The key issues of apartheid and Rhodesian independence remained on Britain's African agenda, but they were marginalized out of frustration in solving them.

Margaret Thatcher (1979-90)

The Thatcher administration shared the past consensus on avoiding open-ended commitments in Africa. From Wilson to Thatcher, there was continuity in the decline of British military presence and operations in sub-Saharan Africa. The Thatcher government had no interest in becoming a global power and did not try to acquire the military tools and facilities to be one. Any British involvement in the Third World during the Thatcher years was exceptional. With the end of the Rhodesian UDI and Zimbabwe's transition toward majority rule, Britain seemed to have gotten rid of all its colonial responsibilities in Africa with a sigh of relief. Subsequently, Africa became further marginalized in British foreign policy priorities as British policies toward Africa were viewed under a more critical and pragmatic eye.

In terms of military cooperation, the Thatcher government consciously limited the allocation of advisors and military training personnel to short-term renewable periods with no open-ended time commitments. Overall, military programs were marginal during the Thatcher years, with the exception of the Commonwealth Monitoring Force in Rhodesia and subsequent assistance to Front Line States which border South Africa. Other aid efforts carried a new 'ideological' orientation in assessing their impact on British interests. Economic efficiency and market-responsiveness were the standards which the Thatcher government introduced as "a means of reinforcing the continent-wide tide now flowing strongly against previous excessive centralization, irrespective of any other consideration."[34]

Prime Minster Thatcher's rejection of economic sanctions as a means of bringing an end to apartheid in South Africa caused heated debate. Her strong stand against sanctions isolated her in international fora, whether at the U.N., the Commonwealth or even the European Community. Her premiership, marked by a series of modest but politically significant military assistance programs in southern Africa, particularly in Zimbabwe, Mozambique, Botswana, and Namibia, advocated the notion that these programs were meant as partial substitutes for sanctions. Both the opposition to sanctions and the various military assistance programs fell under the larger pragmatic objectives of avoiding a radicalization of tensions in the region and preserving the economic fabric of South Africa, where British economic interests were strongest.

John Major (1990-)

Since 1993, Prime Minister Major's record on African policy-making has been marked by a withdrawal from the ideological high ground occupied by his predecessor but was also greatly shaped by rapidly changing circumstances in South Africa. During an October 1991 Commonwealth meeting, John Major appeared less keen to emphasize Britain's position on South African sanctions. The British reservation, wrote *The Economist*, "was perceived as a reasonable dissenting view, not a broadside designed to sink the whole plan."[35] This greater moderation and flexibility compared to Thatcher's approach has been a feature of Major's policy-making style across the board. Major continued Britain's low-key policy toward military assistance to southern Africa. Angola was added to the list of beneficiaries of this military cooperation program.

In the early 1990s, British aid policies were constrained by interests in former colonies and by the need to stress the link between aid and "good governance." Britain tried to promote democracy and human rights by suspending aid, as France did after President Mitterrand's speech at La Baule. In 1991, Britain withdrew aid from Sudan and the next year from Malawi in protest against poor human and political rights records. British aid to Kenya, in conjunction with other western aid, was halted to force President Daniel arap Moi to hold democratic elections. Countries that experimented with free multi-party elections, such as Zambia, received their due rewards. British commitment to promoting human rights and democracy is not dogmatic. Ghana does not have an unblemished record on human rights but "remains the darling of British aid overseers, getting more aid than any other African country except Zimbabwe."[36] Similarly, Uganda's president Yoweri Museveni appeared to have persuaded British authorities that political pluralism would, for the short-to-medium term, be counterproductive to the country's development. Pragmatism prevails in those situations where enlightened "authoritarianism may seem a lesser evil than abject poverty."[37] One important development that occurred during Major's premiership was the general election in May 1994 in South Africa, opening the way for a new era in Britain's relationship with southern Africa.

The most revealing aspect of the change between the policies of Major and Thatcher is the gradual blending of Britain's African policies with those of other western powers such as France and the United States. The geo-strategic marginalization of Africa after the end of the Cold War and the favorable evolution of South Africa's domestic situation has reduced differences in policy objectives among these powers and promoted greater harmonization.

EAST OF SUEZ

The British withdrawal from all colonial possessions and military commitments has been, in geographical terms, the fastest and most thorough transformation of an empire into its next stage of development. Geography alone fails to convey the completeness of the conversion from thriving empire to isolated, declining power. It is the symptom of a deep global change in attitudes. Third World nationalism became an irreversible movement. Britain, in turn, did not possess the willingness or the forces to oppose the Third World's drive for independence. The orchestration of the collapse of the British empire left policy-makers with marginal, but not irrelevant, room for choice. The outcome was not completely left to fate. Over several years, Britain opted for a three-tiered policy: (i) a complete pull-out, leaving almost no open-ended commitments toward former colonies and protectorates; (ii) a transfer to the Commonwealth of whatever responsibilities could be shared from the common imperial past; and (iii) a reduction of British armed forces, the ultimate guarantor of imperial cohesion, as the result of more domestic concerns.

With colonial responsibilities gone, residual, post-colonial overseas commitments could still be arranged. In the mid-1960s, the Wilson government made a series of landmark decisions on the nature and scope of these commitments. His government's decisions hailed the finality of the three-tiered policy; moreover, they structured new attitudes regarding how Britain viewed the world and how the world would view Britain. As a result, Britain had unequivocally moved into a new, post-imperial age.

In a 1965 article, *The Economist* wrote, in what was indicative of the mood at the time: "People ask themselves once again what they think Britain's future place in the world should be. For a lot of them, the answer has turned out to be at home, by the fire."[38] The process of Britain's 50-year withdrawal from east of Suez is divisible into four major steps. The first one is the independence of India, which represented the loss of the most important and lucrative pole of the British empire. Attempts to replace this center of colonial activity with another one, the Persian Gulf, eventually failed. The second phase was the 1956 Franco-British failure in Egypt to regain the Suez Canal zone. The third step, mainly the result of British domestic considerations, was the gradual implementation between 1966-71 of what became the "East of Suez Policy." The fourth and final step will be the independence of Hong Kong in 1997. By then, Britain will have renounced all commitments linked to its former empire in the region, with the exception of a few islands labelled as dependent territories.

The third stage in this retreat from east of Suez was devised against an extremely complex and turbulent background. The Malaysian confrontation had stressed the exhaustion of Britain in its ability to control distant crises. The emerging involvement of the United States in Vietnam was followed by a request from the Johnson Administration that Britain get involved. Consequently, the British government found itself in the delicate position of trying to deflect military participation without offending the United States. Cold War considerations temporarily induced Britain, because of its historic role in India and the Far East, to participate in the containment of China. The most compelling circumstance in the implementation of the withdrawal from east of Suez, however, was the dire economic situation in Britain. Deployment of troops overseas and the development of major weapons systems, such as aircraft carriers and long-range bombers, were among the tools of power projection sacrificed to budget cuts. As a corollary to the East of Suez policy, Britain reoriented its defense effort toward the central European front and the NATO flanks.

An often overlooked effect of this major political and military milestone is that by retreating from east of Suez, Britain also irreversibly consecrated its strategic retreat from south of Suez. British military planners had already eliminated sub-Saharan Africa from their global strategic vision, with the exception of the Simonstown naval facilities in South Africa. With the East of Suez withdrawal, the little that Africa could offer became irrelevant. The Seychelles and Mauritius bases were abandoned after the independence of those two countries. Even military facilities on Diego Garcia, although still in British hands, were leased to the United States for 50 years. Britain maintained only a symbolic military presence on the archipelago.

Was this disengagement inevitable? France, a military power of comparable size, succeeded in keeping a high profile in part of its former colonial empire. France managed its military assets in and around Africa with much greater strategic dynamism, using them effectively in pursuit of control over many African countries. Djibouti and La Réunion are still part of a significant French role east of Suez. French political analysts had little commiseration for Britain's troubles in keeping a presence east of Suez and expressed skepticism on the benefits of its close association with the U.S.: "The United Kingdom accepts in a certain way, to play the role of 'brilliant second' to a more powerful nation, in the hope thereby to gain a larger field of action."[39] In the end, this may have been the real choice which Britain made between 1966-71, and which France, inspired by de Gaulle, stubbornly refused.

The 1956 Suez Crisis

While the loss of India in 1947 may have initiated the end of the British colonial empire, the 1956 Suez Crisis marked the formal and final decline of the *Pax Britannica* as militarily enforceable by Britain. It was this episode that terminated Britain's status as a Great Power, which until then had not been challenged overseas. This rank was not lost in battle, where the Egyptian armed forces had been defeated; rather, it was challenged directly by the U.S., which used all its leverage with devastating effect against the joint Franco-British operation. Keith Kyle, from the Royal Institute for International Affairs, described the trauma's far-reaching effects:

> Judging by the speed with which Britain's African empire was abandoned, it seems clear that after 1956 the British government finally accepted the logic of its decision to grant India independence in 1947, namely that in the post-war world there was no intellectual defence for the continued maintenance of the empire.[...] Even when they resented American intrusion, the British knew that their world role, such as it was, now depended on American support.[40]

Britain drew an important general conclusion from the Suez debacle. The primary one was expressed by General Keightley, commander-in-chief for the joint operation: "The one overriding lesson of the Suez operation is that world opinion is now an absolute principle of war and must be treated as such."[41] World opinion had raised the threshold of feasibility for overseas military interventions, while the presence of the two superpowers reduced the freedom of action for Britain or France. But the political reassessment and outcome of the Suez operation was radically different in both countries. John Newhouse contended that, "whereas the affair divided Britain, it tended to unite France. [...] The French had as their prevailing attitude the belief that Europe must find a way to manage its affairs without reference to the superpowers."[42]

The East of Suez Policy: 1966-71

In the early 1960s, Britain was pursuing manpower-intensive military operations in Cyprus, South Arabia, and Malaysia. Britain's worldwide military commitments came at a heavy cost; the Army was underpowered and overstretched. "To many people in the United Kingdom, and particularly to the Labour Party, it was obvious that the United Kingdom could not continue to devote one-quarter of her defence budget to the region east of Suez."[43] The defense review of 1966, published just after the "Confrontation" between Malaysia and Indonesia, consecrated the first step in the withdrawal process from east of Suez. It contained three essential statements: (i) the withdrawal from the base in Aden, scheduled for 1968; (ii) the cancellation of construction projects for new aircraft carriers; and (iii) the purchase of 50 F-111 bombers from the U.S. The acquisition of these long-range bombers was a form of compensation for the loss of access to distant bases and the abandonment of aircraft carrier projects. Britain assumed that with a retaliatory strike capability, which could be maintained at home and dispatched in time of crisis, it could maintain its international status without the paraphernalia of overseas facilities.

It would take another year before the British government would spell out the policy implications of the comprehensive withdrawal of two brigades from Aden. The thrust of British thinking on that issue was that Britain should not again have to undertake operations outside Europe on the large scale of British military involvement during the "Confrontation" between Malaysia and Indonesia. They went even further, sharing the view that "experience has shown that it is neither wise nor economical to use military force to seek to protect national economic interests in the modern world."[44]

In 1967, a statement of the Ministry of Defence summarized clearly the new orientation of British overseas commitments, with less reliance on the military to promote those policies: "The purpose of our diplomacy is to foster developments which will enable the local peoples to live at peace without the presence of external forces."[45] The time had arrived, according to the Ministry of Defence, to redefine a more restrictive engagement policy for overseas operations:

> We remain responsible for the security of our dependencies; we have obligations to our friends and allies; and we have a political and economic interest in the stability of the world outside Europe, which makes it desirable to retain a capacity for contributing to the maintenance of peace where we can usefully do so. [...] We explained [...] that we would not undertake major operations of war, except in cooperation with allies, and would make our commitments to our friends dependent on the provision in time of whatever facilities we needed on the spot.[46]

These considerations were mixed with the pressing need to limit defense spending. In January 1968, the Wilson government announced the withdrawal of all British forces from the Far East and the Gulf by 1971, and canceled the purchase of F-111s. The decision to withdraw from the Persian Gulf was political, more surprising for its speed of execution than for the policy itself; an earlier Defence White Paper of the British government had suggested the mid-1970s as a potential date for the withdrawal.[47] For the Wilson government, this military and post-imperial budgetary cut "was simply the one sure way to get the Labour party to accept any restraint on domestic consumption."[48]

East of Suez and African Contingencies

Africa was only indirectly involved in the East of Suez debate. Aden had been an important staging post for eastern Africa, especially in colonial times. Afterwards, it continued to serve a useful role as a transit point to facilitate power projection in Africa. Except for some minor post-colonial armed interventions, however, Britain has kept clear of the revolutionary changes which swept through Africa in the 1960s. The interventions at the request of Kenya, Uganda, and Tanganyika in 1964 greatly benefitted from the British bases located east of Suez, mainly Aden. Later, small-scale interventions in Africa were likewise facilitated by the existence of the Aden facilities, but the cost of maintaining them simply outweighed the needs of the small contingents deployed in Africa. Reduced British commitments and security policies east of Suez and in Africa had minimized the operational significance of the South Arabian base, which was consequently eliminated.

The withdrawal from east of Suez also affected British influence in Africa in a less tangible way: It demonstrated the extent and the seriousness of British disengagement from former colonial and post-colonial duties. Not only was Britain announcing that it had lost the willpower to remain involved overseas, it was voluntarily dispossessing itself of all the military tools necessary for overseas operations. Bases were abandoned, long-range bomber programs were canceled, and aircraft carriers were not replaced. The policy was clear in its intention and in its execution. East of Suez was not an effort of decolonization, a movement well past its peak by 1966-71; rather, it was an effort for Britain to abdicate its military influence in a post-colonial world. New policies strove to avoid old patterns of providing troops and military assets for the defense of distant countries.

East of Suez was a mental framework which helped shape Britain's military role and involvement in sub-Saharan Africa. Twenty years after its implementation, the policy has had its advantages. It might have had a salutary effect on avoiding situations in which Britain would have been entangled in African contingencies. For example, Britain has not been drawn into a situation equivalent to France's involvement in Chad. Britain stood aside of the post-colonial turmoil in Africa.[49] British military involvement was sporadic and low-key. The East of Suez policy represented a new era in which Britain started anew. Only with the independence of Zimbabwe did Britain slowly emerge with a new, comprehensive military cooperation policy in southern Africa. Ultimately, all Britain wanted was to facilitate the resumption of trade and investments in South Africa in a more stable and pacified region. Conversely, the lack of such important British interests in East and West Africa have not resulted in a similar involvement in military assistance programs on the part of Britain.

THE COMMONWEALTH

Successor to the Empire?

> It was the past that suggested, first in a limited and mainly British colonial context, that in the face of quasi-nationalist or nationalist demands for autonomy, there was a possibility other than counter-resistance or abdication. That possibility was association, ultimately to be interpreted in terms of equality.[50]

For Nicolas Mansergh, from whom the previous passage was quoted, the Commonwealth became accepted as national policy in post-war Britain due mainly to two factors: "positively, the prospect of Commonwealth which softened the sharp edge of finality, and negatively, earlier Commonwealth experience which warned of the hazards of attempted repression."[51] The evolutionary transformation of the Empire into the Commonwealth, after a protracted period where both existed side by side, has "culminated in the national freedom and association in partnership [...]. It may be that in the accomplishment of this end, the Commonwealth either lost its *raison d'être* or still had other causes to advance."[52]

The quest for an identity and a cause grew more acute as more countries joined the Commonwealth. As it became less Anglo-centric over time, it lost its value as an exclusive tool for British foreign policy-making; with the dramatic increase of the membership, the Commonwealth proved too successful for its own good, becoming unfocused through over-extension. The juxtaposition of countries such as India or Canada next to others like Vanuatu or Saint Christopher and Nevis shows not only disparities in ideology, culture, population and wealth, but also stresses the divergence of geo-political concerns. The main members of the Commonwealth have global, or at least regional, interests, while the micro-states do not have to withstand the consequences of their votes on issues in areas beyond parochial concerns. The result is that each new membership diluted the commonalities, and that the Commonwealth has become a body without real power on the international arena. *The Times* commented as early as 1965, just after the Commonwealth had absorbed a cluster of newly independent countries, that "the political unlikeness, or incompatibility, of Commonwealth members is now its most obvious feature."[53]

Surviving the Late 20th Century

The savvy comments of A.P. Thornton on the status of the Commonwealth verge on contempt for the organization's ability to play any significant role at all in world politics: "The Commonwealth, [...] remains today in the world, revolving around no axis, a presence if not a force, a project more than an achievement."[54] He added in the same vein: "The Commonwealth deals less in power than in hope, and does not seem to be directed toward anything more concrete than its own continuation."[55] The history of the Commonwealth may at times appear as the history of self-centered disputes and squabbles among its members. For 40 years the Commonwealth "has developed a 'special relationship' within itself, between a small group of secondary powers and a swathe of the totally powerless."[56] Some concrete achievements can be paraded, however. The unusual role played by the Commonwealth during the transition process of Rhodesia into Zimbabwe was a remarkable achievement. In terms of services to its members, the Commonwealth created a structure composed of a permanent secretariat and offering mutual aid programs, technical cooperation and educational developments.

Sometimes, the Commonwealth does not shy away from engaging in a military training program, as in Uganda in 1981, when 14 members, mainly Kenya, Sierra Leone, and Tanzania, contributed either personnel or funds. Another instance of Commonwealth military involvement was in Zimbabwe, where it assisted in reshaping the guerrilla armies into regular armed forces. Countries feeling a need for military assistance without wanting to pay the political price of British military patronage have received military contingents from a few selected Commonwealth members. Ghana, for instance, has received this type of military aid. Although the assistance team was initially multinational, the British advisors after some time were left under only nominal Commonwealth authority. Outside the military realm, the Commonwealth also contributed election-monitoring teams to Third World countries that engaged in democratic reforms, including Bangladesh, Guyana, Malaysia, and Zambia.

Despite its poor record on concrete achievements, the Commonwealth sometimes fares better in displays of diplomatic solidarity. When President Ronald Reagan launched U.S. troops to invade Grenada in October 1983, he drew the sharp criticism of Margaret Thatcher, his friend and staunch ally. British authorities were angered at the fact that they had received no advance warning of an invasion plan against a member of the Commonwealth.[57] More recently, during the election process of a new U.N. secretary-general in late 1991, two strong candidates remained in the race toward the end: Bernard Chidzero, Zimbabwe's finance minister, and Boutros Boutros-Ghali, Egyptian deputy prime minister. Chidzero, who eventually lost the race, could count on British support "since Zimbabwe is a member of the Commonwealth."[58] These expressions of solidarity are often limited to symbols and diplomatic posturing.

The Permanent Structure of the Commonwealth

The Commonwealth is a free association of 50 nation states: 16 African, 13 American, 10 Pacific, and eight Asian, and three European. It boasts a total population of 1.2 billion, of which 70 percent is located in Asia, 15 percent in Africa, 10 percent in Europe, and 5 percent elsewhere.[59] There is no founding treaty, charter, or constitution. Ghana became the first black African member of the Commonwealth upon achieving independence in 1957. Twelve more sub-Saharan countries were to join over the next eleven years, completing the bulk of African members to the Commonwealth. The only African states to have joined since then are the Seychelles in 1976, Zimbabwe in 1980, and Namibia in 1990, bringing the total of African countries in the Commonwealth to 16.[60]

The institutionalization of the Commonwealth occurred with the creation of the Secretariat. Established in 1965, the Secretariat is located in London and in 1993 was headed by Secretary-General Emeka Anyaoku of Nigeria. While it has observer status at the U.N., the main function of the body is to organize the biennial meetings of Commonwealth heads of governments, annual meetings of finance ministers of member countries, and regular meetings on education, law, health, and other fields as appropriate.

There are today 18 programs managed by the Secretariat, the majority of which are in functional fields such as education, economic cooperation, and science. While the responsibilities and staff of the Commonwealth Economic Committee and the Commonwealth Education Liaison Unit have been absorbed as sub-divisions of the Secretariat, new institutions of the Commonwealth include the Fund for Technical Cooperation and the Commonwealth Foundation. The headquarters in London have approximately 400 staff members. The

1992-93 budget for the Secretariat was £9 million, financed collectively with Britain contributing 30 percent, Canada 19 percent, Australia 10 percent, India over 3 percent, New Zealand over 2 percent, and other members between 1.6 percent and 0.39 percent each.[61] The 1992-93 expenditures of the Commonwealth Fund for Technical Cooperation were an additional £20.7 million. This money is pledged to programs for youth, science, and technical assistance, with the latter absorbing more than 90 percent of the total.[62]

The Heads of State and Government Meetings are another standing feature of the Commonwealth. There have been 14 meetings held since 1965, their locations chosen on the basis of convenience.[63] In October 1991, the Commonwealth Heads of Government Meeting took place in Africa for the third time since its inception, namely in Harare, Zimbabwe. The meeting's final communiqué contained support for maintaining sanctions against South Africa with Britain adding a dissenting note. Prime Minister Major succeeded in avoiding the heated debate which characterized his predecessor's position at prior meetings. Major's dissenting arguments appeared more reasonable. He further announced that Britain would cancel a significant amount of developing countries' debts, with Canada following the move. Finally, the Heads of Government Meeting reaffirmed its objective of more democracy, more respect for human rights, and sounder market-based economic management.[64] The next meeting was held in Nicosia, Cyprus, in October 1993 with 35 participating heads of government. Perhaps in response to President Mitterrand's appeal to francophone solidarity against the cultural aspects of the GATT trade reforms at the *Francophonie* summit held in Mauritius that same month, Britain and Australia used the Commonwealth meeting as a platform to enlist support for the trade reforms from participating members.[65] Preaching for democratic reforms, the Commonwealth's report attacked, without naming him, Captain Valentine Strasser, president of Sierra Leone, who seized power in 1992. His coup was called a "serious setback" to democracy. Captain Strasser promised an early return to democracy.[66]

Britain and the Commonwealth

The British will always see the Commonwealth as "a monument to the vanished empire."[67] The Commonwealth prevented Britain from breaking with the past. While other benefits were welcome, they were ancillary to the role of the Commonwealth as the embodiment of the past in a venerable institution. The strongest case for the additional advantages was made in November 1983 by Foreign Secretary Sir Geoffrey Howe, who declared his satisfaction in the thought that the Commonwealth's existence gave Britain an immediate and privileged entrée to the governments of 30 percent of the U.N. membership.[68] Britain succeeded too well in creating an exclusive forum for its former colonies, neglecting to animate it with a soul and a mission. Over time, Britain has increasingly lost control over its creation, and the Commonwealth in some instances has bypassed Britain altogether:

> An interesting development has been the dispersal of power within the Commonwealth which [...] includes regional foci of power - India in South Asia, Australia and New Zealand in the Pacific, Nigeria in West Africa, Canada in the West Indies. The dispersal is reflected in the holding of a number of Commonwealth Heads of Government *Regional* Conferences, without British participation.[69]

The historic division within the Commonwealth between colonialists and anti-colonialists paralyzed the Commonwealth as a coherent body, thereby denying Britain the use of this forum for pursuing national policies. By the late 1960s, "the virtual completion of the policy of transforming an Empire into a Commonwealth accounted for a new assurance, even an occasional asperity, in British reactions at the United Nations to anti-colonial critics."[70] Britain's role and importance within the Commonwealth reached an all-time low during the meetings of Commonwealth Heads of State and Government in 1987 and 1989, when Britain became isolated in a series of bitter clashes regarding sanctions against South Africa. This separation was so total that Britain had to issue a unilateral dissenting statement after the 1989 Kuala Lumpur meeting. Prime Minister Thatcher firmly rejected sanctions as a tool to bring about changes in the apartheid system. Her contention was that by impoverishing the entire country, including its black population, economic sanctions would not bring the intended political effects. The remarkable aspect of this dissent, from the perspective of the Commonwealth as an institution, is that the Commonwealth was "not dependent on any single member, even one that has always seemed as central as Britain."[71] By challenging the unanimous consent of the other Commonwealth nations so openly, however, Britain seemed to demonstrate its lack of concern in opposing its partners. This attitude, verging on contempt, might, in turn, be interpreted as an indication of the irrelevance of Commonwealth summits in British management of international relations. Were this the case, Britain would have ironically lost not only its dominance in its post-imperial architecture, but also its faith in it. Confidence in post-colonial institutions was perhaps already lacking, as two distinguished British scholars wrote: "There is little expectation that Commonwealth gatherings can be used to urge forward specific British policies. There has in fact been a reversal of intentions. It is the modern Commonwealth which has sought to influence British policy rather than vice-versa."[72] To state the matter even more bluntly, Britain's "commitments toward the Commonwealth are both less precise, and almost certainly ultimately more dispensable, than its commitments toward either the EEC or the Atlantic Alliance."[73]

Despite the often tense relationship with other members, London considers the Commonwealth to be worth its modest costs.[74] Some British officials, however, differ substantially with this view and, during Britain's isolation over sanctions against apartheid, thought the organization "at best futile and at worst damaging to Britain. Each new sanctions-dominated conference increases the minority of officials who would shrug off British departure from the Commonwealth with mild relief."[75] Prime Minister Major's less controversial approach to South African sanctions, together with the rapid dismantlement of apartheid and the prospect of South African membership, gave new hope for finding useful causes to which this old institution could contribute.

French Bilateral Networks and the British Commonwealth

The existence of the Commonwealth prior to the post-war decolonization movements facilitated Britain's ability to cope with demands for independence. Although France tried to establish its *Communauté* along different and more associative lines, it did not succeed. By 1960, France was left with a network of bilateral relationships with its former colonies. Membership in the British Commonwealth, of which the former colonies recognized the Crown as head, is something France was unable or unwilling to match in the early years after decolonization:

Nothing on the French side emerged, *pari passu* with decolonization, to match Commonwealth membership. Britain managed to salvage something which at least resembles empire and expresses in palpable form a surviving unity, arguably an empire's final justification. The Commonwealth, Sir Keith Hancock argued, was "nothing else than the 'nature' of the British Empire defined, in Aristotelian fashion, by its end."[76]

In the early 1990s, the association of France and francophone African states through summits and bilateral defense arrangements seems to have preserved more residue of imperial power than the soft associative club of Commonwealth states. In the Commonwealth, *de jure* equality among members has been achieved, but the cohesion is too weak to justify full recognition of the institution by third parties. While the lack of a pre-existing framework permitted France to take a case-by-case approach to establishing strong bilateral ties, Britain's more systematic method of dealing with former possessions meant that newly decolonized nations had the same status as older and larger members of the Commonwealth. France, on the one hand, was unhindered by precedents in negotiating strong political, economic and military links with each of its former colonies. Britain, on the other hand, was under strong moral and political pressure to grant African countries the same privileges as other Commonwealth members. The trend of loose association had been set by India and Pakistan, and it would have been difficult for Britain to justify double standards within the Commonwealth. As a result of their diverging policies, Britain was able to maintain some solidarity among its former colonies, while France proceeded more selectively. The cases of Indochina and Algeria are examples of this dilution of the unifying force in the former French empire. In contrast, Britain failed to create an association with a strong center while France remains the undisputed hub of francophone countries, especially those in sub-Saharan Africa.

Another distinction between the French and British management of their former colonies lies in the use of a common language. For France, "the extent to which the world makes use of French and thereby takes the opportunity of assimilating French modes of thought is considered a measure of France's own standing in the world. (It is certainly a measure of French self-esteem)."[77] There is an inverse incentive for the common use of a language within each community: In the Commonwealth, it is to the mutual advantage of all members to use English as a common language, while in the *Francophonie*, it is mainly to France's benefit that the language be perpetuated among members. The burden of securing adhesion to a common language is carried by the members in the case of the Commonwealth, and by France in the case of the French-speaking countries.

Chapter 7

British Armed Forces:
Power Projection and Cooperation

In the 1993 "Statement on the Defence Estimates," published by the British Ministry of Defence, military planners emphasized three defense roles for British forces: to protect the United Kingdom and its dependent territories, to ensure against a major external threat to the United Kingdom and its allies through membership of NATO, and to promote the country's wider security interests through the maintenance of international peace and stability. The fundamental assumption underlying the 1993 defense budget estimates "was that the post-Cold War world would be less stable and predictable. The proposals were therefore specifically designed to be sufficiently flexible to respond to changes in the strategic environment which could not be predicted."[1] Starting in July 1990, a Ministry of Defence policy paper entitled "Options for Change" called for severe cuts, especially in ground and tactical air forces assigned to central Europe. The paper suggested an incremental approach to the force reductions. No single type of military capabilities was to be abandoned altogether, despite the cuts involved. The logic behind the choices made was to preserve a wide range of capabilities to tackle uncertain crises in the future.[2]

The Gulf War indicated that the intensity of out-of-area conflicts could require force deployments similar in number and sophistication to those foreseen for continental Europe. The traditional distinction between "in" and "out-of-area" conflicts is no longer relevant for defense planning. "Instead, the criteria will be the depth of British and allied interests and the implications of the crisis for international peace and stability."[3] Military forces in the future will "almost always be employed in conjunction with allies. However, which allies these will be, and what portion of the defence task they should be expected to bear, are matters of considerable controversy."[4]

Britain does not keep troops specifically for out-of-area contingencies. Budget restraints have made this option unfeasible. Out-of-area requirements have to be met by forces with other roles as well. As summarized by the Defence Committee of the House of Commons:

> The inherent contradiction between wanting more capable and flexible forces, while paying for fewer of them, can only begin to be solved if those forces are adaptable, highly mobile, interdependent, and inter-operable, as well as properly trained, equipped and supported.[5]

The troops that might be earmarked for deployment in an overseas emergency have primary tasks within Europe; in conflict or war all out-of-area forces could be brought back with their equipment for deployment in NATO or on home defence tasks.[6] The creation of the new "strategic reserve division" has not changed the dual nature of British mobile forces.

Since 1992, the contribution to international peace-keeping operations have been part of Britain's defense role, although no specific troops have been earmarked for these tasks. "The forces required to meet these requirements will be drawn from those with other roles."[7]

British defense expenditures for 1993-94 were estimated at £23.5 billion, which represents a slight decrease over defense spending under the previous budget of £24 billion, or 4.1 percent of GDP.[8] At this level of defense spending and with the peace-keeping operations in Northern Ireland and the former Yugoslavia, the armed forces complained of overstretch. Defence Minister Malcolm Rifkind warned that certain capabilities are "perilously close to extinction." Further cuts would reduce the number of tasks which could be performed.[9]

POWER PROJECTION: THE ARMY

As of 1993, the total strength of the British Army had fallen to 134,600 troops, a decrease of 18,300 since 1992, yet 15,000 troops above the level expected by the mid-1990s.[10] Traditionally, the main task of the British Army as part of NATO has been to contribute to the stability of western Germany with the 56,000-strong British Army of the Rhine, which will be reduced to about 23,000 troops by the mid-1990s. Britain will be a principal contributor to the NATO Rapid Reaction Corps. Ten percent of the British Army's total strength is deployed overseas: 6,500 troops in Hong Kong until 1997; 4,100 troops in Cyprus, plus 800 troops for the UNFICYP contingent; 1,600 troops in the Falklands; 1,500 in Belize; 1,000 in Brunei as a Gurkha battalion funded by the Sultan of Brunei; and 1,200 in Gibraltar. Britain is participating in several U.N. peace-keeping operations, in the former Yugoslavia, Cambodia, Cyprus, around Iraq, and in the Western Sahara. Absent from this list are troops deployed as part of the U.N. operation in Somalia.

After the 1956 Suez crisis, Britain and France awoke to the reality of their limited ability to influence events overseas militarily. They could no longer mount large-scale operations independently. France absorbed the lessons of Suez by redefining the zones of potential intervention to those which were agreeable, or at least neutral, to U.S. interests; Britain, due to the economic and military constraints of the day, had a tendency to abdicate its residual responsibilities. Allying itself with a superpower and building a small, home-based, air-transportable, strategic reserve was viewed as sufficient to protect the remaining British interests overseas. With British force levels in Europe reduced after the demise of the communist bloc, British defense planners were reconsidering the concept of a new strategic reserve division, 3(UK) Division, to be composed of 5 Airborne Brigade, 3 Royal Marine Commando Brigade, 24 Airmobile Brigade, and two mechanized brigades. In addition to its strategic reserve capability for out-of-area operations, almost all of this division would be assigned to the NATO Rapid Reaction Corps under British command.

5 Airborne Brigade: As the part of 3(UK) division intended for low-intensity conflict, 5 Airborne Brigade is a "go anywhere, anytime force, ready to respond at short notice to an emergency in any part of the world."[11] This brigade is the only airborne and air-trained brigade in the British Army, and its level of readiness is routinely set at five days, although this number can be brought down in times of crises. The brigade includes two battalions of paratroopers selected from a pool of three such existing battalions. The third battalion, which is left out on a rotational basis from the brigade structure, is on semi-reserve status. This rotational structure is premised on the inadequacy of the British capability to airlift three battalions. Intensive parachute training and capabilities are therefore limited to two operational battalions, with the third on rotation. Two light infantry battalions complete the core units of 5 Airborne Brigade: one Gurkha battalion, and one infantry battalion. Although these two battalions can be airlifted, only some of their advanced elements can be parachuted.

3 Commando Brigade: This Navy Brigade is intended for use in higher-intensity conflicts than 5 Airborne Brigade. The following section on the Royal Navy will analyze 3 Commando Brigade in more detail.

24 Airmobile Unit: Conceived as a home-based reserve force for potential projection in central Europe, 24 Airmobile Brigade is Britain's major contribution to the NATO airmobile force. This brigade is in a process of reformation. It includes two airmobile battalions equipped with *Milan* anti-armor missile systems and has important attack helicopter capabilities due to two Aviation Regiments. Each regiment has 12 *Lynx* helicopters equipped with anti-tank weapons, 10 *Lynx* light battlefield helicopters, and 12 *Gazelle* reconnaissance helicopters. The brigade does not have a dedicated support helicopter force to carry the battalions or its artillery.[12]

Special Air Service (SAS): The SAS occupies a special place outside the structure of the strategic reserve, but it is among the forces regularly used in out-of-area contingencies. It was founded in 1941 as a light mobile unit designed to execute sabotage and reconnaissance missions behind enemy lines in North Africa. It has since developed into an elite force to carry out special, often covert, military operations as a "precise cutting tool for political policy."[13] The SAS today is organized into three regiments, each a unit of the British Army. Two of those regiments are part of the Army Reserves. Of the roughly 1,500 troops in the combined regiments, about half serve in the sole permanent regiment, 22 SAS.[14] 22 SAS is divided into numerous operational squadrons of 72 men and six officers each and combines skills in amphibious, air, surveillance, and mountaineering operations, as well as in specialized signal communications.

There has been relatively little British SAS activity in Africa since the original operations in 1941, although there were strong ties with the Rhodesian SAS. Relations between the two forces remained cordial through the late 1970s, but Prime Minister Mugabe disbanded the Rhodesian SAS when majority rule was installed in Rhodesia. The British SAS assisted the Kenyan government in 1965 when an SAS

Training Mission helped organize and train a Special Force Unit for the Police Force. These have been used as presidential bodyguards and in Kenyan anti-revolutionary operations.[15] SAS training teams have also been dispatched in Botswana and Zimbabwe on various occasions in the 1980s to prepare local forces against rebel infiltration techniques. SAS forces are highly regarded in Africa, and there is a long list of African countries hoping to receive SAS training.

POWER PROJECTION: THE ROYAL NAVY

"Now it must be admitted that a good second-class navy is also outside the nation's capacity. For maritime strength depends, as it always did, upon commercial and industrial strength."[16] Thus argues Paul M. Kennedy in his 1989 book *The Rise and Fall of British Naval Mastery*. Post-World War II geo-political concerns, besides economics, also played an important role in sealing the fate of one of the world's most powerful navies. Anthony Eden's historic guarantee to commit British Army troops to NATO indirectly determined the strength of the Royal Navy for the entire duration of the Cold War. The diversion of dwindling post-war resources to a massive army commitment in central Europe was considered contrary to traditional British defense postures. Consequently, "Britain's Royal Navy became a 'NATO Navy.'"[17] Out-of-area contingencies became secondary to containment of the Soviet threat. The Falklands War emphasized the limits of British autonomy for distant maritime operations. According to a report prepared by the House of Commons' Defence Committee, "the Royal Navy is not in general organised in peacetime in units explicitly designed for intervention, with the exception of its amphibious operations."[18] Although the Royal Navy can mount maritime operations at relatively short notice by bringing together a number of warships and support ships, the same report suggested that it needed a naval equivalent to the Army Rapid Reaction Force.

In the early 1990s, the restructuring of the Royal Navy was subject to many uncertainties. The "Options for Change" paper and subsequent defense white papers envisaged less dramatic reductions in Royal Navy/Royal Marines forces than for Army forces, from 63,500 men in 1990 to about 50,000 by 1995.[19] The fleet size would be decreased through the elimination of roughly 20 aging submarines and their escorts, while minesweepers would not be ordered at the rate or in the numbers previously expected.

Warships for Power Projection

Aircraft Carriers: Qualitatively, the decline of British maritime power is illustrated by the decision of Harold Wilson's government to cancel the construction of the *Furious* on February 22, 1966, in the wake of the East of Suez decision. This aircraft carrier was planned to have a displacement of 53,000 tons in order to embark a large number of aircraft. The Royal Navy, with its ambitious plan, priced itself out of gaining enough political support. After careful consideration, the government opted to phase out the old aircraft carriers in the 1970s, when they became obsolete, and "to place no orders for new carriers, relying on shore-based aircraft to support our other arms."[20] For a while, the Royal Navy viewed with favor the declining number of facilities available for shore-based aircraft because it seemed to imply that new aircraft carriers could substitute for them. However, in the aftermath of the East of Suez policy: "the decision against the new carrier in 1966 signalled the retreat; the series of strategic expedients introduced to suggest that this was not the case never carried full conviction."[21]

With the cancellation of the *Furious*, Britain preferred to rely on smaller carriers. The Royal Navy deployed three "through-deck cruisers," which were later designated as anti-submarine warfare (ASW) carriers. Emphasis was put on the need to secure the supply routes in the North Atlantic and to protect the British homeland as a base for NATO forces operating in Europe. The long-range action during the Falklands War tested the full capabilities of the Royal Navy. One valuable conclusion drawn from that conflict was a new appreciation for the advantages of fixed-wing aircraft carriers with sophisticated early-warning electronic warfare systems and interceptors. The limited range of the *Sea Harrier* was one of the concerns that also arose from the Falklands experience.

In addition to their anti-submarine warfare capability, the ASW carriers were given some versatility because they were also conceived as commando cruisers. The ASW carriers can displace up to 19,500 tons and embark only short take-off aircraft. A typical load may include 10 *Sea Harriers* and 9 to 12 *Sea King* helicopters. Currently, the Royal Navy has three ASW carriers: the *Ark Royal*, the *Invincible*, and the

Illustrious. Two of these are operated permanently and the third, the *Illustrious*, is kept on standby in Portsmouth with 30 days notice. Although the Navy has retained three ASW carriers, it has aircraft for only two of them. Their replacement is scheduled in 2010-2015, depending on the carriers' use. The Admiralty has not yet developed any design proposals for a new type of aircraft carrier, although Navy officials would favor a normal-sized, fixed-wing carrier with catapults. Two factors inspired this development: the greater radius of aircraft embarked on a "classic" aircraft carrier (i.e. with conventional take-off capabilities), and the problems related to the aging *Harrier* fleet.

The ongoing review of Europe's security problems may induce the Navy to reconsider the potential roles and applications of its fleet of ASW carriers. No plans exist at this stage to curtail this force in any way. ASW-carriers, equipped with a very comprehensive command center, are ideal for commanding task forces in overseas contingencies.

Helicopter Carriers: The 1993 defense plans and budget estimates made room for the acquisition of Britain's first helicopter carrier. An order was placed in May 1993, although the ship is not scheduled to become operational before 1998.[22] The existing helicopter training ship, the *Argus*, while fitted with substantial hangar space, offers neither the command and control nor the accommodation required. The newly commissioned ship is called an Aviation Support Ship (ASS) or a Landing Platform Helicopter (LPD). It will resemble a flat-top helicopter carrier with a dock. The requirements shaping the ship's specifications were based on the need to be able to airlift a single company group helicopter assault wave while simultaneously engaging in an amphibious attack. Twelve on-board helicopters provide the ability to launch over-the-horizon operations or to shorten the time necessary to disembark the force. The ship will likely carry six *Sea King* helicopters, six *Lynx* helicopters, and four landing crafts. Accommodation for an 800-man commando group is also required.

Amphibious Ships: According to its technical definition, an amphibious force:

> is a flexible and versatile instrument of maritime power, which allows a nation to project, or threaten to project, power ashore, whenever and wherever politically appropriate. [...] An amphibious force can be held at a high state of readiness at home or on the high seas and has considerable deterrent value. [...] It may sail early in a time of tension without commitment and does not require over-flying rights or host

nation support for deployment or resupply. The force is logistically self-sufficient.[23]

Such a force can move 300 nautical miles per day, and thus the extent of its influence upon events ashore is very wide.[24] Given the tactical versatility of an amphibious force, Britain, after lengthy debate, continues to maintain a core of them. The Royal Navy maintains a fleet of two amphibious assault ships, the *Intrepid* and the *Fearless*. Built in the 1960s, these ships are rapidly wearing out and will remain in service only until the mid-1990s. Their versatility is the product of a landing deck which can accept three helicopters, eight landing crafts, 400 embarked troops and 15 tanks. These assault ships give the Royal Marines their uniqueness. Should they be displaced by requisitioned ferries and airliners, the Royal Marines' future "as an elite force with a separate military identity also looks doubtful."[25] The Royal Navy won a new lease for its amphibious force in February 1992, when contracts for project definition and replacement were announced.

In addition to the assault ships, the Royal Navy has also launched five logistic landing ships, four of which were planned and built at the same time as the assault ships. These landing ships have a capacity of 340 troops, 16 tanks, and one helicopter.[26]

Other combat ships and the Royal Fleet Auxiliary: At the end of 1993, the Royal Navy had a large array of ships covering the spectrum of naval warfare capabilities. In addition to the aircraft carriers and amphibious combat ships, the Royal Navy's long-range intervention capability can also draw on 13 destroyers, 27 frigates, 10 support ships, 10 maintenance and logistics ships, five survey ships, and 30 minesweepers and minehunters.[27] Future cuts might reduce the number of destroyers and frigates to a total of about 35.

The Royal Fleet Auxiliary of 23 ships is operated by the Royal Navy Supply and Transport Service, which provides all logistic support for the Royal Navy and is manned by Merchant Navy civilian personnel. The Royal Fleet Auxiliary includes the *Argus* Helicopter Support Ship, which can carry up to six helicopters; Large Fleet Tankers, which can carry two helicopters; smaller tankers; support ships; and five landing ships. British merchant ships were assumed to complement the Royal Fleet Auxiliary in times of war, but the Gulf War proved their almost complete obsolescence for military transportation purposes, a subject of much concern to British military planners and decision-makers. Britain had to rely on foreign merchant ships.[28]

Navy Ground Forces

3 Commando Brigade Royal Marines: The Royal Marines are part of the Royal Navy and are integrated into the new 3(UK) strategic reserve division. As a corps, they control a brigade for amphibious action, deploy battalion-strength commandos worldwide, man Navy ships with small detachments, and provide specialized forces.

In Britain, the Marines are a force for offshore insulation. The main role of 3 Commando Brigade, the primary element of the Marines, is to participate in the defense of NATO's northern flank. Its members are all trained skiers, but the brigade has the flexibility to be deployed anywhere in the world for a duration of 30 days. The 6,900-man Royal Marines include two major formations with two separate headquarters, one for training and reserves and one for operations. Three Commando Brigade, with 3,185 troops, is completely self-contained and includes three battalion-sized Commandos. Some of the other units within the Royal Marines are highly specialized. The Mountain and Arctic Warfare Cadre acts as a deep penetration unit for behind-the-lines reconnaissance and sabotage missions. Two Assault Squadrons, with six landing craft, complete the amphibious role of the Marines. There are also two squadrons of Special Boat Service, which is part of the British Special Forces. The *Commachio* group specializes in defending Britain's offshore oil and gas rigs against terrorist attacks.

The Royal Marines possess a series of advantages over airborne troops in the event of an out-of-area involvement, which partially compensates for their lower mobility. An amphibious assault force may take days or weeks to get to its area of operation, but it can remain there for an extended period. One important advantage of an amphibious force aboard an assault ship is its flexibility to land when and where it chooses, carrying all the necessary equipment and stores. This self-containment and durability is further leveraged by the versatility of the assault ships, which offer a combination of helicopter decks, landing craft docks, and powerful communication outfits.

Fleet Air Arm

Sea Harrier: The Royal Navy benefits greatly from the technological breakthrough that the *Harrier* Short Takeoff Vertical Landing Aircraft (STOVL) represents. This aircraft has made it possible for Britain to continue to operate aircraft carriers after the cancellation of the *Furious* project. The Royal Navy's 37 *Harriers* are quick-response close-air-support planes, which will be outdated by 2010-2015. In the shorter term, plans are to update the aircraft. Despite new designs, which may offer the *Harrier* supersonic speeds, and the impressive record of the *Harriers* in the Falklands war, recent trends are against their use in the long-run. The Falklands air battle success was more the result of the superior training and experience of British pilots and of an excellent air-to-air missile than of superior aircraft. The *Sea Harriers* have a relatively short range of up to 250 miles, which is more limited than conventional fighter aircraft. The *Sea Harriers* also have a smaller payload. It should be recognized, however, that these limitations are compensated by invaluable versatility in sea-land battles. Unlike conventional aircraft leaving from a conventional takeoff carrier, the *Harrier* can land virtually anyplace once ashore. Given sufficient fuel supply lines, a *Harrier* land base can be easily created close to the battlefield. A conventional fighter would need approximately 3,000 to 4,000 feet of runway, which is a rare commodity in some Third World regions, or it has to return to its aircraft carrier.

Sea King Helicopter: By 1993, the Fleet Air Arm disposed of 119 *Sea King* helicopters. Their mission encompasses a variety of tasks: Anti-Submarine (seven squadrons), Airborne Early Warning (one squadron), Commando Assault (three squadrons), and Fleet Support Search and Rescue (two squadrons).[29] During the Falklands conflict, a *Sea King* squadron was used to resupply ships en route to the South Atlantic, and *Sea Kings* were used extensively during combat operations. The Navy's helicopter fleet includes 78 *Lynx* helicopters for anti-submarine warfare, but the Royal Marines use them in an anti-tank capacity. The Navy also has 26 *Gazelles* for training and reconnaissance.[30]

POWER PROJECTION: THE ROYAL AIR FORCE

In its current configuration, the Royal Air Force (RAF) is 80,900-men strong. This figure will be slashed to 75,000 under the "Options for Change" plan. Cuts announced by the minister of defense in April 1993 would reduce the RAF's personnel by another 5,000 by the late 1990s.[31] The RAF is scheduled to reduce the number of its long-range strike aircraft by 45 percent, with a 22 percent cut in fighter squadrons but no reductions in fixed- or rotary-wing air transport.[32] The strength of the RAF in Germany will fall from fifteen squadrons to nine. Despite these quantitative changes, the RAF will retain its full range of capabilities, although reductions point toward significant strategic prioritization. As a senior RAF official said: "The RAF will retain its shape, but there will be more focus now on flexibility."[33] The concern for flexibility reflects the diminished threat from the former Soviet Union and exhibits a gradual, although incomplete, shift in emphasis to out-of-area responsibilities.

A major change which will affect the strike capability of the RAF will be the introduction of the *Eurofighter* 2000. The RAF and the British government are committed to purchase about 250 of these planes. If the full order of the *Eurofighter* 2000 survives the budgetary controversy, its versatile role would mean that it could replace *Jaguars* and *Tornado* F3s. The *Eurofighter* 2000 will become Britain's main attack aircraft and close combat fighter for missions in and outside Europe.[34] In conjunction with the creation of a highly mobile strategic reserve division, the RAF may in the future place orders for a larger, unspecified number of new support helicopters and transport aircraft.

Air Strike Capabilities

Britain has not used strike aircraft to carry out operations in sub-Saharan Africa over the last two decades. There have, however, been several instances where Britain operated strike aircraft in out-of-area theaters, such as during the Falklands War, the Gulf War, and the U.N. peace-keeping mission in the former Yugoslavia.

Tornado: The RAF is equipped with 234 *Tornado* GR-1 and F-2/3 aircraft in either fighter, strike, or reconnaissance configuration. The role of the 66 RAF *Tornado* aircraft deployed in the Gulf was highly publicized. The reconnaissance *Tornado* GR-1A played a key role in the identification of *Scud* missile sites. Their infra-red sensors provided day and night capabilities and allowed data review in real time.[35] Thermal imaging and laser designator pods supplied the *Tornado* with autonomous and accurate designation of targets.

Jaguar: Britain also deployed 12 *Jaguar* GR-1As in the Gulf from an entire active fleet of 44. The *Jaguar* planes will be retained in the foreseeable future to perform their standard reinforcement roles, especially those related to the defense of NATO's northern flank.

Despite their combat versatility, the British *Tornados* and *Jaguars* are not easily deployable in distant overseas theaters of operations.

They were not used in the Falklands War because they could not operate from ASW carriers. *Tornados* assisted by tanker and support aircraft, however, have participated in exercises and demonstrations in the Far East, thereby displaying their long-range capabilities.

Harrier: The RAF maintains 61 *Harriers* in various configurations as fighter or ground attack planes. Britain is committed to retaining the flexible *Harrier*, even in a shrinking Air Force. More purchases of the newer versions of the *Harrier*, the GR-7 which has night attack capabilities, are planned. Fifty planes, out of an estimated total order of 110, were delivered in 1993. Fifteen of the *Harriers* involved in the Falklands War were from the Royal Navy and 16 were from the RAF. The purpose of the RAF *Harriers* was to serve as attrition replacements and to relieve the *Sea Harriers* of ground attack tasks.[36] Neither Royal Navy nor RAF *Harriers* participated in the Gulf War.

Air Transport

The RAF has only enough C-130 *Hercules* to drop a single parachute battalion group in one lift; to deliver and sustain a brigade would require a larger transport fleet. The larger long-range *Tristar* has significant airlift capabilities but cannot be used for tactical parachute operations. The same is true for the RAF's VC-10. The reach of the Army's 5 Airborne Brigade is therefore limited by the RAF's airlift capabilities, which can be enhanced by leasing allied airlift, generally from the U.S., or by resorting to sealift. The RAF has acquired an important tanker fleet with substantial air-to-air refueling capacity.

C-130 Hercules: In 1993, the RAF had 62 C-130H transport planes available. Six C-130s have dual capabilities as transporters or tankers, and sixteen are equipped with air-refueling devices. In the early 1980s, the "stretching" of the C-130 enhanced its out-of-area airlift capabilities. The RAF's new emphasis on flexibility and high mobility will put additional pressure on the need to replace the *Hercules*, but no specific decision had been made as of late 1993. Two likely candidates are the new generation C-130J *Hercules II* and the European Future Large Aircraft, which will be built by a four-nation consortium but was still in the planning stage in late 1993.[37]

During the Falklands conflict, the C-130 established an "air-bridge" between Britain and Ascension, Gibraltar, Dakar and Banjul. Daily flights reached a peak of sixteen. The *Hercules* also performed air-drops to the Task Force ships in and en route to the South Atlantic.

With additional fuel tanks, C-130s even performed long-range supply missions from Ascension to the Task Force, a flight which could last as long as 13 hours.[38] British C-130s were also heavily involved in the Gulf War and participated in supplying emergency relief food to Somalia in 1992-93.

VC-10, Victor, and Tristar: In 1993, there were 27 VC-10 long-range planes in the RAF fleet: nine tankers and the rest assigned to strategic transportation. An additional 12 were also procured. All existing VC-10s are either assigned to air-to-air refueling or are in the process of being converted for that role. The RAF is also equipped with nine *Tristar* tankers/transporters and eight *Victor* tankers. The extensive use of the *Victors* in the Gulf War shortened their lives considerably and the aircraft will probably be phased out by the mid-to-late 1990s, together with the *Buccaneer* and *Jaguar* strike planes.[39]

Long-Range Air Reconnaissance and Space Surveillance

AWACS: One of the main lacunae of the Task Force in the Falklands was the absence of airborne early warning systems. In July 1990, the first E-3D Airborne Warning and Control System (AWACS) arrived in Britain. The RAF took possession of its first AWACS aircraft early in 1991, and six more were delivered before the end of 1992. Despite the relaxation of the Soviet threat, the RAF insisted that it still needed all seven AWACS planes "because of the sheer volume of airspace it needs to monitor, including its NATO commitments," according to Ministry of Defence officials.[40] The aircraft will be split between NATO and national use. For out-of-area missions, they can be supported at a forward operating base for up to one month at a time.

Nimrod: There are about 33 *Nimrods*, three of which are assigned to electronic countermeasures, and the rest to maritime reconnaissance. *Nimrods* were used during the Gulf war for maritime patrols and anti-submarine watch.

SKYNET 4: Over the years, Britain has deployed a military communications network based on the *SKYNET 4* communication satellite. It played a crucial role during the Gulf War. Britain does not have an independent satellite remote sensing capability, but the excellent cooperation in the field of intelligence with the United States has made such an acquisition less important.[41]

POWER PROJECTION FOR AFRICAN THEATERS

Overall, Britain has retained many military instruments to exercise power overseas. The Army units earmarked for rapid action have achieved a level of proficiency among the world's highest. The SAS provides an efficient and discreet tool for swift and timely action in distant corners of the world. The Royal Navy has proved its competence in low-to-mid intensity conflicts during the Falklands War. The versatility of a combination of small aircraft carriers with amphibious assault ships extends the reach of the Royal Navy to virtually all seas. The RAF combines a relatively large fleet of C-130s and tanker aircraft to give it autonomy in military airlift for limited conflicts. The *Jaguar* and *Tornado* strike aircraft, as well as the immensely successful *Harrier*, grant Britain air supremacy against all but a very few air forces. Nevertheless, Britain has shied away from using its armed forces in a sub-Saharan context since the early 1980s, barring a few marginal instances. Overall, British military activity in sub-Saharan Africa has been significantly more restricted than French involvement since the early 1960s. For its part, Britain still regularly trains elite troops in Kenya, but the numbers do not match the vastly larger amounts of French troops which are permanently or semi-permanently deployed in Africa. The reduced number of direct British interventions does not mean that there has been no British military involvement in sub-Saharan Africa. Britain maintains many teams of military advisors in various African countries. Southern Africa has been largely privileged as a recipient of this type of military assistance.

MILITARY COOPERATION

Defining British Priorities

As Britain's global influence diminished after World War II, so too did British military assistance decline as a useful tool for protecting British interests in Africa. In 1981, *The Financial Times* described British policy on military aid in rather derogatory terms:

> Britain's military assistance programme has grown, if not like Topsy, then certainly without real planning. Stemming from the days of empire, it has tended to concentrate on Commonwealth or Third World countries. It is seen by many as highly effective. Yet for 20 years now

it has remained cheap, compact - and peripheral, both to the way Britain sees its own defence needs and to its foreign policy.[42]

Thirty years of military aid confirms the continuity of this downward trend in the African context, although a country-by-country analysis indicates a reversal of this general direction in four specific cases: Zimbabwe, Namibia, Mozambique and, to a lesser degree, Botswana. The resurgence in military assistance to these countries, of which Namibia and Mozambique were not British colonies, was part of Margaret Thatcher's policy of support for Front Line states. As a rule, most military assistance programs appear to be impervious to abrupt changes in the international arena. Small budget allocations for military training in Africa reflected Britain's pragmatic and unambitious policy goals for the region. Dramatic shifts in funding between beneficiaries are infrequent due to bureaucratic inertia and chronic budgetary struggles over the Foreign and Commonwealth Office's Military Training and Assistance Scheme. Country desk turf battles for a larger slice of the military cooperation budget are best described as a zero-sum game because the overall allocations remain roughly the same size every year.

> In practice, the "framework" figure for any recipient is remarkably stable, rising or falling only gently over several years. One reason is inertia. A second is that the occasional proposals to cut aid in response to some provocative statement or gesture by an African leader are generally blocked by on-the-ground British diplomats who in most cases advise that actions speak louder than words, that anti-British action is very rare, and that the existence of an aid program gives access and some influence that would be lost if there were a cutoff.[43]

Criteria for extending British military assistance have developed over time, while the implementation of new programs or continuation of old ones is reviewed in light of their ability to satisfy the basic requirements. These new conditions, of which there are three, are both pragmatic and ideological. First, the assistance programs must encourage good governance; that is, they should not contribute to the repressive capabilities of "bad" governments. In the same vein, British military assistance is intended to contribute to stability. Second, the training provided under the assistance program must make military sense. In other words, British training teams must be able to complete their programs without arbitrary rotations of trainees or high attrition rates. The training must produce military competence. Third, the assistance programs must be cost-effective. This may be the hardest measure of success because it is easy to exaggerate the political importance of these programs. Oddly enough, opponents of expansion in the military assistance program are mainly found at the Ministry of Defence; they argue that all expansion would come at the detriment of resource-starved British forces.[44] The second criterion is purely military, and sometimes clashes with the third requirement, which is a reflection of the Foreign and Commonwealth Office's concern with the price of political influence in an assisted country.

Institutional Actors

"In theory, the Foreign and Commonwealth Office has the policy lead in developing Britain's approach to Africa, including the military component."[45] The Overseas and Defence Sub-Committee of the cabinet, chaired by the prime minister, closely supervises the large military training programs, such as those in Zimbabwe. This division of tasks frequently results in friction within the government bureaucracy. While military officials welcome the experience for their troops, the prime minister and Treasury are anxious to avoid any open-ended commitments.[46] Where no defense interest is served, costs are met either by the country receiving military aid or by the Foreign and Commonwealth Office. By 1990, the latter's share represented about £17-18 million (compared to £9 million in 1981). Half of this budget was spent on Africa, with £7.6 million going to southern Africa alone.[47] The Ministry of Defence carries out any military assistance prescribed by the overseas policy of the government. The specific projects to fulfill government policy are formulated and executed out of the Office of the Director for Military Assistance Overseas by a team of less than 20 officers. The director "has direct tasking authority in the unified British military structure over each of the services for personnel and support for military assistance projects within the resource limits available in the program."[48]

Military assistance, military aid, and defense exports are the three main British contributions to the military development of sub-Saharan states. Military assistance refers to the provision of education, training, and advisory help to indigenous military forces. This is often done through the deployment of training cadres, the creation of schools, and individual instruction both in the recipient country and in Britain.[49]

Military aid consists of outright grants of weapons, equipment or other goods for military development. Defense exports are paid transfers of military goods from British military producers, financed either by cash payments or credit extended to the recipient country.[50]

In early 1993, some 370 British service personnel were loaned to 30 different countries outside NATO (compared to 750 in 1981), and some 3,000 students from non-NATO countries attended military training courses in Britain (compared to 4,000 in 1981). These figures were supplemented by 47 short-term training or advisory teams to 45 non-NATO countries.[51] The number of states benefitting from British training on location has increased since the early 1980s, when only 27 countries outside NATO were involved. In some cases, the British team actually runs the local armed forces. The majority of the countries, including the Gulf states and Nigeria during the oil boom, pay for the assistance they receive. In 1981, Brunei, Kuwait, Oman and Zimbabwe all had British teams of over 100 military personnel. Nigeria and Saudi Arabia paid for teams of more than 50 British officers, while the other countries had teams of less than 50; in most instances there were fewer than six officers per country, as in Ghana, Mauritius, and Swaziland. As is developed below, in the early 1990s, only about 100 British military training personnel were assigned to sub-Saharan Africa.

British military aid comes in the form of equipment, often non-lethal material like radios and vehicles, but never as cash grants. These gifts are often: "more symbolic than significant. Since there is no budget for such assistance and FCO ministers cannot normally extract resources from the Ministry of Defense, these gifts require creative accounting, normally with the prime minister's approval."[52] Within the Ministry of Defence, more significant offers of used equipment and training can be provided to encourage a regular sale with a foreign government.

Traditional British arms export markets have become more sophisticated, both in the type of weapons that are purchased and in the type of financial arrangements and offsets that are part of the deals. "Gone are the days when second-hand British equipment could be gifted to the United Kingdom's former colonies," a British Aerospace official was quoted as saying.[53] This may be true for Asian markets, where at least 35 percent of the value of the purchases has to be injected back into direct or indirect offsets, but sub-Saharan African economies would be hard pressed to handle such large percentages. Sub-Saharan Africa's market potential and financial conditions are not conducive to keeping British defense exports to the region at high levels. The Nigerian market remains one of the most attractive. For instance, in 1983, Britain sold 18 *Jaguar* combat aircraft to the Nigerian Air Force. During the second half of the 1980s, Britain sold $14 billion in arms worldwide, of which only $260 million, or less than 2 percent, went to sub-Saharan Africa. Out of the share for sub-Sahara Africa, Nigeria and Kenya each received $120 million, or 46 percent, while Malawi received $10 million, and Cameroon and Mozambique received $5 million apiece. In comparison, France sold about $605 million in arms to sub-Saharan Africa, which represents less than 3.5 percent of total French arms sales over the same period.[54] In 1990, British arms exports to sub-Saharan Africa reached roughly $60 million, or about 1.8 percent of total British defense equipment exports for that year.[55]

The Ministry of Defense operates a Defence Export Services Office, which has no budget to provide soft credit but, through creative accounting, can offer free training and used equipment. Preferential credit arrangements must be worked out with the Department of Trade and Industry. They are sometimes backed by the Export Credit Guarantee Department with the participation of British banks.

Assistance In-the-Field

The principal effort behind the African military assistance program is embodied in the temporary military units known as the British Military Assistance Training Teams (BMATTs). These offer merely technical advice. In 1993, the size ranged from a few individuals to larger teams of over 50, as in Zimbabwe. While southern African countries host the largest British military assistance teams, countries in West and central Africa host much smaller BMATT squads.

By definition, BMATTs are assigned for temporary missions, which very often means that this commitment is limited to one budgetary year or very short instruction visits. The possibility of renewal does exist, and the large Zimbabwe team has been in place for the last ten years. Margaret Thatcher insisted that training teams should be viewed as operations that should not commit Britain for unspecified periods. "Thus all training programmes have a notional time-scale within which the team is meant to work itself out of a job."[56]

The role of BMATTs is primarily focused on education and training. In some instances, however, the teams are actively involved in running sections of the local military system: "Assistance shades into military support when the recipient is unable to manage the business in hand

and significant numbers of military personnel on loan assume executive positions, but the distinction is sometimes no more than academic."[57]

Overall, the geographic distribution of British military assistance has not changed much over the last decade. Namibia is the most recent addition to the list of beneficiaries. In the 1980s, out of 32 sub-Saharan African states, only nine did not have some form of agreement with London whereby they could receive British military assistance.[58] As for training in Britain, the number of Third World trainees, including Africans, has declined over the past 15 years. This phenomenon reflects the increased emphasis on on-site training, thereby alleviating some of the difficulties in meeting the rising costs of their stay in Britain. Except for a small RAF contingent in Zimbabwe, all British military assistance personnel in sub-Saharan Africa are from the Army.

West Africa: Nigeria formerly had 40 to 50 British instructors at the Jaji Staff College, initially at the request of the Nigerian Army and later of the Air Force and Navy as well. This large British presence in Nigeria began in the mid-1970s, when oil-exporting Nigeria could afford it. Due to the Nigerian inability to maintain payments and an emphasis on domestic forces, the program was terminated in 1983. Only three British trainers remained at the school of infantry. Ghana has preferred to receive assistance from a Commonwealth Military Advisory Team (CMAT) composed of four people. Since the departure of all other Commonwealth contingents, however, the remaining troops are all British, making it for all practical purposes a BMATT team. Finally, five BMATT personnel are posted in Gambia.

East Africa: The British Ministry of Defence regularly subsidizes training in Kenya, mostly for infantry. In 1989, a major exercise was held for an engineer squadron and three infantry battalions which rotated through, one at a time. There are no permanent assistance personnel or BMATT teams in Kenya. Uganda hosted a permanent team of British training personnel, but they were asked to leave in the mid-1980s - coinciding with Museveni's rise to power. In 1986, a 12-member temporary BMATT unit was sent to Uganda, smoothing over relations between Kampala and London after a brief interlude of tense dialogue with the exit of the permanent team. The British military training team pulled out of Sudan in 1990. Until then there had been only four military personnel stationed in Khartoum. The logic behind the withdrawal was that the program failed to fulfill at least two of the three criteria for British military assistance: the training did not make military sense in terms of attendance, and it was not cost-effective

because Britain was not helping to restore a rapidly deteriorating
security situation in the south. The overall evaluation of the program
was disappointing and frustrating.

Southern Africa: In the 1970s Britain paid very close attention to
monitoring the settlement of the transition in Rhodesia-Zimbabwe. The
last British combat forces in Africa left in 1981 when Zimbabwe
became independent. Immediately afterwards, Britain supported its
largest African military assistance program in recent times, sending a
160-man team to integrate and retrain the Zimbabwean armies after the
civil war. That group was still in place by 1993, although with reduced
forces and a dual mission. By then, British assistance personnel
numbered approximately 60. Roughly 35 of them belonged to the
training team for Zimbabwe's armed forces, and 25 were assigned to
the training of Mozambican armed forces inside Zimbabwe. Among
various achievements, the British BMATT advisors designed and helped
build a modern simulation and command center to train entire units of
the Zimbabwe Army in developing command and staff procedures.
BMATT assisted the Zimbabwe Army in operating the military training
camp at Nyanga, near the border with Mozambique. The rate of
graduation was about 120 soldiers per quarter through 1988, at a cost
of about £2 million per year.[59]

Starting in 1986, during Zimbabwe's heavy involvement in
Mozambique to prevent RENAMO rebels from cutting Zimbabwe's
access to the sea, the BMATT team extended its training to
Mozambican troops. Since its inception, this segment of the program
has trained approximately 3,000 Mozambican troops. Strictly speaking,
BMATT is assisting the Zimbabwe National Army in giving aid to a
strategically located neighbor, and some of the training at Nyanga is
provided by Zimbabwe Army instructors. Training conditions were not
optimal during the Mozambican civil war because troops were fielded
back to the theater of operations too quickly. With the 1993 peace
settlement between the Mozambican government and the RENAMO
rebels, BMATT has been training joint units of RENAMO and
government troops. In late 1993, a first unit of 100 troops, 50 from
each side, was close to graduation. Joint training was subsequently
intensified, with intakes of 440 troops per quarter, half of which were
again from Mozambican regular forces and half from RENAMO rebels.
BMATT has been a very efficient instrument for training and
professionalizing Zimbabwean and Mozambican troops.

Four British military assistance personnel were sent to Malawi in 1989 for three months to train the local forces in mine clearance techniques. Malawi has been involved in securing the Nacala railroad inside Mozambique against sabotage attempts by the RENAMO movement. Britain is not eager to commit itself to such operations, having already concentrated on helping Zimbabwe clear the Beira railroad inside Mozambique. Assistance in Malawi remains *ad hoc*. Britain also maintains army training teams of three men in Lesotho and Swaziland, and two men in Mauritius.

The bulk of Ministry of Defense funding for training in Botswana is allocated to the Army. Six British Army personnel were sent to give military assistance, and an SAS team trained Botswanan forces for 16 weeks in 1988.[60] Occasionally, small Air Defense Advisory Teams from the RAF are also sent. In Botswana, Britain is interested in infantry training as an additional means to secure the relations between the two countries. Botswana's training grounds are regarded as a potential replacement for the Kenyan infantry training facilities should the internal domestic situation in Kenya become so repressive as to make British exercises there politically unacceptable.

Training was viewed as a symbol of Britain's good relations with the Front Line States. Despite the frustration of officers in the field with the slowness of progress and the sometimes poor quality of the trainees, the programs have been maintained. This commitment underlined the British government's concern with preserving such a potent tool of influence and good relations. By being discreet, BMATT enhanced its utility to the recipient states and, in turn, served as effective support to British influence in the Front Line States.

The British military assistance plan for Namibia had two phases. In the first phase, the British contingent to the U.N. Transition Assistance Group in Namibia (UNTAG) offered communications support. This included a signal unit of 170 military personnel. After Namibian independence on March 21, 1990 and the establishment of a new government, Britain offered military assistance training on a purely bilateral basis. The assistance, starting in March-April 1990, was carried out by about 50 British military officers who performed three main tasks. First, they assisted the Namibian authorities in setting up an embryonic Ministry of Defense. Second, British assistance personnel helped command and control structures. Third, they provided the new Namibian armed forces with some comprehensive training assistance, including basic training, recruitment counselling and officer selections.

In most assignments, British training teams did more than supervise the Namibian efforts; they often executed the actual operational work. The in-country British assistance is complemented by training in Britain for Namibian armed forces personnel. The assistance to Namibia was initially provided for one year and was followed by a gradual decline in subsequent years. The Namibian program satisfies all criterion for British military assistance in that it is effective, affordable, and self-sufficient while enhancing British influence in the country.

A Cornerstone of Thatcher's African Legacy

Most British military training and assistance programs in sub-Saharan Africa were on the decline by the late 1970s. The independence of Zimbabwe and the highly unstable situation in southern Africa allowed Britain to launch a set of new military cooperation initiatives in the region. The initial deployment of British military advisors came as part of the overall settlement among concerned parties during the independence process in Zimbabwe. By the mid-1980s, Britain was increasingly pilloried in international fora for opposing the intensification of sanctions against South Africa. At the 1987 Commonwealth Heads of Government Meeting in Vancouver, "Mrs. Thatcher, quite unrepentant, argued that Britain preferred constructive policies in the region [...]. In this context, she also pointed out that the British Army was helping to train recruits for the Mozambique Army."[61] The use of military aid to Front Line States as a substitute for sanctions had become a cornerstone of the prime minister's policy in the region. Despite the very high efficiency of the British military aid, governments in sub-Saharan Africa never acknowledged the principle underlying the substitution. During Thatcher's years as prime minister, Britain was continually criticized for not applying sanctions. By the end of 1993, sanctions against South Africa were being lifted, but the BMATT teams in southern Africa remained operational.

Chapter 8

British Overseas Military Facilities

After the independence of India and the demise of the British colonial empire, Britain remained in charge of myriad military bases, either on foreign soil or on small insular British possessions that had been preserved from the general imperial collapse. The bases and possessions gave the British armed forces staging posts in the North and South Atlantic, the Mediterranean, the Caribbean, the Middle East, and even as far as the China Sea and the Pacific Ocean. Through them, British forces could claim to have a global reach. The post-colonial facilities available to Britain in and around Africa can be presented in three parts. Firstly, there are military facilities resulting from agreements with another government, like the Simonstown naval base, the Libyan training facilities, Aden, and Malta. None of these facilities remain available to British armed forces, although some survived well into the 1970s. Secondly, there is Cyprus, which, with two sovereign British bases, is in a category of its own. Finally, there are the British dependent territories, all of which are islands except for Gibraltar. Some of these territories have real or residual military value, others are, from the military perspective, of only historic interest.

With the end of empire and the withdrawal east of Suez, British overseas bases ceased to belong to an integrated strategic ensemble. They were remnants of imperial times, and the rationale for their upkeep was lost. It was not long before Britain began to abandon some of the facilities due to the pressure of both African nationalism and domestic budgetary constraints. After its colonial disengagement, all of the continental British military facilities and bases in Africa were gone except for British island territories surrounding the continent.

In the Mediterranean, Britain was committed in the mid-1960s to assist in the defense of Malta, to consult and cooperate in the defense of Cyprus, and, under the Anglo-Libyan Treaty of 1953, to go to the aid of Libya in the event of it being engaged in war or armed conflicts. In exchange for this defense assistance, Britain was granted access to military facilities in those respective countries. On Africa's periphery, Britain was responsible for the internal and external security of dependent territories such as Gibraltar, Aden, and the High Commission territories of Mauritius, the Seychelles and the Falkland Islands. Britain also kept the colony of St. Helena, with the strategically located islands of Ascension and Tristan da Cunha. The British Indian Ocean Territory, a group of islands including Diego Garcia, was initially administered by Britain from Mauritius and the Seychelles and remained under British control after the independence of these two countries.

In South Africa, the Royal Navy has made effective use of the facilities at its disposal under the Simonstown Agreement. Bending to political pressure to distance itself from the apartheid government, Britain unilaterally denounced the agreement in 1975.

Military Rationale for an Overseas Presence

The British overseas presence in the post-colonial age was in search of a cause to justify its perpetuation, even in a reduced format after the loss of the empire. The primary existential problem was, as Alastair Buchan noted, linked to the "tremendous fallacy wrapped up in the word 'presence.' It is a great mistake to think that a mere military presence deters trouble. It must be backed up either with great authority, in the sense that the presence is representing a number of powerful nations, or it must possess great power itself."[1]

British dependent territories and military bases overseas failed to satisfy either of these conditions completely. The military power available on these territories was usually small, and with the European commitment of the British armed forces there was less power available to back up waning British authority overseas. Moreover, Britain lacked a clear mission. What trouble was the remaining military presence intended to deter? Under what conditions would Britain launch a military operation? There were few overseas commitments left, and even less British military power or political will to support them.

Despite the lack of a clear long-term mission, British military authorities organized the overseas facilities in garrisons and bases, each having different assignments:

> The purpose of a garrison is to guard and help to maintain law and order in the place where the garrison is located. Thus the need for a garrison normally flows from the responsibility of sovereignty or agreement. The military need for an overseas base, however, is determined by the time required to deploy forces and weapons where danger threatens. A base is thus a place where troops, ships, aircraft, heavy equipment, supplies and facilities for maintenance and repair can be kept for military operations elsewhere.[2]

A single overseas facility can be a base for one branch of the armed forces and a garrison for another. Accordingly, in the early 1960s, Britain kept Army garrisons in Malta and Gibraltar because neither of these places was used for Army power projections in the region, but rather as local defense forces. Both locations, however, were naval and air bases. Cyprus was primarily an air base, Aden was an Army and RAF base, and Singapore was a base for all three services.

By the early 1960s, Britain began to question the financial burden of maintaining a vast network of bases and garrisons abroad. Garrisons were particularly expensive because British armed forces were frequently engaged in manpower-intensive constabulary duties overseas. The 1956 Suez Canal crisis further taught the British the limitations of their power, but also demonstrated the vulnerability of their overseas lines of communications in the world order after World War II. Unrestricted access and freedom to use facilities abroad for military purposes could no longer be taken for granted. Military planners first tried to hedge against these limitations by recommending the acquisition of weapons systems designed for power projection. "We must insure against the possible loss of fixed installations overseas by keeping men and heavy equipment afloat, and by increasing the air and sea portability of the Strategic Reserve."[3] This crusade would eventually fail on both accounts: the bases were gradually lost and the strategic reserve was an insufficient replacement. In the absence of bases and enhanced power projection capabilities, the only alternative left to defense planners was to explore whether "some of our burdens can be assumed or shared by our allies."[4] There was an important precedent for this approach. British responsibilities in Greece had already been "shared" with the U.S. in 1947.

CONSENSUAL MILITARY ARRANGEMENTS

The Simonstown Agreement

The Simonstown Agreement between Britain and South Africa provided for the common defense of the sea routes around southern Africa and for the transfer of the formerly British naval base at Simonstown. This agreement was contained in an exchange of letters dated June 30, 1955, and presented before the British parliament in July of that year. Part of the arrangement pertained to the regional defense of the sea routes. Its purposes were to ensure the safety, by the joint operations of the respective maritime forces, of the sea routes round southern Africa.[5] This accord was not a formal agreement, enforceable as a treaty; rather, it was a series of understandings.[6] In exchange for a military commitment to support South Africa's external security with armed forces, Britain obtained the use of the Simonstown naval base; staging and overflight rights throughout the whole territory of South Africa; and a South African concession to allocate its naval units to the Royal Navy in case of international war, including a conflict in which South Africa was not involved. It was an extremely advantageous agreement for Britain.

The agreement remained in force when South Africa became a Republic and withdrew from the British Commonwealth on May 30, 1961. After the U.N. sanctions and embargo on military sales to South Africa, Britain announced in November 1964 its intention to impose an embargo on the export of arms to that country. Prime Minister Harold Wilson, in an answer to a question about sanctions and their effect on the Simonstown Agreement, added: "Nothing I have said in any way involves a breach of the Agreement. Moreover [...] the Agreement is not capable of unilateral denunciation."[7]

Britain continued to deliver arms, including eight *Wasp* anti-submarine helicopters, to the South Africans. These were deemed to fulfill the terms of the agreement. The government of Edward Heath authorized the sale of seven additional *Wasp* helicopters in 1971, after debate on how to balance British strategic and economic interests with international embarrassment about the arms sales. Wilson, back in power in 1974, prohibited the sale of the last two helicopters of the original order. The completion of the east of Suez withdrawal led inevitably to a further strategic consequence: the withdrawal south of Suez.

> In the 1950s, Simonstown's importance stemmed from the support it gave Britain's forward deployment in the Middle East and the protection of the tankers in the Persian Gulf rather than any protection it offered at the Cape. In this respect it was quite logical for Britain to withdraw its last permanently stationed frigate when it opted to redeploy its forces west of Suez in 1967 and to allow the agreement to lapse completely after withdrawing from the Gulf altogether.[8]

When naval maneuvers brought eleven British vessels to Simonstown in October 1974, it caused such a reaction in Leftist circles in Britain that Prime Minister Callaghan had to announce the abrogation of the Simonstown Agreement, which became official as of June 16, 1975. By that time, with new political realities prevailing, the agreement had become "capable of unilateral denunciation."

Libyan Training Area

After the expulsion of the Germans and Italians in 1942 and 1943, Libya was divided under two different military administrations: Tripolitania and Cyrenaica were placed under British control, while Fezzan was under French jurisdiction. On December 24, 1951, Libya became an independent federal kingdom. In 1969, a group of military officers would depose King Idris. The coup led to the decision, in December 1969, to withdraw all remaining British forces from Libya by April 1970 and to close the American Wheelus Air Force Base by July 1970. After that time, there were no longer any British troops stationed permanently on African soil.

Britain had signed a defense treaty with King Idris to help him against external aggression in exchange for the use of training facilities and bases. Britain had maintained the headquarters of 10 Armoured Division in Libya until 1957, although with subsequent reductions in the British military presence the Army headquarters in Malta assumed command of the remaining British troops in Libya after 1963. The British Army kept a small garrison where the British Military Mission trained and expanded the Libyan Army. The British Royal Air Force maintained staging posts at Idris and El Adem. The facility at Idris was closed down in 1966.

The British units in Libya under the Anglo-Libyan Treaty were never used in actual combat. The only minor exception came during the riots of June 5, 1967, when British forces in Benghazi assisted the Libyan Security Forces in protecting British and American expatriates and evacuating the staff of the American Embassy. The Libyan facilities were not used during the 1956 Suez Crisis or in any subsequent post-colonial contingency.

Aden

In the late 1950s, Aden was one of the busiest harbors in the world, with ships stopping for fuel and supplies after crossing the Suez Canal. Aden was initially acquired in response to French ambitions in Egypt dating back to Napoleon. The value of Aden was dubious, as Lord Rawlinson, Indian commander-in-chief, wrote in 1920: "As long as we command the Indian Ocean, Aden is in no danger, and if we do not, I cannot see that it is of any use to us."[9] This rationale was apparently forgotten in 1947, after the independence of India. It would take twenty years, the Suez crisis, and budgetary pressure, for Britain to abandon Aden.

The Suez Crisis in 1956 had two paradoxical consequences on British ability and willingness to control Aden. On the one hand, it seemed normal to compensate for the loss of the British bases in the canal zone by reinforcing Aden. When British authorities found that access through the Suez Canal was no longer unrestricted they decided to establish separate headquarters in Aden to fulfill British commitments in the Arabian Peninsula and in British Somaliland. The "General Headquarters Middle East Land Forces" were to remain in Cyprus. On the other hand, with the closure of the Suez Canal, Aden lost much of its *raison d'être*. It retained only residual value for power projection capabilities in eastern and southern Africa. Although Aden dramatically enhanced Britain's ability to influence events in Africa militarily, the relatively modest British objectives in Africa could not justify the heavy cost of a prolonged stay in Aden.

After the 1956 Suez Crisis, Aden had become, together with Bahrain, the base for the bulk of the British Middle East Land Force. Royal Air Force units stationed in Aden included ground-attack, fighter reconnaissance, tactical transport, and maritime-reconnaissance aircraft and helicopters. Royal Marine Commandos and Army units had been assigned to Aden to keep order and consolidate the local forces. To make matters difficult for British troops in Aden, Nasser's pan-Arabic nationalist movements gained enormous influence in Aden and Yemen. The cost of maintaining peace and order in the immediate vicinity of Aden increased dramatically for Britain when Egypt started sending troops in Yemen, totalling 70,000 men by 1963. Over the years, the pattern of violence would shift from clashes up-country to urban terrorism in Aden. In February 1966, the British government announced that it would completely withdraw from Aden by 1968. As a former chief of staff, Middle East Command in Aden pointed out: "The Aden base became counterproductive strategically once the great proportion of the garrison became locked in combat, first with the Radfan dissidents and then with the urban terrorists."[10]

Under such conditions, "Britain could no longer afford to police the Persian Gulf or the route to India, even to please President Johnson."[11] The last British forces left Aden on November 29, 1967, ahead of their original schedule, after 128 years of British rule. The withdrawal involved 25,000 servicemen and families and included the largest British airlift operation since that in Berlin in 1948.[12] From December 1963 until the withdrawal, 135 British Servicemen were killed and more than 900 were wounded.[13]

Malta

Britain reduced its garrison on Malta in 1962. With independence on September 21, 1964, Malta agreed to guarantee these bases until September 1971. Despite this agreement, Britain determined that there was no longer a military need to retain any substantial forces in Malta, and, in 1967, started to cut its troops there drastically. Both the defense of Malta and Britain's own strategic requirements could be "assured by a combination of limited base facilities in Malta and [...] rapid reinforcement capability in the United Kingdom."[14] The withdrawal was done, however, so as to least disrupt the Maltese economy, which relied heavily on the British defense establishment. As a transition, the British government allowed the run-down period to last for four years instead of the initially planned two years. After four years, Britain formalized its presence in Malta under a modest agreement concluded on March 26, 1972. By threatening to allow Soviet military forces to use facilities on Malta, Maltese prime minister Dom Mintoff pressured Britain into renewing the accords. He granted Britain:

> in peace and war the right to station armed forces and associated British personnel in Malta and to use facilities there for the defence purposes of the United Kingdom and of the North Atlantic Treaty Organisation and for such other purposes as may be agreed between the two governments.[15]

This agreement primarily concerned British naval facilities and the Luga airfield. It prevented the forces of any party to the Warsaw Pact from being stationed in Malta or using military facilities there.[16] Malta's strategic value for Britain had shifted from being a staging post to Suez and the Indian Ocean to being integrated into NATO's southern flank defense system. Potential threats from the region east of Suez or from Africa were not relevant in determining the British defense posture on Malta. All British forces were withdrawn from Malta by March 31, 1979.

SOVEREIGN BASES IN CYPRUS

"Ironically," according to author Brian Lapping, "Cyprus has always proved a strategic disappointment, more ornamental than effective."[17] Once the military bases in Egypt and other British interests in the Middle East were gone, Cyprus lost most of its immediate strategic value for Britain. Cyprus was the site of the General Headquarters Middle East Land Forces responsible for eastern Mediterranean, Arabian Peninsula, and Gulf-area commitments under the Baghdad Pact.[18] With Britain's expulsion from the Suez Canal Zone in 1956 and the accompanying loss of its military facilities in Egypt, Cyprus proved only a partial substitute in the unsuccessful Franco-British attempt to recover the canal. Because the Cypriot harbor of Faragusta was too shallow, much of the Franco-British expeditionary force had to embark at Malta, 960 miles away. Much of the air campaign and airborne assault was run from Cyprus. After the 1956 Suez Crisis, some command duties were transferred to Aden due to disruption in the communication and logistical supply lines to Cyprus. The Cyprus Emergency, which lasted four years before Britain granted independence on August 16, 1960, killed 104 British servicemen and

12 police officers.[19] Britain withdrew from Cyprus, except for a 256 km² territory comprising two sovereign British bases at Akrotiri and Dhekelia and the Retained Areas in the mountains.

During the Cold War, intelligence collection from Cyprus became more intense and produced new roles for the bases, especially the radar and communications centers in the mountains. From the perspective of security planners and the intelligence community:

> What made Cyprus so important was the island's strategic value in a post-Suez empire which had left Britain with world-wide responsibilities, but precious little resources to service them. With Palestine gone, Suez a smouldering memory, Persia overwhelmed by nationalism and the Baghdad Pact in tatters, Britain required solid bases from which to defend its interests. Cyprus was far from ideal, but there simply were no alternative sites in the region; the prospect of two large sovereign bases, plus additional facilities for gathering signals intelligence, must have seemed extremely attractive.[20]

By the end of 1963, British troops were dispatched as a military "green line" to separate the warring Greek and Turkish Cypriots. A U.N. peace-keeping force (UNFICYP) replaced them in March 1964. By 1993, the British contingent to this force was of approximately 800 personnel, in addition to the 3,500-3,800 British military personnel. mainly Army and Air Force, already based at the Sovereign Bases.[21] The British Navy does not maintain ships in Cyprus, but there is a Royal Corps of Transport Maritime Troop with two ramped craft and a patrol boat. The Army presence is in the form of two infantry battalions, including one battalion for UNFICYP, one army reconnaissance squadron, and one engineer support squadron. The land forces were adjusted to the minimum level needed to safeguard the facilities adequately and to maintain stockpiles for rapid reinforcement in the region. The Air Force is equipped with five *Wessex* helicopters and detachments of *Phantom* and *Tornado* aircraft.[22] Signal units are stationed on Mount Olympus and an RAF unit at Troodos.

Cypriot bases are not organized specifically as platforms for out-of-area power projection. Nevertheless, during the Gulf War the British resident garrisons were increased roughly two-and-a-half times, maritime loading facilities at Akrotiri were upgraded, and intelligence cells were maintained to provide up-to-date briefings for all Gulf-bound personnel.[23]

BRITISH DEPENDENT TERRITORIES

Britain retains over a dozen dependent territories scattered all over the world: Anguilla, Ascension, Bermuda, the British Indian Ocean Territory, British Virgin Islands, Cayman Islands, Falkland Islands, Gibraltar, Hong Kong, Montserrat, Pitcairn Island, St. Helena, Tristan da Cunha, and Turks and Caicos Islands. The area of these territories ranges from five km² for Pitcairn to 12,173 km² for the Falklands, and their population ranges from less than 100 (Pitcairn) to six million (Hong Kong). Only half-a-dozen of them are potentially useful for military operations in sub-Saharan Africa.

Britain's dependent territories are "areas at the tail-end of the decolonization process,"[24] and offer the peculiarity of not pursuing independence with the same fervor as earlier nation-states. "Indeed their inhabitants were sometimes worried that they might be forced into independence."[25] In fact, Britain followed a selective approach, serving its own interest by discouraging independence in territories that had an important strategic value such as Gibraltar, Ascension and the British Indian Ocean Territory.

Ascension

Ascension is a small, volcanic island of 34 square miles, with a population of about 1,035 people.[26] It is located approximately 3,800 miles south of Britain, 4,500 miles from the Falklands, and 1,700 miles west of Africa. The territory is supervised by the Foreign and Commonwealth Office through the governor's office on St. Helena. Under an agreement dating back to 1942, the U.S. gained access to military facilities and to the Wideawake airfield. Subsequently, the airstrip was rearranged and extended in connection with the U.S. program for a Long-Range Proving Ground for guided missiles based in Florida. In 1966, NASA opened a tracking station on the island, and the BBC built an Atlantic relay station the same year. Other nations have also benefitted militarily from the Ascension airfield. The Belgian Air Force made use of them during the Stanleyville intervention in 1964.

Britain maintains a small detachment of Royal Air Force *Hercules* C-130K on Ascension. Port facilities on the island are insufficient for use as a military naval base. As the Falkland experience has shown, however, ships cruising in the vicinity of Ascension were resupplied by helicopters based on the island. Ascension became a vital supply base for the Falklands Task Force as it sailed south. Dakar, and to a lesser degree Freetown and Banjul, played an equally vital role in easing the resupply effort of the Task Force. Early in April 1982, the RAF deployed additional *Hercules* and VC-10 Air Transport aircraft to the island. Despite its location 3,750 miles from the Falklands, Ascension served as a base for RAF bombers and reconnaissance aircraft. Construction of a new RAF camp and staging-post for the Falklands 'Air Bridge' was completed in 1984 at a cost of £49 million.

St. Helena

St. Helena, 700 miles southeast of Ascension in the South Atlantic, has a surface of 47 square miles and about 5,000 inhabitants. It has a small port at Jamestown with one 300-foot concrete wharf alongside 10 to 12 feet of water. The coastal waters around the island are almost continuously subject to heavy swells and rollers, but the approaches to the harbor bay are clear and deep. The island does not have a landing strip for conventional airplanes.[27] No permanent British armed forces are reported on the island, which has no use as a base.

Tristan da Cunha

The islands of Tristan da Cunha are a British possession administered from St. Helena. Offering only a very small inhabitable area, it has a population of about 350. Facilities on Tristan da Cunha are sparse, and there are neither seaports nor landing fields for conventional aircraft. Tristan da Cunha does, however, host an important meteorological and radio station. Like St. Helena, Tristan da Cunha is of little military value for British or allied power projection.

Diego Garcia

A tiny necklace of coral islands, uninhabited and unmarked in most atlases, became the focus of mounting U.S. strategic interest in the 1970s and afterwards. Diego Garcia, the largest of these islands which make up the Chagos Archipelago, is a flimsy 30 square mile hairpin of flat palm-strewn coral in the middle of the Indian Ocean, thinly enclosing an extensive lagoon, 1,000 miles from India, 2,000 miles from the Gulf, and 1,600 miles from eastern Africa. Although remote, with a humid climate and incessant winds, it is well formed to accommodate several aircraft runways and natural anchorages.[28]

The British Indian Ocean Territory, a British colony created in 1965, consisted of the Chagos Archipelago (formerly a dependency of Mauritius), Aldabra, Farquhar and Desroches. For a while, British authorities were considering "Diego Garcia as a possible alternative to Aden."[29] Mainland bases, as illustrated by Aden, were deemed to have become a commitment in themselves, swallowing all the forces stationed in them for local self-defense. Island bases were viewed as cheaper and more reliable than mainland bases and more affordable than a new aircraft carrier. The idea was that island bases combined with air mobility (strike-reconnaissance planes and troop-carrying transport aircraft) would suffice to cover British interests in the Indian Ocean. Even this minimalist presence east of Suez was never fully implemented after the British authorities turned over the military use of Diego Garcia to the U.S.

The Johnson administration signed a secret agreement with the Wilson government in 1966 for joint use of the British Indian Ocean Territory. This agreement came in the midst of the first British attempts to withdraw from east of Suez. The pact was revealed in 1970, just before the U.S. build-up on Diego Garcia began.[30] The American military capabilities have been gradually enhanced since 1976, expedited by the redevelopment of a Rapid Deployment Force under the Carter Administration. The Pentagon was relying heavily on the alleged Soviet buildup in Berbera and the expansion of Soviet naval capability in the Indian Ocean to win congressional passage of its Diego Garcia expansion plan.[31] More recently, a new rationale, linked to threats from Iraq or Iran, has replaced the primacy of the Cold War.[32]

In the early 1990s, the Britian's military presence on the island is essentially symbolic to underline British sovereign rights. The Royal Navy keeps one naval party and one Marine detachment on Diego Garcia. No other British forces are permanently deployed on the island.

Gibraltar

Gibraltar officially became a British possession by the Treaty of Utrecht in 1713. In 1967, pursuant to a United Nations resolution on decolonization, a referendum was held in order to ascertain British or Spanish sovereignty. Out of a total electorate of 12,762, an overwhelming majority of 12,138 voted in favor of British sovereignty, while 44 voted for Spain.[33] Matters of domestic concern are left to local authorities, while Britain remains responsible for external affairs, defense and internal security.

Britain maintains only two overseas naval bases: Gibraltar and Hong Kong. The naval presence in Gibraltar amounts to 500 men equipped with two patrol crafts and two twin *Exocet* launchers for coastal defense. The Army keeps 800 troops, with an infantry battalion, a reserve Gibraltar Regiment (a part-time infantry battalion with a small regular cadre), one team of engineers, and one artillery surveillance team. The RAF, with a contingent of 400 men, periodically sends a *Jaguar* detachment to Gibraltar.[34] Gibraltar is equipped with an airfield, built partially on grounds constructed over the sea, and a deep Admiralty Harbor of 440 acres. In 1981, the Ministry of Defence announced that the Royal Navy dockyard in Gibraltar was to close for economic reasons.[35] The dockyard was subsequently converted to commercial use. The Army may follow suit as British troops are expected to be removed by 1997.

Gibraltar has ceased to be a power projection platform for military operations overseas. It is too small and too close to the Britain to offer any benefits for long-range power projection. In the context of sub-Saharan Africa it has been of little use, and will probably be bypassed altogether in any future sub-Saharan contingency.

Falkland Islands

The Falkland Islands would certainly not have been included in a list of bases and military facilities available for British power projection in sub-Saharan Africa if it were not for the new developments after the 1982 war. Before the abandonment of the Simonstown facilities, it was believed in London that the Falklands would benefit from forces from Simonstown in case of an Argentinean attack.[36] The Falklands were conceived as force-consumers rather than a platform for force projection. In the aftermath of the Falklands war, Britain has increased its naval and air force capabilities on the islands. The infrastructure has also been greatly improved. With the possible exception of a crisis in South Africa, however, it is hard to conceive a use for the British Falkland forces in an African context. The Royal Navy units based on the island could possibly play a role in stabilizing the southern Atlantic, but this, too, is improbable.

In 1966, the only British forces on the Falkland Islands were a small detachment of 32 men from the Royal Navy.[37] By 1989, British forces numbered 1,600 with one Infantry Battalion Group, and one to four engineering squadrons. The Royal Navy upgraded its presence with one destroyer-frigate, two patrol boats, and support and auxiliary ships. The Royal Air Force maintains one *Phantom Flight*, six *Hercules* C-130Ks, three *Sea King* HAR-3 helicopters, six CH-47 *Chinook* helicopters, and one RAF regiment equipped with *Rapier* air defense systems.[38]

MILITARY SIGNIFICANCE OF OVERSEAS ASSETS

Of all the territories and overseas bases that Britain has retained from its former Empire, only Ascension, with the Wideawake airfield, still offers militarily significance as a potential platform for power projection in sub-Saharan Africa. All other territories are either too remote or do not offer sufficient infrastructure for strategic considerations. Even Diego Garcia is no longer militarily exploited by Britain. The sovereign bases on Cyprus could potentially offer useful staging posts for flights to eastern Africa should the need arise. Despite the fact that Britain possesses a string of territories and sovereign bases around Africa, little is done to provide them with the capabilities and infrastructure specifically oriented for potential intervention in sub-Saharan Africa. Ascension was reinforced because of the Falklands conflict, and the Falklands because of their need for self-defense. The other territories serve no tactical military purpose whatsoever. Unlike France, Britain does not associate its territories and facilities around Africa with any military policy for their potential application in the sub-Saharan region. There is no military maximization of the use of these assets, although, as in the case of Ascension and Diego Garcia, their transfer to the U.S. does not exclude the possibility of their future use by Britain.

Chapter 9

British Interventions
in Sub-Saharan Africa

From World War II until 1993, the British Army has carried out about 100 operational commitments worldwide.[1] Four of them were conventional, if undeclared, wars: Korea (1950-54), the Suez (1956), the Falklands (1982), and the Gulf (1991). Close to 80 percent were low-intensity operations involving internal security duties, peace-keeping and peace-restoring operations, or counter-insurgency campaigns. The remaining commitments were rescue and relief operations requiring the use of military personnel and resources, albeit in a non-combattant role.

There have been four types of British military operations in post-colonial sub-Saharan Africa. The first classification includes British actions immediately before or soon after independence was granted. This activity must be viewed as part of the colonial disengagement, and not as a new form of neo-colonial control over former dependencies. At best, they represent friendly support to, or the rescue of, nascent governments, and include the clear message that those new governments should become established as soon as possible. The East African mutinies in 1964 are an example of this variety of intervention.

The second variation of British operations in sub-Saharan Africa is exemplified by the attempt to sanction the Rhodesian Unilateral Declaration of Independence (UDI) and counteract the sanctions' negative impact on neighboring countries. These efforts lasted until the creation of Zimbabwe in 1980. Britain had mixed feelings about getting involved militarily in the Rhodesian tangle. No large military action was seriously considered against Rhodesia directly, but, bowing to both international pressure and calls by friendly nations in the region, Britain took some marginally efficient military steps. These were kept at the minimal level, enough to prove Britain's commitment to discouraging the Rhodesian UDI, but insufficient to influence events in any significant way.

As a third means of intervention, Britain got involved, either militarily or through military assistance, in a series of disputes throughout English-speaking sub-Saharan Africa. Direct military involvement was non-existent or limited to the extreme minimum. The Nigerian Civil War is one dramatic case in this category, but a coup in Gambia and unrest in the Seychelles in 1981 provide further examples.

Finally, a new trend seems to have emerged as part of Thatcher's policy of discreet support to Front Line States in sub-Saharan Africa. Either by design or accident, Britain got involved, mainly through military assistance programs, in all countries neighboring South Africa. The process began with assistance to Zimbabwe following its independence in 1980. The military program was then extended to benefit Mozambique, an event made even more remarkable by the fact that the latter was never part of the British Empire. Botswana also received limited but highly visible training and advice from British military personnel, including some training from the SAS. In early 1990, Britain participated in the U.N. force supervising Namibian independence. Subsequently, Britain took the lead in re-organizing Namibian armed forces. This step was again unusual given Britain's lack of enthusiasm at getting involved militarily in its own former colonies, let stand those of others. Finally, at the peace settlement for Angola in 1991, Britain agreed to participate in a U.N. monitoring force in Angola, which resembled the earlier operation in Namibia, and to assist in the reorganization of the Angolan armed forces. With the new political regime slowly taking shape in post-apartheid South Africa, Britain has manoeuvred very well and has fostered as much goodwill in the region as it could from benign military involvement. Beyond this display of military commitment, the consolidation of British interests in southern Africa is left to diplomats and businessmen.

INDEPENDENCE SETTLEMENTS
AND EARLY SUPPORT

Kenya (1963-67)

In March 1963, Britain agreed to grant regional autonomy to the 200,000 Somalis in Kenya's Northern Frontier Province. Elections for Kenya's first African government were to be held in May. The decision to give the Somalis greater autonomy was expected to ease tension with the Somali Republic, which for years had kept British troops on alert. The creation of this Somali region within Kenya caused concern among some political figures that it would become a "British Katanga."[2] Tensions between Kenya and Somalia persisted for years, and Kenya had to defend itself constantly against Somali-sponsored insurgencies. Even after Kenyan independence in December 1963, Britain continued to provide assistance in the form of training and logistical support to the Kenyan armed forces.

On February 5, 1964, after the East African mutinies (see below), Britain and Kenya entered into a defense agreement whereby the Royal Air Force would begin training the first African Flight Cadets for the planned Kenyan Air Force.[3] Britain gave up the Nairobi military facilities the same year, although the Royal Navy maintained refueling capacity in Mombasa. Britain continued, however, to support the Kenyan Air Force whenever problems arose along Kenya's border with Somalia. The last British troops of 24 Infantry Brigade left Kenya in December 1964, and their departure marked the end of the British base in that country. By 1967, Kenya and Somalia had reached a peace agreement to settle concerns over the northwestern territories. Britain continued to maintain a low-profile and informal presence in Kenya for decades by organizing battalion-sized exercises for elite British Army units year after year.

Zanzibar (1964)

Zanzibar in 1960 had a total population of 340,000 people, 15 percent of which was black and the rest mainly Arab and Indian. The population mix has always contained the germs of social upheaval. The political tension was best captured in the laconic description given of the island, where allegedly: "the Arabs owned the land, the Indians controlled the trade and the Africans did the work."[4] Britain had granted autonomous government to Zanzibar in 1960. During January

1961 elections, the legislative seats were equally shared by the Arab-dominated Zanzibar Nationalist Party and by the more moderate Afro-Shierazi Party, supported by neighboring Tanganyika. Internal autonomy was achieved by mid-1963, and full independence was granted in December that same year. Barely one month later, on January 12, 1964, the fragile political balance was shattered when leftist rebels, some of whom had been trained in Cuba, toppled the Arab-led government and proclaimed Zanzibar a republic. The U.S. had maintained a space tracking station on the island, and the American destroyer *Manley* was sent to rescue 61 Americans caught in the revolution, while British authorities were prepared to rescue 300 British subjects. A week after the coup, Britain had deployed a naval force offshore from Zanzibar with the frigate *Rhyl*, the survey ship *Owen* and the aircraft carrier *Centaur*. The *Centaur* had to be re-routed from its original destination in the Far East, where it was going to support the Federation of Malaysia against Indonesian encroachments. Mutinies in three neighboring countries completely overshadowed events related to the evacuation of expatriates from Zanzibar. Britain took no military action in Zanzibar beyond these evacuation measures.

At the political level, events in Zanzibar took a special turn when East Germany and China rushed to recognize the new republic and hurried to send experts to build a radio station.[5] The island's favorable strategic position between South Africa and the Indian Ocean was the reason of so much communist solicitude. The new Zanzibar leader, Abeid Karume, caused surprise by agreeing to a union with Tanganyika on April 23, 1964. Tanganyika's President Nyerere was probably persuaded to join after the ideological about-face in Zanzibar. Nyerere became president of the new entity, with Karume as vice-president. This arrangement reduced western concerns of communist infiltration in Zanzibar.

East African Mutinies (1964)

Britain launched and completed the largest military operation of its post-colonial history in sub-Saharan Africa over the course of a few short hours on the morning of January 25, 1964. Mutinies erupted almost simultaneously in Dar-es-Salaam and Tabora in Tanganyika, Jinja in Uganda, and Lanet in Kenya. The African governments all requested British assistance in quelling the unrest by means of a military intervention.

At the time, Britain's military presence in the region rested on a combination of training teams in support of local army units and combat forces as part of a British brigade group. The Tanganyikan, Ugandan and Kenyan armies were the direct heirs to the seven locally recruited colonial battalions of the King's African Rifles. At the time of independence, five of these battalions were deployed in Kenya, one in Uganda, and one provided garrisons in Tanganyika and Mauritius.[6] For some time, until a complete Africanization could be achieved, the officer corps remained predominantly British. The heavier concentration of British forces in Kenya was a reflection of the large British expatriate community there and the history of trouble after the Mau Mau uprising in the 1950s. The British brigade group, still in place after the independence of the three East African nations, was part of Britain's Middle East Strategic Reserve, which was "available for supporting the civil power in the African territories for which [Britain was] responsible and as a reinforcement for forces in the Middle East, primarily for operations in the Persian Gulf."[7] The brigade group, 24 Infantry Brigade, stationed in Kenya, was composed of the 1st Battalion Staffordshire Regiment, the 2nd Battalion Scots Guards, and the 3rd Regiment Royal Horse Artillery. It was supported by RAF *Beverleys* and *Twin Pioneers*, which contributed to its role as a mobile theater reserve. The brigade was not part of any open-ended commitment or defense agreement to protect the newly independent countries. The Ministry of Defence clearly shied away from such commitments in 1962. It saw its role in support of the local civil governments as a short-term commitment requiring the maintenance of forces in the area, but there was "no long-term requirement for a base."[8] Britain intended only on keeping facilities for air transit, staging and force training "normally accorded by Commonwealth countries to each other."[9]

The mutinies spread clockwise starting in Tanganyika on January 21 and spreading to Uganda and then Kenya in less than four days. The whole crisis took place against the general background of the continuing Congolese post-independence chaos, which had started 30 months earlier with a mutiny. The decision to call an intervention by British forces was made with surprising rapidity. Everything depended on Kenya's approval of a British military role, and that country was equipped with the best infrastructure to act as an intervention platform for quelling the mutinies in the two neighboring countries. President Jomo Kenyatta's initial reluctance to authorize the use of its territory in such an action was soon overruled when trouble erupted in Kenyan military bases. The way was cleared for British forces to intervene in a triple operation on January 25.

Tanganyika: During a visit to Washington in the summer of 1963, Julius K. Nyerere told a questioner at the National Press Club that he still regarded outside military assistance as a "dangerous game" for African states.[10] In January 1964, Nyerere was called to play that game when mutinies broke out at the Colito barracks close to Dar-es-Salaam and in Tabora, killing 14 persons and injuring at least 120.[11] In Tabora, the troops went on strike rather than mutinied, but in Dar-es-Salaam, the mutiny was real. In both places, the immediate cause of the uprisings was discontent over pay levels and the fact that the Africanization of the officer corps was not complete. British officers in Dar-es-Salaam were taken hostage, but their commander fled and later organized the counter-attack by British troops. The mutineers in Dar-es-Salaam took over strategic points in and around the city, including the airport. Having taken them, however, they did not sufficiently secure them, and preferred to participate in the looting downtown.

On January 25, sixty men from the Royal Marines' 45 Commando were dropped at Tabora by helicopters from the British aircraft carrier *Centaur*, initially on standby off Zanzibar, and subdued 800 mutineers in a 40-minute assault. Except for some fireworks, only one bazooka anti-tank rocket was used. Other men of 45 Commando quelled the mutiny at the Colito Barracks in Dar-es-Salaam, while blank powder charges were used in a naval barrage from the *Centaur* and her escort destroyer, the *Cambrian*, off Dar-es-Salaam. "The din was thunderous, but no shells were fired."[12] Helicopters had to be used to airlift commandos from the *Centaur* because the rebels were thought to be in firm control of the airport, and hence troops could not be flown in directly from Britain or Aden. Even the light vehicles of the commandos were airlifted from the *Centaur* by helicopter.[13] Under the circumstances, the aircraft carrier proved to be the ideal tool for power projection in Tanganyika. The alternative would have been to parachute commandos to secure the airport. The planes would have had to come from Kenya or Aden, and the potential risks involved would have been far higher than those resulting from the use of the *Centaur*.

Three Tanganyikan mutineers were killed in the double operation. By noon, a total of 600 British commandos with trucks and equipment had been airlifted to follow up on the initial assault. Most of them were assigned to strategic points in the capital: the state house, the presidential residence, the radio station, the telephone exchange, the overseas cable office, the airport, and the homes of government officials. A last group of British paratroopers landed at Nachingwea, 260 miles to the south near the Mozambican border, and quickly disarmed the mutineers. On the other side of the border, Portuguese troops stood ready to meet the rebels if they were to cross.[14]

The carrier *Centaur* was later relieved by the *Victorious* and *Bulwark* arriving from the Far East. 45 Commando Royal Marines was relieved by 41 Commando Royal Marines, which had been flown from Britain to Nairobi and then on to Dar-es-Salaam. Off the coast of Tanganyika, the survey ship *Owen* and the Royal Fleet Auxiliary *Hebe* were evacuating British subjects from Zanzibar. The destroyer *Cambrian*, which had participated throughout the operations, had left Aden on January 20 with the entire 45 Commando aboard.

Uganda: A little over a year after Uganda's independence and just one day after the mutiny at the Colito barracks in Tanganyika, men of the Ugandan Rifles also mutinied. As in Tanganyika, the Ugandan authorities requested British assistance to control the disorder involving the 1st Battalion of the Ugandan Rifle at Camp Jinja. The reason for discontent was the same as that given in Tanganyika: the troops wanted higher pay. President Milton Obote agreed to the Africanization of the officer corps the same day, January 22. This gesture proved to be too little, too late. The soldiers held the minister of the interior hostage, and detained expatriate officers and NCOs. The British reaction followed on January 25. Thirty men of the 2nd Battalion Scots Guards and the 1st Battalion Staffordshire Regiment, armed with burp guns, burst through the main rebel camp, secured the guards room, and seized the armory before the mutineers awoke. The 450 British troops who were part of the British forces stationed in Kenya soon surrounded the camp.[15] The brief and energetic assault had quelled the mutiny. The women and children of British servicemen were removed from the camp and airlifted to Nairobi via Entebbe.

Kenya: Events in Kenya followed a pattern similar to that in its two neighboring states. Disgruntled soldiers went on strike after hearing the news of the mutinies in Tanganyika and Uganda. The intensity of the crisis was the lowest in Kenya. Only around 150 soldiers of the 11th Battalion of Kenya Rifles participated in what appeared to be fairly harmless sit-down strikes at the Lanet Barracks, near Nakuru. Their discontent never got a chance to propagate among other units in the country. Units of the British 24 Infantry Brigade, specifically the Royal

Horse Artillery's light armored cars, broke up the strike of 150 rebellious troops. The press described the low-intensity combat:

> A sniper fired on the armored cars from a roof. One of the cars moved up closer, brought its turret to bear on a hut with a tiled roof, and with a sustained burst from its .50 caliber machine gun, raked the empty hut. All its windows were smashed, and the sit-down strike collapsed.[16]

Elements of the Scots Guards Battalion secured the airport, the prime minister's office, the police headquarters, the radio station, and the post office in Nairobi, where Kenyan troops had remained loyal. Additionally, 700 men of 41 Royal Marines Commando were flown in from England the same evening. *Shackleton* and *Canberra* reconnaissance aircraft, as well as *Hunters*, were deployed to Kenya, as was the RAF's 38 Regiment field squadron from Aden. With such a deployment of force, order was completely restored the same day.

British troops had succeeded in quelling the three East African mutinies in a single morning with no more than six African soldiers killed. The reasons for this quite unique dispatch of British troops to redress internal problems in an African country can be viewed from the perspective of each side. In the mid-1960s, there was no lack of foreign contenders to rush to the aid of emerging African governments. Soviet and Chinese Cold War strategists were vying for influence in Africa. The East African leaders specifically invited the British, and not, as *The Economist* pointed out, the Ghanaians, Ethiopians, or Russians "because, it must be assumed, they felt sure they could trust the British to get out again."[17] British troops were also the most readily available in the region.

The British went to the rescue of the former colonies for a variety of reasons: to protect British nationals, including British servicemen and their families attached to rebellious East African military units; to avoid the dissolution of East Africa into chaos - bearing in mind the traumatic experience in the Congo after the 1960 mutiny; and to play their part as leader of the Commonwealth, especially since control over the events could be achieved through a fairly low-cost, low-risk operation. The military success of the triple British intervention was complete, and they drew no adverse diplomatic consequences or resentment within the region. Even the Russians maintained a discreet silence after the events.[18] They had earlier warned the British not to intervene in Zanzibar, which was the only place where British troops did not take action.

Militarily speaking, the British were certainly not parsimonious in their use of force. The total number of British troops on alert in the three countries was reported to be 5,300, by far the largest number in Britain's post-colonial military ventures in sub-Saharan Africa.[19] The number of troops dispatched, combined with the British military reputation, overwhelmed the rebels and provoked an almost immediate surrender. The timeliness and speed of the British reaction was greatly enhanced by the fact that British authorities had already started to build strength in the region during the Zanzibar revolution, which, while preceding the mutinies by two weeks, was entirely unrelated to them.

There was a limited degree of consultation between officials in the three East African countries plagued with mutinies, but "the biggest decision of all - to call in British troops - was not a joint one, however coordinated it eventually seemed."[20] The conclusions those countries drew did not appear to include the creation of a common defense and command structure for East Africa. The political cost of the "grievous sham," as the Ugandan leader Milton Obote referred to the mutinies, lingered for some time. The mutinies were an open and irrefutable avowal of the central authorities' weakness because the British troops had moved in on invitation. Nyerere, in whose country the mutinies were the most severe, criticized the events as "most disgraceful" and announced after the British re-established control that the mutinous units would be disbanded. Kenyatta talked about a "grave betrayal."[21] Overlooking the political and economic costs of the rebellion and the accompanying looting and violence, these statements indicated the African leaders' concern for their loss of credibility and the staining of their political image.

Unlike the Zanzibar revolution, the three East African mutinies had nothing to do with communist attempts to gain influence. The mutinies were strictly the result of discontent among soldiers.

Despite some evidence of outside machinations by troublemakers in the wave of East African army mutinies, the facts as known in January 1964 seem to indicate that the chain reaction which began in Tanganyika, shortly after the Zanzibar revolution, and then swept through Uganda and Kenya, was set in motion by the existence of common grievances among all the lower ranks of the former King's African Rifles of East Africa.[22]

Although the mutinous units belonged to different countries, the spread of the rebellion from one country to another should not have been a great surprise. Only two years earlier, these units were jointly administered by British commanders. At the time of the mutinies, each of these units still included dozens of British officers and cadres. They shared not only the same training and instruction manuals, but the same desire for better pay and rapid Africanization. The news of the Dar-es-Salaam mutiny spread very fast through the East African military communities, both British and African, and the media coverage allowed for rapid dispersion of the news throughout the region. It was easy for the mutineers of one unit to empathize with the discontent expressed by another, as they shared similar military, economic, and political conditions within newly independent nations. Only later were these nations further separated by different development paths and divergent public attitudes toward the central authority and the military.

The British intervention in the three East African countries was the first one in Africa since the 1956 invasion of the Suez Canal area. The forces involved were substantial given the threat they faced. In Kenya it involved the troops of all three battalions of 24 Infantry Brigade. The operation was also made possible by troops stationed outside of East Africa, including two Royal Marine Commandos: 41 Commando flown in from England and 45 Commando brought by sea from Aden, initially to help in evacuating British subjects from Zanzibar. Three aircraft carriers were involved; the *Victorious* relieved the *Centaur*, and the *Bulwark* arrived from the Far East for support. One survey ship and one Royal Fleet Auxiliary ship also participated throughout the operations. The air support included *Belvedere* and *Wessex* helicopters, and *Sea Vixen* aircraft. No British commando casualties were reported. The mutinies were quelled in one morning: Britain had played it safe in terms of force deployment and time. A more gradual approach isolating each country for operational purposes might have stiffened the resistance, or have been considered by the mutineers as a last chance for looting and violence before the British arrived.

Mauritius (1965)

In May 1965, a British infantry company was flown from Aden to Mauritius to help local authorities control civil disturbances related to claims for Mauritian independence from Britain. These units were mainly put on guard duties, but they allowed the Mauritian police to concentrate on restoring order. The company was relieved by a company from the infantry battalion in Swaziland, and all British units were withdrawn by the end of 1965. Mauritius attained independence on March 12, 1968.

THE RHODESIAN TANGLE

Rhodesian UDI (1965)

After Ian Smith issued the Rhodesian Unilateral Declaration of Independence (UDI) on November 11, 1965, Britain's prime minister Harold Wilson commissioned a planning paper to deal with the new situation.[23] The paper evaluated the military options open to the British government to reverse the UDI. Wilson felt that, because of his party's narrow majority in parliament, action had to be taken only in the immediate aftermath of UDI; later, the momentum would be lost. The paper was produced in one month, and argued, not to Wilson's displeasure, against a British intervention. The conclusion was that an invasion could not be carried out for technical military reasons and because of the tremendous effort it would require. Perhaps more important than military arguments were the high political risks an intervention in Rhodesia would have represented domestically if things became difficult on the ground.[24] The paper was politically biased under the circumstances, although it also reflected the ideas of the conservative military establishment, which was not eager to get involved in yet another overseas conflict.

One of the main military objections relied on the poor support infrastructure in Zambia, which was viewed as an indispensable staging post for any action in Rhodesia. In the event of an extensive airlift operation, the RAF *Brittania* aircraft would require a hard tarmac surface for landing and refueling. The airport at Lusaka was insufficient to handle heavy air traffic. The suggestion was made to borrow the more adaptable C-130s from the U.S. Air Force for a continuous airlift, but the British RAF authorities, who were disinclined to intervene at all, ignored this option.[25] The intervention ideally should have been performed by two brigades equipped with light armored vehicles.

There were basically only three crossing points from Zambia into Rhodesia: at Kariba, Victoria Falls and Chirundu. Lake Kariba and the

Zambezi River form a major barrier all along the border between the two countries. The three crossing points would have been easy to defend by Rhodesian troops. Other parts of the Wilson paper dealt with the type of resistance that could be expected from the white Rhodesian population backed by a strong South African neighbor. It was feared that the farmers could organize some very tough defense strategies reminiscent of the obstinate resistance of the Afrikaaners during the Boer War.

Part of the reluctance of the British military establishment to fight the Rhodesians might also have resulted from the close military links between British and Rhodesian armed forces, which had often fought side-by-side in World War II and other crises thereafter. To compensate for the image of military inaction, Wilson approved three military operations of limited scope in the region. These narrowly defined operations - the Beira Patrol, Air Force support to Zambia, and limited support to Botswana - would fail to turn the tide of UDI, and achieved only marginal results.

The Beira Patrol (1966-75)

Rhodesia had been virtually independent since 1923; it was "a colony that Britain never governed, [where] Britain had responsibility without power."[26] It is therefore ironic that it was precisely when Britain was to lose Rhodesia that the greatest expectations were raised regarding British ability to influence matters there. After the 1965 UDI declaration, the OAU asked its members to break diplomatic relations with Britain unless the latter crushed the white minority government of Rhodesia. Although the measure was widely ignored - only six countries out of a total of 35 broke relations - it induced Britain to display some military muscle in the area. The Wilson government had made it clear that there would be no direct intervention against Rhodesia. The Wilson government genuinely believed a sanctions package with military backing would be effective.

The Royal Navy was sent to enforce an embargo against oil imports into Rhodesia, in accordance with two U.N. Security Council Resolutions of April and December 1966. The first resolution allowed Britain to use force to prevent oil supplies from reaching Rhodesia, and the second banned U.N. members from either purchasing key Rhodesian exports or supplying oil and oil products to Rhodesia. The patrol of the Mozambique Channel of Beira was maintained for almost nine years, through June 25, 1975, the day Mozambique gained independence. The *Eagle* aircraft carrier participated in this effort in 1966, and was eventually relieved by the *Ark Royal*. The Beira operations also included RAF *Shackleton* aircraft from the Coastal Command operating from Majunga, in the Malagasy Republic, and from the Far East Air Force. The airplanes regularly flew over a wide area to identify tankers. One tanker, the *Manuela*, was prevented from entering the Beira harbor, and the *Joanna V* had to leave before unloading her cargo.

In the end, the Beira patrol was perceived as an exercise in futility. By embargoing oil only from a single point, the pipeline terminal in Beira, the British force completely neglected other points of entry through which oil continued to reach Rhodesia, including the harbor of Maputo and several locations in South Africa. The efficiency of this enforced sanction against Rhodesia was therefore far from successful; its only effect was to increase the price of oil in Rhodesia very marginally, but not enough to damage the Rhodesian economy.

Zambia (1965-66)

Another limited military response from Britain to the UDI came at the Zambian request for British air defense against Rhodesian air strikes. To that effect, the aircraft carrier *Eagle* was dispatched from Singapore, together with escorting destroyers and logistic support ships. The aircraft on the carrier were made available for operations into Zambia. An RAF *Javelin* air defense squadron, together with radar control and communication units in Aden, was also delivered. The entire operation was covered by *Sea Vixens* from *Eagle*. Once the air defense system was in place, it justified the release of the *Eagle* for normal duties. Air defense units were deployed in Zambia from December 1965 until the end of August 1966.

Landlocked Zambia suffered from the Beira patrol and the oil embargo on Rhodesia perhaps even more than Rhodesia itself: the pipeline feeding the Zambian economy ran from Beira through Rhodesia. The main road access to harbors also traversed Rhodesia, and alternative routes were either in bad shape, too long or too dangerous. Zambia soon developed a shortage of oil. The Zambian government blamed Britain for involuntarily harming the Zambian economy. To compensate for this, *Britannia* prop-jet long-range transport aircraft of the British Transport Command were used to airlift fuel into Zambia from December 1965 until October 31, 1966. The *Britannias* transported approximately 11,000 gallons daily, initially from Dar-es-Salaam, and subsequently from Nairobi, to Lusaka and Ndola. Royal Air Force staff supported the airlift. The eventual withdrawal of the British air defense system was partially induced by intelligence reports which had established that Rhodesia was not about to intervene in neighboring countries.[27]

Botswana (1965-67)

In another military development after the Rhodesian UDI, Britain dispatched an infantry company to Francistown, Botswana (then Bechuanaland), to guard the BBC relay station against a feared Rhodesian incursion. This company was initially part of an infantry battalion deployed in Swaziland. The company was withdrawn directly to Britain on August 31, 1967. (The battalion in Swaziland had been gone since 1966.)

The threat to the Francistown radio station was real during the early years of the Rhodesian UDI, and it created serious apprehensions about what Rhodesia could do. Indeed, the BBC was running a propaganda radio station against the Smith regime, with monitors stationed in Francistown to listen to Radio Salisbury. BBC programs were then adjusted accordingly to respond to the Rhodesian announcements.[28] Later, the station was used to pick up signals from guerrillas operating in neighboring Rhodesia as well as from the South African government.[29]

Rhodesia/Zimbabwe (1979-80)

From 1976 onwards, Britain started to assume direct responsibility over the transition to Zimbabwe's independence. British authorities engaged on an arduous reconciliation effort between the warring parties in Rhodesia. It coincided with the arrival to power of the Carter Administration, which opened the way for closer Anglo-American collaboration on southern African issues. It took until 1979 before all parties could agree on a plan for the transition of power from Rhodesia to Zimbabwe, which was finally set out at the Lancaster House Conference in December of that year. The British-sponsored plan, advanced by Foreign Secretary Lord Carrington, called for a British governor to be sent to Rhodesia to arrange a cease-fire and supervise subsequent elections. The governor was charged with re-establishing

British rule after 14 years and leading the country to internationally recognized independence. The governor would become the commander-in-chief of the armed forces from all parties involved. Those forces would gather at various pre-approved points, with the Rhodesian military returning to their barracks before the guerrillas emerged from the bush. Once the plan was approved, it was respected by all parties. A Commonwealth initiative attempted to strengthen the transition plan by dispatching a monitoring force during the election period. The 1,500-man Commonwealth peace force included 1,200 British troops, with token representation from Kenya, New Zealand, Fiji, and Australia.[30] Lord Soames, the newly appointed governor, arrived in Salisbury on December 12, 1979. The governor, "though armed with dictatorial powers, had no means of enforcing his authority if the cease-fire broke down; all he could do was to leave the colony, or else call on either the [guerrilla front] forces or the Rhodesian army to help him enforce his policies, more likely the latter as, in fact, turned out to be the case when minor cease-fire breaches occurred."[31]

Lord Soames had a small military staff acting mainly as liaison officers with the various armed factions. The Commonwealth Monitoring Force and its small Election Commission were thinly spread, especially in the Tribal Trust Lands. Britain had refused to accept a large Commonwealth peace-keeping force:

> supposedly because it would be resisted by the Rhodesians [...] The point is that this proposal was not even entertained by Carrington because he was opposed to allowing any non-British element in the transition arrangements, except for his hand-picked Commonwealth Monitoring force [...] The second reason was Thatcher's adamant insistence that the British presence should be as brief as possible: her 'quick-in-quick-out' argument arose from the fear that Britain would become bogged down in a morass of conflicting interests if the transition were not rushed through at great speed.[32]

The Commonwealth force was instructed not to shoot. Sir Terence Lewin, Britain's chief of defense staff, later defined their duty if hostilities broke out as "to get the hell out of it."[33] The Commonwealth force stayed in Rhodesia/Zimbabwe for about one year, working at 16 assembly points to disarm or reorganize about 20,000 guerrillas. It was simultaneously involved in training the former guerrillas to facilitate their integration into the regular armed forces. Britain has continued to maintain a small Military Advisory Training Team of about 60 men in

Zimbabwe up to the present. They are divided into small teams to provide battalion-level training.

The British-Commonwealth support to the independence transition process in Rhodesia/Zimbabwe was a major diplomatic success. Subsequent U.N. peace-keeping operations in Namibia, Angola, and Cambodia would follow similar disarmament and election procedures. Although the efforts failed completely in Angola, they have achieved impressive results in Namibia and Cambodia by following the model set by Zimbabwe.

NON-INTERFERENCE OR BENIGN POLICING

Nigeria (1967-70)

Nigeria and Britain signed a defense agreement at the time of Nigerian independence in 1960. The treaty was abrogated in January 1962, as Nigeria felt it difficult to sustain a defense agreement with the former metropolitan power while trying to improve its own image as a regional power and encouraging francophone African countries to forsake their defense links with France. In this sense, Nigeria was competing with France for direct influence in West Africa.

On May 30, 1967, the Biafran Republic declared independence and seceded from the Nigerian Federation, thus starting a two-and-a-half year civil war (see Chapter 5 for a more detailed description of the conflict and France's role in it). International support was split among the two factions and formed highly unusual alliances. Britain, the Soviet Union, Egypt and Algeria strongly supported the federal authorities. France, Spain, Portugal, Israel, China, the Republic of South Africa, and Rhodesia sided with the secessionist Ibos, the major ethnic group in Biafra. The support to Biafra was often less formal than that which could be provided to an established government, but through very effective propaganda it succeeded in bolstering favorable public sentiment worldwide.

British authorities, under Prime Minister Wilson, adopted a policy of open support to the Nigerian Federation and agreed to deliver arms, with the exception of aircraft and bombs. The Commonwealth Office hoped that this distinction would demonstrate Britain's restraint in avoiding an escalation in the level of violence. The British arms policy was based on two premises: avoiding Soviet primacy in support of the

Federation, and preventing British loss of influence. Regarding Soviet influence, Wilson noted that: "Nigeria would have been put in the pawn to the Russians had we refused [the supply of arms]. Whatever military supplies we felt it right to withhold, they in fact provided; they were tightening their grip on Nigeria's life."[34] The OAU's overwhelming pro-Nigerian stance helped legitimatize the British government's policy of arms sales to the Federation. Following a middle-of-the-road course which challenged a Soviet pre-eminence while falling short of an open military intervention, Wilson rallied support from right and left.

> African unity had been a popular symbol among British socialists, and the prime minister hoped that African solidarity against Biafra would restrain the mounting antiwar sentiment among British liberals. Wilson did not expect his pro-federal policy to be challenged by a Conservative opposition that was committed to the need to offset the Soviet presence in Lagos, and was anxious about the future of British investments in Nigeria.[35]

Estimated arms supplied by Britain vary between 15 percent of the federal government's military needs, according to official British sources, and 45 percent, according to critics of the British arms deliveries.[36] It was only after the British government refused to deliver modern bomber and fighter aircraft and heavy artillery that the Nigerian federal government turned to the Soviet Union. The latter started to provide 44 modern MiG fighters (piloted by Egyptian mercenaries and probably eastern European pilots), Ilyushin bombers, and 122-mm guns.[37] Thanks to Soviet backing of the Nigerian Air Force, air attacks became a major boost to the Federation's war effort, giving the federal government total control over the air. The guns also played a vital role, as the Biafran army commander, Alexander Madiebo, commented: "When we reached the stage where the Nigerians had the guns and we had not, they simply overran our territory."[38] The Soviet military and economic assistance was a substantial part of the federal government's eventual success; while on the other side, French arms kept Biafra in the field for the last fifteen months of the campaign, but were not enough to avoid the gradual worsening of the situation in Biafra.

The influence Britain could gain through its arms sales policy was marginal and "was not sufficient to end the war."[39] It was certainly not negligible, however, for the offensive capabilities of the federal

Nigerian government. For example, Britain provided 50 tanks used to spearhead offensives, and naval craft to ensure the sea blockade and the eventual capture of the two major Biafran harbors. The Wilson government also dispatched a naval task force off Nigeria during the summer of 1967. The *Bulwark*, with a commando group embarked, spent three months in the area, which indicated Britain's concern with the situation.[40] The task force did not get involved in any military operations.

The Nigerian civil war was a unique case of post-colonial Franco-British rivalry in Africa, each providing weapons to one of the antagonists. Their respective support contrasted the styles of Wilson and de Gaulle; Britain offering cautious but open support while France provided strong but covert backing. Both countries limited their assistance to the supply of weapons, refusing to be dragged into the conflict with troops. The British expatriate community in Nigeria had, since colonial times, been much smaller than those in eastern or southern Africa. During the civil war, Britain maintained no military bases in Nigeria. Given the magnitude and circumstances of the rebellion, any military action within acceptable parameters of casualties and domestic political opposition was deemed impossible by both Britain and France.

Mauritius (1968)

A company from the 3rd Battalion, Light Infantry, was flown to Mauritius from Singapore on January 22, 1968, to assist the Mauritian government in controlling communal disorders which had been exacerbated by economic difficulties. British ships were also moved to the area. The task was to impose order in the urban part of the island, where rival factions were killing civilians. Actions included cordon and search operations, patrolling, and road blocks. Another company was later sent to operate in the plantations and jungle areas. British patrols, aided by helicopters, covered the rural areas in support of the local security forces. Order was restored, and the first company withdrew in August while the remainder left in mid-November.

Kenya (1976)

After the fall of the emperor of Ethiopia, Somalia temporarily became the largest power on the Horn of Africa. Kenya, which had signed a defense agreement with Ethiopia in 1963, feared Somali claims on its Northern Territories and decided to re-equip its armed forces, which were basically suited with only Rover all-terrain vehicles. Kenya ordered arms, including tanks, from Britain, and helicopters from the U.S. The £10 million package Britain agreed to provide took very long to be delivered. The provision of these arms was the full extent of the British military contribution to this Kenyan crisis.

Zaire (1978)

During the Shaba II operation in May 1978, a multinational airlift was undertaken to rescue European hostages of Katangan rebels in Kolwezi (see Chapter 12 for a detailed description of Belgian and French participation in this intervention). Britain contributed with a medical antenna which was flown to Lusaka, Zambia. It involved an RAF Vickers VC-10 and three C-130s with British Army doctors, a field ambulance unit and a field surgical unit. The medical teams remained on stand-by for the duration of the Franco-Belgian operation.

Zambia (1978-79)

Another example of British military sales at a critical time for the beneficiary happened in Zambia in the late 1970s. Since 1977, Zambia had openly supported guerrillas of the Zimbabwe African People's Union (ZAPU). Rhodesia undertook a series of what it called pre-emptive attacks on ZAPU bases in Zambia, including two air raids on Lusaka in 1978 and 1979. The Rhodesians raided the Lusaka airport and a military camp. When Prime Minister James Callaghan met Zambia's President Kenneth Kaunda in September 1978, Britain agreed to an emergency sale of *Rapier* missiles. The raids ceased when a British governor arrived in Salisbury in December 1979 to prepare for Zimbabwe's independence.

Uganda (1980-83)

Dr. Obote was declared president of Uganda on December 15, 1980, after national elections which were monitored by Commonwealth observers. The elections did not, however, bring political or military stability to the country, and random violence continued for two years. A small military training team from three Commonwealth members (Britain, Jamaica and Canada) was sent to support the Uganda National Liberation Army. Failing to bring about cohesion and discipline in

Uganda, this training team was disbanded. Only the British element was left to pursue the effort after 1984.

Gambia (1981)

In July 1981, an attempt to overthrow Sir Dawda Jawara's ruling Peoples' Progressive Party (PPP) occurred during a visit to London by the Gambian president. The insurgents failed to attract support among the population at large. Senegalese military assistance was forthcoming with about 3,000 troops entering Gambia, and the rebellion was thwarted after one week. One of the most dramatic actions occurred when the Senegalese stormed the Field Force Depot in Banjul and the Medical Research Center in Fajara to release hundreds of hostages detained by the rebels. Earlier, about 800 people had been killed during the disturbances, according to official estimates. The alleged leader of the failed rebel coup, Kukoi Samba Sanyang, fled the country with some of his supporters.[41] Some elements of the British SAS also assisted in the operation, apparently to rescue 29 hostages, including 18 children and President Jawara's first wife, who had not accompanied her husband during his visit in London.[42] After the events, Britain dispatched a small training team to help form the Gambian Army.

Botswana (1986-88)

Although this British military action was an extension of military training, the circumstances and the forces used qualify the 1986 Botswana operation as a small-scale intervention. In May 1986, South Africa launched raids aimed at what it considered to be terrorist ANC bases in Gaborone, the capital of Botswana, and its vicinity. Britain and the U.S. had promised military aid against South African attacks and anti-apartheid guerilla infiltration.[43] The same year, 90 men of the British SAS went to train the Botswana Defence Force in techniques to resist future South African raids. The SAS training exercises made use of an RAF C-130. The SAS session, which took place in a remote corner of the Botswanan desert, lasted about six weeks.[44] After the South African raid of March 1988, the SAS went back to train Botswanan forces for sixteen weeks. In the early 1990s, the SAS apparently returned for exercises in Botswana, although, as for most of its activities, little information is available from open sources on the type of exercise this elite force performed. One can only surmise that it was in line with previous actions to bolster Botswana's ability to defend itself against armed infiltrations.

Liberia (1990)

During the insurgency that rebel leader Charles Taylor initiated on December 24, 1989 against the regime of President Samuel Doe, Britain sent one frigate and one tanker ship to evacuate British citizens. Britain had no intention of intervening in the conflict, but was merely concerned with the protection and evacuation of British and other expatriates from Liberia. The British ships were withdrawn by late July 1990, by which time all 700 members of the British community had left Liberia. On August 5, 1990, the assault ship *Saipan* arrived to evacuate U.S. embassy personnel and other civilians from Monrovia in operation *Sharp Edge*.

MILITARY PURSUITS IN SOUTHERN AFRICA

Namibia (1989-90)

Britain's role in southern Africa at the time of the Namibia-Angola settlement received some strong backing from Chester Crocker, U.S. assistant secretary of state for African affairs. In early 1989, he stated his belief that the U.S., having taken the lead role in "creating the realities" that led to the settlement, should now let others - British prime minister Margaret Thatcher in particular - shoulder greater responsibility in its implementation.[45] Crocker was quoted as saying:

> I think the British, as probably the world's most experienced external power on this set of issues, have been the quickest to pick up on it. [...] I think [Margaret Thatcher] is quite prepared to make it known that the British have a contribution to make and I think she is absolutely right. In fact, in some respects, she has within her grasp more of the elements of creating things than almost anybody else.[46]

Britain paralleled Crocker's aspirations with objectives of its own. The assistance programs to Front Line States, in the economic and military fields, aimed at gaining influence. Military assistance was perceived as a substitute for other, more radical forms of anti-apartheid solidarity that Britain could not accept, such as military intervention. Direct British interests in the Front Line States were relatively minor and second to its interests in South Africa. Overall, British military aid programs sought primarily to avoid excessive violence between all parties concerned in that region. Order and stability were the best means of serving British interests in southern Africa, within acceptable parameters of the gradual dismantlement of the apartheid regime. Britain's involvement in the Namibian independence settlement and in the Angolan peace process has to be viewed in light of this general policy objective.

In early 1989, after South Africa and the U.N. negotiated a settlement on the transition to Namibian independence and agreed on a date for its implementation, the U.N. Transition Assistance Group in Namibia (UNTAG) was deployed. UNTAG's purpose was to create the necessary conditions for free and fair elections in Namibia. At maximum strength during the November 1989 elections, UNTAG's civilian and military personnel numbered about 8,000 individuals from 27 countries. In addition to the civilian component, there was a police force of 1,500 men and a military force of roughly 4,500.[47] The responsibilities of the military branch included: "monitoring the cease-fire and the confinement of the parties' armed forces to base; monitoring the dismantling of the South African military presence in Namibia; and maintaining some degree of surveillance over the Territory's borders."[48]

Overall, UNTAG's deployment and operation ran without problems. Some fighting broke out between South African forces and heavily armed SWAPO groups that had infiltrated Namibia in April 1989, before UNTAG was fully deployed. At least 200 people were killed as a result of this fighting, and the U.N. was blamed for the slowness of its deployment.[49] By May, the crisis was over and the rest of UNTAG's operation proceeded smoothly. UNTAG's forces were never directly involved in any of the combat. On March 21, 1990, Namibia became independent and UNTAG was completely disbanded.

Britain contributed to the military component of UNTAG with a single squadron, which peaked at 170 people during the elections in November 1989; by March 1990, there were only six people left. In early April 1990, a team of 32 British instructors arrived in Windhoek to begin a bilateral military aid program to train and organize an initial Namibian force of 4,500 to 5,000 troops.[50] This effort was beyond the framework of U.N. assistance.

Angola (1991-92)

On May 31, 1991, the government of Angola and the rebel faction that it had battled for 16 years, known under its Portuguese acronym as UNITA, signed a peace agreement in Lisbon ending the civil war and paving the way for free democratic elections. Under the agreement, a U.N. force of 440 military and police officers and 175 civilians monitored the cease-fire during preparations for internationally supervised elections to be held in the fall of 1992. The two warring factions had agreed to create a single 50,000-member armed force, composed of joint units. Portugal, Britain and France offered to assist in building the new forces. Members of the British Army participated with their Portuguese and French counterparts in training Angolan forces as part of the Angolan peace accords. Several British soldiers were sent for a brief period, although not as part of a particular Army unit. Their main purpose was to provide engineering and motor transport training to members of the Angolan military.

The outbreak of fighting in the wake of the September 1992 Angolan elections destroyed all plans for the immediate creation of an integrated national army. The situation deteriorated very quickly, and Britain organized an airlift operation in November 1992, during which the Royal Air Force evacuated 149 British citizens from Angola.[51]

Somalia (1992-93)

From December 1992 to February 1993, during the early deployment of U.S.-led operation *Restore Hope*, Britain dispatched an RAF detachment to Mombasa, Kenya, to mount relief sorties to several destinations in Somalia under the code-name operation *Vigour*.[52] The detachment included two *Hercules* transport aircraft and up to 88 personnel (27 aircrew, 13 engineers, 12 movement personnel, 16 communications personnel, seven security personnel, and the remainder in operations, intelligence, administration and medicine). The two *Hercules* moved approximately 3,000 tons of aid.

Although the U.S. had been actively seeking British participation in the ground operations at battalion or brigade level, the Ministry of Defence and the Foreign and Commonwealth Office made it clear that such forces would not be offered. The decision was related to the extent of existing British commitments, "and in particular uncertainty over escalation of the situation in Bosnia."[53] The British secretary of state stated that:

The decision not to send ground forces to Somalia was not taken because of the absence of such forces. We would have sent a battalion if we had thought it appropriate. We decided that the best contribution that we could make to Somalia was with RAF *Hercules*.[54]

The Defence Committee of the House of Commons, investigating British peace-keeping and intervention forces, deplored that "an opportunity for a valuable contribution from both a military and humanitarian perspective was lost."[55]

PRAGMATISM AND AVERSION TO INTERVENTION

Britain's ambivalence in getting militarily involved in its former colonies contrasts highly with the French and Belgian approaches. For instance, in the case of operation *Restore Hope*, both France and Belgium sent troops to Somalia, even though both had also committed troops in the former Yugoslavia. The history of British intervention in post-colonial sub-Saharan Africa is divisible into three periods, each reinforcing the downward trend in British military involvement in African affairs: (i) the period between 1960 and 1964, which witnessed the peak of Britain's post-colonial military engagement in sub-Saharan Africa; (ii) 1965-79, when the Rhodesian tangle called on Britain's capabilities as mediator and peace-keeper; and (iii) the 1980s and early 1990s, when Britain seemed committed to a *de facto* policy of pragmatic non-interference in Africa.

Unlike France and Belgium, Britain did not react militarily to Soviet expansionism in Africa during the 1970s. This was in part a reflection of the fact that former British colonies were not the primary targets of the Soviets and Cubans. British authorities felt that the Soviet-Cuban presence did not endanger their vital interests on the continent. More precisely, Britain did not have vital or strategic interests in sub-Saharan Africa. Britain's largest military operation, during the East African mutinies, was undertaken at a time when Britain still thought it had to assume a leadership role in the Commonwealth. When even this last self-imposed duty was eventually abandoned, right after the Zimbabwean independence, the last remnant of Britain's post-imperial responsibilities vanished. Sub-Saharan Africa could have qualified as a vital, or at least higher level, interest in Britain's foreign policy if authorities in London had been seriously committed to playing a leadership role in the Commonwealth, or even in perhaps a more narrowly defined British-African Commonwealth. This, however, was not a concern for British policy-makers.

The stakes were different for French authorities, who regarded their French-African relationships as one of the cornerstones of French influence in the world and an essential dimension of French linguistic and cultural radiance outside France. Nothing else could better differentiate French and British policy toward sub-Saharan Africa than the respective endorsement of a regional role by Paris and the reluctance to play such a role by London. In many other aspects, both European powers shared significant similarities: an important colonial legacy, economic interests, at least implicit demands from former colonies for continued involvement, sufficient power projection capabilities, sovereign island-bases around the continent, and secure access to host-nation support during military interventions. The instrumentalities and global environment for post-colonial influence were identical in the case of both powers, but they differed in their approach toward how to manipulate the global environment effectively. Britain did not need, or chose not to need, a post-colonial sub-Saharan zone of influence the way France did.

After Britain renounced a leading role in a sub-Saharan zone of influence, it did not completely abdicate all other forms of involvement. Interests in the region were defined more narrowly. Economic considerations assumed a much larger role, and hence South Africa became the focus of British policy-making in Africa. The trend was particularly evident in the 1980s and 1990s. Britain's approach to southern Africa increasingly resembled Belgian policy with regard to Zaire: avoiding serious destabilization in a zone of high economic interest. Events in the field and the weight of history would allow Britain to preserve a low-key profile in such a role, while Belgium had to resort to more dramatic actions, including repeated military interventions. In the early 1990s, Britain's economic interests in South Africa were more secure than Belgium's in Zaire.

Chapter 10

Belgian Political and Military Involvement in Africa

Belgium's political structure rests on a combination of constitutional monarchy, proportional representation, and the division of the country into French-speaking and Flemish-speaking communities. Executive responsibilities lies with the government's ministers, and no act of the king can have effect unless countersigned by one of the ministers. The system of proportional representation in both the Senate and the House of Representatives prevents *de facto* a single political party from gaining an absolute majority in either assembly. Multiple parties co-exist and compete for votes, fragmenting the electorate into a plethora of political constituencies. In some legislative elections the Belgian electorate has been offered an electoral menu listing the acronyms of no less than 42 political parties from which to choose.[1] Not surprisingly, there has only been one instance since 1919 of a single political party gaining a 50 percent majority in the Belgian parliament, the Christian Social Party between 1950 and 1954.

Historically, political parties in Belgium organized themselves along ideological or religious lines, from which emerged the centrist Christian Social Party, the conservative Liberal Party, the Socialist Party, and the now-defunct Communist Party. Regardless of the fact that parties may have shared the same ideology, they later split along linguistic lines into French and Flemish-speaking factions. This particularity has generated additional political parties organized exclusively around linguistic-nationalist agendas.[2] Linguistic nationalism brought about the federalization of Belgium in 1993. Ecological and other small parties have also added to the variety of political forces represented in the country's legislative branches.

Under the constraints of proportional representation, multi-partism and linguistic differences, Belgium is characterized by a weaker executive branch than countries with two main political parties or with a strong presidency. Governments in Belgium have to rely on coalitions of four to six parties on average in order to gain a majority in parliament. Ministerial portfolios at the federal level (since 1993) are then distributed among the coalition participants, usually a combination of Flemish and French-speaking members of the Christian Social party, with Socialist and/or Liberal partners and the occasional addition of a French or Flemish nationalist party. The prime minister, usually a member of the party which collected the greatest number of votes, presides over a politically heterogeneous cabinet. In many ways, the cabinet acts as a collegial body of party representatives from the winning coalition whose objective is to supervise the execution of the coalition government's mandate. Ministers are responsible before parliament, where they have to rely heavily on the endorsement of their respective parties. "Government stability requires a disciplined majority, which, for important matters, often results in party-line voting."[3] The system of close political control by the parties has sometimes been dubbed "partycracy." Consequently, party discipline is easily enforceable by party authorities, who, although influential actors, are not constitutional policy-making participants. Over time, parties have been able to reinforce their position and have weakened the role of the Belgian parliament. Xavier Mabille, an authoritative source on the Belgian political system, explained this shift as:

> due to the fact that the coalition practice obliges the parties in the government to devise an agreement specifying the intentions of the new team. This agreement is a binding contract on the members of the government. [...] Consequently, the freedom of the major parliamentary groups is restricted, for any initiative that might upset the balance behind the coalition is untenable.[4]

The room for maneuverability is restricted to the greatest common denominator among the coalition members in the government. Many decisions are compromises and the results of consultations and reciprocal concessions. Belgian governments are inherently unstable, and have succeeded each other in the post-war era at a rate of one new government per 15 months, or 39 governments in 49 years. Developing grand strategies and attempting to achieve long-term continuity of political goals is an almost impossible task. The complexity of the Belgian decision-making system tends to muddy the situation. "A compromise *à la belge* is generally so complex that it is difficult to shed light on all its aspects. It is also an expensive system [and] can give rise to wariness about politics or even a rejection of politics."[5]

BELGIAN DECISION-MAKING

Crisis Management

During the late 1970s and early 1980s, Belgium became involved in a series of domestic and international crises, ranging in intensity from small-scale terrorist attacks in Belgium to low-level combat situations, as in Shaba in 1978. The need to be able to respond militarily to such a wide spectrum of situations provided an occasion to restructure and refine crisis management procedures, especially at the highest political level. The contingency procedures for problems, especially in central Africa, have been streamlined and improved over time. Nevertheless, Belgian reactions to crises continue to rely on a fair amount of improvisation. A special room is reserved for emergency situations and crisis management at the Ministry of the Interior. The room is equipped with all types of communication equipment and crisis monitoring facilities geared primarily to domestic crises but also useful in external ones.

The crisis cabinet regroups different sets of officials according to the type of contingency. Belgium does not have an institutionalized equivalent of the U.S. government's National Security Council, and there exists no formal mechanism to convene a group of national security authorities. A contingency in central Africa will usually require the core participation of the prime minister, the minister of foreign affairs, the minister of defense, the minister of external commerce, the secretary of state for cooperation and development, and occasionally the ministers of the interior and of justice. Non-cabinet authorities such as the chief of staff and the chief of the security service may also be called to participate.

In cases of military intervention, the crisis cabinet issues directives specifying the objectives of the action, its duration, and the rules of engagement for the forces in the field. The opinion of the chief of staff at the cabinet level merely serves to assess the military feasibility of the operation. Much of the decision-making is centered around the minister of defense and the crisis cabinet. While the military authorities produce a plan and suggest a means of execution, there has traditionally been much cabinet-level interference once an operation has been launched. For instance, during the 1964 Stanleyville rescue operation, troops were already in the air when the cabinet was still haggling about the necessity and extent of the intervention. Once on the spot, military commanders sometimes receive conflicting orders from the Belgian ambassador, the military attaché at the embassy, the General Staff, the minister of defense, and the prime minister. The cabinet often operates in parallel with the regular lines of command. Such micro-management of intervention by the cabinet in Brussels sometimes results in damaging delays and a lack of flexibility for military commanders in the field. The latter usually follow the orders cautiously and have little room, or incentive, to change them according to local developments.

Policy-Making and African Affairs

As a small industrial nation with limited international objectives, Belgium's foreign relations are largely dominated by trade, and, in the case of developing countries, aid programs. The ministerial portfolios reflect these priorities by consolidating foreign relations, international trade and development cooperation in one ministry, the Ministry of Foreign Affairs, but with two ministers and one state secretary. Among them, the minister of foreign affairs has precedence over both the minister for external commerce and European affairs and the state secretary for cooperation and development. The minister of foreign affairs defines the broad lines of all foreign policies and programs.[6] While he - no woman has ever held this position - has the overall lead, he has to cooperate with his counterparts from either commerce and European affairs or from cooperation and development, who can be expected to protect their turf with all the bureaucratic means at their disposal and by calling on their respective political parties. Indeed, as part of the formation of the coalition government, the ministerial and adjunct portfolios may be awarded to members of different political parties. Party interference in foreign policy decision-making often complicates and encumbers cooperation among the three top foreign policy-makers.

There are three institutional levels at which foreign policy-making can be coordinated. At the first level of coordination, the two ministers and the state secretary meet within the Ministerial Committee of Foreign Affairs. This committee meets once or twice a month and reviews all matters which overlap the authority of one or more of the three foreign policy branches; it also considers other general objectives. The committee also reviews the sale of arms and ammunition to foreign countries. The second level of coordination is done during full government cabinet sessions, or within a more restricted crisis cabinet. Concerning sub-Saharan Africa, the full cabinet interferes only in highly political matters or when major decisions have to be made. Belgium's difficult relationship with Zaire - the country with which Belgium has the closest ties in sub-Saharan Africa - is often subject to discussion at the cabinet level given the great dissent on which policies to adopt. The crisis cabinet, as described further below, convenes among other reasons when Belgium is considering a military intervention abroad. Finally, a third level of foreign policy coordination is at the European level. More and more foreign policy issues are deferred, to or at least discussed within, the framework of the European Community or, since late 1993, the European Union. African affairs are discussed periodically at the European level, especially with regard to preferential trade agreements, crisis situations or human rights abuses. For instance, the sensitive relationship with South Africa or military involvement in Somalia has been discussed and coordinated among European partners in the EC/EU Council of Ministers.

In many ways, the geographic areas and fields of interest of Belgium's contemporary relationship with Africa are the direct product of policy priorities developed in colonial times. During the 75 years of Belgian colonial rule in the Congo, either under the direct authority of King Léopold II (1885-1908) or under the Belgian government's colonial administration (1908-1960), Belgians have typically manifested two parallel approaches toward their central African possession, which is eighty times the size of the metropole. The first approach was inspired by pure mercantilisml, applied ruthlessly and with the aim of outright exploitation of all exportable resources in the colony. The methods of some of the Belgians and other foreigners - the Congo was a Free State open to all - were so brutal as to provoke an international outcry dramatized by Joseph Conrad's novel *The Heart of Darkness*.

The protest was not purely righteous, however, and to some degree merely disguised attempts from envious powers to snatch the Congo away from the Belgians. The outcry later subsided and Belgium continued the same commercial exploitation of its colony as its European neighbors did in theirs. On the positive side, the mercantilist drive was at the origin of large investments in infrastructure and extraction industries. Because the investments were profitable, the infrastructure was well kept; at Zairian independence in 1960, Belgium could be proud of its achievements in that field, especially when compared to the average French or British equivalent in Africa.

The second approach which permeated, and often conflicted with, the early mercantilist drive was more idealistic. Missionaries, teachers, and young colonial bureaucrats left Belgium to settle in the Congo. They brought basic education - though not at university level, built hospitals, and provided the backbone for a responsible program of social growth and nation-building. Despite the fact that the Congo was a colonial possession and was ruled by Belgians, it was managed as an autonomous entity. The internal autonomy of the colony vis-a-vis the metropole left colonial managers with an unusual freedom to develop a rather paternalistic development model, combining a strong dose of idealism with a condescending view of the local population's political aspirations. This scheme is different from the French assimilationist approach or the British self-rule system. Slowly, the Belgian elements were bringing western ideas and public management methods to a population that they generally regarded as lacking political maturity. Their entire development agenda was shaken by the sudden drive to independence and the ensuing five years of political turmoil.

Post-colonial relations continued to be clearly marked by the dualist mercantilist/missionary approach, which remains part of Belgium's trade and aid policies thirty years later. Remarkably, no new approach has been added, although the two existing ones have undergone basic mutations due to sensitive North-South relations in the world after 1960.

The Economist once wrote that "Zaire is the only foreign country where visiting Belgian politicians have a chance to feel important."[7] Indeed, Belgium's place on the international scene has been enhanced by the influence it could continue to exercise in its giant former colony. On the contrary, Belgium's post-war international image was at its lowest when it failed to solve the Congolese crisis between 1960 and 1965. Belgium was ostracized in international meetings, and it took several years to recover.[8] From its independence in 1960 until 1991-92, the Congo, and later Zaire, has dominated Belgian policy-making for sub-Saharan Africa, even though other concerns in Africa have gradually eroded this virtually exclusive focus.

The relationship with Zaire has never been easy and has been marked by the forceful and erratic personality of President Mobutu. The latter's uninterrupted hold on power since the mid-1960s contrasts with the ex-metropole's rapid succession of fragile coalition governments. Despite the many changes in governments, Belgian authorities have adopted a policy that stressed the pursuance of strong involvement in Zaire through economic interests and aid programs, at least until late 1991.

The relationship was seriously shaken in 1989. Starting with a dispute over Zaire's debt toward Belgium, the complete breakdown of diplomatic relations was prevented only through the skillful mediation of Morocco. The scars of this argument led the Belgian parliament to re-evaluate the terms and conditions of Belgium's dependency on Zaire and of Belgian sycophantic behavior toward Mobutu. The parliament concluded that Belgian economic dependency on Zaire was not so high as to compensate for all of President Mobutu's abuses. The threshold of tolerance had been reached, and Belgium gave a new reading to Mobutu's twenty-five years of ruthless and corrupt rule. The alleged massacre by Zairian troops of dozens of students on the university campus of Lubumbashi in May 1990 provided the pretext for a more critical Belgian re-evaluation.[9] Subsequent Zairian investigations failed to uncover conclusive evidence against the Mobutu regime, and a Belgian request for an international investigation was denied.[10] Outraged at Belgium's request, Mobutu took, among other actions, the drastic step of banning all Belgian-sponsored assistance programs, both civilian and military. Belgian aid through non-governmental organizations was also included in this ban, which involved about 700 Belgian assistance personnel, 440 of whom were paid by the Belgian government and 250 from government-sponsored personnel in NGOs.[11] The final blow to the Belgian presence in Zaire came during the Zairian armed forces mutinies of October-November 1991. Most Belgian private interests in the country were abandoned by the hastily evacuated expatriates.

Combined with an aversion toward President Mobutu - mainly by left-of-center political parties in Belgium - Belgian politicians distanced themselves from too strong a focus on Zaire. Since then, there have

been few indicators pointing toward a reversal of this trend. Former
Foreign Minister Mark Eyskens, in an interview to the newspaper *La
Libre Belgique* in March 1992, regretted this abdication, which he felt
was inspired more by short-term considerations than by an exact
appreciation of Belgium's potential role in central Africa.[12] After 1992,
the Belgian government's policy concerning the Zairian situation was
that President Mobutu was a liability and that development programs
and other types of assistance should not be reactivated. Belgian
authorities felt that Mobutu should either resign or retain only
symbolic, transitional powers. The concurrent withdrawal of the World
Bank's assistance to Zaire and the stern warnings of the IMF created
an impasse. The Zairian authorities need the assistance to restart the
economy, but the international development assistance is on hold until
Zaire proves its goodwill and respects its agreements. According to a
1994 interview with Belgian Foreign Minister Willy Claes, once the
political chaos is resolved, the solution of the impasse may require
Belgium, in coordination with France and the U.S., to play a leading
role in preparing for the resumption of aid flows.[13]

Private commercial Belgian interests in Zaire have also dwindled in
the wake of the 1991 expatriate evacuation. Traditionally, trade and
development aid figure among the primary ongoing interests and are
supported by a fairly large expatriate community. Belgian expatriates
in sub-Saharan Africa numbered roughly 45,000 people, although this
figure included about 10,000 in Zaire who left the country during the
1991 and 1992 mutinies and who, for the most part, have not returned
because the situation has remained precarious. Since the early 1980s,
trade with the whole African continent has amounted to about 2-3
percent of total Belgian exports and 4-6 percent of the imports. A
decade later, the numbers were respectively 3.7 percent and 2.5 percent
(respectively $4.5 billion and $3 billion). The Belgian trade balance
with Africa is chronically negative, by a ratio of 3-to-2 for imports
against exports.[14] Zaire (until the end of 1991), Nigeria and South
Africa are Belgium's three main trading partners in Africa, and
represent more than 45 percent of Belgian exports to sub-Saharan
Africa.[15] The biggest trade deficit was with Zaire in 1991, for a total
of about $500 million, although the figure declined dramatically during
the subsequent turmoil. Belgium's commercial priorities are not exactly
reflected in its aid policy. Trade relations between Belgium and sub-
Saharan Africa are naturally dominated by the three economic giants in

that part of the world, with Zaire coming first for historical reasons, followed by Nigeria and South Africa.

Belgium's aid policy reflects the weight of history. The three former Belgian colonies, Zaire, Rwanda and Burundi, have traditionally received the lion's share of Belgian aid funds. The Belgian annual public aid budget to developing countries, for both bilateral and multilateral assistance, reached a total of close to BEF 24 billion ($800 million) in 1992. Aid money has steadily dropped as a percentage of the Belgian GNP from the high in 1983, when it reached 0.59 percent, to 1992, when it was only 0.38 percent. In 1992 the Belgian agency in charge of cooperation and development, *Administration générale de la Coopération au Développement - Algemeen Bestuur van de Ontwikkelingssamenwerking*, or AGCD-ABOS, absorbed about 80 percent of the total aid package, compared to 60 percent the previous year. The bulk of the remaining money goes principally to the Ministry of Finance and other ministries, including Defense.[16] Sub-Saharan Africa is by far the largest recipient of Belgium's aid. Of the AGCD-ABOS assistance in 1992 that can be identified by country (roughly half of the agency's budget), Zaire received 2.6 percent (compared to 20 percent in 1990), Burundi received 16 percent (11 percent in 1990), and Rwanda received 11 percent (unchanged since 1990). All the rest of the sub-Saharan region had to be satisfied with a few percentage points less than the three former Belgian colonies. Aid recipients belonging to the former group, i.e. 45 countries, each received on average 0.6 percent of the AGCD-ABOS budget.[17] The dilution of Belgian aid over such a large community of nations has begged the question of what impact Belgium can command with the respective beneficiaries. Experts wonder whether it would not be better to target African countries where Belgian aid level could make more of a difference and enhance Belgian influence.

Starting in the 1980s, Belgian diplomacy in Africa developed in parallel with the adjustment programs imposed by the International Monetary Fund, the World Bank, and groups of donor countries. In the case of Zaire, the link between multilateral aid programs and Belgian cooperation programs was formalized in 1989 with the signature of a Belgo-Zairian agreement in Rabat, Morocco.[18] IMF-type economic soundness and stability programs became a component of Belgium's approach to central Africa, and mainly Zaire. In 1990-91, a new brand of diplomacy emphasized the respect for human rights and democratic rule. This orientation became "a new imperative, morally more

defendable, but not so easy to implement."[19] The issue of human rights
achieved a central status in Belgian policy toward Zaire after the May
1990 massacres of students on the Lubumbashi university campus by
soldiers allegedly from the presidential guard. The subsequent turmoil
caused by the hasty introduction of multipartism and other democratic
reforms in Zaire, as well as in Rwanda and Burundi, has cautioned
Belgian policy-makers to reconsider their priorities in view of the
appalling human rights abuses caused by the failure of the reforms.
Willy Claes, Belgium's minister for foreign affairs, commented in the
press that in the government's approach: "We first talk about human
rights before even talking about democracy."[20] The uncontrolled
changes in the three former Belgian colonies in central Africa between
1990 and 1994 has produced a feeling of discouragement and impotence
among the Belgian authorities, which is shared by international lending
organizations. Despite the region's gloomy prospects, there continues
to be a general expectation in the world's diplomatic community that
Belgium would pursue its role as one of the influential actors in central
African affairs. France has challenged this role since the mid-1970s,
and Paris succeeded in equalling or even overtaking Brussels as one of
the centers of European influence in the three former Belgian colonies.
The heavy cost of sustaining the ailing African economies has
subsequently demonstrated that both countries stood to gain from
coordinating, to the extent possible, their policies in central Africa, and
including the U.S. in the coordination effort. Perhaps unable to sever
all historical ties, Belgium continues to harbor a residual willingness to
pursue an active role in the region and has preserved some of the
indispensable means, including a military option, for living up to
international expectations.

MILITARY INVOLVEMENT IN AFRICA

Belgium claims few, if any, strategic ambitions in Africa. The
Belgian Ministry of Foreign Affairs was quite outspoken in a 1983
document specifying that: "Belgium's goal in Africa is not to create
zones of influence. [Belgium] does not have the will nor the means,
however little that may be, to limit the sovereignty of a country it is
assisting." The same document added that: "We are not threatening; no
one fears, on our part, imperialist designs and we have a track record

which is generally speaking well appreciated."[21] Although Belgium may not have pursued a consistent effort to establish and organize a zone of influence in central Africa, it has clearly succeeded in maintaining a zone of interest where it has yielded considerable influence. In fact, Belgium's influence in the region has not been wholly passive, and one should not regard Belgian intentions in central Africa as completely devoid of ambitions to consolidate existing power. The difference with France is obvious, however, both in the size of the effort to play an influential role and in the political drive behind that effort. As a small power with limited means to assist countries either economically or militarily, and without a global cultural mission, Belgium approaches its involvement in central Africa with much more limited ambitions than France. In addition, the powers of the Belgian executive branch are inherently more diffuse and less stable compared to the strong, centralized authority vested in the French executive. The consistent pursuit of a long-term strategic ambition in regions outside Belgium's zone of interests becomes impossible. Africa does not fall within the core category of Belgian vital strategic or even economic interests. The more peripheral importance of Africa in Belgian foreign policy-making provides for greater flexibility because the cost of an error is reduced. The differing views among Belgian political parties give rise to African policies at least as numerous as the parties themselves. The key elements in their respective policy approaches to Africa, and central Africa in particular, revolve around their evaluation of three issues: the human rights and humanitarian aspects (the latter includes the security and well-being of Belgian expatriates), the importance of Belgian economic and commercial interests, and the criteria for the use of force in crisis situations. Progress in democratic reforms have recently been added to the list. Policies concerning central Africa and military intervention can be categorized according to the three main ideological trends in Belgian politics.

The Christian Social constituency has a long tradition of involvement in central Africa through missionaries, schools, and hospitals, as well as through the many Catholic non-governmental organizations (NGOs). Parallel to the work of the NGOs, Christian Social constituents have created many businesses in Africa and are therefore concerned with promoting their commercial interests on the continent. The Christian Social parties, both French- and Flemish-speaking, often find themselves caught between the conflicting interests of their respective electorates: on the one hand are people concerned with human rights and Christian solidarity toward less favored populations, and, on the other hand, are the commercial operators whose interests favor continuity in the relationships with Third World suppliers and markets, even at the cost of turning a blind eye toward human rights violations and corruption. The dilemma in itself is not one over which the Christian Social parties have a monopoly, but no other political party is so acutely torn between the two conflicting interests. For these reasons, military interventions in central Africa are usually approved by the Christian Social party, French- and Flemish-speaking alike. However, military deployments in Africa cannot be endorsed unless there is a serious threat to Belgian interests. The only politically acceptable threat for military operations in Africa is when Belgian expatriates are directly endangered. Historically, this has been an essential condition for launching a Belgian military operation. Commercial and political interests could also be secured at the same time. The Christian Social party's endorsement of the occasional use of force is best illustrated by its participation in every government decision favoring military engagement in former African colonies.

The French and Flemish Liberal-conservative parties are traditionally more business-oriented with regard to overseas policies and have far weaker connections to NGOs involved in the Third World than the Christian Social parties. They subscribe to humanitarian military interventions, but are inclined to go further in recognizing the need to protect Belgian commercial and economic interests abroad. Such goals would be particularly acceptable if an operation could, with good reason, be presented as a humanitarian cause. Belgian conservative parties tend, in this sense, to share the views of policy-makers in France. During the 1978 Shaba II intervention, when many Belgians felt they were pushed aside from their central African turf by a covetous France, a Belgian, French-speaking, conservative magazine explicitly endorsed the French approach in saying:

> As to the French, if they have other African ambitions, it is not for us [Belgians] to judge them. First because we owe them some thanks for the prompt and efficient intervention of the [Foreign] Légion. Even if there are people to insinuate that the action of France is not pure and disinterested, one could legitimately answer: 'So what? All work deserves a salary! Where do you think you are? In a world of choir boys?' Who would obstinately try to help Mobutu if there was not some copper to be gained?[22]

This radical approach at a time the Liberal party was in the opposition may not reflect the view held by all conservatives. What it does reflect is that Liberals may be more outspoken about the commercial realities that surround an intervention. The Liberals' approach to interventions has not been tested in practice. Except during the Congo's transition to independence in 1960, the Liberal party was never in power during any of the overseas crisis situations requiring the use of force. However, they have often endorsed overseas military action from the opposition benches in parliament, even though they may have been critical of the modalities of its execution.

On the Socialist side, the views on military interventions differ by linguistic region, with the French-speaking Socialist party being less radical than the Flemish-speaking party. Both, however, have few historic links with central African affairs. They were not involved in the colonial ventures and drew almost none of their constituency from people involved in colonial activities. Traditionally, Socialist parties have considered it their duty to concentrate first on social injustices at home. Gradually, they have shaped their policy toward central Africa in terms of the political acceptability of the governments receiving Belgian assistance funds. The poor human rights record of the Mobutu regime has made it a target of criticism from the Belgian Socialists. Karel Van Miert, a former chairman of the Flemish Socialist party, was one of the most virulent anti-Mobutu political figures in Belgium and was quoted as saying, after a minor crisis in 1985, that: "The Flemish Socialists will not give in to the Zairian president, the most corrupt man in the world."[23] Although not necessarily against military intervention, the Socialists are adamant about keeping such actions within a strictly defined humanitarian focus. This orientation was demonstrated by the 1990 intervention in Rwanda and the 1991 intervention in Zaire, which the French-speaking Socialist minister of defense, Guy Coëme, fully endorsed. The Belgian participation in the Gulf War, the U.N. intervention in Somalia and the U.N. peace-keeping force in the former Yugoslavia were also endorsed by Socialist cabinet members.

Besides the ideological approaches to Africa and military interventions, the cultural differences between the two linguistic communities in Belgium produced two additional sets of attitudes which cut through ideological differences. The Flemish population in Belgium has historically been less involved in the political, military, and commercial build-up of the colonies than the French-speaking community. With the notable exceptions of Catholic missions and educational or charitable work, Flemings have traditionally kept a lower profile in pursuing post-colonial interests in central Africa. With Zaire's declining importance to the Belgian economy, "many Flemish-speaking Belgians are impatient with the French-speakers' eagerness to please Mr. Mobutu."[24] The attitudes of the two linguistic communities are also traditionally different with regard to military matters. As an American observer of Belgian policy processes described it: "Policy decisions in the arms sales and security assistance arena are complicated further by the fact that most Belgians (but especially the Flemings) share a general aversion for military matters."[25]

Despite their ideological and linguistic differences, political parties in Belgium have remained close with regard to their views on military interventions. Their positions fluctuated in unison with public opinion, shifting from a strong support toward interventions in the early 1960s, to a reluctance to intervene in the 1970s, and finally to a new zeal in the late 1980s and early 1990s. This renewed enthusiasm grew in intensity to the point where Belgium became simultaneously involved in up to three military interventions in Europe, the Middle East and Africa.

Belgium has intervened about ten times in crisis situations in post-colonial sub-Saharan Africa. The political consensus on the need to intervene militarily has sometimes taken shape amidst heated debates within the coalition governments, especially in the early 1960s and in the 1970s. During the series of interventions in Africa and elsewhere between 1990 and 1994, an agreement among government partners to intervene militarily was reached relatively easily. The untarnished success rate of past interventions, starting in 1960 until 1993, has infused the Belgian population with an unusually high degree of confidence in the capability of Belgian troops to intervene abroad. With the death of ten soldiers in the U.N.-led peace-keeping operation in Rwanda, however, this confidence may have been shattered. After 1960, Belgium participated in more military interventions abroad than any other European state, with the exception of France and Britain. A consensus on the need to intervene derived directly from two main factors: either the danger to which Belgian expatriates were subjected or the call for humanitarian peace-keeping missions, as in Somalia and the former Yugoslavia. According to an opinion poll prepared in late January 1994, before the Rwanda disaster, the Belgian population showed an extraordinarily strong endorsement for this second type of military operation. The Belgian troops in Somalia were just back from their difficult assignment, and the troops in the former Yugoslavia were still carrying out their mission under frustrating conditions and despite having suffered several casualties. The results of the poll, as described in the table below, demonstrate a clear backing of the prerogative for Belgium to intervene abroad.[26] Reactions to such a poll after the Rwanda events were not available at the time of writing.

TABLE 6: Survey of Belgian Attitudes Toward Interventions

	Yes	No	?
Are military interventions acceptable to put an end to conflicts or to protect civilians?	71%	17%	12%
Do you approve of Belgian military interventions abroad?	62%	33%	5%
Do you think Belgium should increase its military presence in the former Yugoslavia?	53%	33%	14%
Are Belgian losses in lives justified in the former Yugoslavia?	41%	49%	10%

Source: Survey & Action

Belgian interventions do not result from previous defense agreements with a central African country, and no such accords have been signed between Belgium and any overseas countries. Military contingency plans exist, but there are no automatic bilateral provisions that can trigger an operation in a given central African state. There is a widely accepted rationale for humanitarian military intervention based on the fact that the armed forces of central African countries, especially Zaire and Rwanda, are deemed too weak to assume responsibility for the defense of Belgian expatriates at times of serious trouble.

For Belgium, unlike for France and Britain, it is hard to identify a distinct African policy, or a policy toward foreign intervention, for each of the 25 government coalitions in power since 1960. No strong personalities emerge in the Belgian decision-making process the way they tend to appear in French or British politics. African policy-making, like on most other topics, is the result of compromises between parties in government. Two consecutive governments led by Gaston Eyskens became involved in the immediate consequences of the Congolese independence and the Belgian withdrawal. The dramatic Stanleyville rescue operation in 1964 occurred during the premiership of the Christian Socialist Théo Lefèvre, with the Socialist Paul-Henri Spaak in charge of foreign affairs. The Lefèvre government marked the peak of Belgium's post-colonial involvement in sub-Saharan Africa's political development. The government's strategy was to avoid an open confrontation with the U.N. policy of support to the territorial integrity of the Congo, while pursuing a policy of discreet support to the Katangese secessionists at the same time, at least to help them negotiate from a stronger position with the authorities in Kinshasa.

For the next 14 years Belgium did not participate actively in an overseas military operation. In 1978, the stakes revolved around the mineral-rich Katanga province, renamed Shaba, at a time of intense Soviet-Cuban expansionism on the African continent. Next to its participation in NATO, Belgium's role in Shaba can be considered one of its main contributions to containing Soviet influence during the Cold War. The instability of Belgian governments deprived the country's authorities of the ability to act quickly and resolutely. The Belgians were unable to participate in the French-sponsored 1977 Shaba operation, and Belgian paratroopers arrived a few hours after French *Légionnaires* in Kolwezi during the second Shaba operation in 1978. Nonetheless, the international context was not propitious for outright unilateral interventions, which may account for the hesitancy of the two governments of the Christian Socialist prime minister Léo Tindemans to act at all in the 1977 crisis, and to be delayed by domestic contradictions in the 1978 crisis. During the latter case, the strong personalities of Paul Vanden Boeynants, the Christian Socialist minister of defense, and Henri Simonet, the Socialist minister of foreign affairs, played up these contradictions.

In the years that followed until the end of the Cold War, Belgium did not engage in any military interventions at all. Then, between 1989 and 1994, in an unexpected flurry of overseas military activity, Belgium became involved in rapid succession in no less than eight foreign military operations, six of which were in Africa. Five of these operations were U.N.-sponsored: Namibia (1989-90), the Gulf War (1991-92), Somalia (1992-94), the former Yugoslavia (1991-), and Rwanda (1993-94). In three instances, Belgium acted outside a U.N. mandate, in conjunction with France, to rescue European expatriates caught in local mutinies or ethnic combats: Rwanda (1990), Zaire (1991) and Zaire (1993). The last two operations also benefitted from the active support of the U.S. Air Force. As a small European nation, Belgium has contributed its share to U.N. military operations. This policy was pursued by three governments, each regrouping a Christian Socialist and Socialist coalition: first, from May 1988 until September 1991, under Prime Minister Wilfried Martens, with Léo Tindemans as minister of foreign affairs and Guy Coëme as minister of defense; then under a second Martens government from September 1990 until March 1992; and finally under the premiership of Jean-Luc Dehaene, with Willy Claes at foreign affairs and Léo Delcroix at defense. Belgium's military involvement in the early 1990s is made even more remarkable by the fact that half of these actions took place outside Belgium's traditional area of intervention in central Africa. The sense of international and humanitarian responsibility that pervades Belgium's actions may point to a new role for Belgian forces. The security horizon as viewed from Brussels has moved away from the old border between the two Germanies to a more remote circle of explosive areas that have a less immediate impact on Belgian security. As long as international military operations could be conducted with virtually no loss of life, participation was forthcoming. After the Rwanda operation in 1994, cautious risk appraisal can be expected and enthusiasm will undoubtedly ebb.

Chapter 11

Belgian Armed Forces: Power Projection and Cooperation

Belgian armed forces are primarily oriented toward the defense of the homeland and the support of NATO's overall force posture. In parallel, Belgium has maintained a modest intervention capability geared mainly to its interests in Africa. Although small in comparison to the power projection capabilities of France and Britain, this Belgian force for overseas contingencies has proved efficient and adequate for operations in central Africa and participation in U.N. peace-keeping.

In 1990, the Belgian armed forces totaled about 92,000 troops, of whom 36,200 were conscripts. Belgium also claimed an additional 450,000 reserves, 146,500 of whom have served within the past three years.[1] The reserve was basically composed of former conscripts who had served their time and had been reintegrated into civilian life. Following a series of extensive reviews of Belgium's defense posture in the aftermath of the Cold War, drastic changes were made to the composition of the armed forces. Budget considerations were paramount in bringing about these transformations. The total manpower in all three services of the armed forces is gradually being cut by more than half, to reach the goal of a professional force of 40,000 troops in 1997: 27,500 for the Army, 10,000 for the Air Force, and 2,500 for the Navy. In early 1993, total manpower was already down to 80,700. Starting with the class of 1994, conscription service was to be abolished. In view of the reduced East-West threat, mass conscription was abandoned in favor of an entirely professional army. Professor De

Vos of the Belgian Royal Military Academy explained this move as an attempt to make more efficient use of the available manpower. The period of conscript service had become so short that the armed forces did not invest in extensively training the draftees, and instead employed them at small, menial services. This further reduced the morale and commitment of young draftees.[2]

The defense reduction plans also called for capping the budget at BEF 98 billion ($2.8 billion in 1994 prices) from 1994 until 1997. This is BEF 4 billion lower than the 1992 budget. Belgium's defense budget as a share of its gross domestic product had already steadily decreased during the 1980s, usually hovering at or below 3 percent. Comparing these figures with that of other NATO allies, Belgium ranked among the lowest quarter of the NATO contributors. The low level of defense funding in Belgium and the rush to cash in the peace dividend have been a consequence of an enormous public-sector debt which represented over 140 percent of the estimated 1994 GDP, the highest among OECD countries.[3] The public debt problem has become endemic and, because of it, the low level of defense spending has always been perceived as one of funding rather than one of political commitment.[4]

The drastic budget restrictions are also going to affect the future investments in new equipment and weapons systems. Personnel costs, previously kept at around 50 percent of the overall defense budget, may rise to 60-65 percent, representing a larger share of a smaller pie. Consequently, new weapons acquisitions will have to be curtailed to one major procurement plan per service branch.[5] As the Army chief of staff, Lieutenant-General José Charlier, pointed out: "With a budget of less than BEF 100 billion per year, high-tech armed forces are out of the question."[6]

The armed forces restructuring will be concluded by 1997, and, though inevitable, will have far-reaching consequences. Military authorities estimated that in the future Belgium would not be able to honor its existing NATO and international commitments.[7] Paradoxically, at the time when the country was cutting its military capabilities to a post-World War low, Belgium participated in no less than eight military operations abroad between 1989 and 1994. The unusual military activism illustrates two characteristics of Belgium's strategic outlook. On the one hand, it demonstrates a firm Belgian commitment to playing a responsible role among western allies in shaping a new world order, or at least avoid the excesses of a chaotic transition. On the other hand, it shows that there is a Belgian interest in Africa which will not be abandoned lightly.

POWER PROJECTION: THE ARMY

When Belgium became a signatory of the North Atlantic Treaty in 1949, its contribution to NATO reflected an interdependent approach to its own and western Europe's security. In this allied framework, Belgium agreed to retain a small but not insignificant Navy and Air Force while directing its major military effort toward maintaining its Army. The latter consisted of an Army Corps assigned to NATO, land forces designated for home defense, and a tactical reserve of one Para-Commando Regiment. In 1990, just before major restructuring programs were being implemented, the Belgian Army was about 68,700 troops strong and absorbed the largest amount of conscripts among the three armed services (29,100 draftees, or 80 percent).[8] The new reforms of the Belgian Army will bring the number of troops down to 27,500 professionals by 1997. The Army's combat capabilities will then be limited to one 12,000-strong mechanized infantry division of three brigades (one of which will be partly stationed in Germany) and one 3,500-strong Para-Commando brigade. The mechanized infantry division will be made available to the Eurocorps by January 1995; it will also be directly linked to NATO as a "Central Region Ready Maneuver Division."

Although NATO allies at times had wished that Belgium would dedicate more resources to its NATO commitments by not taking out-of-area roles upon itself, there are no indications that Belgium might relinquish its relatively modest but efficient overseas force projection capability.[9] In fact, rather than consider its out-of-area role as a diversion of military resources away from allied objectives, Belgian authorities have described it as an important, although discreet, contribution to allied interests in Africa.[10]

The Para-Commando Regiment

The only Army unit with training suitable for overseas action is the Para-Commando Regiment, which will be brought to brigade strength by 1997. This unit is extremely versatile and can be called upon to intervene on the European Central Front, to assist in the defense of the homeland, to participate in Allied rapid deployment forces, or to operate independently overseas. In early 1993, the Para-Commando Regiment consisted of three combat battalions of light infantry units which could all be air-dropped. Three support units complement the combat battalions: an anti-tank company, an artillery battery, and a reconnaissance squadron. This regiment also provides its own training center for all of its personnel. About one-third of the regiment is in training at all times.

In early 1994, the total peacetime strength of the Para-Commando Regiment was about 2,500 troops. The regiment was always a highly professional unit whose personnel were about 80 percent career servicemen and 20 percent conscripts. Conscripts serving with the Para-Commandos had a term of service of 15 months, three-to-five months longer than the regular service term, and had to volunteer to join the regiment. Under the new armed forces configuration, the force will be increased to 3,500 career servicemen.

Once on the ground, the Para-Commandos operate as a light infantry unit. The anti-tank elements are equipped with French-made *Milan* missiles, and the artillery battery is equipped with 105-mm light howitzers. During airborne operations, the Para-Commandos must rely on light vehicles only, due to the limited air transport capacity of the Belgian Air Force.

In June 1991, NATO developed plans to organize mobile forces for rapid deployment anywhere within the alliance, and possibly further afield. Two concepts were defined: a Rapid Reaction Force (RRF) of division size, deployable on five to seven days notice; and an Immediate Reaction Force (IRF) of brigade size, deployable within 72 hours.[11] The Belgian contribution of ground forces to the RRF will consist of the Para-Commando forces. One battalion of Para-Commandos will be assigned to the IRF. These forces, the only airborne unit within the Belgian Army, will continue to be available for national contingencies as is customary under NATO procedures.

Army Airmobile Units

The Army possesses by far the largest helicopter fleet in the Belgian armed forces. The former fleet of 59 SA-313/318 *Alouette* helicopters is gradually being phased out and replaced by the 46 newly acquired A-109 *Agusta* helicopters. These light helicopters can fit into the cargo hold of the C-130H cargo plane flown by the Belgian Air Force. One

Alouette was used during the 1978 Shaba II military intervention. The Air Force does not, however, have the capacity to transport a full light aviation squadron to an overseas theater of operation.

POWER PROJECTION: THE AIR FORCE

In 1990, the Air Force had a strength of 19,900, 5,100 of whom were conscripts. The strength figures for 1993 were 17,300 in total, with 4,300 conscripts. By 1997, the total will be brought down to a fully professional force of 10,000 men. The fighter and ground attack aircraft used by the Belgian Air Force are the U.S. F-16 and the French *Mirage* 5BR. The latter aircraft will be phased out, leaving only 72 active F-16s divided into two wings, plus another 18 F-16s in reserve. None of these planes have been used for interventions outside NATO, except for the Gulf War, when they operated from Turkey, and for enforcing the U.N. no-fly zone in the former Yugoslavia. Belgium may contribute one squadron of F-16s as part of the newly created NATO Immediate Reaction Force.

The main contribution of the Air Force to out-of-area operations is through military air transport. All air transport capabilities are grouped under the 15th Wing for Transport and Communication, an amalgam of five different types of planes subdivided into two squadrons. The Belgian Air Force does not possess of any aircraft dedicated to fuel transport, although during certain operations a C-130 has been converted to a fuel transporter through the use of rubber containers provided by the United States.

C-130H: Between 1972 and 1973, the Belgian Air Force received twelve C-130s. These cargo planes have since been refitted with new wings which store more fuel and permit greater range efficiency. The C-130Hs form the bulk of Belgian military air transport and have been involved in all sub-Saharan military interventions, as well as in numerous humanitarian rescue missions. The C-130Hs have no in-flight refueling capability, and are not equipped with decoy flare systems to protect against light, heat-seeking anti-aircraft missiles such as the *Stinger*. Despite certain cuts affecting the Belgian armed forces, the number of available C-130Hs is not expected to decrease.

B-727: The two Boeing B-727s of the Air Force can each transport up to one hundred passengers or can be converted to carry cargo. They have a range of only 3,000 km. The Air Force tried unsuccessfully to sell the planes under a restructuring plan implemented in 1990. Four years later the planes were still for sale and no other plane had been earmarked for purchase to replace them. It remains unclear whether these planes will be replaced at all. The loss of the two B-727s might deprive the Air Force of the capability to deploy a complete battalion of para-commandos with full gear to an overseas destination in one lift, especially given the maintenance and refitting schedules of the limited C-130H fleet. If the B-727s are not replaced, the Air Force will have to rely more heavily on chartered civilian air planes and/or allied military transport capabilities. The alternative for Belgium is an even greater reduction in the types of interventions it can afford.

Other Aircraft of the 15th Wing: The other aircraft of the 15th Wing have little value for overseas operations due to their size and/or range. The single HS-748 is conceived as short-range courier plane with a capacity of 2.5 tons or 28 passengers. The five available *Merlin* III-As and the two *Mystère* 20s are too small to be used for anything other than VIP transport and are therefore irrelevant to overseas power projection capabilities.

POWER PROJECTION: THE NAVY

The Belgian Navy is the least developed service of the Belgian armed forces. With a total of 4,400 men (1,000 of which are conscripts) in 1993, the Belgian Navy maintains four frigates, 17 seagoing mine warfare ships, and two support ships. The rest of the fleet includes inshore minesweepers, research vessels, and auxiliary ships. With the restructuring of the Navy scheduled for 1997, only 2,500 sailors will remain, with three frigates (of which one will be sold), seven minehunters, four minesweepers and two command ships.[12]

The four frigates existing as of 1994 are well-armed and designed entirely by the Belgian Navy. The first two frigates were delivered in December 1976. Their armament includes four *Exocet* MM 38 surface-to-surface anti-ship missiles, *Sea Sparrow* surface-to-air missiles, one *Creusot Loire* 100-mm gun, and *ECAN* L5 anti-submarine torpedoes. The frigates are also equipped with decoys, infra-red flares, and electronic support measures. Under post-Cold War restructuring, plans to modernize the frigates have been canceled to cut future costs.[13]

The forces for seagoing mine warfare consist of six ocean minesweepers, four coastal minesweepers, and seven coastal minehunters. The mineclearing fleet has occasionally been involved in overseas operations, such as the Gulf crises in 1987-88 and 1990-91. In these situations, Belgium usually contributes a small number of minesweepers with a support ship. Despite the cost-cutting measures, in 1993 the Navy won approval for three new minesweepers plus one prototype.

The only combat operation of the Belgian Navy in post-colonial Africa came during an assault on the harbor of Matadi, immediately after Congolese independence. The Belgian Navy was never a key player for Belgian military operations in sub-Saharan Africa, even during colonial times. The Congo was virtually landlocked, except for a small outlet on the South Atlantic, where Matadi is located. Belgium never had any overseas naval facilities outside the Congo river estuary, and that one was lost in 1960. The Belgian Navy played only a supporting role during the Zairian operations in the late 1970s. Its main contribution was a supply ship with, among other things, spare parts for the C-130s and the capability to provide limited hospital care to evacuees. The problem for Belgian maritime missions to central Africa is time. It takes a minimum of 15 days to organize sea transportation and arrive there from Belgium, and no permanent pre-positioning scheme exists by which to shorten this period. During the 1992-94 Belgian participation in the U.N. peace-keeping force in Somalia, the Navy dispatched one command and supply ship off the Kenyan-Somali coast.

CHARACTERISTICS OF BELGIAN POWER PROJECTION

Of the three countries under review in this study, Belgium has the least to offer in terms of military power projection capabilities. The Belgian armed forces cannot rely on any type of foreign bases, permanently manned staging facilities, or units dedicated exclusively to overseas assignments. Yet, among western European countries, Belgium is second only to France in terms of military activity in sub-Saharan Africa. This fact is perhaps more an indication of how little the other European powers have been involved militarily in that region rather than of the strength of Belgium's military involvement. By concentrating its efforts on a specific section of Africa, Belgium has been able to conduct the only type of military intervention feasible for a small country with limited resources for power projection. Through post-colonial military assistance programs, Belgium has become well acquainted with the operational environment of central Africa. Furthermore, by earmarking only one unit, the Para-Commando Regiment, for possible action in that part of the world, Belgium has avoided excessive dispersion of the resources necessary for action in its primary intervention theater outside Europe.

Another element in Belgian intervention has been the relatively sizable military transportation fleet of the Belgian Air Force. The combination of specialized Army skills with almost complete military self-sufficiency for low-intensity operations in central Africa has yielded some success.[14] After the turmoil following Congolese independence in 1960, Belgium has intervened several times in central Africa. In each case, Belgian ground forces have successfully accomplished their missions. Casualties on the Belgian side have been extremely low, with none at all in the operations of Kolwezi (1978) and Rwanda (1990), and one accidental casualty during the 1991 and 1993 interventions in Zaire. Some casualties were reported in the case of Somalia. The ten casualties in Rwanda (1994) have darkened this record. In comparison to the French actions in Kolwezi and Rwanda (1990), Belgium prefers to send excessive numbers of troops to ensure an overwhelming capability in the field rather than risk losses through inadequate force levels. The absence of permanently deployed troops in sub-Saharan Africa makes Belgian intervention dramatic and exceptional. Consequently, public opinion in Belgium is highly emotional about the dispatch of troops, particularly before interventions became more frequent in the early 1990s.

In the past, poor management of public relations by the political and military authorities has unnecessarily jeopardized some Belgian interventions. The success of the 1978 operation in Shaba could have been threatened by the Belgian press, which aired all the details of departing troops on evening news programs before the forces had arrived in Zaire, giving ample warning time to friends and foes alike. Only the low combat skills of the Katangese rebels prevented them from exploiting the situation. The government quite sensibly concluded that the next operation would depart from a more hidden military facility instead of from Belgium's international airport. The earlier public relations incidents showed how poor the institutional understanding was of the non-combat aspects of an intervention. Until 1978, the military had, through lack of practice, neglected both the need to monitor the political context at home and abroad closely, and the importance of managing the interface with the public.

BELGIAN MILITARY ASSISTANCE

A small power like Belgium must be particularly selective in the choice of countries it wants to assist militarily. Belgium has therefore chosen to sign cooperation agreements with two of its former colonies: Zaire and Rwanda. Burundi was denied a similar agreement because of government perpetrated massacres in 1972. Belgian authorities have renewed military assistance to Zaire and Rwanda. In the case of Zaire, the assistance was canceled after President Mobutu terminated all forms of Belgian aid in July 1990. The bloody events in Rwanda in 1994 also led to the evacuation of Belgian military assistance personnel. Before that, a consensus had been reached across the Belgian political spectrum, and nuances between the parties were not strong enough to jeopardize the existence of the programs themselves. When the Socialist Guy Coëme became the Belgian minister of defense on May 9, 1988, military assistance programs to Zaire were maintained despite the lack of improvements in that country's human rights record. All political parties have understood that even small, inexpensive military assistance programs could buy a lot of influence and stability in central Africa. The loss of political influence from unilaterally reducing these programs was also well understood in Brussels, as was the corollary that increased assistance would not yield a correspondingly larger share of influence. The assistance effort has therefore fluctuated very little over the last two decades.

Military assistance programs aim primarily at strengthening and stabilizing the armed forces of the assisted country. By doing so, they accomplish many more objectives that bear favorably on five parameters with national, regional, or international significance. First, highly disorganized military structures, such as the Zairian armed forces, can use any type of assistance they can get. More than equipment and new weapons systems, there is a need for greater professionalism and efficiency. The assistance contributes, although

sometimes very modestly, to fighting corruption and disorder in forces
that are grossly underpaid and neglected. A second stabilizing effect of
Belgian military training teams is the psychological reassurance they
give to Belgian or western expatriates by their mere presence, although
the teams have no operational command position and are explicitly
prohibited from interfering in conflicts. A third stabilizing role of
military assistance programs, this time at the regional level, is to show
the solidarity of the former metropolitan power with the beneficiary.
This form of aid strengthens the independence of young states vis-a-vis
their neighbors, although often at the expense of greater dependency
toward the former colonial power. This phenomenon is particularly
evident in countries with French assistance programs, and is a means
of leverage held by France over the assisted country. The same is true
with Belgium, although to a lesser degree. The withdrawal of military
advisors is the most obvious way of showing one's loss of confidence
in the beneficiary country. Although the amount of training personnel
involved might be limited, the impact of their withdrawal is far from
symbolic. A fourth benefit of military cooperation derives indirectly
from a more secure political and economic climate in the area, which
is a distinct benefit to both parties. Finally, military assistance
programs are an unacknowledged yet notable element in allied burden
sharing. Although out-of-area contributions cannot be formally included
within the individual responsibilities of NATO allies, it is undeniable
that they are appreciated by other allies. Such activities relieve a global
power, like the U.S., from the political and even military costs of
monitoring and influencing events in specific sub-regions. During the
Cold War, continued Belgian and French military involvement in sub-
Saharan Africa demonstrated that they retained influence in their
respective former colonies. In other areas, such as in the Horn of
Africa, Angola and Mozambique, a power vacuum invited superpower
interference, thus providing an additional arena for confrontation during
the Cold War.

The Legal Framework

Unlike France, Belgium has never signed formal defense agreements
with some of its former sub-Saharan colonies. The only military
accords which Belgium has kept with sub-Saharan Africa are the two
military cooperation agreements with Zaire and Rwanda.

The Law of April 4, 1972, enacted by the Belgian parliament, formalized a July 22, 1968 exchange of letters between the Belgian and Congolese authorities with regard to technical military cooperation.[15] Simultaneously, the Belgian parliament conferred legal authority to similar arrangements with the Republic of Burundi (following a government-to-government arrangement of December 10, 1968) and with Rwanda (following a technical military cooperation convention signed by the two governments on August 22, 1969).[16] The agreement with Burundi was never implemented. The emphasis was placed on the instruction role of Belgian assistance personnel, excluding any operational activity. The cooperation agreement with Rwanda was further reinforced by a Friendship Treaty, enacted on April 15, 1973. The approval of the Belgian parliament was deemed necessary in view of the fact that it is not the task of the Belgian armed forces to put its units at the disposal of foreign governments. Military personnel abroad are regrouped in the *Corps de Coopération Technique Militaire*, which benefits from extraterritoriality and comes under the authority of a Belgian commander. The latter is in constant contact with the Ministries of Defense of both signatory countries. The military cooperation programs are managed directly by the Belgian Ministry of Defense. Additional advisors could also be sent, but their cost would be covered by the host government.

Routinely, the ceiling of personnel recommended in the bilateral agreements was not reached in the field. Belgium often dispatched only 80 percent of the troops authorized by parliament. The Belgian parliament, for instance, allowed for a contingent of 110 military advisors for Zaire, but the actual number in the field was consistently lower, with 84 in the first half of 1990 until they were asked to leave the country. The lower staffing level is justified as "a cost-cutting measure which frees up additional funds that can be used for operations (rather than salaries and personal needs)."[17]

The Belgian Ministry of Defense also provides non-lethal operational support and equipment to Third World countries. This assistance represents about 25 percent of the total military cooperation budget, against 75 percent for personnel, and is primarily spent on infrastructure and financial aid, the remainder going to follow-up operational aid. The 1990 budget for military assistance, the last to include Zaire, was about BEF 500 million ($16 million), of which BEF 320 million ($10.6 million) went to Zaire and the rest to Rwanda. After Zaire was dropped from this list of beneficiaries, Belgium did not

replace it with another country. In 1993, the Rwanda program cost
BEF 196 million ($5.5 million).

A last part of Belgian assistance programs includes scholarships and
specialized internships. These are managed by the Belgian Ministry of
Defense, but paid for by funds from the Belgian Ministry of Foreign
Affairs. Just before July 1990, there were 52 students from Zaire and
29 from Rwanda studying in Belgium. In contrast, only one specialized
training internship had been granted to Zaire against 11 to Rwanda.
The contribution of the Ministry of Foreign Affairs amounted to $1.2
million for scholarships and internships in Belgium.

Zaire

Before President Mobutu eventually carried out his threat to cut civil
assistance programs, he submitted the Belgian aid programs to the
changing moods of the two countries' relationship; one day cutting the
programs down, and the other inviting back the assistance personnel.
Military assistance programs, on the other hand, have always managed
to remain beyond the scope of the turmoil. While the Belgian state
secretary for cooperation and development at times had to cut or
modify drastically some highly visible civilian assistance programs,
military programs continued while keeping as low a profile as possible.
Visits by the Belgian defense minister were usually met with great
ceremony by the Zairian authorities, who put aside any disputes with
Belgium to mark the occasion. The state secretary for cooperation and
development, in contrast, has often been received coolly as an
indication of Zairian displeasure with Belgium. The deference shown
by Zaire to Belgian military assistance, when compared to the
manipulative behavior when dealing with civilian assistance, illustrates
the higher level of influence that western countries can derive from
military versus civilian assistance, even when the former represents a
much smaller financial burden.

Military cooperation between Belgium and Zaire started in 1960.
The primary emphasis was on Katanga, where 500 of the 507 Belgian
military personnel in the Congo were sent. The legal basis for their
presence, according to the Belgian government, was Article 250 of the
pre-independence *loi fondamentale* of May 19, 1960 on the future
organization of the Congo.[18] Under strong pressure from the U.N., all
Belgian military advisors left Katanga by late 1961.[19] The government
of Prime Minister Adoula restarted an embryonic cooperation program

after an agreement signed in June 1963, whereby the Belgian technical assistance personnel would be integrated within the Congolese armed forces. The arrival of Tschombé as prime minister saw the program significantly expanded to 390 Belgian advisors. An arrangement between the Congolese Republic, Belgium and the U.S. subsequently reinforced this presence. The Belgian Air Force detachment of 158 troops maintained and operated the 30 aircraft that the U.S. had placed at the disposal of the Congolese.[20]

The golden age of military assistance to the Congo was then in full swing. Belgian military personnel organized and operated logistics teams, and efforts were made to create "integrated battalions" with Belgian military instructors in command positions. The results of the latter initiative were mixed because the Belgians did not appear eager to exercise the command role.[21] By 1967, when the country was emerging from the chaos and rebellions which marked its early stages after independence, the momentum had turned and assistance started decreasing again. Belgian military advisors were cut down to 117 and occupied more traditional roles such as training and instruction. Military justice advisors were withdrawn and all assistance to the Congolese Air Force was suspended.

With the normalization of Belgo-Congolese relations in June 1968, military assistance programs received a new framework, which became the basis for all further cooperation programs. The exchange of letters in July 1968 defined the new status of military cooperation, with Belgium now concentrating its assistance on instruction and technical tasks as well as on high-level advisory support at the Zairian Ministry of Defense in Kinshasa. The number of advisors gradually declined from 220 in 1970 to about 84 in early 1990, including 53 officers and 31 non-commissioned officers (NCOs).

Over the years, the focus of the training has been modified in view of local priorities and also as a function of Belgian budgetary constraints. Just before his eviction in 1990, there was only one General Staff advisor left with Zaire's armed forces, down from 28 in 1972.[22] However, the Officers School in Katanga, the Technical-Logistics Training School in Kinshasa, the Commando Center north of Kotakoli, and the Navy School at Banane continued to be staffed with Belgian advisors. Twenty-two Belgian advisors were also posted with the 21st Infantry Brigade deployed in the Shaba province. This latter direct support to a combat unit was a result of the two Shaba crises in the late 1970s. For security reasons, Belgium agreed to support one operational unit in the region, though its mobility and combat-readiness remained questionable.[23] Belgium also sponsored some mechanics and other technical advisors.

In another category of military cooperation, one finds the continued presence of a Belgian C-130 in Zaire. By early 1980, Belgium had instituted the practice of maintaining one C-130 in Zaire on a monthly rotational basis. The C-130 was intended to resupply the various military assistance missions that Belgium maintained throughout the country. The aircraft was also used to fly Belgian advisors to their Zairian units, as well as to train Zairian paratroopers. Of the four C-130s Zaire received from the U.S., only one remained in flying condition. Unfortunately for the Zairian paratroopers, the plane was reserved for the personal use of the Zairian president and was converted for that purpose, preventing its employment for parachute training missions. For Belgium, an additional benefit of having a Belgian C-130 permanently on-station was to provide updated information on Zaire's infrastructure.

Mobutu's sudden unilateral decision to put an end to all Belgian assistance to Zaire - civilian and military, public and private - was implemented without delay. By the end of the summer in 1990, no Belgian military advisors remained. These advisors had constituted by far the single largest overseas Belgian military assistance program, representing approximately 70 percent of the worldwide Belgian military assistance effort. The Zairian dependency on Belgian military assistance was diluted over time. Belgium was exposed to competition from France, North Korea, China, Israel, Italy and some others. Only French support would prove durable and would seriously dent Belgian influence in Zaire. Notwithstanding the competition, Belgian military assistance proved to be reliable, efficient, and non-threatening for the recipient. Starting in the mid-1970s and all through the 1980s, Belgian officials at the Foreign Ministry and on the General Staff were anxious to avoid any prolonged disruption in military ties with Zaire, lest the vacuum in security assistance be filled by less restrained suppliers, notably France and China.[24]

With the collapse of central authority in Zaire after 1991, western governments have adopted a more cautious and reserved approach toward military assistance to Zaire. The power vacuum at the national level was replicated in the provision of foreign military assistance. French or Belgian post-colonial influence and military involvement thrive on stability, with the occasional occurrence of small, manageable crises. When faced with serious disruptions of stability or civil wars, western influence and military involvement have a tendency to decrease until better times.

Rwanda and Burundi

The history of Belgian military assistance to Rwanda has been less mercurial than that with Congo/Zaire. In 1993, the Rwanda program included 20 Belgian advisors (ten officers and ten NCOs). In the opinion of many Belgian advisors, compared to the aid program in Zaire, the Rwanda program "supports a much better trained and better equipped local army. The Hutu mountain tribe leaders of Rwanda, it is said, take a far more serious, hardworking approach to [technical military cooperation] than do the Zairians."[25] Although the Belgian parliament allows a ceiling of 32 advisors, this number has not been supplied for reasons similar to those applicable in Zaire. The 20-man Belgian team managed three main projects: a military academy, a military hospital, and a commando training center. With the end of military assistance to Zaire, Rwanda became the sole recipient of Belgian military advisors. The termination of Zaire's program and the rebel invasion of Rwanda in 1990 did not result in an increase in the strength of the Belgian advisory team in Rwanda until 1994, when it was withdrawn altogether.

Despite the existence of a legal structure for military cooperation between Belgium and Burundi, which was created by the Law of April 4, 1972, Burundi did not benefit from any Belgian assistance after President Micombero took power in Bujumbura on April 29 of that same year. This coup was followed by one of the bloodiest episodes in African history, when in a matter of a few months an estimated 120,000 people were killed, and millions more took refuge in neighboring countries. Belgium never reactivated the military assistance programs to Burundi thereafter. (The 1994 events in Rwanda brought similar consequences to that country, except that the death toll was estimated at 200,000.) The only Belgian military personnel in the country are the military attachés at the Belgian embassy.

Arms Sales

Belgian-sponsored military assistance programs do not include any transfer or subsidy for the purchase of arms. The only type of equipment that the Ministry of Defense provides under its assistance programs is related to military training material and non-lethal equipment. The Belgian government considers the sale of lethal equipment as private business between Belgian arms exporters and interested foreign governments. The official Belgian role is limited to monitoring and approving the types of sales and the acceptability of the recipient country. The press has repeatedly denounced the laxity of Belgian authorities with regard to control over arms exports.[26] An export license is required under the 1962 "Law on the Export, Import and Transit of Goods," which was complemented by the ministerial decrees of 1987 and 1988 on the transfer of specific technologies. The Ministries of Foreign Trade, Economic Affairs (through a Central Licensing Office), and Foreign Affairs are competent to review export licenses. For exports outside NATO, the review process relies on a political-military evaluation at the Ministry of Foreign Affairs and approval by an inter-cabinet committee.[27] Complicated cases can be further referred to an inter-ministerial meeting under the chairmanship of the prime minister. Other ministries such as Justice, Interior and Defense can also become involved. The competence of the latter is in advising on technological, security, and military balance issues.

Belgian arms industries are ill-equipped to gain large export markets: government purchases are declining; the arms industry is in competition with emerging arms producers (Brazil, Israel, South Africa, etc.); and the technological content of Belgian weapons remains relatively low, which gradually increases their vulnerability vis-a-vis new weapons-producing countries. In the early 1970s, the defense industry directly or indirectly employed 66,000 Belgians. Twenty years later, this number has been cut in half.[28] Large segments of Belgium's defense industry have been acquired by foreign companies. Among them is Fabrique Nationale, taken over by the French weapons manufacturer GIAT. Due to its ailing defense industry, Belgium's share of overseas weapons markets dropped. In the 1980s, arms production represented about 1 percent of GDP.[29] Arms exports were less than half a percent of total Belgian exports. Seventy percent of those arms exports went to Third World countries; sub-Saharan Africa accounted for only 17 percent of total arms exports.[30] In the same decade, purchases by Zaire fluctuated between $1 million and $10 million, well below the level reached by some other sub-Saharan countries. In 1987, for instance, Angola purchased $37 million out of a total of $60 million in Belgian arms sales to the region. In the same year, Rwanda spent only $262,000 on Belgian arms, and Burundi recorded no purchases.[31]

At times Nigeria also bought far more Belgian weaponry than Zaire or Rwanda. From this data, one cannot draw a correlation between Belgian arms sales and military assistance programs.

WHAT FUTURE MILITARY ROLE FOR BELGIUM IN AFRICA?

Belgium has maintained only one rapid deployment unit, the Para-Commando Regiment, and has given it the necessary air transport capability to move at least part of its forces overseas. Unlike Britain or France, Belgium does not have a Marine unit with amphibious capabilities. The traditional theater of overseas operations for Belgium has been the landlocked countries of central Africa, which have poor communication networks. An airborne, light-infantry unit has been given the responsibility of executing the limited scope of Belgian interventions in this area. These interventions have always been of limited duration, and troops engaged in overseas operations have been posted only as long as necessary to evacuate or protect endangered Belgian citizens. Only in the framework of U.N. operations after 1989 were Belgian troops dispatched for long periods of time.

Belgian military interventions in Africa differ dramatically from French actions in many African countries. France's use of military involvement in Africa serves far broader policy objectives than the mere protection of French expatriates. This difference in approach was clearly evidenced during the 1978 intervention by France and Belgium in Zaire: French troops had the explicit order to secure the Shaba region, while Belgian troops were under strict orders not to interfere with the local conflict, but only to evacuate the expatriate community in Kolwezi.

Belgium has been able to intervene without encountering any serious resistance. The particular context of armed insurgencies in central Africa has proven to require only low-intensity combat or evacuation operations. With time, potential African antagonists may acquire more sophisticated weapons, especially air defense systems or armored vehicles. By then, Belgium will have to review its means of projecting force independently. The air transport fleet is very vulnerable and is too small to transport even a light armored battalion in one lift without outside assistance. Other problems may arise from dispatching units other than the Para-Commando Regiment due to their lack of specialized skills and experience in foreign interventions.

In evaluating Belgium's future military involvement in sub-Saharan Africa, a distinction will have to be made between unilateral operations, those undertaken only with close allies such as France or the U.S., and multilateral operations. Some indicators point toward a possible reduction in years to come of Belgium's willingness to intervene in Africa unilaterally or with close allies. The main reason for the decline in unilateral actions is linked to external events, mainly the political chaos that took place in Zaire in 1991 and 1993. Politically, the circumstances in Zaire after 1993 made an intervention less likely because only a small fraction of the former Belgian expatriate community remained there and few Belgian economic interests have been preserved after the destruction brought by the mutinies. A change in Zaire's political situation, especially significant progress toward democracy and the resignation of Mobutu, could signal a resumption of Belgian development and military assistance programs to Zaire.

On the contrary, Belgium's military participation in U.N. peace-keeping operations initially appeared remarkably assiduous. Since 1989, the bulk, both qualitatively and quantitatively, of Belgium's military involvement in sub-Saharan Africa has consisted of its participation in the U.N. operations in Namibia, Somalia and Rwanda. Belgian public support for these new types of foreign military roles was unusually strong. The casualties under the 1994 U.N. peace-keeping operation in Rwanda, however, may have eroded this support dramatically.

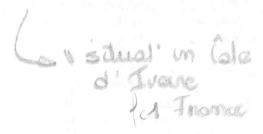

Chapter 12

Belgian Interventions in Sub-Saharan Africa

Belgium's military interventions in sub-Saharan Africa can be divided into three distinct periods, following a pattern that is not completely different from French or even British interventions in the region. The first period, from 1960 through 1965, covers the post-independence settlement of the Congo. The new African authorities in Léopoldville had to deal with two major crises: the disintegration of the administrative structure put in place by the Belgians to rule the country, and several secessionist and rebel movements. Belgium's military involvement in those crises was very dramatic. The circumstances under which the intervention occurred and the role Belgium played or failed to play have been recorded among the most traumatic experiences of post-colonial African history. The chaos that resulted from Congolese mutinies, domestic political volatility, Belgian interventions, the Katangese secession, and the U.N. involvement created a lasting trauma for remaining colonial powers, new African governments, and U.N. bureaucrats alike. The second Belgian intervention took place in Stanleyville in 1964 to rescue the European and American hostages held by rebels belonging to a movement inspired by Patrice Lumumba, the former Congolese leader. The Stanleyville intervention left a bitter aftertaste: many Belgian hostages were killed, and the operation, supported by the U.S., was severely criticized by Soviet-bloc and Third World countries.

The second cycle of Belgian interventions, from 1977 through 1979, again took place in Zaire, the new name given to the Congo in 1971. Belgian military involvement in central Africa at the time was heavily conditioned by the international context and France's intrusiveness. Soviet-Cuban influence in Angola after the collapse of the Portuguese colonial power directly threatened the political regime in Zaire. France took the leading role in containing Soviet-Cuban penetration of the Shaba province in southern Zaire in 1977 and again in 1978. Belgium resented the French action within its traditional zone of influence, but failed to take any action in 1977; it intervened in 1978 only after long delays which contrasted with French initiative. Although militarily successful, the 1978 Belgian operation was a diplomatic and public relations disaster which aggravated tensions between Belgian and Zairian authorities. The Belgian intervention was executed simultaneously with the French one, but the two European powers failed to coordinate their actions. France consequently reaped all the glory and dramatically increased its influence in the area to the detriment of Belgium. The latter was castigated by the Zairian president, who became more bold in his criticism of Belgium after receiving French support.

The third period of Belgian military interventions in Africa runs from 1989 until 1994. The collapse of Soviet-Cuban influence in various regions of Africa left a power vacuum. In parallel, unconditional U.S. or allied support to autocratic anti-communist regimes dropped rapidly. These evolutions opened the way for two new types of development. Firstly, within the framework of U.N. peace-keeping operations, they made western military involvement possible in regions previously unaccessible for such activities, as in Angola, Somalia or Mozambique. Secondly, the political chaos in several African countries under autocratic rule was favored by western powers insofar as it would engage them on the path to democratic reform. The risk of encouraging political changes had become more acceptable since no heir to the Soviets or Cubans could take advantage of Africa's unavoidable vulnerability during the transition from autocracy to some form of democratic government. The unwritten rules of foreign military engagement in Africa were becoming very clear. The settlement of civil wars and crises in territories formerly under Soviet-Cuban influence or outside French or Belgian zones of influence was referred to multilateral organizations, mainly the U.N., for potential action. U.N. operations in Namibia, Angola, Somalia, Mozambique and Rwanda fell under this category. The civil war in Liberia was handled by the Economic Organization of West African States (ECOWAS). When developments within the French or Belgian zones of influence reached unacceptable levels and put the expatriate communities at risk, then military action was decided unilaterally or jointly by a core group of western countries, specifically France, Belgium and the U.S. Operations with Belgian involvement in Rwanda (1990) and in Zaire (1991 and 1993) fell under this latter category. The exception to this informal division of tasks in post-Soviet Africa is the U.N.-sponsored peace-keeping operation in Rwanda in 1993-94. In this case, Belgium agreed to be part of a U.N. peace-monitoring force in its former colony.

THE CONGOLESE TRAUMA

Congolese Independence (1960)

On July 5, 1960, only five days after the Congo gained its independence from Belgium, the Congolese armed forces, known under their colonial denomination of *Force publique*, mutinied in the garrisons of Léopoldville and Thysville (now Kinshasa and M'banza N'gungu). These mutinies were provoked by the fact that the *Force publique*'s wages were generally inferior to what politicians and public servants received, despite the often superior education of the military personnel. Members of the *Force publique* viewed the Congolese politicians with defiance and contempt, and could not bring themselves to be put at the service of civilian authorities. The hostility toward ministers and parliamentarians was the first cause of the mutiny in early July.[1] Additional reasons included the denial of command positions to Congolese military personnel. The Belgian commander's uncompromising attitude only exacerbated tensions. Bowing to the pressure, the Congolese prime minister, Patrice Lumumba, dismissed the commander on July 6 and subsequently upgraded all Congolese soldiers and non-commissioned officers (NCOs) by one rank. Nevertheless, these measures did not suffice to quell the growing rebellion. In another attempt to appease the soldiers, Lumumba decided on July 9 to africanize the *Force publique* completely. Higher ranking black officers were to be promoted through election by the various garrisons. Congolese troops could also vote to retain their Belgian officers as technical advisors. About 40 percent of them failed to pass their electoral test and had to leave the country.[2] Joseph-Désiré Mobutu was one of the Congolese who benefitted from Lumumba's decision and was promoted from NCO to colonel. He would later become the Army chief of staff, and, in 1965, president.

The mutinous troops regarded the lack of central authority as a license to molest Belgian citizens, to loot, and, in some instances, to rape. The victimization of white European women by Congolese soldiers during the first days of the mutiny exacerbated the panic in the expatriate population of Léopoldville.[3] The exodus of the Belgian population was massive: about 10,000 during the first days and 38,000 by the end of the month. This outflow represented a significant drain of qualified administrators from a total European population of 100,000. Radio stations relayed the news of the mutinies and aggression against the white population throughout the country, which contributed to the spiraling sense of fear and desperation.

The rapid degradation of the situation caught Belgium completely by surprise. The country had always thought of its African colony as a model of colonial administration. Belgium had never kept military forces in the Congo before 1953, when it sent a first contingency to bolster local forces. The colony had its own military structure, called the *Force publique*, which was independent of Belgium's armed forces and financed by the colonial budget. Only Belgian officers on leave from their regular assignments in the Belgian military commanded the Congolese troops. Prior to July 8, 1960, four battalions and three companies formed the core of the metropolitan forces deployed in the colonies, which were commanded from headquarters in Léopoldville and Usumbura. Belgium also operated three metropolitan bases in the Congo: Kitona and Kamina, each with a landing strip, and the naval base of Banane. Belgium rushed additional forces to the Congo during the ensuing days of July 1960, when the situation ran completely out of control. Eventually, up to 10,000 metropolitan soldiers were deployed in central Africa.[4] A naval task force had been dispatched for the Congolese independence. The Air Force maintained a few *Harvard* and *Fouga Magister* aircraft in the Congo, as well as some DC-3 and C-119 transport planes.[5]

The only legal framework that had been worked out by the Belgian and Congolese authorities to organize the transition from colony to sovereign state was the Friendship Treaty, which provided guidelines for future Belgo-Congolese cooperation. The text, however, did not mention the possibility of continued Belgian use of military bases in the Congo, nor did it concern itself with the rules of engagement for metropolitan forces already present in the Congo.[6] The treaty specified that the Congolese minister of defense had to approve all future Belgian interventions. Belgium did not establish a transitional government to provide interim measures for the new Congolese state. Belgian authorities had trapped themselves into subjecting the presence of their troops in an independent Congo to the whim of the new Congolese government and not to the binding articles of a defense agreement. As expected, Lumumba requested the departure of the Belgian troops only days after independence and brought the matter to the U.N. to prevent seditious behavior by the Belgian military.

By that time the internal situation in the Congo had worsened dramatically, and the massive exodus of the Belgian population had begun. On July 10, Belgian metropolitan forces intervened in Elisabethville, Luluabourg and Matadi. The situation in Elisabethville, in the southern province of Katanga, had remained relatively quiet until the announcement of the africanization of the *Force publique*. The Katangese provincial civilian authorities and some of the Belgian officers wanted to avoid a sudden africanization of the *Force publique* in Katanga. Because the majority of these forces were not of Katangese origin, the Katangese government feared that an africanized military force might be hostile and uncontrollable. These concerns did not apply to the police forces, which were recruited locally to form the core of the Katangese gendarmerie. Belgian officers in Elisabethville, on hearing exaggerated accounts of atrocities throughout the country, tried to strip their troops of ammunition. This measure inevitably made the Congolese soldiers extremely apprehensive.

On July 9, shooting broke out between the Belgian and Congolese troops. The forceful reaction of the Belgian officers in Elisabethville was atypical because the transfer of authority had happened relatively quietly in most other garrisons around the country. After Katangese authorities appealed to the metropolitan forces, Belgian paratroopers landed in Elisabethville on July 10. The operation involved ten transport planes and two companies of paratroopers. The political and psychological barriers against the use of force had been broken for the first time; many more Belgian interventions would follow. Although they had little room to manoeuvre, the Katangese political authorities were extremely reluctant to call upon the Congolese central government to quell the crisis. The only alternative was to call upon metropolitan forces. In this respect, the metropolitan intervention might be considered as being, in the words of one Belgian military historian, "directly at the origin of the Katangese secession."[7]

Katanga declared itself an independent state on July 11, 1960 and asked Belgian troops to remain in place. Metropolitan troops at one point occupied 14 locations in Katanga, sometimes supervising the disarmament and dismissal of Congolese Army units. By July 21, most of the 6,000 Congolese soldiers stationed in Katanga were on "indefinite leave."[8]

Some 1,200 European had meanwhile taken refuge in downtown Luluabourg. Ambiguous reports of attacks on them by rebels of the *Force publique* triggered a purely humanitarian action from the metropolitan forces based at Kamina. This second operation was carried out on July 10 without major incident by an airdrop of paratroopers.

The third large-scale operation during the first half of July took place in Matadi, the only significant harbor in the Congo River estuary. The Belgian authorities considered Matadi a great strategic asset for the supply of Léopoldville because the Congo would be virtually landlocked without the Matadi port infrastructure. Metropolitan forces were called there to rescue the remaining Europeans, but also to prevent rebellious soldiers from taking over or blockading the harbor. On July 11, metropolitan army forces disembarked at Matadi. The operation, involving all three services of the Belgian armed forces, was unique. The Navy was involved with four light escort ships (*algérines*), four river patrol boats, and one cargo ship;[9] the Army assigned three-and-a-half companies; and the Air Force intervened with its *Harvard* airplanes. Belgian troops came from metropolitan bases at Kitona and Banane, both about 100 km from Matadi.

Although the operation was conceived to secure the city and its infrastructure, the situation quickly soured. The Congolese troops were extremely nervous at the sight of Belgian troop movements, and firmly believed it was an attempt by the Belgians to recapture their lost colony. Once ashore, the troops engaged in limited fighting, but spent most of their time observing the opponent. The Congolese troops, after the Belgian landing operation, unsuccessfully started to use their batteries against one of the three Belgian Navy units in the harbor. Retaliation did not take long, and the guns aboard the Belgian ships quickly destroyed the Congolese artillery. The whole operation, which had been conceived as a preventive measure, had quickly escalated into open combat.

Belgian military commanders had still not grasped the potentially catastrophic political effects of such a direct intervention. They launched an air attack against part of the Congolese position, losing one plane to enemy ground fire. The Belgians also fired on a Portuguese settlement across the border. When the commander-in-chief of the metropolitan forces in Léopoldville heard about the extent of the attack, he immediately ordered a complete withdrawal of all Belgian troops. The operation had lasted about 36 hours. All of the casualties were on the Congolese side with 19 dead and 31 wounded, including civilians.

From then on, the rapid succession of interventions became a race against time to evacuate as many Europeans as possible from the Congo. The metropolitan forces were called to intervene at least nineteen times in fifteen days, excluding the operations in Katanga.[10] The gradual withdrawal of Belgian troops would last until August 4, 1960, again with the exception of Katanga. Most members of the Belgian cadre within the Congolese National Army left before July 31. By August 19, the last Belgian technicians, with the exception of a handful acting as advisors to Colonel Mobutu, had departed. Those remaining technicians became the core through which Belgium would later reorganize its military aid to the Congo.

By the time Lumumba requested immediate Belgian withdrawal and the international community appeared to lend legitimacy to his claim by replacing Belgian troops with U.N. contingents, the Belgians had become the mutinous element in the Congo. In fact, Lieutenant-General Cumont, the Belgian Army chief of staff, developed the idea of reconquering the entire Congo.[11] His rationale for this aberration was simple. The first set of interventions was conducted to protect Belgians. Having done that, the Belgian troops in fact endangered all Belgians in the Congo. A spiral of Belgian interventions and angry Congolese reactions was set in motion. The more the Belgians intervened, the more they angered the Congolese and the more reason there was to protect Belgian citizens, although this was sometimes done prematurely and unnecessarily. By securing strategic points all over the country and disarming local Congolese troops, General Cumont wanted to retain the permanent capacity to evacuate Belgian citizens. Belgian Minister of Defense Gilson, although also prone to favor intervention, eventually put a stop to Cumont's scheme.

In retrospect, relatively modest levels of disorder and violence in the Congo had produced a disproportionate reaction. The Congolese soldiers firmly believed the metropolitan troops had returned to kill them and sometimes responded with brutality to misinformation about an imagined Belgian takeover. The European exodus was triggered by relatively few and localized instances of aggression and rape. The casualties among the resident Europeans, including Belgian officers in the *Force publique*, were estimated at only 12 dead and several wounded for the entire month of July. The metropolitan forces suffered six dead and 19 wounded. On the Congolese side, 70 men were killed and at least an equal number were wounded. Casualties on both sides were mainly incurred during combat.[12]

The relatively modest number of casualties and the unnecessary exacerbation of panic indicate that the Congolese disaster could possibly have been avoided. It seems to have been more the result of misinformation and mutually anticipated fears than of an objective assessment of the facts. The discontent among the Congolese military exploded during a transition period when Europeans expected trouble, enhancing their fears and suspicions. Despite the overall chaos, various units of the Congolese Army remained in their barracks throughout the crisis. Many Europeans saw no reason to flee the country, and metropolitan forces virtually had to coerce some into leaving. The metropolitan forces executed their orders from Brussels very professionally, with the exception of the overreaction in Matadi. "Still, and except for Matadi, the way they intervened had in general less impact than the very fact of intervening."[13]

The mismanagement of the crisis was attributable to both the new Congolese government and the Belgian authorities. Prime Minister Lumumba overreacted in his handling of the armed forces' strikes and mutinies in Léopoldville on July 6 and 7, and he overestimated the beneficial effect of the subsequent africanization of the military. His anger at the Belgians became manifest only after a long brooding period which came to a boiling point the moment Belgium expressed support for the Katangese secession. Understanding the Congolese Army's fears, he sided with them in calling for an end to Belgian aggression. Congolese and Belgian inexperience was mutually reinforcing. Governing a nascent nation-state, the Congolese authorities obviously lacked practice managing governmental affairs. Belgium had no imperial tradition, and could not have countered the July unrest in a comprehensive counter-insurgency operation, either as advisors to the new Congolese government or as direct participants with metropolitan forces. In its colonial history, Belgium had dealt successfully with numerous tribal uprisings, but the scale and extent of the July unrest was something new. Belgian officers of the *Force publique* could not find the right combination of force and diplomacy to stifle the mutinies at an early stage.

The early deployment of metropolitan troops from bases within the Congo had catastrophic effects on the country's political stability. It was not a military disaster for Belgium, but rather an example of its diplomatic myopia. Beyond humanitarian aid, the troops had no grounds for staying in the Congo; no legal provisions had been made before Congolese independence to justify a later Belgian presence. The Brussels government was not against the Congolese central government as such, but it found the chaos and destructiveness of the whole crisis intolerable.

Belgian assistance to Katanga was pursued as long as the U.N. forces did not exercise any control over that region. The Belgian troops, except for advisors, left Katanga in August 1960. Meanwhile, Katanga acquired an embryonic military through the reorganization and reinforcement of its police forces. The Belgian assistance to the gendarmerie would last another year before Belgian military personnel were expelled from the Katanga region, which from then on survived on mercenary assistance.

The overall failure of Belgium's post-independence policy was not only due to a very poorly planned transition, but also to Belgium's inability to influence events in a post-colonial world.

In July 1960, Belgium [had] neither the internal political means, nor the military forces, nor the diplomatic relationships to assist her former colony to make the first steps in its history as an independent country.[14]

Belgium was unable to exert a *de facto* tutelage over its former colonies as France or Britain had done. A Belgian analyst, J. Vanderlinden, summarized it in saying that:

Belgium, once deprived of the status and the means of power, was too weak externally, and too divided internally to exert this tutelage and protect the Congo. The latter was too big, its economy too developed, its wealth too coveted, its administration too complex to be able to do so without a metropole [...] The Congo, during the first years, was a country in search of her metropole.[15]

The Stanleyville Rescue (1964)

On April 15, 1964, two-and-a-half months before the departure of the last U.N. troops from the Congo, rebel forces claiming to succeed Lumumba's movement started trouble in eastern Congo, close to the border with Burundi. Six months later, after rapid advances went virtually unopposed, the insurgents controlled more than one-third of the Congolese territory. On September 5, 1964, the rebels declared Stanleyville, captured on August 4, the capital of an independent government. The astonishing success of the poorly armed rebels was largely due to the extreme fear they instilled in the soldiers of the *Armée nationale congolaise* (ANC), the National Congolese Army. The Simbas, or Lions, as the rebel forces called themselves, had a reputation of invincibility based on the belief that they possessed magical powers which made them immune to bullets. Patrick Nothomb, Belgian consul in Stanleyville, described the Simbas' arrival in the city as follows:

> Whoever has not witnessed this event will never be able to fully imagine or understand the terrorizing power emanating from such an appearance. Try to imagine two lines of 25 men, each on a sidewalk; in the center of the street, an officer, and ten meters further, a gesticulating old man, the sorcerer. The fifty men, armed with ten guns and forty sticks, walk at 2 km an hour while waddling elastically; they are bare-chested and carry long herbs bundled around the torso and attached by strings to the head. [...] the terrorizing effect is obtained through the hoarse and monotone cries coming rhythmically from their throats. [...] Stanleyville will be taken by three such groups of fifty robots, but these robots move directly to the key points in town.[16]

The Simba officers were not taken by the witchery their troops claimed to possess, and were careful to avoid combat in zones where the ANC did not fear the alleged supranatural powers of the Simbas. One of the counter-insurgency tactics the central government used to defeat the rebels was to capture some of the Simba sorcerers and force them to immunize the ANC soldiers or to curse the Simbas.

The decline of the insurrection was as sudden as its success. The rebel leaders could not administer the conquered regions, make the economy function, transform the rebel army into a modern and efficient combat force, or even obtain international recognition and support. The revolutionary administration proved "as corrupt and powerless as the previous one; it did not succeed in mobilizing or uniting the population for the realization of the political and economic objectives of the new leaders."[17] Rebel authorities accumulated tactical mistakes and completely misjudged the international reaction when they took hostage the expatriate population of Stanleyville, including numerous Belgians and Americans.

From the moment of the hostage-taking, four military elements became involved in carrying out the defeat of the Simbas: the ANC, mercenary forces, Belgian troops, and the U.S. Air Force.

By the end of 1961, the ANC, based on the remnants of the *Force publique*, counted about 29,600 men under a unified command. In addition to this there were approximately 15,000 police troops. A U.N. report of June 29, 1964, described the state of the ANC at that time as follows:

An examination of the general situation in the Congo since 1961 shows that the ANC is still insufficiently instructed and unified to face a major crisis. In emergency situations, most Congolese soldiers are still insufficiently disciplined and do not show a great attachment to their duty and their country. Competent and devoted officers are the exception rather than the rule. The result is that authority is lacking at the top and that the troops do not possess a military *esprit de corps*. The penury of good commanders and the absence of an organic hierarchy may be the principal reasons for the present deficiencies of the ANC. The lack of logistical organization and the absence of method within the military staff also constitutes a grave obstacle to a more efficient operation.[18]

The ANC was unpopular because of its extreme repression and brutality toward civilians in the search for insurgents.[19] Many soldiers, subdued by Simba witchcraft, deserted the ANC to join the ranks of the rebels. Once the rebels lost the momentum of their attack, however, the ANC was able to organize a counter-attack. Meanwhile, many changes had taken place in the Congo's overall political context. Prime Minister Adoula ended his term of office on June 30, 1964, which coincided with the departure of the U.N. troops. During attempts to form a new government, an extraordinary reversal of circumstances took place. Moïse Tschombé, the former Katangese secessionist, was asked to head the new Congolese government. He was to become Congo's strongman in the summer of 1964, when the hostage rescue operation was being prepared and implemented.

Taking advantage of their good relations with the new prime minister, Belgian authorities started to devise an entirely new military assistance program. It consisted of a small group of special military advisors under the direction of Colonel Vandewalle. They were to provide advice to Tschombé himself. Vandewalle developed a plan for the liberation of Stanleyville using 4,200 troops, mostly ex-Katangese gendarmes, supported by 62 Belgian advisors and 390 foreign volunteers. Vandewalle found the Katangese soldiers more reliable than other ethnic groups in the regular Army and more obedient to the prime minister. Under the plan, all operations would be under his direct control and would benefit from Belgian logistical support. Belgian foreign minister Spaak signed the mission order for Vandewalle on August 24, 1964, seventeen days after the Simbas captured Stanleyville. The operation, later known as *Ommegang* after a biennual folkloric parade in Brussels, was initially based in Kamina, a pivotal position between Katanga and the Congo's centrally controlled northwestern zone.

Two months later, on October 27, the first elements of the *Ommegang* operation were flown to the edge of the rebel territory by a U.S. Air Force C-130 military transport aircraft. The tactic adopted by the *Ommegang* operation was quite simple: to maneuver as quickly as possible and hustle the rebels away ahead of them as they went. "From an orthodox military point of view, it was a joke."[20] The *Ommegang* forces covered 400 km in five days on bad roads and trails. They arrived at Stanleyville, another 620 km to the north, on November 24, the day after the airdrop of Belgian para-commandos.

The use of mercenaries proved extremely efficient, in military terms, in the reconquest of Stanleyville. The key to success was their very close supervision by non-mercenary Belgian officers, who ensured compliance with official Belgian directives. On the one hand, resorting to mercenaries offered the important advantage of reducing formal Belgian exposure and military casualties in a delicate operation. On the other hand, the official Belgian presence in key command position provided a coordination and disciplinary framework to the whole operation and prevented mercenaries from pursuing independent goals. The rebels were completely unable to resist the well-organized and well-supported force advancing against them. They organized ambushes rather than real defensive manoeuvres to attempt to stop the *Ommegang* operation, but to no avail. The insurgents showed little tactical understanding when they did not inflict any real damage to bridges and ferries, thereby failing to impede the advance of the *Ommegang*.

Although the Belgian-supported mercenary column had already made some rapid progress toward rescuing the European and American hostages in Stanleyville, alarming rumors regarding the fate of those hostages in the rebel-controlled area led the Belgian government to contemplate the possibility of an air rescue operation with U.S. assistance. Consequently, Under-Secretary of State W. Averell Harriman, a partisan of intervention, met with Belgian foreign minister Spaak in New York on November 1, 1964. A few days later the U.S. and Belgium agreed to cooperate in preparing a joint operation.

On November 17, 1964, 140 Belgian commandos of the 12th Independent Company of Commandos and 400 paratroopers (three companies of the 1st Para-Commando Regiment) were ferried aboard thirteen U.S. Air Force C-130s. An additional C-130 was reserved for the U.S. Air Force command and control element. The first landing stop was made at the U.S. Air Force Strategic Air Command base in Moron de la Frontera in Spain. The planes arrived on Ascension Island on November 18 and left for Kamina on November 21. Two more USAF C-130s joined the expedition in Ascension, one for maintenance and one for telecommunication transmissions. As soon as the Belgo-American expedition arrived in Kamina, the four C-130s, which had been at the disposal of the ANC, were retrieved for the airdrop operation, bringing the total number of planes available to 20. At 4:00 a.m. on November 24, the first group of 320 paratroopers descended on the airfield of Stanleyville and secured it for the C-130s, which landed 45 minutes later. The Belgian troops suffered no major injuries, and only a few small-caliber bullet holes in some of the C-130s bespoke of any reaction by the rebels.[21] In town, however, the rebels moved a large group of hostages out of the hotel where they had been kept. Later, rebels on the road started shooting the group at random, killing 20 Belgians and two Americans and wounding another 40 Belgians, five of whom later died from their wounds. The rebels quickly disbanded after the arrival of the para-commandos downtown. At 9:00 a.m. the same morning, the *Ommegang* arrived in Stanleyville.

A couple of days later, two companies of Belgian para-commandos were dropped on Paulis, 380 km northeast of Stanleyville, where 19 hostages had already been executed during the two previous days. The para-commandos evacuated more than 100 expatriates and then left the town. Other towns were also considered as sites for air rescue operations, but the highly critical and vociferous international reaction to the joint Belgian-U.S. intervention considerably increased the pressure to terminate the whole operation quickly. About 300 of the estimated 600 expatriates left in rebel territory were killed before the end of the insurgency, most of them Belgians.[22] The Belgian para-commandos suffered only three dead and twelve wounded.[23] By December 1, all Belgian paratroopers had returned home.

Washington's role in the events of 1964 was not limited to air transport of Belgian troops. Earlier in the year, it became obvious that the Italians who were to train the Congolese pilots would fail to produce results in time for the counter-insurgency operations. As part of the U.S. support, the Central Intelligence Agency created a front company, the Western International Ground Maintenance Operation (WIGMO), based in Liechtenstein, to hire Cuban refugee pilots in Florida. These mercenary pilots flew many missions and were extremely effective in support of the advance of the mercenary column under Colonel Vandewalle. Through the Military Aid Program, the U.S. also provided the Congolese forces with six propeller-driven T-28 training aircraft (outfitted as light ground attack aircraft), and some relatively long-range, World War II-era, twin-engined B-26 attack bombers. With the withdrawal of the Simbas, reconnaissance flights of longer range had to be executed.[24] It took until June 16, 1964 for the U.S. State Department to concede, after several denials, that "some American civilian pilots under contract with the Congolese government have flown T-28 sorties in the last few days in the eastern part of the Congo."[25] The U.S. also operated a small group of four U.S. Air Force C-130 transport planes with their 56 crew and maintenance personnel, which was vital for resupplying the ANC and moving the *Ommegang* troops.[26] With a complete monopoly over military air transport, the U.S. was instrumental in defeating the Simba insurgency.

In evaluating the hostage rescue operation, its success was far from complete given the high number of casualties among the hostages. In terms of its unofficial goal of defeating the rebels and reuniting the Congo, the operation was highly successful. The Belgo-American airdrop mission was geared primarily toward the rescue of hostages, The mercenary *Ommegang* force, although initially only approved for rescuing hostages, was far more effective at liberating and occupying large expanses of territory. They remained in place until the almost total defeat of the rebels. In addition, their actions did not have to be officially endorsed by the Belgian government, unlike the Belgian-U.S.

airdrop operation. What gave the *Ommegang* campaign its military originality was its unique combination of Belgian Army officers with both mercenaries and local armed forces. Despite the *Ommegang*'s success in defeating the rebels, the image of mercenaries interfering in Congolese internal affairs would stick for a long time. It was partly the use of the mercenaries, both by Belgium and the U.S., that provoked the violent international rejection of the air rescue operation.

At the political level, the Stanleyville events opened the way for the power takeover by Mobutu, then the commander-in-chief of the armed forces. Belgium and the U.S. were favorable to his accession to power. They appreciated his pro-western sympathies and viewed him as a strongman capable of keeping the Congo under centralized control. Until the late 1970s, Mobutu more than lived up to these expectations.

TO SHABA, RELUCTANTLY

Shaba I (1977)

During the first Shaba crisis in March-May 1977, Belgium abstained from direct intervention in Zaire. As described in Chapter 5, France organized the airlift of Moroccan troops to rescue the Zairian armed forces, which were unable to deal with the invasion of Katangese rebels from Angola. The only military action taken by the Belgian defense minister Paul Vanden Boeynants was to dispatch a C-130 military transport plane to Kigali, Rwanda, with ten para-commandos on board. Their mission was to stand by and, if called upon, to assist in the evacuation of Belgian civilians in the Shaba region. It proved impossible to contact Belgian expatriates in that region, and subsequent developments made an evacuation attempt superfluous. The mission was canceled after the success of the Franco-Moroccan operation.

Shaba II (1978)

In 1978, France and Belgium intervened in the southern part of Zaire. With the exception of Chad, it was, with over 1,800 troops, the largest military intervention in sub-Saharan Africa by western powers since the British quelled the East African mutinies in the early 1960s. It was also one of the very few instances where the intervening powers participated in actual, although limited, combat. Both contingents had different agendas. French troops were eager to reinstall the Zairian government's authority in the rebel-controlled area, while Belgian forces were initially under strict orders only to evacuate the expatriate community trapped in Kolwezi.

In Zaire, things had not improved since the first Shaba crisis. The economy did not recover from poor reorganization plans and badly implemented austerity programs. The Zairian armed forces (renamed FAZ, or *Forces Armées Zairoïses*, in 1971) were also being reorganized. This was long overdue, but insufficient. France undertook the responsibility of forming and training a parachute battalion. Belgium, which already had the responsibility of schooling Zairian officers, was also charged with organizing an infantry brigade in Kitona. After the 1977 Shaba crisis, a line of defensive positions was established along the southern part of the approximately 2,220 km border with Angola. The distances alone, not to mention the condition of the FAZ, left many holes in their defensive position. Zaire was convinced that the victory over the rebels in 1977 would suffice to deter them from returning.[27] This strategy proved to be counter-productive, deterring only the FAZ, and not the enemy, from better preparation.

The rebel FNLC (*Front National de la Libération du Congo*) repeated its attack on Shaba in May 1978. (See Chapter 5 for their first invasion in Shaba.) This time, they moved covertly into Zambian territory to strike Mutshatsha and Kolwezi in Zaire. It was intended as an economic hostage operation aimed at cutting the rest of Zaire off from access to the vast export revenues generated by Gécamines, the mining consortium based in Kolwezi. By traversing Zambia, the rebels bypassed the newly erected Zairian defense line on the Angolan border.[28] On May 13, 1978 the rebels occupied and secured their hold over Kolwezi. At the time, their force strength was estimated at 2,500 men. However, local recruiting raised the total rebel force to 4,000-4,500, with varied levels of military discipline and training. They were lightly armed, with only a few heavy machine guns and 81-mm mortars.

After the rebels entered Shaba and took the city of Kolwezi virtually unopposed, Mobutu's first appeal to foreign powers was directed to French president Giscard d'Estaing.[29] Another Shaba I-type intervention with western logistics and African soldiers was rejected for reasons of speed and Moroccan intervention fatigue. The King of Morocco, Hassan II, failed to see the reason why his countrymen should protect European expatriates while Europeans seemed so much better at doing it themselves. In response to the Zairian demand for assistance, the French authorities first deferred to Brussels before undertaking any action. French president Giscard d'Estaing initially showed little enthusiasm for engaging French troops in Shaba.[30] The Belgian authorities, however, were in a state of utter confusion. Initial rumors indicated that the expatriate population had not been harassed, denying Belgium any reason to act on humanitarian principles. The prospect of even remotely appearing to endorse the Mobutu regime with Belgian troops paralyzed Belgian authorities. Economic interests alone could not trigger enough political support for an intervention. The crisis cabinet was split into interventionist and non-interventionist factions. The lack of integrity of the Mobutu regime was part of the debate, as was the traditional anti-interventionist position of certain political groupings. Additionally, some attitudes in Belgium, such as that held by the Flemish Nationalist party, "were allergic to any collusion with France."[31]

In Kinshasa, Colonel Yves Gras, the head of the French military mission, advocated forceful and immediate action to avoid a further spread of the rebellion.[32] Paris, through the voice of Mr. Journiac, then head of the Elysée's African Affairs Office, responded with reticence to such an initiative, arguing that it was up to the Belgians to take the lead.[33] The Belgian crisis cabinet could not come up with a decision. On May 15, it was reported that the six French military assistance personnel posted in Kolwezi had been abducted.[34] Diplomatic channels between France and Belgium remained active throughout the crisis, although there was growing irritation with each other's decision-making process. While the Belgian decision was slow in coming, the French decision-making circle was limited to the president and a few others without external interference. Little was done to coordinate the radically different French and Belgian approaches.

France was eager to restore stability in Zaire by pushing the rebels back to Angola. President Giscard d'Estaing, more than any of his predecessors, wanted to conclude a multilateral Euro-African solidarity pact which would have institutionalized France's leadership in Zaire.[35] Other motivating factors for France included geo-strategic concerns and the impact of a Katangese-Cuban-Angolan takeover of Zaire's richest province. Furthermore, Zaire's claim of being the second largest French-speaking community in the world made it an obvious part of the francophone realm.[36]

With news about European casualties in Kolwezi, the Belgian cabinet on May 16 authorized its Ministry of Defense to go ahead with the preparation of a contingency plan while putting the Para-Commando Regiment on a higher state of alert. It was not until two days later that the first planes left Belgium. During those two days, no concerted action was taken between the French and Belgium military staffs. Belgium planned its intervention independent of any potential French action, with the specific goal of evacuating the Europeans from Kolwezi within 72 hours. As a result of their poor intelligence sources and lack of information as to whether or not Cubans were also deployed, the Belgian authorities decided to play it safe by dispatching 1,180 troops of the Para-Commando Regiment with 20 assorted transport utility and support vehicles.[37] All of this was to be transported by eight C-130s and two Boeing 727 civilian airliners to Kamina, an important military airport in southern Zaire. As part of this effort two different air routes were adopted. The shorter of the two flights between Brussels and Kamina was flown by the C-130s with extra fuel tanks and eight civilian Boeing 747s. It included stopovers at Porto Santo, Madeira, and Libreville, Gabon; the other route included two additional stopovers at Dakar and Abidjan.[38] It would take until almost midnight on May 19 before the Para-Commando Regiment could assemble its entire force at Kamina.

As of May 17, while Belgium was preparing for its intervention, France simultaneously took action by putting 2 *Régiment Etranger de Parachutistes* (2 REP) on a high degree of alert. President Giscard d'Estaing favored an intervention but wanted to be informed of Belgian intentions prior to committing French troops.[39] As soon as the Belgian decision to intervene was announced on May 17, Giscard followed with a similar decision that same day. Samy Cohen, a long-time observer of the French political decision-making system, viewed Giscard's order as motivated by a desire to pre-empt the Belgian intervention once he knew that France would not have to act alone.[40] It would be up to the minister of foreign affairs, Louis de Guiringaud, to plead unsuccessfully for a greater coordination between the two intervening forces. French troops arrived at Kolwezi on the evening of May 19, about 12 hours before the Belgian troops. The French advocated an airdrop directly to the north of Kolwezi as a way to achieve greater surprise because it was unclear whether or not the Zairian Army had retained control over the airport. French troops were flown by three

UTA DC-8s, an Air France Boeing 707, and a military DC-8. The planes flew to Kinshasa with only one stopover in Abidjan.[41]

Meanwhile, chaos reigned in Kolwezi. The FNLC seemed to have gradually lost control over the situation, prompting the French president to authorize the operation for May 19, one day earlier than planned. The Belgians could not be ready that early. The first wave of about 405 French paratroopers embarked from Kinshasa on four Zairian C-130s and two French *Transalls*. They were dropped only one-and-a-half hours before sunset; to avoid the higher risks of a night drop, the second wave of 233 paratroopers did not occur until the next morning. Consequently, the French troops on the ground only had time to conduct very limited military operations within the vicinity of the town. They then took position at night and waited for reinforcements.

At 6:30 a.m. on May 20, at exactly the same time as the drop of the second wave of French paratroopers, eight Belgian C-130s landed in Kolwezi; two hours later the planes brought supplies and the remaining Belgian troops. The whole regiment landed and entered the town a few hours later. The C-130s then started evacuating the refugees to Kamina, where civilian airplanes flew them to Brussels. The Belgians preferred a regular landing at the Kamina airport secured by Zairian troops to a paradrop because it was a faster way of getting the troops to their objective with less risk of casualties. A highly visible paradrop, instead of a discreet landing at a sufficiently remote landing strip, would have also unnecessarily put the lives of the hostages at risk. A Belgian major who participated in the operation was highly critical of the French paradrop: "We think that from our perspective, the airdrop was not the result of a correct appreciation at the military level."[42]

Although organized and executed independently, the French operation was conceived to complement the Belgian action. On the contrary, the Belgian operation was planned to be completely self-sufficient. The French minister of foreign affairs confirmed this complementarity after the fact: "We took the decision to intervene as a first step within an apparatus later to be completed by the Belgian intervention, destined to evacuate those who wished."[43] The French did not plan to evacuate the expatriate population and had not prepared the means to do so. Thanks to the Belgian support, France was able to plan for a relatively small-scale, low-cost operation, knowing that the Belgians would follow with all the impedimenta. For France, it was militarily cost-effective and politically rewarding. The French were credited for the full success of the operation and for chasing the rebels out of Zaire. The Belgian authorities had not been in favor of a joint operation mainly for political reasons. They did not support the French idea of an intervention geared toward the rescue of the Mobutu regime. Belgium's approach focusing on the evacuation of the expatriates antagonized Mobutu, although it undeniably contributed to the liberation of Kolwezi.

During the earlier stages of the crisis, the Elysée had in fact given its approval to a joint operation, but under French command.[44] Irrespective of the differing general objectives, the command issue might have been another divisive complication. Joint military operations are usually led by the commanding officer of the country with the greatest contribution to the joint force. In the case of the Kolwezi operation, the Belgian contingent of 1,200 was almost double that of the French, who had fewer than 650 men. It would be logical to assume, therefore, that the Belgians might have taken command over the whole operation. Belgium also contributed more planes than France. At the time, however, it was inconceivable that France would put its troops under a Belgian commander for an operation in which prestige and visibility were deemed so important. An integrated joint operation was not feasible due to the lack of agreement on the common objectives of the intervention and the impracticality of organizing a formal integrated command structure for a single Franco-Belgian operation.

On the ground in Kolwezi, the two foreign contingents worked well together, each respecting the other's military goals. They were able to delimit exclusive zones of operation for their respective forces, thereby ignoring each other as much as possible.[45] Belgian medical assistance to French soldiers was more forthcoming. Although the French saw little reason to evacuate the Europeans after the situation had stabilized, they did not oppose the Belgian officers who scrupulously, yet unimaginatively, executed their orders to evacuate the European population. These officers might have transferred the expatriates to Kamina and then waited to see how things developed in Kolwezi, but instead evacuated them, as ordered, directly to Europe. The evacuation was not forced upon the Europeans in Kolwezi, but the haste of the Belgian operation created an "evacuation-psychosis" which resulted in the transfer of 2,269 refugees to Europe in three days.[46] The first departure of the Europeans was understandable, because the rebels had killed about 900 people, including 11 French soldiers and military personnel, 120 civilian Europeans, 500 Zairian soldiers and civilians, and 247 Katangese.[47] There was no selective evacuation, however, and no options were presented other than evacuating to Europe or remaining in Kolwezi. As the Belgian ambassador in Kinshasa pointed out at the time, Belgium had committed a double psychological error by ordering an evacuation: first, detaching itself so blatantly from Mobutu by taking away the personnel who kept the industry running in Kolwezi; and second, abandoning Belgian interests in Shaba, with the possibility of others moving in.[48] From a purely military perspective, the Belgian armed forces had achieved all of the objectives assigned to them without casualties or gunfire.

Indeed, despite the high dramatization of the Kolwezi intervention in the press and in a subsequent French action movie, events on the ground had gone rather smoothly. Order was rapidly restored in Kolwezi after the arrival of the French and Belgian troops. The Katangese-Angolan rebels had already started to leave the city early on May 19 upon hearing about the imminent Belgian and French intervention. The only rebels left were those recruited locally after Kolwezi had been conquered.[49] They formed no lasting threat to elite French and Belgian forces. The Belgian troops left immediately following the three-day evacuation, except for one battalion of para-commandos which remained in Kamina to patrol the southwestern provinces of Zaire. Their function was more to reassure the local population than to fight rebels. No serious casualties were reported on the Belgian side. It has been alleged that the presence of this 600-man battalion was partly due to the prolonged stay of the French paratroopers. Belgium did not want to leave the whole field to the French because, as the head of the French Military Mission at the time commented in hindsight, Paris might have reaped - as it eventually did - "all the benefits of this operation in the eyes of Mobutu."[50] The entire French 2 REP would stay for an additional three weeks, with the first elements leaving as early as June 7, 1978. Casualties on the French side were significant: 11 dead, including the six military advisors in Kolwezi, and 20 wounded.[51]

In June, an Inter-African Force relieved the French and Belgian troops. This 2,684-man Inter-African Force was composed of contingents from Morocco (1,511 troops), Senegal (500), the Central African Republic (300), Togo (159), Côte d'Ivoire (110), Egypt (60), and Gabon (44).[52] All of the troops, equipped with French arms and vehicles, were transported to Lubumbashi by U.S. Air Force C-141 and C-5 transport planes.[53] The official ceremony marking the transition to the Inter-African Force occurred on June 22. Three days later, the last

Belgian para-commando unit left Zaire. External support for the Inter-African Force was limited to the U.S. and France. Belgium remained uninvolved.

The U.S. viewed the active participation of its allies in containing Soviet influence with favor. The fact that the allies had agendas of their own which differed from those of the U.S. did not matter as long as Soviet-Cuban influence was checked and American objectives were not opposed. The 1956 Suez Crisis had provided an example of the consequences of U.S. displeasure, but since then not one post-colonial sub-Saharan African operation by France, Britain or Belgium was rejected or countered by the U.S. On the contrary, the U.S. often sided diplomatically, and occasionally militarily, with these three countries in their military interventions.

The U.S. actively contributed to the Belgian military operation. President Carter gave direct authorization for the use of American transport planes and equipment. This assistance was indispensable for Belgium given the scope of the operation it had in mind. Had Belgium planned for a one-battalion intervention with lighter equipment, Belgian Air Force transport planes might have been sufficient. Due to over-cautiousness and a lack of precise intelligence on what was happening in Kolwezi, Belgium conditioned the launching of its operation upon a U.S. approval of air transport. The Belgian request to the U.S. was not made reluctantly; Belgium was keen on internationalizing its intervention. Additionally, Belgium was eager to dilute French predominance in the operation.[54] U.S. logistical assistance was coordinated from U.S. European Command Headquarters in Stuttgart, Germany.

On May 19, only hours after the first Belgian military plane arrived in Kamina, the first American C-141 unloaded a mobile refuelling installation. The Americans also contributed equipment to convert one Belgian C-130 into a tanker rapidly so the Belgian Air Force would be able to resupply itself.[55] In total, it is estimated that the U.S. supported the Belgian operation with eight C-141 sorties, used mainly for the transport of fuel equipment.[56] Also among the equipment transported by U.S. C-141s was one unarmed Belgian *Alouette* helicopter, (a type which is air-transportable by C-130 aircraft, such as those flown by the Belgians). Another practical U.S. contribution to the Belgian operation was the installation of a satellite communications (SATCOM) station. This station functioned for the duration of the Belgian operation to link Europe with the base in Kamina.

France benefitted to an even greater extent than Belgium from U.S. military assistance. The French chairman of the joint chiefs of staff, General Jeannou Lacaze, asked the Americans for long-range air transport for use between the French basis of Solenzara in Corsica and Zaire. The U.S. provided ten C-141s, which flew 23 sorties, plus one giant C-5 for fuel. The U.S. Air Force sent crews to Solenzara, Dakar and Kinshasa at the start of the operation.[57] U.S. planes did not carry any French troops and the French insisted that this American assistance served more as a matter of convenience than necessity.[58] This insistence illustrates how sensitive French authorities were to appear as acting independently of any superpower, especially in Africa.

Belgian relations with Zaire, and with Mobutu in particular, were at a historic low after the Shaba intervention. Belgium's poor political and diplomatic handling of the crisis and its ill-conceived evacuation plan would result in lasting damage. All the European executives of Gécamines, the gigantic mineral complex in Kolwezi, had been evacuated to Europe with their families. Their replacement or return was conducted on terms immensely more favorable to the Zairian executives. The latter's participation in management positions jumped from 24 percent before the crisis to 87 percent after the crisis. Within the 13 percent of remaining European managers, a reshuffling drastically diminished the Belgian share in favor of increased French involvement.[59]

At all levels, France came out the winner in the Shaba operation. Mobutu congratulated the French for their zeal in coming to the rescue of his country and rapidly stabilizing the situation. France's subsequent access to Zaire's commercial and economic assets served to further French influence in the region. For the West, the operation was a landmark event in the containment of Soviet-Cuban influence in sub-Saharan Africa. Twelve years later, the Soviet and Cuban presence had completely subsided.

From the perspective of the rebels, the attack was their final attempt to recover the Shaba province and destabilize the regime of President Mobutu. The initial attack on Kolwezi had been a tactically brilliant action for a slow-moving, lightly armed guerrilla force. Kolwezi was the proper target because of its major economic value. The surrounding population was very much allied with the rebels, providing them with supplies and furnishing a widespread intelligence base. Nevertheless, except for the initial attack, everything the rebels did was destructive, if not outright disastrous, to their cause. The Katangese rebels completely misjudged African and western solidarity. More damaging still was their inability to control their own troops, particularly the new local recruits. The ensuing massacres only strengthened western resolve to intervene. The summary execution of six French military advisors posted in Kolwezi was another indication of their political and diplomatic inexperience.

At the tactical level, the rebels seemed more bent on destruction than the pursuit of their own advantage. They demolished large amounts of military equipment and planes, but failed to perceive the need to sabotage the airfield once they knew about the French and Belgian intervention. On the contrary, the gratuitous destruction of civil and industrial infrastructure indicated that the rebels were not prepared to rule the territory. It is probable that the Zairian armed forces would have have defeated the rebels even without outside assistance, although at a considerably higher cost and after a much longer period. The poor transportation network in Zaire was one of the main reasons for the inertia of Zairian forces.

The conclusion of the rebels' handling of the Shaba II campaign is puzzling. It indicated either a considerable sense of despair and impatience on the part of the Katangese community in Angola, or a great vulnerability to Soviet-Cuban manipulation. Except for the strategic advantage of moving through Zambia directly toward Kolwezi, the rebels had learned nothing from the Shaba I campaign.

Zaire (1979)

In February 1979, less than one year after the Kolwezi operation, the Belgian prime minister Vanden Boeynants sent a two-company Belgian contingent (about 250 soldiers) to the army-navy base in Kitona, roughly 200 miles west of Kinshasa. Technically, these troops were dispatched to train Zairian forces in the use of mortars and were supposed to participate in joint maneuvers. The operation, baptized *Green Apple*, was launched as alarming reports of rebel infiltration from Angola, Zambia, and Rwanda reached Brussels. Mercenaries, mostly Belgians, were spotted and eventually arrested in Rwanda. According to official sources in Belgium, the Belgian action was partly motivated by the discovery of a plot led by mercenaries to overthrow President Mobutu. The situation in Kinshasa was alarming. Generalized poverty and scarcity of food, combined with accelerating inflation, created an explosive environment. Serious riots were feared, and the

Zairian forces were deemed unable to guarantee the security of the Europeans.[60]

The Belgian decision to send troops was taken without major political problems and the secret was better safeguarded than during the 1978 Shaba II operation. The Belgian troops, ferried by 12 C-130 sorties, arrived on February 12, 1979. One of the tasks of the Belgian troops was "to set up refugee camps for possible regrouping and evacuation of the European population."[61] Belgium did not have to implement a humanitarian rescue action. The 1,705-ton Belgian command support vessel *Zinnia* sailed from Ostend in February to provide logistic facilities at the mouth of the Zaire River, close to the base of Kitona.

The Inter-African Force, put in place after the 1978 Shaba crisis, was still present at the time. The chaotic and quickly deteriorating condition in the capital explained why the Belgian forces were sent to a base relatively close to Kinshasa. The troops were withdrawn by the middle of March 1979. The circumstances that triggered the Belgian operation are unclear, but assuring the stability in Kinshasa was considered the best way to provide for the overall security of Belgian expatriates, which was the primary objective of the Belgian government. Given Belgium's difficult relationship with Mobutu, his political survival must have been a secondary concern to Belgian politicians. The operation proved to be a mere precautionary measure, but one which prevented further degradation of the volatile situation, pre-empted a French action, and signaled a reassertion of Belgium's role in Zaire.

OPERATING IN A NEW WORLD ORDER

Namibia (1989-90)

Belgium participated in the U.N. Transition Assistance Group (UNTAG) with a small contingent which was deployed in Namibia in early 1989 and disbanded in March 1990. (See section on Namibia in Chapter 9 for more detailed information). The Belgian military contribution was limited to 15 members of the Military Police and 15 officers from the Belgian Gendarmerie, which falls under the authority of the Ministry of Defense. The peace-monitoring operation went without incident for the Belgian contingent.

Rwanda (1990)

"The boys from Brussels are going in," quoted *West Africa* magazine in mid-October 1990, adding: "It is not often that Belgium gets the chance to roll up its sleeves for an imperial adventure, so perhaps one should not be too harsh on the government for its decision to dispatch troops to Rwanda."[62] During the night of September 30 to October 1, 1990, between 1,500 and 3,000 armed Rwandese refugees entered Rwanda from neighboring Uganda.[63] Their leader was a Ugandan major-general of Rwandese origin, Fred Rwigyema. The rebels, belonging to the Tutsi tribe, advanced to 40 miles northeast of Kigali, the capital. They sought to overthrow the regime of President Juvénal Habyarimana, a Hutu who had been in power since 1973 and whom they accused of corruption and disregard for democratic reforms. The underlying issue, however, had tribal origins. Since its independence in 1962, Rwanda had been dominated by the Hutu tribe, which comprised 85 percent of the population. The invading refugees were of the Tutsi minority tribe, who had been expelled or had fled in successive waves from 1959 until 1962. During this period, 100,000 people were massacred in tribal upheavals that shifted control of the country from the Tutsis to the Hutus. The Rwandese Tutsis had taken refuge in Burundi, Tanzania, Uganda, and other neighboring states. In 1990 the Tutsi diaspora totaled about two million individuals, of whom 250,000 lived in Uganda. Some of them had joined Yoweri Museveni, himself a Ugandan Tutsi, in his quest for power in Uganda during the mid-1980s. When Museveni became president of Uganda in January 1986, many Rwandese Tutsis continued to serve in his regular armed forces. The Rwandese refugee leader Rwigyema served as deputy commander-in-chief of the Ugandan Army before resigning this position and leading his troops into Rwanda.

Initially, the 5,000-man Rwandese Army proved unable to cope with the invasion. Morale was low, and the troops were better known for their skills at smuggling than for their prowess in combat.[64] The rebels progressed rapidly. Belgium, concerned for the security of its 1,630 citizens living in Rwanda, sent ammunition to help the Rwandese Army.[65] For almost 30 years, Belgium had continuously pursued a military assistance program in Rwanda. By 1990, this program had about 20 military personnel assigned while a similar, although more recent, French program consisted of 69 military advisors. Belgian policy-makers reacted rapidly. On October 4, 1990, the first 180 Para-

Commandos had already left Brussels. Following its low-risk approach to such contingencies, Belgium dispatched a total of 540 soldiers, or four companies of men, from the 2nd and 3rd Battalions of the Para-Commando Regiment. The task force also included a reconnaissance platoon, a mortar platoon, a signal communications team, and a medical team.[66] The airlift was executed with eight C-130 sorties, a Belgian Air Force Boeing 727, and one DC-10 civilian transport aircraft. In the early morning of October 6, all Belgian troops in Kigali were operational. The U.S. did not provide any transport aircraft, but assisted Belgium with secure satellite communication. The remarkable thing about the Belgian force deployment was that it was simultaneous with Belgian operations in the Persian Gulf, where Belgium had dispatched four ships and two C-130s.

France also decided to launch a humanitarian intervention to ensure the security of its 700 citizens in Rwanda. One-hundred fifty Légionnaires of 2 REP flew from Bangui and began operations in Rwanda on October 5, almost simultaneously with the Belgians. The two foreign contingents did not engage in any fighting. Some skirmishes had apparently taken place the previous night around the presidential palace, although they were soon silenced by the Rwandese Army.[67] These relatively minor fire fights seemed to have been precipitated by a few infiltrated groups with no direct link to the rebels in the northeast.[68] A curfew was declared over the city. Another company of 150 French Légionnaires from N'Djamena arrived to reinforce the first detachment. In the following days, French troops evacuated some 170 compatriots from northern Rwanda. Belgium also evacuated its 77 citizens from northeastern Rwanda to Kigali.[69]

The main task of the Belgian troops was to secure the airport in order to maintain a free escape route for the evacuation of the civilian European population. The Belgian embassy also received some military protection because it was a potential gathering point for evacuees. The French troops were sent with similar instructions regarding the humanitarian aspect of their operation. The coordination between the two contingents, initiated at the General Staff level but also on the ground, was much more effective than in 1978. The two contingents shared similar operational plans and arranged for a distribution of tasks in assigned zones.[70] The Belgians were assigned the protection of the airport, and a small French contingent was left there under Belgian command.[71] At the political level, the coordination of the two efforts was greatly facilitated by the common humanitarian objectives. The

Franco-Belgian intervention calmed the situation in the government-held area and bolstered government forces by allowing them to concentrate on fighting the rebels. The Rwandese military also benefitted from advice from the newly arrived Belgian and French troops, as well as from a more abundant stock of ammunition and equipment. Government troops profited from superior firepower, which included French-supplied *Gazelle* helicopters manned by Rwandese.[72]

A third intervening force was flown in from Zaire, which is linked to Rwanda and Burundi in a regional mutual defense treaty through participation in the *Communauté Economique des Pays des Grands Lacs*. The troops were part of Zaire's elite presidential guard and officially numbered about 500 men. Unlike their French and Belgian counterparts, the Zairian troops were sent to the front line and actually participated in the fighting. Ten days after their arrival, the Rwandese authorities requested their departure due to the Zairians alleged involvement in pillaging.

It was later learned that an unusual occurrence favored the government forces: the rebel leader Rwigyema died on the second day of the invasion. According to rebel sources, he stumbled on a mine while crossing into Rwandese territory, although the Rwandese authorities claimed that he was killed by one of his followers in a rift over which strategy was more appropriate: guerrilla tactics or a rapid drive toward Kigali.[73] Given the unlikelihood that the surprised Rwandese Army had the opportunity to mine key points to the capital, the rift seems the more credible explanation for Rwigyema's death. The rebels were extremely successful at concealing the disappearance of their leader, although they pursued their offensive with less aggressiveness and organization than if Rwigyema had survived. His successor was Paul Kagame, a man in his thirties who was a former chief of the intelligence and security services of the Ugandan armed forces. The main brake to a rapid rebel expansion was the lack of support among the local non-Tutsi population. The Hutus were not keen on seeing their former rulers return to power, despite their reservations about Habyarimana's presidency in Rwanda.

Rumors of massacres of 2,000 to 4,000 Tutsis, spread by the Rwandese regular forces and Hutu peasants, brought the Belgian political consensus temporarily into question.[74] The data about possible government involvement was inconclusive, and neither France nor Belgium withdrew its soldiers, which might have permitted even greater atrocities against Rwandese civilians on the front. Diplomatic efforts were undertaken as the situation grew calmer.[75] The rebels had ceased to be a threat to the capital or to the Rwandese government. They had apparently settled into limited guerrilla warfare with an effective force reduced to only about 800 men. The area under their control had shrunk to a section in the northeast of the country in the national park of Kagera.

During the month of October, a high-level Belgian delegation led by the prime minister conducted two rounds of "safari-diplomacy," visiting Rwanda, Burundi, Kenya, Uganda, and Tanzania. It failed to produce conditions for a lasting peace. By November 1, 1990, the Belgian paratroopers left Rwanda under pressure from several parties in the government coalition in Brussels.[76] For a while thereafter, Belgium maintained two C-130s in Nairobi for possible evacuation of civilians from Rwanda.[77] A subsequent high-level French diplomatic mission, led by Jacques Pelletier, minister of cooperation, and Jean-Christophe Mitterrand, the president's advisor for African affairs, produced equally inconclusive results. Both countries promoted the idea of a regional conference on the refugee problems. The role of Uganda in support of the rebellion was still unclear, but no permanent solution could exist until all forms of outside support were withdrawn. On January 22, 1991, a group of 400 to 600 rebels seized part of Ruhengeri, a city 12 miles from the Rwandese border with Uganda. A detachment of 100 French paratroopers was sent to the region to evacuate 210 French and other expatriates.[78]

By late March 1991, Zaire had succeeded in negotiating a cease-fire agreement between the Rwandese authorities and the rebels.[79] This agreement also provided for the creation of an all-African OAU observation and monitoring force of about 135 men, with Zaire, Uganda, and Burundi providing 45 men each. Belgium and France were not to participate in this force, but agreed, together with Germany, to assist with financial and logistical support. Once this force was in place, all other foreign forces would be required to leave Rwanda. However, it took close to three years of negotiations before a much larger force, under the auspices of the U.N., would eventually move into the country. Belgium agreed to contribute troops to the U.N. peace-monitoring force. France had maintained the equivalent of one and sometimes two companies of paratroopers (150 men each) permanently stationed in Kigali from the 1990 intervention until December 1993. French troops left once an effective neutral interposition force was in place.

Zaire (1991)

By September 1991, the Zairian government's financial situation had reached a new low, with huge budget deficits and runaway inflation. One consequence of the country's economic disintegration was that military personnel from the regular armed forces did not receive their monthly pay for several months in a row. The elite and more highly paid presidential guard was not concerned with the delay in payment. The 31st Parachutist Brigade of the Zairian Army, a French trained unit which until a few months before had been commanded by French officers, mutinied and thereby started a movement that soon spread to other units. Led by elements of the 31st Parachutist Brigade, 3,000 dissatisfied soldiers stationed in the vicinity of Kinshasa swept into the capital and began pillaging on a large scale. The local residents joined in systematically sacking the city stores and residences of well-to-do citizens and foreigners. The news spread rapidly throughout the country. Other major cities, including Kolwezi, were reported to be subjected to uncontrolled violence and plundering. Mobutu's power base was no longer strong enough to oppose the chaos.

President Mobutu had convened a National Conference before the mutinies to promote democratic reform. The conference gathered all political parties, business leaders and religious institutions in Zaire. On September 20, after weeks of wrangling which ended amidst three days of violence, the conference was suspended. Opposition parties denounced the unfair treatment they received from the Mobutu regime during the conference. It was against this hectic political background that the soldiers mutinied on September 23. Nevertheless, the subsequent military and popular discontent was purely spontaneous and opportunistic. No political motives could be attributed to those who participated in it during the early stages. Economic hardship and declining living standards made a looting bonanza impossible to resist.

In view of the rapidly deteriorating situation, the French and Belgian governments decided to act by sending troops with the initial objective of protecting and evacuating the foreign nationals. During the night of September 23-24, the first French troops arrived in Brazzaville from the CAR and Chad. This was a remarkably short reaction time, made possible by the prepositioning of troops and *Transall* aircraft in both countries. The French contingent crossed the Zaire River and moved toward Kinshasa the next morning. Additional troops were later flown in from France. The 600-strong French contingent consisted of Marine

Infantry units and elements of the Foreign Legion.[80] The code name of the French operation was *Baumier*. The French Air Force participated in the intervention with ten *Transalls*, two C-130s, and one DC-8.[81] The French paratroopers moved rapidly toward the Zairian capital's airport and the French embassy compound; one soldier was shot in an apparently random incident with mutinied Zairian soldiers. Eventually, the French armed forces moved into town and started evacuating the expatriate population of Kinshasa to Brazzaville by boat.

Belgian troops left Brussels on September 24 and arrived in Brazzaville the next day after stopovers in Ghardaïa, Algeria, and Niamey, Niger. In total Belgium sent 1,145 troops, mainly Para-Commandos from the Regiment's 1st and 3rd Battalion, as well as a reconnaissance squadron and an anti-tank company. A month into the operation, 140 troops from the 2nd Battalion Commandos were stationed in Libreville, Gabon, to facilitate the evacuation of civilians. A surgical unit, communications specialists, and a logistics detachment completed the Belgian deployment.[82] The Belgian intervention was code-named *Blue Beam*. The Belgian Air Force used ten C-130s and two Boeing 727s for the operation. The Belgian C-130s and their crews were particularly well-prepared for a Zairian contingency. Between 1982 and 1989, one C-130 had been permanently stationed in Zaire with rotating Belgian crews.[83]

Two other nations, the U.S. and Portugal, also contributed to the rescue operation with military means. The U.S. Air Force contributed seven C-141 military transport airplanes. On September 27, Portugal, with a large community of its citizens residing in Zaire, put one of its C-130s and 25 men under Belgian command with a credit of 150 hours of flight time. This would be the first Portuguese military operation in Africa since 1975. The three main military participants in the evacuation, Belgium, France and the U.S., cooperated to a degree never before achieved between intervening powers in post-colonial sub-Saharan Africa. From the beginning of the crisis, a French military officer was assigned to the Belgian operational center, and a Belgian officer was dispatched to the French center. A U.S. officer joined the Belgian center a few days later.[84] On September 25, a joint Franco-Belgian operation under Belgian command landed in Kolwezi to evacuate all expatriates who expressed the desire to leave.[85] In Kinshasa, Belgian troops reported to French officers.[86] French paratroopers, aboard American C-141s, organized assault landings in some of Zaire's remote corners to evacuate U.S. and other expatriates.

Politically and diplomatically, the cooperation between Brussels, Paris, and Washington was closer than in any previous French or Belgian intervention in Africa. With the collapse of order in Kinshasa, the three allies tried to steer Zairian authorities in the direction of democratic reform, with Mobutu either resigning or relinquishing most of his powers to a transitional government before general elections could take place. The French, Belgian and American ambassadors in Kinshasa, whose power the press compared with that of pro-consuls,[87] consulted each other regularly and delivered joint messages to President Mobutu at various instances during and after the military intervention. On the day of the uprising, the Belgian foreign minister Mark Eyskens, then in Washington, met with Secretary of State James Baker and contacted French foreign minister Roland Dumas.[88] The three agreed to implement joint evacuation plans. There was a convergence between Paris, Brussels and Washington on essential aspects of long-term, fundamental reforms needed in Zaire, particularly economic stringency and democratization. However, divergences appeared on the future role reserved to President Mobutu, with the Belgians most eager to see him replaced while France and the U.S. felt more cautious. These differences did not affect the joint operation; they became completely irrelevant a few weeks later when Mobutu reasserted his grip on the government.

Initially, France's role in influencing Mobutu seemed preponderant. The Belgian disengagement from Zaire, including military and civilian aid, had been completed a year earlier, leaving Belgian authorities with little leverage over Mobutu. The U.S. had also terminated its military assistance programs in Zaire in June 1991. After the Angolan peace settlement and the subsequent withdrawal of Cuban troops, the strategic value of Zaire to the U.S. was drastically reduced. Only France maintained an active military program in Zaire at the time of the mutiny. It is therefore not surprising that the French ambassador in Kinshasa took the lead as Zaire's strongman during the early days of the disorder.[89] In the words of a Belgian journalist, it was then obvious that: "The French policy was much more active than the Belgian and the intervention by the [French] parachutists put Mobutu's regime virtually under the tutelage of Paris."[90] The French advantage gradually eroded due to the lasting chaos in Zaire and Mobutu's adroit handling of the weaknesses of his political adversaries.

The evacuation of all expatriates who wished to leave was terminated on October 2, although order in Zaire was far from restored. Food shortages and a latent sense of insecurity persisted, especially in the capital. On October 4, French and Belgian authorities together decided to reduce their numbers of troops and assign supplementary missions to the remaining forces. These missions consisted of "assuring by their passive presence a certain dissuasive force [and] assuring the surveillance of certain vital points as well as the distribution of humanitarian aid."[91] This approach was a departure from the initial plan to evacuate foreigners; it officially prolonged the military presence, but the presence of foreign troops barely sufficed to settle the situation. In a pre-emptive move, Belgian para-commandos were positioned on the Atlantic Coast around the oil rigs owned by the Belgian oil company Petrofina.[92]

To ease the political tension resulting from the riots, President Mobutu reluctantly named an old political adversary and member of the opposition, Etienne Tshisekedi, as the new prime minister on September 29. France and Belgium, on the presumption that the political compromise was the correct move for the nation, started to withdraw part of their forces in early October: about 150 men for each contingent, as a first step toward a complete withdrawal. The new prime minister pleaded for French and Belgian forces to prolong their stay in Zaire to avoid a confrontation between opposition groups and Mobutu's presidential guard or his numerous covert agents.[93] The Belgian and French authorities did not heed the prime minister's appeal, but later events proved that their withdrawal was indeed premature.

The Mobutu-Tshisekedi coalition crumbled when the two leaders failed to bridge their many differences, especially with regard to the allocation of the ministerial portfolios of defense, interior, and mines. No other structure existed to fill the void left when the prime minister was dismissed and Bernardin Mungul-Diaka was named to replace him on October 23. Government opponents took to the streets to protest the arbitrary dismissal of Tshisekedi and Mobutu's unilateral nomination of the new prime minister, whom they rejected even though he was part of the opposition. Kinshasa again became the theater of violent demonstrations. The homes of three of Tshisekedi's supporters were bombed. In the meantime, Lubumbashi, the capital of the Shaba province, was plundered.

The new commotion that shook the country convinced most of the remaining expatriates to leave. A tripartite decision made on October 24 between the Belgian minister for foreign affairs, the deputy minister for African affairs at the French Foreign Ministry, and the American assistant secretary of state for African affairs strongly advocated the evacuation of all nationals of their respective countries and agreed to the subsequent withdrawal of French and Belgian troops. Numerous other countries gave similar orders to their expatriate communities in Zaire. France in turn ended all its civilian and military cooperation programs with Zaire on October 25 to mark its strong disagreement with Mobutu's arbitrary rule. On October 30, the voluntary evacuation was completed; an estimated 10,000 to 15,000 expatriates had left the country. The withdrawal of French citizens was completed on October 31. The Belgian government made a similar decision the same day, but only completed the withdrawal of its troops on November 4.

The withdrawal occurred amidst strong political pressure on President Mobutu. While Belgium and France unequivocally requested his departure at a trilateral meeting in Brussels on October 24, the U.S. lapsed behind in requesting Mobutu's complete removal from power. The U.S. position was made public at a hearing before the Senate Foreign Relations Subcommittee on Africa on November 6. Herman Cohen, the U.S. assistant secretary of state for African affairs, indicated that the U.S. had not ruled out a role for President Mobutu, albeit under a new regime:

> The best hope for Zaire now is genuine power sharing between President Mobutu and the opposition. In particular, President Mobutu must break with the past and allow a transitional government to run the economic and domestic political affairs of the country without interference, including control over finance.[94]

By then, France had adopted an even tougher stance toward Mobutu after a period of circumspection in late September and early October. The French minister of cooperation, Edwige Avice, declared in Paris that she could not conceive, "under the current circumstances, how France would invite Mobutu to the *Francophonie* Summit to be held in Paris in November 1991."[95] Belgium had already dissociated itself from the Mobutu regime in July 1990.

From the point of view of the intervening powers, the Zairian operation was remarkable in several aspects. Four allied countries had contributed to a massive evacuation of refugees in an explosive environment and suffered only two casualties, a French Marine and a Belgian paratrooper. The integration in the field between the operations of these four countries is without precedent in Africa. The cooperation was also unique from a political perspective. High-level political leaders of the three principal countries involved met in Brussels and accepted common objectives. Nevertheless, their united force, both military and diplomatic, was still insufficient to re-establish order in Zaire or to obtain Mobutu's resignation. It also failed to persuade him to respect the power of his prime minister. The opposition, due to its own inability to present a common front, appeared to be weaker after the intervention than before. In weeks following the departure of French and Belgian troops, Mobutu succeeded in restoring the essential aspects of his power base at the cost of increased political, bureaucratic and economic chaos throughout Zaire.

Zaire (1993)

In January 1993, France and Belgium once again sent troops to Congo-Brazzaville and Zaire to evacuate European citizens endangered by army mutinies and riots. In a sadly familiar scenario, mutinous troops rampaged through the capital on January 28. French refugees gathered at the French embassy in Kinshasa. That evening, in a never-explained incident, Philippe Barnard, the ambassador, was killed. Soldiers firing automatic weapons randomly plundered shops and homes, stealing money from civilians at gunpoint. Troops loyal to the president fought fierce street battles to put down the mutiny. The Army camps of Ceta and Kokolo, where the mutiny originated, were completely encircled on Friday, January 29, as was the office of Prime Minister Tshisekedi, who had been restored to his previous position.

Spontaneous violence erupted among soldiers after the pro-Mobutu Central Bank introduced 5 million Zairian banknotes to settle a two-month payroll for the military. The Central Bank was injecting massive liquidity without any accountability to the government. Inflation soared to more than 6,000 percent in 1992 for goods purchased in stores. The new banknotes, worth less than $2 each, were declared illegal tender by the prime minister. Consequently, many shops, gas stations and commercial banks refused to accept them, and soldiers were deprived of their purchasing power.

The French minister of foreign affairs accused the Zairian troops of deliberately killing the French ambassador.[96] On January 29, France dispatched about 150 soldiers from the 21st Regiment of Marine Infantry stationed in Bangui. A dozen men from these troops arrived in Kinshasa the same day, securing the French embassy and evacuating some of the 400 expatriates who took refuge in the compound. Another 60 French soldiers followed on Sunday, January 31.[97] In cooperation with the Belgian government, French defense strategists had also planned for the French troops to secure the airport of N'Djili to allow for the safe arrival of four C-130s and two Boeing 727s of the Belgian Air Force.[98] A C-5 *Galaxy* military transport plane from the U.S. Air Force participated in carrying the Belgian forces' heavy equipment to Brazzaville, just across the Zaire River from Kinshasa.[99] The Belgian rescue and evacuation forces never arrived in Zaire. Although the first 100 out of a total of 550 troops flew from Belgium on January 29, they landed in Brazzaville and remained there. Prior to the arrival of those troops, only 14 Belgian para-commandos and five gendarmes had been assigned to protect of the Belgian embassy. President Mobutu strongly opposed the Belgian intervention on Zairian territory. On the contrary, the prime minister and the political parties supporting him pleaded for a Belgian military intervention by troops stationed in Brazzaville. Tshisekedi launched an appeal to the international community to send soldiers into the country "to guarantee our security."[100]

Presidential troops took precautions to prevent Belgian military planes from landing at the N'Djili airport. Air-defense batteries were deployed along the landing strip, and Belgian military analysts suspected the presence of American *Stinger* missiles supplied by the UNITA movement in Angola.[101] In a further move to prevent a Belgian military evacuation operation, the president opposed any crossing of the river by Belgian troops and put the presidential yacht at the disposal of Belgian, French and other civilians who wanted to be evacuated to Brazzaville. In the meantime, Zairian troops had succeeded in quelling the mutiny. French troops considered their mission completed on February 4, and the bulk of Belgian troops started leaving Brazzaville the next day. The withdrawal was completed about ten days later. The Zairian opposition parties estimated the death toll due to the mutinies and riots at 1,000, most of whom were military men. The toll included five Europeans.

The U.S. remained absent during the crisis, as President Clinton had barely had the opportunity to put in place a new administration. The Belgian foreign minister visited Washington in mid-February, and Secretary of State Warren Christopher seemed to recognize the need for Belgium to play a leading role in solving the crisis.[102] In the weeks following the withdrawal of French and Belgian troops, the three western powers took little concerted action. The Zairian situation was reminiscent of the Togolese crisis in 1991, when French troops were sent to neighboring Benin but did not intervene to support the beleaguered prime minister against an uprising of Army troops backing the Togolese president. Despite appeals from the political opposition to President Mobutu, Belgian authorities shied away from openly intervening *manu militari* against Zaire's president. In comments to the press, Willy Claes, Belgium's minister of foreign affairs, offered a triple explanation for this inaction:[103]

> We do not have the necessary legal framework. Intervention, but under what mandate? Secondly, the government's policy, as decided during [the latest] council of ministers, rests on a purely humanitarian basis. Finally, it would be irresponsible to put in danger the lives of the Belgians still in the country.

The writing on the wall must have become clear to African dictators and democratic opposition parties alike: military intervention by former colonial powers in sub-Saharan Africa stops short of operations to support processes for democratic reform. Such actions were left to diplomatic pressure, reduced development aid, and, whenever feasible, U.N. military action. The Zairian prime minister had officially requested the presence of U.N. observers and technical assistance to organize elections. Belgium remained cautious and did not want to support a request for a U.N. initiative without prior approval from Washington. France was said to be even less enthusiastic about a U.N. operation in Zaire to organize and monitor elections lest it open the door to similar U.N. involvement in France's zone of influence in Africa.[104]

Somalia (1992-94)

Operations *Restore Hope* and UNOSOM II in Somalia were analyzed in Chapter 5. The bulk of the Belgian contingent, which had peaked at over 900 troops, was withdrawn by the end of 1993. The remaining forces and the command and support ship were to be withdrawn before mid-February 1994.

Rwanda (1993-94)

The U.N. Security Council initially authorized the dispatch of 1,000 troops on October 5, 1993 to monitor the peace agreement reached three months earlier between the Rwandese government and the rebel *Front Patriotique Rwandais* (FPR) in Arusha, Tanzania, on August 4, 1993. By April 1994, the U.N. force was 2,500 strong and composed of contingents from twenty different countries. The peace-monitoring force was planned to remain in Rwanda until after general elections took place in 1995. As a former colonial power, Belgium agreed to participate in the U.N. force with a contingent which eventually reached 430 troops. This figure fell well short of the 800 troops requested by the U.N. but which Belgium failed to supply by invoking budgetary restraints.[105] Besides troops, Belgium also contributed equipment and logistical support, including two helicopters.[106]

Among its various operational assignments before the elections, the U.N. force escorted FPR officials to Kigali so they could be integrated into the Rwandese transition government. U.N. forces did the same for FPR guerrilla troops to integrate them into the regular Rwandese military. The transition process subsequently ran into problems due to the difficulty of establishing an interim government.

The Belgian participation may at first appear as a logical extension of its 1990 intervention and of the various peace initiatives Belgian authorities had tried to present soon afterwards. The novelty of the situation is that for the first time, Belgium contributed to a U.N. operation within its traditional zone of interest in central Africa. Mediating an end to the Rwandese civil war and introducing democratic reforms in the country were among the objectives that the Belgian government tried to help the opposing parties achieve. In 1991-92, however, Belgium failed in its unilateral brokering efforts, as did France. Regional efforts under the aegis of the OAU also failed. Finally, the U.N. agreed to monitor the peace process following the Arusha settlement. Belgium and France went along with this decision in view of their lack of diplomatic success and the high cost of covering the peace process unilaterally, which would require maintaining a large monitoring force in Rwanda. The complexity and deep roots of the Rwandese civil war did not permit a rapid solution through negotiations, and neither of the two European powers were willing or able to muster enough clout to enforce the terms of earlier peace accords.

On April 6, 1994, events took a turn for the worse. President Habyarimana of Rwanda and President Ntaryamira of Burundi were both killed when a rocket attack caused their plane to crash near Kigali. The immediate result of Habyarimana's death was panic and heavy fighting in the streets of the Rwandese capital between increasingly disoriented government forces and the rapidly advancing columns of the rebel FPR. Violence erupted between Rwanda's two main ethnic communities, the Tutsi and the Hutu, leading to mass slaughter and anarchy. Refugees of both communities fled to neighboring countries by the hundreds of thousands. In a matter of two weeks, civilian casualties were conservatively estimated at 200,000, with some sources suggesting figures twice that amount.

Belgian soldiers within the U.N. force were among the first casualties. Ten soldiers assigned to the protection of the Rwandese prime minister after the president's assassination were executed after being disarmed by local forces. The shock of these killings was deeply felt in Belgium, and the government came under strong pressure to cease all participation in the U.N. peace-keeping force.

The international reaction to the increasing violence was to organize a multinational evacuation operation for the fearful expatriate community trapped in the country. Seven allied nations participated in this operation. France sent 460 troops (among which one company of the 3 RPIMA) and five *Transall* planes. The first elements of this force arrived as early as April 8. In an unusual move, Prime Minister Balladur, and not President Mitterrand, supervised the execution of the French intervention directly. Belgium sent another 600 men, independent of the U.N. force, and the bulk of its military air transport fleet: seven C-130s and two Boeing 727s. Germany and Canada each supplied one military transport plane, and Italy provided three C-130s and 80 troops. The Netherlands participated with four C-130s. The United States kept one ship, the *Peleliu*, with 330 Marines on board, on alert off the Kenyan shore and provided C-130 and C-141 aircraft for evacuating expatriates. Most allied operations were coordinated from Nairobi, which acted as a hub for the various evacuation efforts; France used Bangui as the center for its operation.

In the face of the complete breakdown of order and peace in the country, and under pressure at home, the Belgian government informed the U.N. Security Council on April 13 of its intention to repatriate its contingent to the U.N. force in Rwanda. The decision came into effect the next day and was equally applicable to the evacuation force, which had been sent a week earlier. By April 15, Belgian, French and Italian troops were completing their withdrawal. The U.N. retained a much-reduced force in Rwanda, although it was considering proposals to send a much larger force to bring peace to the country.

Belgium's unilateral decision to withdraw altogether from the U.N. force, combined with the evacuation of Belgian aid personnel, amounted to a *de facto* suspension of all assistance programs to Rwanda for the foreseeable future, even if there was a declared willingness to resume aid programs whenever conditions would permit. The brutal execution of the ten soldiers created a national trauma that put into question Belgium's ability to gain sufficient public support for future contributions in U.N. peace-keeping operations.

The remarkable feature of the evacuation operation, which was organized outside the framework of the U.N. peace-keeping force, was the direct participation of seven allied countries, including Germany, and the dispatching of Italian troops on the ground to protect evacuation points inside Rwanda. The multilateralization of such a non-U.N. military operation may well become a more common element of future crises in sub-Saharan Africa.

THE SPECIFIC ENVIRONMENT FOR BELGIAN MILITARY INTERVENTIONS IN AFRICA

Belgium's record of military involvement in sub-Saharan Africa is surprisingly long for a small power with only 10 million inhabitants and no overseas strategic ambitions. Belgium's military role can be divided into a series of commitments covering three concentric circles: the defense of the homeland, NATO responsibilities, and out-of-area interventions. The latter type includes two different roles: either as part of a U.N. or regional peace-keeping operations, or as protector of Belgian interests in central Africa. Belgium has participated in three U.N.-sponsored operations in Africa; only in one instance have the two roles overlapped, during the military operation in Rwanda starting in 1993 under a U.N. mandate. Alone among smaller European powers, Belgium has continued to view a selected area in the world as a place in which some crises might require the use of force. Central Africa became the theater of eight military interventions, decided by Belgium alone and executed either unilaterally or with France and the U.S.

With such an unusual record among western powers, except when compared to French or British military involvement in Africa, one wonders what reasons were compelling enough to justify the repeated Belgian military interventions in the region. For the Belgian participation in U.N. operations in Namibia, Somalia and Rwanda, the answer is a combination of peer pressure and a sense of responsibility to accept a fair share of the collective burden. The payoffs may include the accumulation of goodwill and influence within the U.N. system.

These explanations leave the question of why Belgium intervened so frequently, either unilaterally or in conjunction with the U.S. and France. Post-colonial ties do not provide the full answer, although they are a necessary condition for this type of intervention. Belgium never intervened in Burundi, despite that country's record of massacres and coups in the post-colonial era. The interests at stake are defined through a combination of objective factors and political motives. In summary, the following conditions have to be partly or completely fulfilled for a Belgian intervention to occur:

1. Belgium must have considerable interests and a sizable concentration of Belgian expatriates in the country in question.
2. The regular local armed forces must be unable to provide satisfactory protection to the Belgian expatriate community.
3. The official authorities must request foreign military intervention.
4. A military intervention must be justifiable on humanitarian grounds.
5. A Belgian intervention must be feasible without incurring more than limited casualties.
6. Belgium must not be isolated diplomatically, and must obtain allied logistical support if needed, mainly from the U.S.

The first condition eliminates most African countries with the exception of Zaire, Rwanda, Burundi, and South Africa. South Africa hosts the greatest number of Belgian expatriates, with more than 20,000. Before 1991, Zaire was second with over 15,000 Belgian expatriates, followed by Rwanda, Côte d'Ivoire, and Burundi with 1,500-1,700 each.[107] Except for Zaire, where the vast majority of the expatriate community was evacuated in 1991-92, the number of Belgian citizens in these countries has remained stable in recent years. Other countries with significant numbers of Belgians, such as Gabon with about 500 or Nigeria with about 700, fall within the French or British spheres of influence. It is unlikely that Belgians would be targeted specifically within the European expatriate community if a crisis occurred in any of those latter countries.

The second condition, the inability of an African country to defend the expatriate community, applies almost automatically to Zaire, and to a lesser extent to Rwanda and Burundi. The Zairian armed forces have on various occasions been unable to protect the expatriate community. In fact, those forces have often been a threat themselves. It can therefore be expected that Belgian forces would be put on some type of stand-by alert immediately following the eruption of a rebellion, mutiny, or other destabilizing crisis in Zaire, but also in Rwanda.

The condition relative to the approval of the official local government is almost absolute. Belgium would be unlikely to intervene in support of rebels against a recognized government. To reach central Africa, Belgium has to negotiate overflight rights over several African countries, including North African states. The OAU has a record of not lending its support to rebellious movements, and most African states do not accept any western action that is openly hostile to the legal authorities of another African country, even when in strong disagreement with that country. The only practical possibility for a Belgian military action without the approval of the local authorities or a request from an African regional organization would be either in collaboration with a powerful ally like the U.S. or France, or within the framework of a multinational force.

The fourth condition, the humanitarian grounds for intervention, is essential in two ways: it pre-conditions the endorsement by the Belgian public and the majority of political forces; and it warrants at least tacit support from key African countries, particularly those granting overflight rights and allowing stopovers.

The low casualty rate among Belgian troops during the course of past interventions has facilitated subsequent decisions to intervene. This extreme aversion for casualty risk explains the Belgian military commanders' insistence on having an overwhelming force on the spot. In each of the instances where Belgium and France intervened together, Belgium deployed roughly twice as many troops to the crisis area as did France. In this respect, the execution of ten soldiers in Rwanda in 1994 has been the exception that may not only jeopardize Belgium's willingness to participate in future U.N. peace-keeping operations, but may also enhance Belgium's caution in unilaterally dispatching troops to central Africa.

The final condition, which predicates a Belgian military intervention on allied, or more precisely American, diplomatic patronage and logistical support, is necessary in the event of a serious crisis in Africa.

Belgium is not in a position to handle a major crisis in central Africa on its own. Diplomatically, it does not have the clout to be isolated and ignore international criticism. Militarily, it has only limited means for power projection over very long distances. The U.S. has been Belgium's most reliable partner, from the 1964 Stanleyville rescue operation to the evacuation operations conducted in conjunction with France in the early 1990s. For Belgium, organizing a military operation in coordination with France, as for instance in Rwanda or in Zaire, presents an important logistical advantage. It grants Belgium the quasi-automatic endorsement of about a dozen francophone African countries that support actions taken by France, and, by extension, Belgium. This francophone African support may take the form of putting military facilities at the disposal of Belgian forces, as was the case with Gabonese and Congolese airports during the Franco-Belgian evacuations from Zaire in both 1991 and 1993.

Belgian unilateral interventions, or those with key allies, have always been low-intensity operations with limited objectives. Labeled as humanitarian operations, these military actions have been reasonably successful at removing or protecting expatriates involved in crises in central Africa. A common thread seems to run throughout these Belgian interventions: the circumstances in which they take place are quite dramatic. Part of the explanation for this resides in Belgian crisis management and its tools for executing contingency operations. The multipolar nature of Belgian coalition governments slows decision-making. To gain enough political momentum for an intervention, conditions in a given crisis area must be critical. Because Belgium does not maintain troops in or around its customary zone of intervention in central Africa, it cannot undertake small, low-key preventive measures to control or even monitor disorders. France, on the contrary, has retained this ability and, by the mere presence of its troops in Africa, can deter nascent troubles.

An almost constant by-product of Belgian action in Africa, even if such a result is not part of the official mission and has never been acknowledged publicly, is the reinforcement of local political regimes. During the 1978 Shaba crisis this inevitable effect was conceded reluctantly to the Mobutu regime. If Belgian interventions have at times succeeded in reinforcing or saving the political regimes of President Mobutu and President Habyarimana, they have been unable to obtain the departure of the former after 1991.

Belgium has often failed to reap any political, diplomatic, economic, or commercial benefits from its militarily successful interventions. The 1960 and 1964 actions aroused ire from some members of the international community. The 1978 intervention in Kolwezi ended in badly damaged relations with Mobutu, the loss of economic advantages in Zaire, and an unnecessary political humiliation when France arrived first in Kolwezi and received all the credit from Mobutu. The political handling of the interventions in Rwanda and Zaire in the early 1990s illustrates the improvements in Belgium's self-perception as an intervening power. Until April 1994, public opinion was very supportive of the later interventions in central Africa and of actions within the framework of U.N. operations. The government has been in tune with the general public. The distancing from Mobutu has cleared the ambiguity about the moral aspects surrounding the Shaba II operation in 1978. The government's military actions unambiguously ceased to be interpreted as regime support operations, but were in fact kept within the strict confines of humanitarian operations. At the diplomatic level, Belgian authorities have clearly stated their support for democratic reforms, which is tantamount to bolstering the political opponents of Mobutu. These reforms are the true stakes of the central African policy that Belgium initiated in 1990. Only if this approach is successful will Belgian investors and expatriates return to Zaire. Belgium must restore its military credibility after the panicked withdrawal from Rwanda in April 1994, however, before it will reappear as a center of influence in central Africa.

Chapter 13

Men's Fear of the Unknown

> Even then the empire retained the loyalties of many, for the alternative was chaos. When this ceased to be so, when organized barbarian states capable of providing a measure of security began to emerge in the lands that had once been Roman, then the last system of imperial security lost its last support, men's fear of the unknown.
>
> Edward N. Luttwak
> *The Grand Strategy of the Roman Empire*[1]

On March 6, 1957, Ghana shed the colonial system and took a bold step into the unknown. Guinea followed suit the next year. 1960 was the key year in which no less than 17 colonies in sub-Saharan Africa gained independence: 14 French, one Belgian, one Italian and one British. By that time, France no longer had sovereign possessions in the region, except for Djibouti. Belgium left the continent completely in 1962. Britain proceeded at a slower pace and left the continent in 1968, but was invited back for a brief colonial interlude in 1980 to ease Zimbabwe's independence process.

When confronted with the rapid pace of the transition from colonies to sovereign states, former colonizers and colonies alike have feared the unknown. How could it have been otherwise given the close interrelation resulting from the colonial bond? France managed to offer its colonies the most comprehensive framework for post-colonial relations, bringing back some measure of security and predictability after independence. The offer was extended simultaneously to all aspiring sovereign states: first through a community project with France, then through strong bilateral ties. Britain's pragmatic view was devoid of such a systematic character; a case-by-case approach tried to preserve remnants of British post-imperial dignity and emphasized links with a set of core ex-colonies where British interests were the strongest. Belgium, perhaps in over-reaction to domestic and international pressures, left its main colony precipitously, opening the way to chaos by failing to devise a post-colonial structure immediately to deal with the unknown.

Subsequent evolutions have shown that the post-colonial ties between the three former metropoles and their ex-colonies rested on similar instrumentalities of influence, even if the manner in which this influence was structured and pursued varied widely from one former metropole to another. A common feature was that the vast majority of newly independent states in the French, British or Belgian zones of influence failed to organize their own security and development independently. Many socio-cultural, commercial and personal ties would inevitably have survived the demise of colonial empires, but the military and economic weakness of the new states became the venue for special links. This weakness of the African states, combined with the willingness of ex-metropoles to pursue the greatest level of influence within the limits of domestic and international constraints, was embodied in a new international regime. Zones of influence, commonwealths, or bilateral agreements structured a new order. Post-colonialism was not synonymous with international chaos and *laisser-faire*.

The contention elaborated in this study is that the African empires of the three European metropoles did not expire after the independence ceremonies. Each metropole actively pursued a policy to build a new foundation for its post-colonial interests in Africa. Institutional inertia cannot explain the continuance of very structured links between ex-colonies and ex-metropoles, nor can commercial ties alone justify the extensive and complex set of instruments which France, Britain and Belgium retained to enhance their influence in their former African possessions. Things did not happen accidentally or by bureaucratic negligence. On the contrary, former metropoles actively sought influence by all available means, including military links and interventions. The three European powers independently pursued their self-interest in the post-colonial world order. The parameters shaping their respective quests for influence varied widely according to each power's domestic and international policy priorities. The divergence of interests and approaches was not, however, of such a magnitude that common patterns failed to appear. In fact, the three countries fashioned a new international regime, unique to post-colonial empires, which respected very specific rules and relied on a pre-defined set of instrumentalities. The large variety of political and military actions undertaken by France, Britain or Belgium, the wide spectrum of their motives, and the variations in their respective means of influence should not hide the fact that all three countries fall under a single regime in their dealings with sub-Saharan Africa.

The French, British and Belgian relationships toward their former African colonies stand out among the many other North-South relationships. A combination of two factors distinguished them from the rest: firstly, the relationships were foremost post-colonial and, secondly, they were premised on military involvement. The matrix of the new regime is a direct consequence of the colonial legacy. In addition, the regime's survival relies on the willingness to commit troops and military assistance on the part of the centers of influence. The use of force is not accidental, even though the situations requiring force may have been. The three European powers have always remained prepared for an overseas military role, even if only a limited one, in times of crises.

Nowhere else has this special dual bond defined an international regime, except perhaps in Russia's relationship with other former Soviet republics in the early 1990s or in the United States' role in the Philippines. With regard to Africa, however, the United States, the Soviet Union and China could not rely on historic colonial ties; and former colonial powers such as Portugal, Spain, Italy, Germany, the Netherlands and Japan have all broken the links tying them to former colonial possessions. The latter countries also did not consider military involvement as a means of post-colonial influence - at least not until the early 1990s.

A EUROPEAN POST-COLONIAL REGIME

Returning to Stephen D. Krasner's definition as first quoted in Chapter 1 , international regimes are: "a set of implicit or explicit principles, norms, rules and decision-making procedures around which actors' expectations converge in a given area of international relations."[2] France, Britain and Belgium, together, are three pillars of a specific international regime, which for convenience will be called the European Post-colonial Influence, or EPI, regime. The three European powers are the cores of three respective international zones of influence in sub-Saharan Africa. The basic actors of the regime are: (i) the three European powers, referred to as the centers; (ii) the sovereign nations of the former sub-Saharan African colonial empires, referred to as the zones of influence, the post-imperial equivalent of the empire's periphery; and, (iii) third countries that have had to adjust their international expectations to the realities and constraints of the EPI regime.

A Given Area of International Relations

The immediate field of application - the zone of influence - of the EPI regime is limited to the centers' respective relationships with former colonies in sub-Saharan Africa. Other areas formerly under their control do not, for the most part, fall under consideration for this regime. This concerns, for example, France's post-colonial relationship with Algeria or Indochina, and Britain's ties with India or Australia. The EPI regime's area of application is restricted geographically, but is much less confined functionally. The relationships between the three European powers and the new sub-Saharan African nations touch on many aspects of domestic and international life. Cultural, financial, commercial, social, military, political, humanitarian, educational, and other fields are all affected by the regime. The EPI regime benefits from the multi-disciplinary networks in all of the above mentioned functional domains; it draws its specificity from the essential political and military dimensions. These aspects give French, British and Belgian relationships with Africa a fundamentally different depth and intensity than can be found, for instance, in Portuguese or German relationships with Africa.

The EPI regime emerged in a new global world order in which the North-South dimension had become more complex than under the old imperial system. It was marked by a considerably greater diversity of actors and decision-making centers. The role played by a variety of international institutions was unique in history. After 1960, all non-colonial western countries had the opportunity to play a part in the independent countries. The combined pressure and weight of these new actors interacted with the way the EPI regime found its place in North-South relationships.

Principles and Norms

The EPI regime grew out of a radical change in the principles, norms and rules that conditioned the previous regime. Colonialism amounted to the imposition of a metropolitan order on distant territories. The principles of international conduct emanated from the European centers, with little or no room for the concerns of the periphery. The competition among scrambling colonial powers determined the geography of influence. It legitimized international coercion in all areas except for Europe and a few other places strong enough to resist the shuffle. Colonial possessions came to embody the sublimated weakness and frustration of continental European nations hungry for status and power. "Competition for empire became a surrogate for more direct confrontation in Europe."[3] Economic exploitation and expansive evangelization provided the means and constituencies to assert colonial authority better. The diplomatic, economic and religious interests grew, mutually reinforcing each other and cementing a large political support base for the pursuance of the colonial regime.

Sovereignty was the colonial periphery's only outlet to express its rights. Other channels were either not allowed by the colonizer or were opened too late, as in the case of de Gaulle's *Communauté* project. The sanctification of sovereign equality and the rejection of open international coercion as a means of international conduct came in response to pressure from the periphery. The subsequent achievements on the path to independence and self-determination at all levels are a matter of gradation. Formal acknowledgment of sovereignty, the building block of the new international order, did not and could not end dependency in many functional areas of international relations. A new interaction between the old colonial center and periphery could now be redefined on the basis of the new relationship between sovereign entities. Purged of superfluous colonial paraphernalia and legacies, a novel framework emerged between the center and the now-sovereign periphery. The approach tried to preserve as much of the former colonial interests as was compatible with the formal respect of sovereign rights. The ensuing order reflects not only the centers' protective approach to its vested interests, but also the new nations' limited capacity to revolutionize all aspects of their dependency on the former metropoles.

The distinctive character of the EPI principles and norms holds not only when compared with other contemporary international regimes, but also when evaluated against other historical regimes. The EPI center-to-periphery interactions occupy a separate place in North-South relationships and are not a form of diluted colonialism or imperialism. They are the re-invention of the colonial links of influence in a new world order. The EPI regime is immersed in fundamentally different norms of international behavior compared to imperialism and colonialism. The sovereignty of the periphery radically altered the symbolism of its relationship with the center. This feature arguably represents the most important and genuine achievement of the independence movements. The overriding sense of legitimacy, that imperialism and colonialism were right and justified, was irrevocably destroyed. Direct alien rule became unacceptable, subject to international scrutiny and sanction. Two World Wars challenged European world supremacy and revealed the power of the United States and the Soviet Union, both of which claimed to champion anti-colonial policies, although the United States watered down its anti-colonialism in the interest of western unity.

The historical analysis provided in the preceding chapters indicates the existence of six basic principles and norms underlying the EPI regime. Under these theoretical principles, members are committed to respect each other's sovereignty, to act in a mutually beneficial way, to redress inequalities of wealth and power, to accept the realities and constraints of zones of influence, to limit the resort to force, and to refrain from interfering in each other's intra-zonal affairs.

Principle 1: The legitimacy of self-determination and the sanctity of sovereign equality among participating members, all pursuing their self-interest, is an exogenous condition imposed by the world order emergent in the 1960s. An international regime among sovereign entities is necessarily founded on a mixture of self-interest and solidarity. Such a framework outlaws outright domination, but permits the establishment of zones of influence.

Principle 2: Under the EPI regime, actions undertaken by members must, by definition, be mutually beneficial because there exists no enforcement mechanism within the regime and all members, as sovereign entities, have in theory the option to opt out at any time. A regime must help solve common problems. The fact that the EPI regime has to be a mutually beneficial framework for both the centers and the periphery - or at least the periphery's elites - stems from the pursuit of self-interest by all parties. The possibility of opting out of the regime is used either by design or by benign neglect. Central powers can exclude some nations from their zone, as de Gaulle did forcefully with Guinea, or as successive British governments did by gradual disinterest in most of their East and West African ex-colonies. Similarly, the newly independent nations retain the option of changing patrons, and many have taken advantage of this possibility. This opt-out clause enhances the degree of freedom of all parties and forces those committed to the regime's survival to pay greater attention to the demands and aspirations of other members.

Principle 3: The EPI regime is a North-South regime. It shares with other North-South regimes the commitment to help redress the unequal distribution of power and wealth between European and African members through flows of assistance in virtually all areas, including security. The African members receive what is usually a disproportionately large share of the funds from European members' foreign assistance programs. For the Europeans, this contribution is an essential requirement for their participation in the regime and a pre-condition for playing a continuing role in the sub-Saharan region. The former colonial link continue to inspire a sense of post-colonial responsibility that is not due to European guilt resulting from the huge disparity in wealth, but rather was based on common history and convergent interests.

Principle 4: The voluntary participation of African members in a formal or informal European zone of influence requires them, at times, to align their foreign policy objectives with those of the patron state. They must also, on occasion, prolong or concede favorable commercial and cultural advantages. The EPI regime is built on the sub-Saharan African nations' acknowledgement of their limited ability to sever all ties with the former colonial powers without incurring high costs. For the new African elites, the regime is a substitute for revolutionary changes without the uncertain outcomes, and it provides a familiar structure in which to organize their interests and bring back some measure of predictability in international relations.

Principle 5: The effective or potential European military involvement on the side of African members is an essential component of the regime. In theory, military force cannot be exercised at the expense of an African member of the regime, but only at its invitation - although the decision on whether or not to intervene is left to the discretion of the European power. Hence, the objective of using military power is not to dominate or to enlarge the domain of influence, but to assist in the security of the African member of the regime. The aggrandizement of a given zone of influence is achieved through persuasion and negotiation, but not through wars of conquest.

Paradoxically, the recourse to military intervention has been the path of least resistance for all parties concerned. For the centers, it amounted to an inexpensive means of achieving larger political or economic ambitions. For the African partners, it has provided a security guarantee, courtesy of the European taxpayers, with the additional advantage of being redeemable at a moment's notice.

Principle 6: The European members respect each other's role in their respective zones of influence and do not interfere with each other's management of intra-zonal affairs. Like colonialism, the EPI regime implicitly endorses a weaker version of continued sharing and subdivision of African zones of influence among the three European powers. This norm has certainly held in the case of France's influence over its former colonies, which other western powers have never challenged. For Belgium, the case is less clear given the extensive role of France in former Belgian colonies. However, Belgium's loss of monopoly in central Africa is as much the result of its gradual abdication to fully play its part as of France's eagerness to expand its influence in all of francophone Africa. Britain has reduced its influence to far less comprehensive levels than France or even Belgium, but its pre-eminence in anglophone Africa remains fairly unchallenged by other EPI powers. The main exception was Nigeria, especially during the Biafran secession.

By and large, the six principles have been respected, although there have been important deviations. All members of the regime have had to compromise on some of the principles and adapt their expectations to existing geo-political and economic realities. After more than three decades, however, the system is still in place. This in itself is a sign of success, as the members have remained committed to the continued existence of the EPI regime. Over time, the regime has gained in stability as its norms were better understood and reactions among members became more predictable.

Rules and Decision-Making Procedures

The EPI regime shows only a limited degree of systemic formalization and institutionalization. The system remains informal because it was created and maintained mostly by convergence or consensus over the objectives among participants, enforced by mutual interest and occasionally by formal agreements. No single institution was ever founded to represent the interests of all three European members and/or their African partners. In fact, the community of nations covered by the EPI regime is not aware of the regime's existence as a specific joint system. Participants feel they belong to one - and sometimes two - of its three main branches: the French, British or Belgian zones of influence. The three northern powers meet frequently in different international fora, particularly within the European Union and NATO, although there has been no post-colonial equivalent of the Berlin Conference, which regrouped as such all participants in former colonial regimes. Instead, there are three parallel mechanisms, two of which have an embryonic institutionalization. For France, the Franco-African meetings are the most structured manifestation of a formal collective regime. The Commonwealth plays a similar role for Britain, although its geographic reach is far wider than just sub-Saharan Africa. Belgium has not created a forum for periodic meetings with former colonies. Most of the decision-making under the EPI regime results from bilateral negotiations and agreements. Rights and obligations, whether contractual or not, are defined by bilateral understandings. As a rule, there exists no collective responsibility under the EPI regime, although there have been multilateral decisions and actions. For instance, France and Belgium cooperated in several interventions in central Africa; and it was in response to an urgent request from its African partners that France launched operation *Manta* in 1983. This Franco-Belgium cooperation demonstrates the North-North solidarity among members of the EPI regime, while the 1983 intervention in Chad was a showcase for South-South solidarity in reaction to an aggression by Libya, an outsider to the regime, against one of the African members.

From the inception of the EPI regime, the past has continued to shape present and future bilateral relations. Post-colonial influence resulted partially from administrative inertia and the absence of alternative channels for commercial, cultural and other exchanges. Post-colonial links proved easy to preserve or reactivate once the passion and rhetoric which immediately followed independence had abated. Both the European and the African bureaucracies and economic actors were geared toward the pursuance of relationships, albeit unequal ones. In the end, the day-to-day instrumentalities of the center's influence remained virtually unchanged, resting on a mix of technological superiority and economic predominance.

At the national level, each country has developed its institutions to cope with the demands and responsibilities inherent to the EPI regime. Most of the bureaucracy was already in place, dating back from colonial times. In some instances, special institutions or procedures were created in the 1960s. Again, France provides the best example when de Gaulle installed an advisor on African affairs at the Elysée Palace. In addition, the new French Ministry of Cooperation was created to deal exclusively with the African zone of influence and coordinate all forms of aid, including military assistance. France also launched a unique framework to ensure the monetary cohesion of its zone of influence. The EPI regime has not received such highly distinctive bureaucratic recognition in Britain and Belgium, but public spending on development aid proves the special status of the African ex-colonies. For more than three decades, they remained the primary beneficiaries of development funds. Occasionally, one African country or another has fallen out of favor, although former colonies as a group have received highly favorable treatment.

Military cooperation has benefitted from special attention in all three European countries, testifying to the vitality of an essential component of the EPI regime. African countries dominate the list of beneficiaries of French, British or Belgian military assistance, even, as in the case of Belgium, to the exclusion of any other Third World area. Military cooperation agreements define in detail the nature and importance of the assistance provided. During crises, emergency decision-making procedures are well-established at all levels of authority. Contingency plans exist for overseas military intervention, especially in areas such as Chad or Zaire, where such actions have taken place repeatedly. Troops designated for African theaters of operations can be put immediately on high alert. The network of overseas bases is, to the extent necessary, integrated in the planning and implementation of military operations. France has undoubtedly achieved the highest level of preparedness for African contingencies, but Belgium and Britain are both capable of moving rapidly with troops into a given crisis area, either on their own or with logistic support from the United States.

A remarkable evolution in the EPI regime is linked to the growing role and influence of international institutions. At the United Nations, the French, British or Belgian permanent representatives often act as the representatives of their respective African partners on issues that are otherwise of little or no relevance to their respective countries. Similarly, the French, British and Belgian representatives at the major international lending institutions, the IMF and the World Bank, spend considerable amounts of energy trying to channel development funds to their respective zones of interest in Africa. The rationale is, firstly, that those institutions play a central role in orienting development efforts and priorities throughout the Third World, and, secondly, that every dollar of development funds paid by the international lending institutions is, up to a point, a dollar less to be paid by the French, British or Belgian taxpayers. This substitution effect has been in place especially during years of economic hardship and budgetary cuts in Europe. Unable to assume all of the development needs of their zones, the European powers use their leverage at the IMF and the World Bank to distribute the burden.

Special recognition is given to the existence of the EPI regime within the decision-making and bureaucratic apparatus of each member country. It perpetuates a structured zone of European influence in sub-Saharan Africa. The means through which European powers exercise their influence at the political and military levels are formidable, as has been illustrated in this study of French, British and Belgian policies toward sub-Saharan Africa. Influence did not come as an accidental legacy of colonial empires. It was an implicit objective, involving political choices and the commitment of resources and manpower. Undoubtedly, the goal was pursued with more vigor by France than by Britain, and both could commit more means than Belgium.

Expectations and Outcomes

D.K. Fieldhouse, in his comparative survey on colonial empires, argues that colonial empires were seldom deliberately acquired to produce wealth, and that they were retained irrespective of their "profitability."[4]

> Empire in the modern period was the product of European power: its reward was power or the sense of power. The end of empire did not mean economic loss to the one-time imperial states: on the contrary, it meant that the economic advantage of operating in other parts of the world was no longer offset by the cost and inconvenience of political responsibilities. [...] The west retained its economic preponderance: some even held that the margin of wealth between advanced and 'developing' countries widened as empire ended. If Europe in fact derived her wealth from her colonies, their loss made remarkably little difference to her.

What was true for colonial empires remained so for post-colonial zones of influence. Financial profitability, while never disdained, was not the primary reason for European powers to pursue influence in sub-Saharan Africa. In fact, it often seemed that in the post-colonial era, profitability was disconnected from the search for influence, as western powers often yielded less influence in the more profitable areas of the Third World than in sub-Saharan Africa. More predominant in European justifications for continuing the pursuit of influence were, in Chester Crocker's words, "Cold War concerns, the desire to maintain spheres of predominance, the urge to assure continuity for its own sake, and the prestige of extra-European military roles."[5]

In trying to achieve these objectives, France, Britain and Belgium spontaneously developed a new international regime. They found an opportunity to realize gains through the creation of and adhesion to a whole set of norms and rules. The regime's outcomes were a function of the distribution of power among the European and African members. The EPI regime was created at a time of fundamental discontinuity in the international order. Hence, the main expectation was that the regime would bring predictability and stability to the interactions between the three European powers and their former African colonies. The regime was negotiated along mostly bilateral lines, although the relationships between the center and the individual countries belonging to its zone of influence were complex. There were significant opportunity costs associated with the role of center. Trade-offs were equally difficult to reconcile for African nations.

From the onset, the zone of influence was conceived as a source of diplomatic status on the international scene for all parties of the EPI regime. For France and Britain, a zone of influence is one of the elements, in addition to their nuclear status, that justifies their permanent seats at the U.N. Security Council. France can mobilize a dozen or more votes at the U.N. General Assembly or in other international fora such as the International Monetary Fund, the World Bank, and the General Agreement on Tariffs and Trade. Britain's reliance on Commonwealth votes is less secure, but signs of Commonwealth solidarity abound on the international scene. Even Belgium achieves a status in North-South relationships greater than that accorded to other western powers of similar size due to its continued role in central Africa. African members of the EPI regime gain from their association with a more powerful patron who will often advocate their position in international institutions.

The French-British-Belgian paradigm for North-South relations provides a framework to shape the expectations of both participating and non-participating international actors. The regime is acknowledged and often recognized by the world community. When a crisis erupts in a sub-Saharan African country that is part of the French, British or Belgian zone of influence, international attention quickly converges on the former metropole to determine its intentions. Even the United States, the only remaining superpower, defers to ex-metropoles on the appropriate course of action to solve crises within their zones of influence, as occurred with regard to France's actions in Chad. Other friendly international actors move into the arena only if the ex-metropole declines to act. Regional powers such as Libya or Nigeria may have resented the influence and tried to counter it, but even their hostility was an acknowledgement of a special link between the ex-metropoles and their former colonies. The EPI regime was never intended to be an alliance against a common threat, despite its temporary and incidental anti-Soviet orientation during the 1970s and 1980s.

SEPARATE APPROACHES IN THE E.P.I. REGIME

All participants in the EPI regime have developed idiosyncracies stemming from their respective vantage points and the benefits of the regime. Beyond the common goals and outcomes described in the previous sections, each member of the regime tries to pursue independent objectives of national interest while adhering *de facto* to the general principles and rules of the EPI regime.

France: Not Losing its "Exalted" Place in World Affairs

According to the French philosopher Pascal Bruckner, France's incurable *malaise* is caused by the feeling that the country "is afraid of becoming a nation like any other, pursuing a destiny that it doesn't control. For two centuries, France - like the United States - has constituted one of the few messianic nationalisms that set out to save humanity and regenerate the world."[6] As a medium power, it is hard for France to reconcile the self-proclaimed universalism of its *mission civilisatrice* with the inherent limitation of its means. John Chipman has related this frustration to the elemental logic of French power in Africa. "To compensate for an incapacity to exert influence in all parts of the globe, as would a superpower, a medium power, such as France, must try to preserve for itself a certain exclusive influence in a region."[7]

International influence also secures the French linguistic realm, a factor of considerable importance for France. The survival of French as an international language, and hence as a means for French culture to radiate, is dependent on the continued adhesion of a large constituency outside French borders committed to the use of French as a main language. In this field, francophone Africa plays a vital role as host to a considerable proportion of the francophone community in the world, although the mastery of French can vary widely from one segment of the population to another. The vulnerability of France's cultural position in view of the anglo-saxon preeminence has exacerbated French cultural nationalism and has rendered the French "particularly sensitive of the danger of losing their 'exalted' place in human and world affairs."[8]

France's staying power in Africa has been called one of the political and economic wonders of the post-imperial era.[9] What makes this situation even more remarkable is the enthusiastic endorsement of France's influence by most francophone African countries. According to John Chipman, French leaders have claimed, not entirely without reason, that for francophone African countries:

> their share of French power, grandeur and independence, which gives them a special status. On the other hand, a good deal of French activity in Africa has been taken not only with the compliance, but at the request of the Africans. French influence in the region has therefore come to be

related not only to the nature of power as deployed by French leaders, but also to the definition given that power by the Africans. Indeed the Africans have to some degree been the determinants of French power in Africa in that they have given sanction [...] to the importance of France on the continent.[10]

By its capacity to co-opt African elites, France has managed to create a relationship with francophone sub-Saharan Africa that defines the upper limits of the potential for cooperation within the EPI regime. France's continuing large presence in most of its former colonies produced a certain stability. This is not the least of France's achievements and reasons for its lasting power in post-imperial Africa. Hence, the African endorsement of French culture and vision is directly related to France's ability to guarantee security and stability. The general pattern has been for France to regulate the levels of violence and disorder within its zone of influence and to maintain them within acceptable limits. In general, where the French maintained garrisons "there were fewer military coups in the early years of independence than in either the former British possessions or those countries that rejected a continuing close relationship with France."[11]

France to this day is essentially a *status quo* power in its military approach to Africa. Stability has been the primary objective, justified initially by the need to assist fragile young governments. This was followed by attempts to contain Soviet-Cuban or Libyan forays into Black Africa, and then by efforts to smooth the potentially disruptive transition to democracy. Many African observers contend that French aid is destabilizing in the long run, because without French military intervention it is unlikely that any of the African armies supported by France could meet national or regional security challenges.[12]

Of all the EPI powers, only France has carried out an African strategy that had the advantage of best serving its own global interests and world vision. In 1982, President Mitterrand said to one of his advisors: "My real project is to build the unity of Europe so it can muster the courage to help the South, and Africa in particular. It is worrisome to see the amount of expectations which are addressed to our country. One wonders if we can satisfy them."[13]

Britain: Damage Limitation

"Since the late 1960s," according to James Mayall of the London School of Economics, "the contemporary problem for British governments in their relations with the non-European world can be fairly accurately, if somewhat negatively, described as damage limitation."[14] Britain had gradually shifted its economic power and diplomatic orientation toward Europe and away from Africa. Starting from this basic policy choice, Britain developed an African policy which would depart on many aspects from French policy in Africa. The post-imperial mindset of British policy-makers was one of seemingly reluctant involvement in overseas areas. Britain's adhesion to the EPI principles and rules was never as extensive as French adhesion; nevertheless, Britain has avoided abandoning all pretensions to a distinctive role in influencing events in sub-Saharan Africa. Britain's involvement over more than three decades was far more than just an honorable and graceful withdrawal from its African possessions. At the same time, British policies were less sanguine about Britain's involvement than was the case in France.

This attitude did not signal a complete abandonment of British policy objectives in Britain's approach to Africa. The residual concerns "were the protection of trade and investment and the provision of aid both as an inducement to African governments to stay within the liberal market order and as a more direct buttress to British exports."[15] Two geographic areas emerged naturally in the field of trade and investment: firstly, the important British investments in South Africa, and, at a later stage, the irresistible oil bounty in Nigeria. Involvement in each of these countries placed Britain in a delicate situation. Nigeria's importance to Britain faded with the gradual decline in oil prices during the 1980s, its chronic political instability, and the discovery of the North Sea oil fields. Relations with South Africa required a balancing act between economic involvement with that country and the inevitable international condemnation resulting from any association with the apartheid regime. Britain's qualified support (including military) to various Front Line States was partially thwarted by its resistance to trade sanctions against South Africa. The British government has tried "to have it both ways; i.e. to cooperate and contain simultaneously."[16] This dilemma in Britain's African policy disappeared after the May 1994 general elections in South Africa.

The British policy focus on trade and investment in selected zones presents a radical difference with France's indiscriminate approach to former colonies in Africa. This selectivity was possible because Britain did not have to preserve a central cultural or linguistic position in an anglophone African realm. Francophone Africa would be much more prone to divergent linguistic tendencies if support and direction were not forthcoming from Paris.

At the political level, Britain offered its former colonies membership in the Commonwealth. Nicholas Mansergh has best described the true expectations and stakes related to this unique institution:

> It was the past that suggested, first in a limited and mainly British colonial context, that in the face of quasi-nationalist or nationalist demands of autonomy, there was a possibility other than counter-resistance or abdication. That possibility was association, ultimately to be interpreted in terms of equality. [...] The extent to which there was an element of illusion on the British side about what was taking place, remains debatable. But even conceding that there was apt to be an over-sanguine interpretation of what the Commonwealth that superseded Empire would mean in terms of continuing British influence, that fictional ingredient served only to reinforce the fact in easing psychologically, and in a way that would otherwise have been inconceivable, the concluding stages of British colonisation.[17]

At the military level, Britain's pragmatic disengagement from Africa was followed by not much more than benign policing of a few selected areas. No home-based troops were specifically earmarked to contribute to missions in sub-Saharan Africa. After Britain's withdrawal from east of Suez, the whole continent ceased to figure among the security priorities of the British armed forces. French territories, on the contrary, were fundamentally more dependent on the ex-metropole for security than their British counterparts, and specialized French troops were earmarked for assignments in Africa.[18] Britain favored diplomacy over military interventions, even preventive ones, during crisis situations. Resources for peacetime military assistance programs were very limited compared to France's programs. Still, Britain has remained militarily involved in southern Africa through modest but highly valued military assistance programs and through its participation with Namibian and Angolan U.N. monitoring forces. The in-the-field impact of British involvement is largely political, a symbol of Britain's desire to continue to be counted as a force in Africa, albeit a moderate one. For African nations, the high-quality and superior professionalism of British training personnel and instructors make even modest assistance programs a much appreciated contribution. Britain's limited military presence in Africa is not subject to controversy at home. After the 1964 East African mutinies, British authorities never had to evacuate British citizens from the region for humanitarian purposes. Corollary to the almost complete political and military disengagement of Britain from Africa is the fact that British citizens were not often the targets of vindictive crowds, dissatisfied governments or frustrated rebels in any of sub-Saharan Africa's crises.

Belgium: Recovering from the Congolese Trauma

Belgium's approach to decolonization and subsequent crises in central Africa has been reactive rather than preventive. The sudden independence of the Congo found Belgium unprepared for a post-imperial role, despite its large economic interests in one of Africa's richest countries. The violent rejection of Belgian involvement and cooperation after Congolese independence delayed a comprehensive understanding between the ex-metropole and its immense former colony. The 1960 trauma was compounded by the 1964 Stanleyville rescue operation, which faced international condemnation although several hundred Belgians had been massacred. Subsequently, Belgium adopted a lower political-military profile and concentrated instead on its economic interests. It shied away from taking any role in the first Shaba crisis in 1977, thereby opening the door for French military involvement in Zaire.

From then on, Belgium lost its exclusive influence in Zaire. This represented a unique development under the EPI regime: it was a case of a joint zone of influence. Three of the more recent interventions, in Shaba (1978), Rwanda (1990), and Zaire (1991) have all been executed in conjunction with France. The latter gradually took the political lead in military interventions in the former Belgian colony. During the early phase of the 1991 operation in Zaire, France completely supplanted Belgium as the only true external power-broker in that country.[19] A similar development occurred during crises in Rwanda in 1992 and in Burundi in 1993.

If upset in the late 1970s by France's assertiveness in its traditional zone of interest, Belgium gradually learned to appreciate the advantages of joint management. By the early 1990s, with the political situation in a state of crises and confusion in Burundi, Rwanda and Zaire, Belgium and France began to cooperate, at times in exemplary fashion.

The international military activism of Belgium in the early 1990s is remarkable given the size and weight of the country on the world scene: Zaire, Rwanda, the Gulf War, the former Yugoslavia, Somalia and Rwanda again. In terms of military operations in sub-Saharan Africa, Belgium is far more active than Britain, and second only to France among foreign powers. This is partly a reflection of central Africa's chronic political and ethnic instability, but also of Belgium's commitment to continued influence in the region.

Africa: The Price of Stability

The impact of the EPI regime on African nations has been the subject of much controversy because the regime has been associated with neo-colonialism. There has been a growing chasm between the accusations of neo-colonialism and the decrease in Europe's real impact and authority in sub-Saharan Africa. President Kwame Nkrumah of Ghana was among the first to sense this gap when he warned that neo-colonialism was the worst kind of imperialism because, unlike the real thing, it constituted the exercise of power without responsibility.[20] By this definition, the EPI regime would fall somewhere between imperialism and neo-colonialism, as its principal achievement is precisely to re-inject a sense of responsibility in exchange for European influence in Africa.

The European responsibility in Africa derives somewhat from a moralistic impulse to support less developed countries, but the prime factor is self-interest. European powers had a stake in preserving and regulating stability in their zones of influence. From the time of independence, no alternative system was readily available to replace the EPI regime. African elites, once in power, endorsed the need for stability and worried about more radical changes. It appeared simpler and cheaper to deal with humbled former colonizers than to be left alone in an uncontrolled international environment.

Were African expectations with regard to the benefits of the EPI regime fulfilled? Was the European military involvement in post-colonial sub-Saharan Africa beneficial in terms of stability and peace-waging? Given the extremely limited number of international wars within the French, British or Belgian zones of influence, the benefits to African states must be measured in terms of domestic stability and levels of violent dissent. France's active management of stability in its African zone of influence seems to have produced statistically significant results when compared to political or even economic developments in the British or Belgian zones, or elsewhere in Africa. Studies based on data from 1960 to 1980 for thirty African countries found that the incidence of political instability in countries with a French colonial history is significantly lower than for countries with a non-French colonial history.[21] The French edge is particularly evident in reducing the levels of so-called communal instability (civil wars, rebellions and ethnic conflicts), as compared to elite instability through coups, attempted coups and plots. In other words, France's military and political role in Africa, as well as its substantial development aid, may only marginally reduce elite instability in the francophone zone compared to other zones, but it significantly reduces the communal expression of dissent.

Additional effects of France's presence in Africa can also be recorded. It is no coincidence that the four countries where France has constantly maintained garrisons (*forces de présence*), Senegal, Côte d'Ivoire, Gabon, and Djibouti, have all had uninterrupted civilian governments. Cameroon, with no permanent French bases, but with a French defense agreement, has also been ruled by civilian governments since its independence. The presence of French forces in these five African countries challenges the authority and influence of local military establishments and provides civilian authorities with insurance against military takeovers. The cases of Togo and the CAR challenge the otherwise strong correlation which exists between lasting French defense agreements and uninterrupted African civilian authority. The four African countries hosting French military bases, plus Cameroon, also figure among the top eight economically better-off countries in Black Africa.[22] This statement can be interpreted in different ways. On the one hand, lasting military stability enhances a country's prospects for economic development, as in Côte d'Ivoire and Senegal. On the other hand, French troop deployments can be a function of the host country's economic potential (Gabon's petroleum) or can be the cause of the host country's prosperity (as was the case with Djibouti, which thrived on French military spending).

The evidence for former British colonies is less conclusive and varies by region. English speaking West Africa has witnessed a lot of elite and communal instability. East Africa, with the exception of Uganda, has provided a politically more stable environment, no doubt partly triggered by the quelling of the East African mutinies in 1964. Southern Africa has been dominated by the destabilizing policies of South Africa, which in turn favored stability among the Front Line States. Belgium's former colonies in central Africa have enjoyed strong elite stability, although amidst a great deal of ethnic discontent.

The argument that the EPI powers favored elite stability has been used against the continuation of the EPI regime. Critics contend that by providing zealous support to African elites which were sometimes hand-picked, France and Belgium, and to a lesser degree Britain, may have smothered dissent in African countries and hence impeded democratic political changes. While there is little doubt that French, Belgian and British policies usually sought to avert elite turnover in their respective zones of influence, the record demonstrates without ambiguity that African countries outside the EPI regime, and hence with higher elite turnover, did not become more democratic. Again, the evidence through 1993 shows that former francophone colonies have been far more receptive to the wave of democratic reform than any other region of Africa. By that time, autocrats were voted out in Benin, Burundi, the Central African Republic, the Comoros, Congo, Mali, Niger, and Madagascar. A French impulse to advocate reform was not absent in promoting those changes, however imperfect or transient some may be. In anglophone Africa only Lesotho and Zambia succeeded in overthrowing an autocratic regime through elections.[23] According to a French academic, Jean-Louis Triaud, francophone constituencies in Africa have shown a greater initial enthusiasm for embracing the democratization movements than their anglophone counterparts precisely because they were locked in a very static political environment.[24] For better or worse, anglophone Africa has been subjected to greater political changes, a freer press, and often a more independent judiciary system than in many francophone countries. These virtues have been very unevenly distributed, but they may explain why anglophone countries have chosen a different, more independent road to democratization than francophone countries. The lesson to be drawn from this evidence is that strongest EPI power, France, is better than the weaker ones, Britain or Belgium, at managing stability, when such is its objective; France is also better at promoting change when transformations are overdue.

The African nations soon learned to master the advantages of belonging to EPI zones of influence. They were also aware of the regime's vulnerabilities, especially during the Cold War, and sometimes took full advantage of them. Ultimately, however, they were not successful in using the EPI regime as leverage to improve their general condition relative to the developed world.

A CHANGING E.P.I. REGIME

Regimes are "all arrangements reflecting policy contingency" and "mirror the evolving capacity of man to redefine and perhaps solve common problems."[25] After a period of persistence, regimes become interactive. The theorists of international regimes have established that a regime disappears or changes to a new regime when its fundamental norms and principles are abandoned. Changes of rules and decision-making procedures are merely changes within the regime. The regime is weakened when actual practice becomes increasingly inconsistent with principles, norms, rules and procedures.[26]

The essence of the EPI regime is the capacity of European powers to exercise influence over a part of sub-Saharan Africa. Hence, the regime's survival is linked to the critical leadership role played by the three European powers and the way such leadership can be upheld. Consequently, the European powers' lasting search for influence is at the core of the regime's rationale. The search is pursued with different intensity, ranging from France's voluntarist policies to Britain's moderate course, which is just sufficient to keep its options open. The EPI powers are also the providers of the collective goods needed to make the regime function smoothly and efficiently.

Have we reached a breaking point in the EPI regime where incongruencies between the regime and its causal variables are becoming so significant and lengthy that they fundamentally alter the regime itself? The answer is negative, although many variables and developments in international affairs have altered the regime's outlook. The question seems more pertinent since the fall of the Berlin Wall in 1989. The Cold War represented an exogenous force in intra-African relations and on western influence in Africa. The vehement anti-colonial position of the Soviet Union hastened the pace of decolonization. The EPI regime predates the African version of the Cold War, which started in the mid-1970s, and has also survived it, although superpower rivalry had an undeniable impact on the regime's development. The distortions in the regional balance of power which were the result of heavy Soviet-bloc involvement disappeared abruptly. Three important changes occurred almost simultaneously following the demise of the Soviet Union: greater assertiveness by the European EPI powers to reform Africa's political landscape, enlargement of the EPI regime to new European powers, and a resurgence of U.N. initiatives on the African continent.

Firstly, moralism, opportunism, and perhaps excessive exaltation pervaded western efforts to encourage democratic reform in sub-Saharan Africa. Typically, the first serious attempts to tilt political systems toward greater openness came through a French presidential "decree," when President Mitterrand, in a 1990 speech at La Baule, declared that democracy would be the new key word in Franco-African assistance programs. The urgency of democratization was later dropped quietly, and a more workable course was adopted. By gradually shifting their political support from old, unpopular African elites to democratically elected governments, France, Britain and Belgium have made an important gamble. If democratic reform is successful, they may eventually avert the collapse of the EPI regime by enhancing its popular appeal in Africa and giving it a new dynamism.

Secondly, while the Soviet bloc's influence in the Third World repressed or dwarfed the attempts of many former colonial powers to retain any type of bond with their former possessions that could resemble anything close to what France, Britain or Belgium have achieved, the collapse of the Soviet Union allowed these powers to recuperate some of the lost political space. Portugal's timid attempts to provid military advisors to Angola and Mozambique, Italy's impressive military contribution of 2,300 troops to the U.N. force in Somalia, and the arrival of the first German troops in sub-Saharan Africa since World War I as part of its 1,200-troop contingent to U.N. forces in Somalia, indicate some initial movement in those countries to join the EPI regime. To a lesser extent, the same was true for the German and Italian contributions to the Rwanda evacuation operation in April 1994. For both Portugal and Italy, military involvement has become an instrument to mark a special responsibility and quest for influence in former colonies, even after absences of 16 and 50 years, respectively. Their attempts are an extraordinary testimony to the highly uncommon bond created by former colonial links, and to the fact that this bond has to be embodied by some kind of military involvement when needed.

Finally, the end of Soviet involvement in sub-Saharan Africa favored a renewed U.N. activism in the region. The Soviet Union's first steps into sub-Saharan Africa came during the 1960 U.N. military operation in the Congo, the largest U.N. military operation up to that point. The pro-western orientation of the subsequent Congolese regime must have cautioned leaders in Moscow, because thereafter the superpowers could never agree to launch a U.N. operation of that magnitude during the Cold War. Not surprisingly, the post-Soviet world saw a resurgence of large U.N. operations, including in sub-Saharan Africa. In its dealings with Somalia or Cambodia, the U.N. displays a behavior that commentators, regardless of whether they favor or oppose such operations, have at times labeled as colonial.[27] Perhaps it would be more accurate to consider U.N. operations as a multilateral version of the EPI regime, with stronger idealistic or moralistic overtones. Influence is sought to pursue the universal interests of humanitarian relief and a basic framework for good governance.

The enlargement of the EPI regime to newcomers and the multilateralization of its norms and decision-making procedures testify to its endorsement by a larger community as a viable, if imperfect, model for conducting North-South relations. Democratization, enlargement and multilateralization may change the EPI regime, but they do not fundamentally weaken it. The EPI regime is based on the notion of influence. It thrives on international disparities in power, which are often due to disparities in wealth. At the end of the 20th century, Africa is characterized by two numbers: 8 percent of the world population for 1 percent of world trade. The day this continent, endowed with vast resources, can reverse its marginalization on the international chessboard, and the day it is fully in charge of its own security, will be the day Africa will cease to be a target for foreign influence. Nothing would be more upsetting to the architects and defenders of the post-imperial EPI regime. For them, that would be a day to be in a disconsolate mood indeed.

Notes

Chapter 1

1. Michael W. Doyle, *Empires* (Ithaca, NY: Cornell University Press, 1986), 12.

2. Ibid.

3. "Colonisation," *Encyclopaedia Universalis* vol. 4 (Paris: Encyclopaedia Universalis, 1980), 709.

4. Ibid., 710.

5. D.K. Fieldhouse, *The Colonial Empires* (London: Weidenfield and Nicolson, 1966), 395.

6. George Kennan, *Russia, the Atom and the West* (New York: Harper & Brothers Publishers, 1958), 74.

7. Hon. Alastair Buchan, M.B.E., "Britain East of Suez: Part One - The Problem of Power," *RUSI* CXII, no. 647 (August 1967): 209.

8. Christopher Coker, "South Africa's Strategic Importance: a Re-assessment," *RUSI* 124, no. 4 (December 1979): 24.

9. George H.T. Kimble, "Colonialism: The Good, the Bad, the Lessons," *The New York Times*, 26 August 1962.

10. *The Oxford English Dictionary, Second Edition* (Oxford: Clarendon Press, 1989) Volume VII, 939-40.

11. Doyle, 19-50; Adapted from Doyle's classification of international political inequalities.

12. Ibid., 40.

13. Brian Barry, *Economic Approach to the Analysis of Power*, in Doyle, 41.

14. "The Great Dance resumes," *The Economist*, 21 December 1991 - 3 January 1992, 62.

15. Adapted from *Encyclopaedia Universalis* vol. 11, 668.

16. "Impérialisme et anti-impérialisme," *Encyclopaedia Universalis* vol. 8, 753.

17. Lord Beloff, "The End of the British Empire," in W.M. Roger Louis and Hedley Bull, *The Special Relationship: Anglo-American Relationships since 1945* (Oxford: Clarendon Press, 1986), 257.

18. Cited by André Fontaine, "Y a-t-il encore un 'Super-Grand'," *Sélection hebdomadaire du journal "le Monde"*, 25-31 October 1990, 3.

19. Edward Mortimer, "America, Europe, and the Imperial Legacy," in Louis and Bull, 357.

20. James Mayall, "Africa in Anglo-American Relations," in Louis and Bull, 331.

21. Raymond Aron, "Qu'est-ce qu'une Théorie des Relations Internationales?" *Revue française de Science politique*, October 1967, 843.

22. Robert E. Osgood, "The Nature of Alliances," *U.S. National Security Policy*, edited by Daniel J. Kaufman, Jeffrey S. McKitrich and Thomas J. Lency (Lexington, MA: Lexington Books, 1985), 63.

23. Quote from Josef Joffe, "You can't go home again," *U.S. News & World Report*, 4 February 1991, 56.

24. Joseph Conrad, *The Heart of Darkness* (New York: Bantam Books, 1989), 9.

25. Louis de Guiringaud as quoted by Christian d'Epenoux and Christian Hoche, "Giscard l'Africain" *L'Express*, 22 December 1979, 38.

26. Chester A. Crocker, "Military Dependence: the Colonial Legacy in Africa," *The Journal of Modern African Studies* 12, no. 2 (1974), 265-86. The article derived from his earlier, unpublished doctoral thesis "The Military Transfer of Power in Africa: a comparative study of change in the British and French systems of order," Johns Hopkins University, Washington, D.C., 1969. The following section draws on some of his conclusions.

27. Ibid., 268.

28. Chef de bataillon Le Seigneur, statement collected by J. Guillemin, "Coopération internationale: politique militaire de la France en Afrique noire francophone et Madagascar," (Ph.D. diss., University of Nice, 1979), 8; as quoted by Tshiyembe Mwayila, "Théorie et pratique de la stratégie Est-Ouest en Afrique : première partie," *Le mois en Afrique*, June-July 1986.

29. According to a source for 1926; quoted in Michel Martin, "From Algiers to N'Djamena: France's Adaptation to Low-Intensity Wars, 1830-1987," in David Charters and Maurice Tugwell, *Armies in Low-Intensity Conflict* (London: Brassey's Defence Publishers, 1989), 94.

30. Crocker, 276.

31. Louis and Bull, 279.

32. Crocker, 273.

33. A.F. Mullins, Jr., *Born Arming: Development and Military Power in New States* (Stanford, CA: Stanford University Press, 1987), 17.

34. Ibid., 18.

35. Simon Baynham, *The Military and Politics in Nkrumah's Ghana* (Boulder, CO: Westview Press, 1988), 25.

36. Ibid., 277.

37. Ibid.

38. Martin, "From Algiers to N'Djamena: France's Adaptation to Low-Intensity Wars, 1830-1987," 94.

39. Mullins, 20.

40. This is in addition to six battalions of King's African Rifles, 21,000 police and more than 20,000 Kikuyu Home Guardsmen. Before the end of the Mau Mau insurgency, the RAF dropped a total of 50,000 tons of bombs. For more details, see Robert B. Edgerton, *Mau-Mau: An African Crucible* (New York: The Free Press, 1989), 85-7.

41. Crocker, 283.

42. Mullins, 111.

43. Ibid.

44. Crocker, 284.

45. Stephen D. Krasner, *International Regimes* (Ithaca: Cornell University Press, 1983), 2.

46. Ibid., 3.

47. Ibid., 5.

48. Ibid., 15-6.

49. Donald J. Puchala and Raymond F. Hopkins, "International Regimes: Lessons form Inductive Analysis," in Krasner, 68.

50. Ibid., 70-2.

Chapter 2

1. Louis de Guiringaud as quoted in Christian d'Epenoux and Christian Hoche, "Giscard l'Africain" *L'Express*, 22 December 1979, 38.

2. Jacques Attali, *Verbatim I: 1981-1986* (Paris: Fayard, 1993), 378.

3. Michel Schifres and Michel Sarazin, *L'Elysée de Mitterrand, secrets de la maison du Prince* (Paris: Alain Moreau, 1985), 178.

4. Samy Cohen, "Monarchie nucléaire, dyarchie conventionelle," *Pouvoirs* 38 (1986): 13. France's first woman prime minister, Edith Cresson, was appointed only in May 1991, explaining the sole use of the masculine pronoun.

5. CREST/Ecole Polytechnique, *Quelles structures pour les interventions militaires multinationales?* (Paris: CREST/Ecole Polytechnique, 1992), 6.

6. Jean Guisnel and Bernard Violet, *Services secrets: Le pouvoir et les services de renseignement sous François Mitterrand* (Paris: Editions la Découverte, 1988), 135.

7. "Au Sommet," *Armées d'aujourd'hui*, no. 128 (March 1988): 24-25; 1986 figure for personnel in Guisnel and Violet, 133.

8. CREST/Ecole Polytechnique, 9.

9. Colonel Jean-Pierre Goze, "Préparation interarmées," *Armées d'aujourd'hui*, no. 83 (September 1983): 30.

10. Schifres and Sarazin, 178.

11. Ibid., 168.

12. Epenoux and Hoche, 37.

13. Jacques Amalric, "Plaies d'Afrique: V. - La France embourbée," *Le Monde* (Paris), Edition international - Sélection hebdomadaire, 14-20 June 1990, 2.

14. Francis Terry McNamara, *France in Black Africa* (Washington, D.C.: National Defense University Press, 1989), 203.

15. *Tuned into the South - France, a Positive Partner for Developing Countries* (Paris: French Government, April 1990), section 2.

16. "La politique française de coopération," Communiqué, *Marchés Tropicaux* (25 December 1987).

17. *Tuned into the South*, section 5.

18. Benin, Burkina Faso, Cameroon, the Central African Republic, Chad, the Comoros, Congo, Côte d'Ivoire, Equatorial Guinea, Gabon, Mali, Niger, Senegal, and Togo.

19. Richard Joseph, *Gaullist Africa: Cameroon under Ahmadu Ahidjo* (New York: Fourth Dimension Publishers, 1978), 18.

20. *Tuned into the South*, section 4.

21. Refers to "Communauté Financière Africaine" in West Africa and "Coopération Financière en Afrique centrale" in central Africa.

22. *Tuned into the South*, section 4.

23. "La Caisse centrale de Coopération économique," *Marché tropicaux et mediterranéens*, 17 April 1992, 969-70.

24. Quoted in J. Coleman Kitchen and Jean-Paul Paddack, "The 1990 Franco-African Summit," *CSIS Africa Notes*, no. 115 (30 August 1990): 2-3.

25. Mark B. Hayne, "The Quai d'Orsay and the Formation of French Foreign Policy in Historical Context," in *France in World Politics*, ed. Robert Aldrich and John Connell (New York: Routledge, 1987), 194.

26. Ibid., 198.

27. Malawi, an anglophone country, received limited assistance, including some military advisers, to cope with Mozambican RENAMO rebels.

28. François Soudan, "Roland Dumas: l'ami du Prince," *Jeune Afrique* (25 May 1988): 16.

29. Ibid.

30. Frédéric Dorce, "L'Afrique, un marché profitable," *Jeune Afrique*, 13-26 August 1992, 133-5.

31. Frédéric Dorce, "Les deux mamelles de la France en Afrique," Ibid., 100.

32. Géraldine Faes, "Dix ans d'immobilisme politique," *Jeune Afrique*, 13-26 August 1992, 107.

33. Jacques Foccart as quoted in Lavroff, *La politique africaine du Général de Gaulle (1958-1969)* (Paris: A. Pedone, 1979), 402.

34. McNamara, 80-81. After asking a question about the prospects of French Community, Jean Mauriac reported the following comment by General de Gaulle in 1958: "At that moment, [de Gaulle] looked at me with condescension: 'The Community, you may say, is rubbish...These people, once part of it, will only have one idea, that is to quit it.' And he added: 'But anyway, it had to be done.'" (Lavroff, 387.)

35. Gilbert Pilleul, quoted in Lavroff, 387.

36. Pierre Lellouche and Dominique Moisi, "French Policy in Africa: A Lonely Battle Against Destabilization," *International Security* 3, no. 4 (Spring 1979): 111.

37. Ibid.

38. John Chipman, *French Power in Africa* (Cambridge, MA: Basil Blackwell, 1989), 109.

39. Tamar Golan, "A Certain Mystery: How Can France Do Everything That It Does In Africa - And Get Away With It?," *African Affairs* 80, no. 318 (London: The Royal African Society, January 1981): 3.

40. William Zartman, "French Policies," Paper presented at the Herbert Wilson Griffin Seminar in International Affairs by the Dacor Bacon House Foundation entitled "*Sub-Saharan Africa in the 1990s*," Washington, D.C., 27 September 1988, 160-4.

41. There is the well-known declaration of Gaston Monnerville before the *Assemblée Consultative* on May 25, 1945, which is quite explicit in acknowledging France's debt to its colonies: "Without its Empire, today France would only be a liberated country. Thanks to its Empire, France is a victorious country." Quoted in Pascal Chaigneau, *La politique militaire de la France* (Paris: Publications du CHEAM, 1984), 13.

42. Zartman, 161.

43. "France's fading affair with Africa," *The Economist*, 22 April 1989, 39.

44. Lellouche and Moisi, 114.

45. Jacques Foccart, quoted in Lavroff, 403.

46. McNamara, 191.

47. Pierre Haski, "Business as Usual?," *Africa Report* (July-August 1986): 17.

48. McNamara, 195.

49. Général Gallois presented another argument on how France's membership in the club of nuclear-armed nations could affect its policies in the Third World. "These nuclear powers are keener on using this freedom of action and to intervene wherever they can in the world because of the total impunity, at least at home, which the atom is giving them. They know that the conflicts which they provoke [...] cannot harm them, that the combats which decide the

extent of their spheres of influence, do not risk accelerating into higher intensity conflicts in which their own territory would become the theater and the victim [...]. While nuclear weapons allow for risk-free actions abroad, decolonization has given them vast areas of instability where to intervene." Général Gallois, *Le Renoncement* (Paris: Plon, 1977), 81; quoted in Chaigneau, 85.

50. Lellouche and Moisi, 116.
51. Michel L. Martin, "From Algiers to N'Djamena: France's adaptation to low-intensity wars, 1830-1987," in *Armies in Low-Intensity Conflict*, ed. David Charters and Maurice Tugwell (London: Brassey's Defence Publishers, 1989), 109.
52. Chaigneau, 70.
53. John Chipman, *La République et Défense de l'Afrique* (Paris: Bosquet, 1986), 29-30.
54. Ibid., 30.
55. Chipman, *French Power in Africa*, 126-7.
56. The new nomination of Foccart by Pompidou apparently did not go without strong initial objections by the latter. It was necessary to invoke the wish of General de Gaulle to have Pompidou accept this "legacy." Pierre Péan, *L'homme de l'ombre* (Paris: Fayard, 1990), 439-40.
57. Chipman, *French Power in Africa*, 129.
58. Examples of this are Zaire in 1977 and 1978 and Rwanda in 1990. The military dimension of the Franco-African special relationship continued to receive enough support from African countries so as not to significantly affect overall French military policies in sub-Saharan Africa.
59. Pascal Chaigneau, 14-15. Since the situation in Europe was frozen due to the U.S. nuclear umbrella, Soviet expansionism could only be directed toward Asia and Africa.
60. Kitchen and Paddack, 1.
61. Chipman, *French Power in Africa*, 127.
62. McNamara, 184.
63. Louis de Guiringaud, "La politique africaine de la France," *Politique étrangère* (June 1982): 445.
64. Lellouche and Moisi, 119.
65. Général Méry, "L'Avenir de nos Armées," *Défense nationale* (June 1978): 21, quoted in Lellouche and Moisi, 120.
66. Robin Luckham, "Le militarisme français," *Politique africaine* 2, no. 6 (May 1982): 59.
67. "Then, I noted in this respect that one talked about 'NATO-ization'! I will tell you, when the thinking is weak, it hides behind slogans....The question of knowing whether France decided to send a unit to assist threatened Europeans or compatriots by herself, in a territory not covered by NATO, has no relationship whatsoever with any problems which NATO is competent to

address." President Giscard d'Estaing in *Le Monde*, 16 June 1978, quoted in Luckham, 57-58.

68. Lellouche and Moisi, 133.

69. Romain Yakemtchouk, "Les Deux Guerres du Shaba," *Studia Diplomatica* 41, no. 4-5-6 (Brussels: Institut Royal des Relations Internationales, 1988), 458.

70. Ibid., 467.

71. Ibid., 130.

72. Daniel C. Bach, "La France et la sécurité du continent africain: du bilatéralisme au multilatéralisme bien tempéré" [draft], Paper prepared for the PISA Conference, Tangier, 2-6 July 1989, 6.

73. Luckham, 62.

74. McNamara, 184.

75. Belgian foreign minister Van Elslande, in "Van Elslande: Maar wat gebeurt er nu juist?," *Knack* (20 April 1977), quoted in Yakemtchouk, 464. Van Elslande responded to a question on whether there was a conflictual situation between France and Belgium: "For two years, we have suggested to France not to engage in overbidding in Africa. We have indicated to them that the Belgians have not disturbed them in regions where France has historic interests and we asked them in turn not to do this to the Belgians elsewhere in Africa....There exists between the two countries an international economic rivalry. We continually experience the result of their interest in the riches of Zaire."

76. Chipman, *French Power in Africa*, 130.

77. Chaigneau, 53.

78. Lellouche and Moisi, 121.

79. Chaigneau, 81.

80. Ibid., 80 and 86.

81. Lellouche and Moisi, 123.

82. McNamara, 166.

83. *Le Monde*, 13 June 1978; in Luckham, 58.

84. Bach, 6.

85. McNamara, 169.

86. Jean-Marie Colombani and Jean-Yves Lhomeau, *Le Mariage Blanc* (Paris: Grasset, 1986), 168.

87. Bach, 7.

88. Albert Lebacqz, *Le Septennat* (Paris: Editions France-Empire, 1980), 64.

89. J.J. Jonas and A. Noury, *Giscard de tous les jours* (Paris: Fayolle, 1978), 100, quoted in Yakemtchouk, 407.

90. Lebacqz, 63.

91. Lellouche and Moisi, 126.

92. Martin Staniland, "Francophone Africa: The Enduring French Connection," *The Annals of the American Academy*, no. 489 (AAPSS, January 1987): 58.

93. Jean-Pierre Cot, "What Change?" *Africa Report* (May-June 1983): 12.

94. Jean-Pierre Cot, *A l'épreuve du pouvoir: Le tiers-mondisme, pour quoi faire?* (Paris: Seuil, 1984), 10.

95. Ibid., 23.

96. Ibid., 85-86.

97. Jean-Marc Kalflèche, "Mitterrand et l'Afrique: De la 'stratégie' à la réalité," *Le Figaro* (Paris), 4 August 1981, 3.

98. Jean-François Bayart, *La politique africaine de François Mitterrand* (Paris: Editions Karthala, 1984), 26.

99. Ibid., 28.

100. McNamara, 202.

101. Bayart, 36.

102. Ibid., 75-76.

103. Philippe Decraene, "Viewing Africa from the Elysée," *Optima* (30 March 1984): 5.

104. In 1993, the *Epervier* system was still in place.

105. McNamara, 206.

106. See next chapter for details.

107. In an article by J.C. Pomonti entitled, "M. Mitterrand entend dédramatiser les relations franco-africaines," in *Le Monde*, 20 January 1983. Mitterrand was quoted as declaring: "I am the one who determines French foreign policy, not my ministers [...]. It is not forbidden for Ministers to think or to have an opinion [...]. It is not conceivable that a policy would be implemented without my agreement, or more precisely, without my impulsion." Bayart, 48.

108. Colombani and Lhomeau, 156.

109. Ibid.

110. Press articles quoted by J. Coleman Kitchen, "The Enduring French Connection," *CSIS Africa Notes*, no. 68 (26 January 1987): 2.

111. Interview by the author.

112. Haski, 20.

113. McNamara, 215.

114. Bach, 11.

115. Chipman, *French Power in Africa*, 136.

116. Stéphane Hessel, "Il faut réviser, réformer, réfléchir...," interview by Hugo Sada, *Jeune Afrique* (11 June 1990): 20.

117. Ibid., 21.

118. A report by Jean-Pierre Prouteau on behalf of the French business leaders' syndicate entitled, *Rapport patronal 1988 France-Afrique*, (Paris: Comité ACP-CNPF & Conseil des Investisseurs français en Afrique-noire, 1987) analyses these trends in greater detail.

119. France responds to this by trying to shape multilateral policies from within. See Serge Degallaix, "Les nouveaux rapports franco-africains," *Revue des deux mondes* (May 1989): 30-32.

120. François Soudan, "Mais que veut donc la France quand l'Afrique bouge?" *Jeune Afrique* (11 June 1990): 6.

121. François Mitterrand, quoted in Kitchen and Paddack, 2.

122. François Mitterrand in "Un entretien avec François Mitterrand," *Le Monde* (Paris), Edition internationale - Sélection hebdomadaire, 14-20 June 1990, 7.

123. Hugo Sada, "Chaillot n'est pas La Baule," *Jeune Afrique* (27 November - 3 December 1991): 4.

124. "Under slow notice to quit," *The Economist*, 6 July 1991, 39.

125. François Soudan, "Jacques Pelletier: pas de préjugés," *Jeune Afrique* (25 May 1988): 14.

126. Soudan, "Mais que veut donc la France quand l"Afrique bouge?" 7.

127. François Soudan, "Paul Biya: 'Il' nous a compris," *Jeune Afrique* (27 November - 3 December 1991): 7.

128. Colette Braeckman, "Démocraties africaines: un temps d'arrêt..." *Le Soir*, 17 December 1991.

129. Pierre Haski, "La ligne de partage des domaines 'réservés'," *Libération*, 31 March 1993, 10.

130. Dominique Garraud, "Défense: pas de guerre de tranchée," *Libération*, 31 March 1993, 10.

131. "France, The African village waits for the polls," *Africa Confidential*, 4 December 1992, 5.

132. Ibid.

133. Bach, 17.

134. Bayart, 54.

135. J.-B. Duroselle, *Histoire diplomatique de 1919 à nos jours* (Paris: Dalloz, 1978), 729.

136. Emeka Nwokedi, "Franco-African summits: a new instrument for France's African strategy?" *The World Today* 38, no. 12 (December 1982): 478.

137. Malyn Newitt, *The Comoro Islands* (Boulder, CO: Westview Press, 1984), 127.

138. Stephen Smith, "Le sommet perd sa base," *Africa International*, no. 115 (January 1989): 25.

139. Nwokedi, 478.

140. Ibid., 482.

141. Smith, 24.

142. Ibid.

143. Kitchen and Paddack, 1-2.

144. Marie-Pierre Subtil, "M. Bérégovoy invite ses interlocuteurs africains à une gestion plus rigoureuse," *Le Monde*, 9 October 1993, 7.

145. Elimane Fall, "Le sommet des désillusions," *Jeune Afrique*, 15-21 Octobeer 1992, 5.

146. Subtil, 7.

147. Golan, 4-5. "Two days after Cecil Dennis returned to Monrovia, the coup d'état of Master-Sergeant Samuel Doe took place. Cecil Dennis was arrested (and later executed). The only intervention on his behalf was that of France."

148. See Chapter 6 on the British Commonwealth.

149. Cot, *A l'épreuve du pouvoir*, 130.

150. "Rwanda's perpetual war," *The Economist*, 6 June 1992, 54.

151. "133,840,000 locuteurs dans le monde," *Jeune Afrique* (27 November - 3 December 1991): 73.

152. Quoted by Jacques Hislaire, "La France mène le bal du Dodo (mauricien)," *La Libre Belgique*, 19 October 1993, 5.

153. Andrei Magheru, a member of the Romanian delegation, declared at the occasion of the Paris meeting that for his country: "*Francophonie* means a return to our roots." The Bulgarian spokesman, Gregory Spassov, made no secret of his country's motivations to join the Summit: "We would join any international grouping which would want us. If it were possible, we would adhere to the Commonwealth." Quoted by Sophie Boukhari in "Ils ont dit" *Jeune Afrique* (27 November - 3 December 1991): 10.

154. Ibid., 5.

155. "Il faut montrer la francophonie," *Africa International* (November 1991): 86.

156. Marie-Roger Biloa, "Un premier bilan," *Africa International* (November 1991): 84.

157. Ibid., 84.

158. Nwokedi, 482.

159. Dennis Austin and Keith Panter-Brick, *Post-Colonialism*, University of Manchester, unpublished paper, sine loco, sine dato, 2.

160. Kitchen and Paddack, 3.

Chapter 3

1. "Budget 93," *Armées d'aujourd'hui*, February 1993, 38-9.

2. International Institute of Strategic Studies, *The Military Balance: 1993-4* (London: Brassey's, 1993), 41-4.

3. Dominique Garraud, "L'Armée: la réforme avance en tenue de camouflage," *Libération*, 31 March 1993, 3.

4. Dominique Garraud, "Joxe renforce l'état-major des armées," *Libération*, 11 February 1993, 9.

5. Pierre-Yves Le Bail, "Nouvelle dynamique de défense," *Armées d'aujourd'hui* (May 1990): 13; and J. A. C. Lewis, "France to Begin Force Pull-Out," *Jane's Defence Weekly* (1 September 1990): 301.

6. Giovanni de Briganti, "Government Review Aims To Pare Military Force," *Defense News*, 27 September - 3 October 1993, 12.

7. J. L. P. Nouvel, "From the Land That Created the Word 'élite'," *National Defense* (December 1990): 58; and J. A. C. Lewis, "France: Fighting to Maintain a Credible Deterrence," *Jane's Defence Weekly* (4 May 1991): 728.

8. *Force d'Action Rapide*, FAR, Maisons-Laffitte, sine loco, sine dato, presentation brochure.

9. Francis Terry McNamara, *France in Black Africa* (Washington, D.C.: National Defense University Press, 1989), 161.

10. General Jeannou Lacaze, interviewed by Jean de Gallard, "La FAR et l'utilisation des satellites militaires," *Air et Cosmos* no. 1002 (19 May 1984): 42.

11. Général de corps d'armée Préaud, "La Force d'Action Rapide (FAR)," *Bulletin Trimestriel de l'Association des Amis de l'Ecole Supérieure de Guerre* (1st Trimester 1989): 21.

12. Colonel Bertrand de la Croix de Vaubois, "Commander en temps réel," *Armées d'aujourd'hui* (December 1984): 36.

13. General Fricaud-Chagnaud, *Origine, moyens, signification de la Force d'Action Rapide*, Conference Paper, Woodrow Wilson Center, Washington, D.C., 30 October 1984, 8.

14. "Quand tout a commencé," *Armées d'aujourd'hui* (June-July 1991): 14.

15. Erwan Bergot, *Opération Daguet: les Français dans la Guerre du Golfe* (Paris: Presses de la Cité, 1991), 274.

16. The theoretical mobility of the 4th Airmobile Division confers it with an ability to engage enemy forces up to 350 km away within half a day. However, if one takes into account the war conditions, the fighting maneuvers, and the return trip, the combat range of these helicopters is closer to 100 km without refueling.

17. "The French Army: Shield and sword for Europe?" *The Economist*, 23 June 1984, 38.

18. Fricaud-Chagnaud, 7.

19. "The French Army: Shield and sword for Europe?," 39.

20. Bergot, 267.

21. Diego Ruiz Palmer, "France," in Jeffrey Simon, *NATO-Warsaw Pact Force Mobilization* (Washington, D.C.: National Defense University Press, September 1988), 287.

22. Préaud, 21.

23. Dominique David, "La FAR en Europe: le dire des armes," *Défense nationale* (June 1984): 46.

24. Source: International Institute of Strategic Studies, London.

25. Norman Friedman, "Regional Naval Reviews: Western Europe," *Proceedings* (March 1991): 101.

26. *Dossier d'information de la Marine* (Paris: Etat-Major de la Marine, Bureau "Etudes Générales," 1990), 6-7.

27. Friedman, 101.

28. *Dossier d'information de la Marine*, 10.

29. Jean-Michel Boucheron, *Rapport Fait au Nom de la Commission de la Défense Nationale et des Forces Armées (1) Sur le Projet de Loi de Programmation (no. 733) relatif à l'équipment militaire pour les années 1990-1993*, Constitution du 4 October 1958, Assemblée Nationale, Neuvième Législature, Première Session Ordinaire de 1989-1990, 340.

30. A study by the Congressional Research Service found that U.S. carriers spend only 20% or less of their time actively deployed overseas. This assumes that it takes about 4.5 carriers to maintain one carrier permanently deployed in a given location. The U.S. Navy's traditional claim has been that the ratio was closer to 33%. (*Inside the Pentagon* [April 27, 1990]: 6). France does not have such requirements and does not try to have a carrier continuously deployed at a specific location; rather, the criterion is to maintain one carrier in a permanent 24 hour state of alert at a home port, which represents 50% readiness for a fleet of two carriers.

31. The maximum continuous deployment period for a French carrier is about 150 days. This does not mean that the carrier can remain autonomous for that long. With one tanker as supply ship, the carrier must remain within 1,000 nautical miles of a supply base; with two tankers, the distance increases to 2,500 nautical miles.

32. Boucheron, 121.

33. Ibid., 127.

34. Captain Richard Sharpe RN, ed., *Jane's Fighting Ships: 1990-91* (Surrey: Jane's Information Group, 1990), 181.

35. *Dossier d'information de la Marine*, 76.

36. Sharpe, 183.

37. Ibid., 194.

38. Admiral B. Louzeau, "La Marine aujourd'hui et demain," *Revue Maritime* (Fall 1988): 25.

39. A.D. Baker III, "Combat Fleets of the World," *Proceedings* (May 1991): 245.

40. "OSD Officials Quietly Explore Using Conventional Subs for Some Navy Missions," *Inside the Pentagon* (24 October 1991): 6.

41. Christopher Chant, *Super Etendard* (Sparkford: Haynes Publishing Group, 1983), 54.

42. Chris Bishop and David Donald, *The Encyclopedia of World Military Power* (New York: The Military Press, 1986), 61.

43. Louzeau, 27.

44. *Dossier d'information de la marine*, 40.

45. Ibid.

46. "Gulf Prompts WEU Panel to Urge New Airlift, Satellite Agencies," *Aerospace Daily* (20 June 1991): 483.

47. "Transports and Tankers," *Air Force Magazine* (May 1991): 170.

48. Interview by the author with a former French Air Force general in charge of airlift, Paris, February 1990.

49. General Henri Paris, "La stratégie militaire française en Afrique subsaharienne," *Relations internationales et stratégiques* 4 (Winter 1991): 105.

50. Giovanni de Briganti, "French Near Completion of Air Transport Update Plan," *Defense News* (26 March 1990): 7.

51. IISS, 65-66; and "French Buy Two More Lockheed Giant Transports," *Defense Week* (19 November 1990): 11.

52. Boucheron, 393.

53. Group Captain Keith Chapman, "Military Air Transport Operations," *Brassey's Air Power Series 6* (London: Brassey's Ltd., 1989), 72-80.

54. Needs for the CN-235 were estimated at 15 aircraft. Boucheron, 393.

55. Konrad Alder, "A Survey of Western Air Transport Capabilities," *Armada International* (March 1989): 49.

56. De Briganti, "French Near Completion of Air Transport Update Plan," 7.

57. To circumvent this requirement, the regular tanks of cargo planes are often filled completely with fuel, which is then siphoned out at the destination for use in military aircraft.

58. Interview by author with former French Air Force General, Paris, February 1990.

59. *Super Profile: SEPECAT Jaguar* (Somerset: Haynes, 1984), 56.

60. Jeffrey M. Lenorovitz, "French Use Jaguar Fighter/Bombers To Strike Desert Storm Targets," *Aviation Week & Space Technology* (28 January 1991): 23.

61. Général d'armée de l'air Jean Fleury, "Stratégie aérienne et armée de l'air," *Défense nationale* (April 1990): 19.

62. Jeffrey M. Lenorovitz, "French AS30L Laser Missiles Scored High Hit Rate in Air-Ground Attacks," *Aviation Week & Space Technology* (22 April 1991): 109.

63. Jeffrey M. Lenorowitz, "France Uses C.160G Aircraft To Perform Elint, ESM Missions," *Aviation Week & Space Technology* (21 January 1991): 62.

64. The E-3F is the French version of the E-3A AWACS. "French Getting First AWACS," *Aviation Week & Space Technology* (21 January 1991): 15.

65. Brigadier General Jay D. Blume, "The E-3A Component - A Unique Multinational Element," *NATO's Sixteen Nations - Special Edition* 35, no.7 (December 1990): 11.

66. Boucheron, 398.

67. Peter de Selding, "Defense Minister Invites French Emphasis on Spy Satellites," *Defense News* (13 May 1991): 50.

68. Ibid.

69. John Chipman, "French Military Policy and African Security," *Adelphi Papers*, no. 201 (Summer 1985): 6.

70. Pascal Chaigneau, *La politique militaire de la France*, (Paris: Publications du CHEAM, 1984), 22.

71. French government official, interview by author, Paris, February 1990.

72. Chaigneau, 23.

73. John Chipman, "French Military Assistance to Sub-Saharan Africa," in *Final Report: U.S.-Allied Cooperation in Security Assistance to Sub-Saharan Africa* (Washington, D.C.: Center for Strategic and International Studies, 27 February 1991): 9.

74. John Chipman, "French Military Policy and African Security," *Adelphi Papers*, no. 201 (Summer 1985): 6.

75. Jacques Guillemin, "L'Importance des Bases dans la Politique Militaire de la France en Afrique Noire Francophone et Madagascar," *Le Mois en Afrique* (August-September 1981): 33.

76. Fondation pour les Etudes de Défense Nationale, *France, Océan, Mer Rouge* (Paris: *Fondation pour les Etudes de Défense Nationale*, 1986), 321-2. However, the mobility of French forces deployed "temporarily" in Chad and the CAR are greater, as demonstrated by the 1990 operation in Rwanda.

77. Chaigneau, 41.

78. "Huit traités de défense et vingt-trois accords d'assistance," *Le Monde*, 25 November 1991.

79. Stephen Smith, "La France perd son âme africaine," *Africa International* (January 1989): 22.

80. The Ministry of Foreign Affairs manages the military cooperation programs in North Africa, the Middle East, and Ecuador.

81. Colonel Michel Sabourault, "Aider sans aliéner," *Armées d'aujourd'hui*, no. 143 (September 1989): 33-34.

82. Chipman, "French Military Assistance to Sub-Saharan Africa," 14.

83. Sabourault, 34.

84. Chipman, "French Military Assistance to Sub-Saharan Africa," 20; based on figures from the French Ministry of Cooperation.

85. "Huits traités de défense et vingt-trois accords d'assistance."

86. Ibid.

87. Chipman, "French Military Assistance to Sub-Saharan Africa," 23.

88. Ibid., 13.

89. U.S. Arms Control and Disarmament Agency, *World Military Expenditures and Arms Transfers: 1989* (Washington, D.C.: Government Printing Office, October 1990), 119.

90. Ibid., 120.

91. John Chipman, *French Power in Africa* (Cambridge, MA: Basil Blackwell, 1989), 147; and a French Army officer, interview by author, Paris, February 1990.

92. Chipman, "French Military Assistance to Sub-Saharan Africa," 17 and 38.

Chapter 4

1. Général Revol, *Communauté et stratégie mondial* (Paris: Centre Militaire d'Information et de Spécialisation pour l'Outre-Mer, 1961), 16, in Jacques Guillemin, "L'importance des bases dans la politique militaire de la France en Afrique Noire francophone et à Madagascar," *Le Mois en Afrique* (August-September 1981): 31.

2. George Weeks, "The Armies of Africa," *Africa Report* 9, no. 1 (January 1964): 11.

3. Pascal Chaigneau, *La politique militaire de la France* (Paris: Publications du CHEAM, 1984), 50.

4. Guillemin, 33.

5. Ibid., 49.

6. Admiral Castex, quoted by General Mitterrand in "La place de l'action militaire extérieure dans la stratégie française," *Revue de Défense National* (June 1970): 896.

7. Guillemin, 34.

8. Chaigneau, 52.

9. France would briefly reoccupy the base between 1977 and 1981.

10. These categories are adapted from the French colonial military infrastructure for the period immediately following decolonization as described in Guillemin, 39. Currently, all African bases are considered "principal bases" in official accounts, although this may be more for historic reasons than a reflection of their recent roles and performance.

11. Louis Le Pensec, "Une politique pour l'outre-mer français," *Revue de défense nationale* (August-September 1990): 15-16.

12. Fondation pour les Etudes de Défense Nationale, *France Océan Indien Mer Rouge* (Paris: Fondation pour les Etudes de Défense Nationale, 1986): 117.

13. *Africa South of the Sahara 1991*, 20th ed., (London: Europa Publications Limited, 1990), 815.

14. Jacques Amalric, "M. Mitterrand pose des conditions à l'aide aux régimes africains," *Sélection hebdomadaire du journal "Le Monde,"* 14 June 1990, 5.

15. M. Jean-Michel Boucheron, *Rapport fait au nom de la Commission de la Défense Nationale et des Forces Armées (1) sur le projet de loi de Programmation (n° 733) Relatif à l'Equipement militaire pour les années 1990-1993*, Assemblée Nationale, Neuvième Legislature, Première session ordinaire, 2 Octobre 1989, 340-2; and International Institute for Strategic Studies, *The Military Balance 1990-1991* (London: Brassey's, 1990), 66.

16. "Indian Ocean: French subtlety," *Africa Confidential* (3 November 1978): 8.

17. Amalric, 5.

18. Fondation pour les Etudes de Défense Nationale (FEDN), 122.

19. France partly justifies holding these small pieces of territory by negative incentives. H. Labrousse wrote that these lost islands in the Indian Ocean must possess "an indisputable value. To be able to realize this, it is sufficient to stress the American and British efforts to ensure their sovereignty on any visible territories anywhere in the Indian Ocean which could host an airstrip, an anchor place, or which could serve as a transit facility." Quoted by Guillemin, 43, from M. Labrousse, *Le Golfe et le Canal* (Paris: PUF, 1973), 33.

20. Malyn Newitt, *The Comoro Islands: Struggle Against Dependency in the Indian Ocean* (Boulder, CO: Westview Press, 1984), 126.

21. Ibid., 59.

22. *Africa South of the Sahara 1991*, 393.

23. Newitt, 126.

24. Boucheron, 339.

25. "A Farewell to French Arms," *Africa Confidential* (17 November 1989): 4; FEDN, 36.

26. *Africa South of the Sahara 1991*, 435.

27. Marc Yared, "Djibouti à son tour," *Jeune Afrique* (27 November-3 December 1991): 18.

28. "Protocole provisoire fixant les conditions de stationnement des forces françaises sur le territoire de la République de Djibouti," Publié par décret No. 85-1171 du 5 novembre 1985, *Journal Officiel*, 10 novembre 1985, 13060.

29. The French still recall with resentment the British decision in 1966 to remove all British military bases east of Suez. Aden, which was a valuable asset in the British network of military bases, was included in the British withdrawal which left France alone in the region.

30. Guillemin, 43.

31. Ibid.

32. "Les forces françaises stationnées à Djibouti" *SIRPA Actualités, no. 42* (6 December 1991): 14.

33. FEDN, 321.

34. Ibid., 325.

35. Boucheron, 340.

36. Guillemin, 40.

37. Chaigneau, 31.

38. "NATO Airlift Deficiencies Seen in Zaire Evacuation," *Aviation Week & Space Technology* (29 May 1978): 22.

39. Sources: SIRPA; Boucheron, 341; IISS.

40. Francis Terry McNamara, *France in Black Africa* (Washington, D.C.: National Defense University Press, 1989), 148.

41. Source: SIRPA; Boucheron, 341; and IISS.

42. Boucheron, 341; IISS.

43. General Henri Paris, "La stratégie militaire française en Afrique subsaharienne," *Relations internationales et stratégiques* 4 (Winter 1991): 101.

Chapter 5

1. As of 1991, eight African countries maintained defense agreements and over 25 had cooperation agreements with France.

2. Pierre Dabezies, *Les interventions françaises hors d'Europe*, (Paris: Fondation des études de défense nationale, December 1988), 11.

3. Ibid., 17.

4. Two hundred French soldiers died overseas between the Gabon operation in 1964 and that in Chad ending in 1984. Général Fricaud-Chagnaud in the preface to André Foures, *Au-delà du sanctuaire* (Paris: Economica, 1986), 13.

5. Christian d'Epenoux and Christian Hoche, "Giscard l'Africain," *L'Express*, 22 December 1979, 36.

6. Richard Joseph, *Gaullist Africa: Cameroon under Ahmadu Ahidjo* (Enugu, Nigeria: Fourth Dimension Publishers, 1978), 25.

7. Ibid., 26.

8. *Africa South of the Sahara: 1991*, 20th ed., (London: Europa Publication Limited, 1990), 316.

9. Pierre Péan, *L'homme de l'ombre* (Paris: Fayard, 1990), 284-5.

10. Georges Chaffard, *Les Carnets secrets de la décolonisation*, quoted in Péan, 286.

11. "Mauritania's Bow," *The Economist*, 3 December 1960, 1009.

12. J.H.A. Watson, "Mauritania: Problems and Prospects," *Africa Report* (February 1963): 4.

13. "Le gouvernement mauritanien s'est réuni après l'attentat qui coûta la vie à trois Français dans un mess," *Le Monde*, 3 April 1962, 8.

14. "Les attentats de Mauritanie," *Le Monde*, 26 April 1962, 5.

15. Ibid.

16. "Les événements du Gabon: M. Peyrefitte indique que les troupes françaises étaient intervenues dans d'autres pays d'Afrique," *Le Monde*, 28 February 1964.

17. "France's Military Role in Africa," *Africa Report* (January 1964): 10.

18. William J. Foltz, *From French West Africa to the Mali Federation* (New Haven: Yale University Press, 1965), 187.

19. Ibid., 180.

20. George Weeks, "The Armies of Africa," *Africa Report* (January 1964): 7.

21. "Le film des événements," *Le Monde*, 17 August 1963, 4.

22. "Les manifestations se poursuivent contre le gouvernement de Fulbert Youlou," *Le Monde*, 16 August 1963, 1.

23. "Le 'gouvernement provisoire' du Congo-Brazzaville est présidé par M. Massemba-Débat," *Le Monde*, 17 August 1963, 1.

24. "Fulbert Youlou avait appelé Colombey," *Le Monde*, 17 August 1963, 4.

25. Péan, 303.

26. "Un précédent ?" *Le Monde*, 17 August 1963, 1.

27. Richard Synge, quoted in *Africa South of the Sahara: 1991*, 756.

28. Philippe Decraene, "Le gouvernement de Niamey expulse plusieurs milliers de Dahoméens fixés au Niger," *Le Monde*, 24 December 1963, 5.

29. John Chipman, *French Power in Africa* (Cambridge, MA: Basil Blackwell, 1989), 123.

30. "Le film des événements," *Le Monde*, 21 February 1964.

31. Chipman, 123.

32. Péan, 306.

33. *Le Monde*, 28 February 1964, quoted in Pierre Lellouche and Dominique Moisi, "French Policy in Africa: A Lonely Battle Against Destabilization," *International Security* 3, no. 4 (Spring 1979): 117.

34. Franck Terraine, *Les 56 Afriques* (Paris: Maspero, 1979), 169, quoted in Dabezies, 12.

35. Béchir Ben Yamed, "Des paras pour M'ba," *Jeune Afrique* 172 (24 February 1964): 5.

36. Jean Lacouture, "Leçons d'une aventure," *Le Monde*, 22 February 1964, 8.

37. Pierre Lellouche and Dominique Moisi, "French Policy in Africa: A Lonely Battle Against Destabilization," *International Security* 3, no. 4 (Spring 1979): 118.

38. M.J.V. Bell, "Army and Nation in Sub-Saharan Africa," *Adelphi Paper* 21 (August 1965): 14.

39. Philippe Decraene, "Un détachement français a été mis en place en République Centrafricaine," *Le Monde*, 17 November 1967, 5.

40. Lloyd Garrison, "French Army Aids a Regime in Africa," *New York Times*, 17 November 1967, 1.

41. Thomas O'Toole, *The Central African Republic: The Continent's Hidden Heart* (Boulder, CO: Westview Press, 1986), 50. Bokassa kept his French citizenship even after becoming president, despite the vagaries of his love-hate relationship with France.

42. Ibid; and Richard Booth, "The Armed Forces of African States, 1970," *Adelphi Papers*, no. 67 (May 1970): 15.

43. Keith Somerville, *Foreign Military Intervention in Africa* (New York: St Martin's Press, 1990), 54.

44. Ibid., 59.

45. John Stremlau, *The Internal Politics of the Nigerian Civil War, 1967-1970* (Princeton, NJ: Princeton University Press, 1977), 11.

46. Ralph Uwechue, former official of the Biafran foreign service, quoted in Stremlau, 225.

47. A.H.M. Kirk-Greene, *Crisis and Conflict in Nigeria*, vol. 2 (London: Oxford University Press, 1971), 245.

48. It is difficult to determine whether the pressure on de Gaulle by the Côte d'Ivoire and Gabon was genuinely inspired or rather a triangular influence exerted by de Gaulle's own entourage and his minister Foccart.

49. Stremlau, 229.

50. Ibid., 231.

51. The higher figure comes from the *Manchester Guardian*, 1 October 1968, quoted in Peter Schwab, *Biafra*, (New York: Facts on File, 1971), 73.

52. Stremlau, 231.

53. Péan, 322.

54. Stremlau, 229-230; and Péan, 321.

55. Hervé Coutau-Bégarie, *Le problème du porte avions* (Paris: Economica, 1990), 126.

56. Stremlau, 233.

57. "Le Tchad," *Politique africaine* (December 1984): 9.

58. Jacques Attali, *Verbatim I: 1981-1986* (Paris: Fayard, 1993), 34.

59. Ibid., 484.

60. Philippe Decraene, "Chad at World's End," *Africa Report* (January 1968): 56.

61. Ibrahim Signate, "Les rebelles, le minerai et la France," *Jeune Afrique* (9-15 September 1968): 19.

62. Rajen Harshe, "Political Implications of French Military Interventions in Africa - Three Case Studies," *IDSA Journal* 12, no. 3 (January-March 1980): 274.

63. John Wright, *Libya, Chad and the Central Sahara* (Totowa, NJ: Barnes and Noble Books, 1989), 127.

64. G.B. Crouse, "Libya's Desert Defeat," *Soldiers of Fortune* (February 1989): 54; and *Africa South of the Sahara*, 363.

65. Crouse, 54.

66. Nelly Mouric, "La politique tchadienne de la France sous Valéry Giscard d'Estaing," *Politique africaine* (December 1984): 88.

67. *Africa South of the Sahara 1991*, 364.

68. René Lemarchand, "The Crisis in Chad," in Gerald Bender, et. al. *African Crisis Areas* (Los Angeles: University of California Press, 1985), 246.

69. Agnes Thivent, "L'impossible mission de l'armée française," *Le Monde Diplomatique*, March 1980, 21.

70. Mouric, 96.

71. *Africa South of the Sahara 1991*, 364.

72. Agence France Presse, *Bulletin d'Afrique*, 6 November 1981.

73. C. Castéran, "La troisième guerre du Tchad," *Le Matin* (11 August 1983).

74. "Des Américains au Tchad," *Le Monde*, 5 August 1983, 1.

75. A call by President Mitterrand for a negotiated settlement was greeted the following day by the Libyan ambassador in Paris, perhaps too quickly. (David Marsh, "Mitterrand in Chad federation call," *Financial Times*, 26 August 1983, 26.)

76. Jean-Claude Pomonti, "Un déluge de feu," *Le Monde*, 12 August 1983, 1.

77. *Africa South of the Sahara*, 368.

78. *West Africa*, 22 August 1983.

79. Much of the information pertaining to the operational deployment of French forces in Chad and neighboring countries was supplied during an interview by the author in February 1990, with a former French Air Force general.

80. Crouse, 56.

81. "OAU's Chad Initiative," *Africa Research Bulletin* (January 1984): 7089.

82. Bernard Brionne, "Tchad: Fin de l'opération Manta," *Défense nationale* (November 1984): 181.

83. The 2,000-strong Zairian contingent, still in Chad at the time, would pull out soon afterwards.

84. Coutau-Bégarie, 121.

85. "Chad: Fighting Flares Again," *Africa Research Bulletin* (March 1986): 7975.

86. Alain Crosnier, "Le dispositif 'Epervier' au Tchad," *Air Fan*, no. 132 (November 1989): 16.

87. Ibid., 17.

88. Crouse, 57.

89. Crosnier, 20.

90. Crouse, 59.

91. Laurent Zecchini, "Surenchère au Tchad," *Le Monde*, 9 January 1987, 1 and 4.

92. Crouse, 61.

93. Jacques Amalric, "Paris pourrait aider le Tchad à 'reconquérir son intégrité,'" *Le Monde*, 14 November 1986, 6.

94. Mireille Duteil, "Paris mise sur l'enlisement libyen," *Le Point*, 5 January 1987, 76.

95. "Chad's Toyota war," *The Economist*, 12 September 1987, 43.

96. "Chad: France hedges its bets," *Africa Confidential* 31, no.8 (20 April 1990).

97. Crosnier, 20.

98. "Chad: France hedges its bets."

99. "Le Tchad toujours...," *Le Monde*, 18-19 November 1990.

100. "La France 'n'est pas impliquée dans les combats' déclare le Quai d'Orsay," *Le Monde*, 27 November 1990.

101. Jacques de Barrin, "Les dirigeants de N'Djamena seraient en fuite," *Le Monde*, 2 December 1990.

102. "La France renforce le dispositif 'Epervier,'" *Le Monde*, 30 November 1990.

103. "Hissène Habré a évacué N'Djamena," *Le Monde*, 2 December 1990.

104. "Hissène Habré contraint à fuir," *Progrès*, 2 December 1990.

105. Jonathan C. Randall, "France Sends Troops To Reinforce Chad," *The Washington Post*, 4 January 1992, A13.

106. Stephen Smith, "La France au secours du régime tchadien," *Libération*, 4-5 January 1992, 2.

107. Randall, A13.

108. Stephen Smith, "La tactique du gendarme africain," *Libération*, 4-5 January 1992, 3.

109. Lellouche and Moisi, 119.

110. Robin Luckham, "Le militarisme français," *Politique africaine* (May 1982): 52.

111. Coutau-Bégarie, 124.

112. Ibid.

113. Ibid., 129.

114. FEDN, *France, Océan Indien, Mer Rouge* (Paris: CHEAM, Fondation pour les Études de Défense Nationale, 1986), 312.

115. Jean-Michel Boucheron, *Rapport fait au nom de la Commission de la Défense Nationale et des Forces Armées (1) sur le projet de loi de Programmation (n° 733) relatif à l'Equipment militaire pour les années 1990-1993*. Assemblée Nationale, Neuvième Legislature, Première session ordinaire, 2 October 1989, 386 and 390.

116. Somerville, 116.

117. "Les Jaguar français ont essuyé le tir d'armes antiaériennes du Polisario," *Le Monde*, 23 December 1977, 4.

118. Coutau-Bégarie, 127.

119. Ibid.

120. "M. de Guiringaud minimise les interventions françaises au Tchad et en Mauritanie," *Le Monde*, 9 May 1978, 8.

121. Boucheron, 389.

122. Somerville, 116-7; and Boucheron, 387-8.

123. Robert E. Handloff, *Mauritania: A Country Study* (Washington, D.C.: Federal Research Division, Library of Congress, 1990), 175.

124. Romain Yakemtchouk, "Les Deux Guerres du Shaba" *Studia Diplomatica* 41, no. 4-5-6 (Brussels: Institut Royal des Relations Internationales, 1988), 426.

125. The International Institute for Strategic Studies, *The Military Balance 1977-1978* (London: Adlard & Sons, Bartholomew Press, 1977), 48.

126. The superpower which France tried to keep at a distance was the former Soviet Union, acting through proxies, although this does not mean that there was not also an effort to keep the United States at bay.

127. Yakemtchouk, 406.

128. Ibid., 452 and 458.

129. Valéry Giscard d'Estaing, *Le pouvoir et la vie* (Paris: Editions Compagnie, 1988), 239.

130. Yakemtchouk, 471.

131. See the compilation of Belgian and European reactions in Yakemtchouk, 464-6.

132. Renaat Van Elslande, "Maar wat gebeurt er nu juist?," *Knack* (20 April 1977), in Ibid., 464.

133. Dabezies, 14.

134. Thomas O'Toole, *The Central African Republic* (Boulder, CO: Westview Press, 1986), 55.

135. "Coup de canne à Franceville," *Jeune Afrique* (10 October 1979): 32.

136. Jos-Blaise Alima, "La semaine où tout s'est joué," *Jeune Afrique* (3 October 1979): 28.

137. "The Gabon intervention," *West Africa* (3 June 1990): 926.

138. Siradiou Diallo, "L'Afrique humiliée," *Jeune Afrique* (3 October 1979): 38.

139. Mohamed Selhami, "Lettre de Bangui-en-France," *Jeune Afrique* (10 October 1979): 30.

140. Béchir Ben Yahmed, "Tous comptes faits...," *Jeune Afrique* (3 October 1979): 22.

141. Jean-François Bayart, *La politique africaine de François Mitterrand* (Paris: Editions Karthala, 1984), 29.

142. Coutau-Bégarie, 129.

143. Siradiou Diallo, "La guerre ?" *Jeune Afrique* (15 July 1981): 40.

144. Ibid., 41.

145. Philippe Decraene, "Viewing Africa from the Elysée," *Optima* (30 March 1984): 5.

146. *Africa South of the Sahara*, 848.

147. "Gambie: la France avait bien donné le feu vert...," *Le quotidien de Paris* (3 August 1981): 1; and "Coup Plot Discovered," *Africa Research Bulletin* (15 March 1988): 8788.

148. Hamza Kaïdi, "L'armée sénégalaise," *Jeune Afrique* (12 August 1981): 25.

149. "Togo: High drama," *Africa Confidential* (1 October 1986): 4.

150. Ibid., 6.

151. Mohamed Selhami, "Un commando venu du Ghana pour tuer," *Jeune Afrique* (8 October 1986): 29.

152. Coutau-Bégarie, 127.

153. *Africa South of the Sahara*, 1034.

154. "Togo: Laying the blame," *Africa Confidential* (10 December 1986): 10.

155. "Congo: Family Feud," *Africa Confidential* (23 September 1987): 8.

156. Ibid.

157. "Congo: Unpopular Anga," *Africa Confidential* (21 October 1987): 8.

158. "Congo: Moroccans replace Cubans," *Africa Confidential* (7 December 1990): 6.

159. Hugo Sada, "A chacun ses 'Africains,'" *Jeune Afrique* (27 April 1988): 33.

160. Ibid.

161. Somerville, 109.

162. "Les mensonges de Bob Denard," *Le Figaro* (Paris), 6-7 January 1990, 1.

163. "President Assassinated," *Africa Research Bulletin* (15 December 1989): 9489.

164. Ibid.

165. Mayotte decided to stay French when the other three Comoro Islands unilaterally declared independence in July 1975.

166. Edward Cody, "France Sends Force to Oust Mercenary," *The Washington Post*, 14 December 1989; "International Isolation," *Africa Research Bulletin* (15 January 1990): 9523.

167. Ibid.

168. "South Africa Slighted," *Africa Research Bulletin* (15 January 1990): 9525.

169. Christopher S. Wren, "Mercenaries Quit Indian Ocean Isles," *The New York Times*, 16 December 1989, 6.

170. "La grande peur des petits Blancs," *Jeune Afrique* (11 June 1990): 11.

171. "Emeutes et pillages au Gabon," *Sélection hebdomadaire du journal "Le Monde,"* 24-30 May 1990, 3.

172. Christian Casteran, "Gabon : La France s'en mêle," *Jeune Afrique* (4 June 1990): 6.

173. "Un remake," *Le Monde*, 26 May 1990, 1.

174. Jean de la Guérivière, "Le dispositif militaire français au Gabon va être allégé," *Le Monde*, 2 June 1990, 30.

175. Lt-Col. T.W. Parker, "Operation Sharp Edge," *Proceedings* (May 1991): 103.

176. Libby Lukes, "French Navy ship sails to rescue expatriate workers," *The Financial Times*, 1 June 1990.

177. "Djibouti Squeezed," *The Economist*, 12 October 1991, 44; and Catherine Simon, "Le gouvernement français invite les autorités locales à 'engager le dialogue avec l'opposition,'" *Sélection hebdomadaire du journal "le Monde,"* 14-20 November 1991, 5.

178. "Djibouti calls upon France for help," *News from France* (Washington, D.C.: French Embassy, 6 December 1991), 2.

179. "France Mobilizes Troops in Togo Crisis," *The Washington Post*, 30 November 1991, A24.

180. "Togo: ultimatum au Premier ministre," *Echo de la Bourse* (30 November 1991).

181. "Togo's Premier Is Said to Rule On Short Tether," *The Washington Post*, 5 December 1991, A42.

182. "France seeks a peaceful solution," *News from France* (Washington, D.C.: French Embassy, 6 December 1991), 1.

183. Jacques Isnard, "Une armée encadrée par des Français," *Le Monde*, 5 December 1991.

184. Sada, "Pourquoi la France n'a pas bougé," *Jeune Afrique* (27 April 1988): 8.

185. "Opération Oryx," *Armées d'Aujourd'hui*, January 1993, 13.

186. "La Belgique va envoyer 250 hommes de plus en Somalie," *Le Soir*, 6-7 February 1993, 7.

187. "Mitterrand's muddle," *The Economist*, 27 February 1993, 50.

188. Ibid.

189. "Quelques cent mille Rwandais fuient les zones de combat," *Libération*, 11 February 1993, 18; and Catherine Simon, "Quatre-vingts personnes ont été tuées lors de nouvelles violences tribales," *Le Monde*, 29 January 1993, 5.

190. "Le gouvernement s'installe... à l'hôtel," *La Libre Belgique*, 8 November 1993.

191. President François Mitterrand, interviewed in *Le Monde*, Edition internationale - Sélection hebdomadaire, 14-20 June 1990, 7.

192. Yakemtchouk, 593.

193. Albert Bourgi, "Du bon usage des paras," *Jeune Afrique* (11 June 1990): 7.

194. "A New World Order: To the Victors, the Spoils - and the Headaches," *The Economist*, 28 September 1991, 24.

195. General Henri Paris, "La stratégie militaire française en Afrique subsaharienne," *Relations internationales et stratégiques* 4 (Winter 1991): 105.

Chapter 6

1. Roger Martin, "How British Policy Toward Africa Is Shaped and Executed," *CSIS Africa Notes* 87 (27 July 1988): 2.

2. P. Weiler, "British Labour and the Cold War: the Foreign Policy of the Labour Governments, 1945-1951," *Journal of British Studies* 26 (1987): 57.

3. The cabinet is a "product of convention rather than statute." R.M. Punnett, *British Government and Politics* (London: Heinemenn, 1975), 186.

4. Frank Stacey, *The Government of Modern Britain* (Oxford: Clarendon Press, 1968), 257.

5. Philip Stevens, "Minister reveals style of Major's cabinet government," *The Financial Times*, 12 November 1993, 8.

6. Richard H.S. Crossman, *The Myths of Cabinet Government* (Cambridge: Harvard University Press, 1972), 43.

7. Stevens, 8.

8. Ibid., 281.

9. Joe Rogaly, "Nails in the cabinet," *The Financial Times*, 12 November 1993, 14.

10. The Defence and Overseas Policy Committee of the cabinet is chaired by the prime minister with the participation of the secretary of state for defense, the foreign and commonwealth secretary, and the home secretary.

11. "The Empire Strikes Back," *The New York Times Magazine*, 10 March 1991, 34.

12. "The War Leader" *The Economist*, 19 January 1991, 56.

13. Martin, 1.

14. Ibid.

15. Ibid., 2.

16. Ibid., 7.

17. Alistair Horne, *Harold Macmillan, Volume II: 1957-1986* (New York: Viking, 1989), 29.

18. Robert B. Edgerton, *Mau Mau: An African Crucible* (New York: The Free Press, 1989), 237.

19. Horne, 177.

20. Ibid.

21. Ibid., 409.

22. It must be said that, having left office, Macmillan disagreed with the British disengagement East of Suez, considering it to be "the most disastrous thing that has happened in twenty years." He claimed in later years that he would have been tougher on the Aden issue. Ibid., 421.

23. Ibid., 195.

24. Ibid., 198.

25. Ibid., 393.

26. Ibid., 401.

27. Macmillan apparently was influenced by Sir James Robertson, a retired British governor-general, as demonstrated by a conversation he recorded with Robertson: "After attending some meeting of the so-called cabinet or council, I said, 'Are these people fit for self-government?" and he said, 'No, of course not.' I said, 'When will they be ready?' He said, 'Twenty years, twenty-five years.' Then I said, 'What do you recommend me to do?' He said, 'I

recommend you to give it to them at once.' I said, 'Why, that seems strange.' 'Well,' he said, 'if they were twenty years well spent, if they would be learning administration, if they were getting experience, I would say wait, but what will happen? All the most intelligent people, all the ones I've been training on will become rebels. I shall have to put them all in prison. There will be violence, bitterness and hatred. They won't spend the twenty years learning. We shall simply have us twenty years of repression, and therefore, in my view, they'd better start learning [to rule themselves] at once.' I thought that was very sensible." Ibid., 190.

28. Harold Wilson, *A Personal Record: The Labour Government 1964-1970* (Boston: Little, Brown and Company, 1971), 180.

29. Ibid., 181.

30. Ibid., 196.

31. Ibid., 558.

32. Ibid., 556.

33. Ibid., 559.

34. Martin, 3.

35. "Resounding tinkle," *The Economist*, 26 October 1991, 49.

36. "Aid for Africa: If you're good," *The Economist*, 29 May 1993, 44.

37. Ibid.

38. "Per Ardua ad Aspidistram," *The Economist*, 30 October 1965, 472.

39. François Honti, "La Grande-Bretagne brillant second?" *Le Monde Diplomatique*, March 1966, 1.

40. James Mayall, "Africa in Anglo-American Relations," in *The Special Relationship: Anglo-American Relations since 1945*, ed. William Roger Lois and Hedley Bull (Oxford: Clarendon Press, 1986), 322.

41. Keith Kyle, "Britain and the Crisis, 1955-56," in Lois and Bull, 130.

42. John Newhouse, *De Gaulle and the Anglo-Saxons* (New York: The Viking Press, 1970), 8.

43. D.E. Kennedy, *The Security of Southern Asia* (New York: Praeger, 1965), 47.

44. Ministry of Defence, *Statement on the Defence Estimates: 1965*, London: Her Majesty's Stationery Office, February 1965, 8.

45. Ministry of Defence, *Statement on the Defence Estimates: 1967*, London: Her Majesty's Stationery Office, February 1967, 7.

46. Ministry of Defence, *Supplementary Statement on Defence Policy 1967*, London: Her Majesty's Stationery Office, July 1967, Ch. III.

47. Harold Wilson, *Harold Wilson: A Personal Record* (Boston: Atlantic Monthly Press, 1971), 483.

48. "The Washing of Hands," *The Economist*, 20 January 1968, 18.

49. Although the Kenyan Unilateral Declaration of Independence and the South African problem are vaguely similar, they certainly did not involve the extent of military machinery used by France in Chad.

50. Nicholas Mansergh, *The Commonwealth Experience* (London: Weidenfeld and Nicolson, 1969), 401.

51. Ibid., 402.

52. Ibid., 413.

53. "Tools for a New Age," *The Times*, 4 January 1965; quoted in J.D.B. Miller, *Survey of Commonwealth Affairs* (London: Oxford University Press, 1974), 399.

54. A.P. Thornton, "The Transformation of the Commonwealth and the 'Special Relationship,'" in Lois and Bull, 377.

55. Ibid., 367.

56. Ibid., 377.

57. Pierre Courtiade, "Le Royaume-Uni dans l'ombre de l'aigle américain," *l'Armement*, December 1989, 57.

58. John M. Goshko, "Field Narrows in Race for Top U.N. Job," *The Washington Post*, 14 November 1991, A47.

59. "Commonwealth Summit" *Africa Research Bulletin* (15 November 1989): 9437.

60. All African participants to the Commonwealth are located south of the Sahara: Botswana, Gambia, Ghana, Kenya, Lesotho, Malawi, Mauritius, Nigeria, Seychelles, Sierra Leone, Swaziland, Tanzania, Uganda, Zambia, and Zimbabwe. A number of African territories, formerly under British jurisdiction or mandate, did not join the Commonwealth: Egypt, Sudan, British Somaliland, and South Cameroon. South Africa left the Commonwealth in 1961 after becoming a republic.

61. *Report of the Commonwealth Secretary-General 1993* (Commonwealth Secretariat: London, 1993): 137.

62. Ibid.

63. The holding of conferences outside the United Kingdom was made possible by the creation of the permanent secretariat. The locations have been: Lagos (1966); Singapore (1971); Ottawa (1973); Kingston (1975); Lusaka (1979); Melbourne (1981); New Delhi (1983); Nassau (1985); Vancouver (1987); and Kuala Lumpur (1989).

64. "Resounding tinkle," 49.

65. Michael Holman, "Commonwealth focuses on Gatt and rights," *The Financial Times*, 22 October 1993, 5.

66. Michael Holman, "Bland leading the bland as Commonwealth meets," *The Financial Times*, 22 October 1993, 16.

67. Thornton, in Lois and Bull, 377.

68. Ibid.

69. Dennis Austin and Keith Panter-Brick, *Post-Colonialism*, unpublished paper, sine loco, sine dato, 23.

70. Mansergh, 352.

71. "Commonwealth Summit," *Africa Research Bulletin* (15 November 1987): 8656.

72. Austin and Panter-Brick, 18.

73. Mayall, in Lois and Bull, 331.

74. Martin, 5.

75. Ibid.

76. Austin and Panter-Brick, 2.

77. Ibid., 10.

Chapter 7

1. Ministry of Defence, *Defending our Future: Statement on the Defence Estimates 1993*, (London: HMSO, July 1993), 7.

2. Philip A.G. Sabin, "British defence choices beyond 'Options for Change,'" *International Affairs* 69, 2 (1993), 272.

3. *Defending Our Future*, 10.

4. Sabin, 270.

5. House of Commons, Defence Committee, *United Kingdom Peacekeeping and Intervention Forces* (London: HMSO, 1993): x.

6. Ministry of Defence, *British Defence Policy: 1989-90*, London: Her Majesty's Stationery Office, February 1989, 24.

7. Sabin, 281, quoting the 1992 Defence White Paper.

8. *Defending Our Future*, 75.

9. Charles Miller and Michael J. Witt, "Defense Spending Spirals Down," *Defense News*, 12-18 July 1993, 12.

10. International Institute of Strategic Studies, *The Military Balance 1993-1994* (Brassey's: London, 1993), 62.

11. Bruce Quarrie, *Special Forces* (New Jersey: Chartwell Books, Inc., 1990), 34.

12. House of Commons, ix.

13. Jonathan Block and Patrick Fitzgerald, *British Intelligence and Covert Action: Africa, Middle East and Europe since 1945* (Dublin: Brandon, 1983), 40.

14. Ibid., 41.

15. John Strawson, *A History of the SAS Regiment* (London: Secker and Warburg, 1984), 213.

16. Paul M. Kennedy, *The Rise and Fall of British Naval Mastery* (London: The Ashfield Press, 1989), 337.

17. James L. Lacy, *Between Worlds: Europe and the Seas in Arms Control* (Santa Monica: RAND Strategy Assessment Center, 1991), 43.

18. House of Commons, x.

19. Alison Smith and David White, "Government under fire over Navy cuts," *The Financial Times*, 3-4 April 1993, 8.

20. Harold Wilson, *A Personal Record: The Labour Government 1964-1970* (Boston: Little, Brown and Company, 1971), 212.

21. L.W. Martin, "British Defence Policy: The Long Recessional," *Adelphi Paper* 61, (London: Institute for Strategic Studies, 1969): 6.

22. House of Commons, xiv.

23. R.S. Tailyour, "The Future of Amphibious Warfare," *RUSI Journal* (Spring 1991): 33.

24. Ibid.

25. David Fairhall, "Unhappy Landing for the Royal Marines," *The Guardian*, 16 September 1985.

26. The International Institute for Strategic Studies, *The Military Balance 1989-1990* (London: Brassey's, 1989), 80.

27. IISS, *The Military Balance 1993-1994*, 63.

28. Ian Kemp, "UK 'could not fight alone,' says study," *Jane's Defence Weekly* (17 August 1991): 261.

29. Ministry of Defence, *Statement on the Defence Estimates: 1989*, London: Her Majesty's Stationery Office, 1989, 56.

30. IISS, *The Military Balance 1993-1994*, 64, and House of Commons, 115.

31. Smith and White, 8.

32. Sabin, 272.

33. Nick Cook, "Cuts, but no role change for RAF," *Jane's Defence Weekly* (4 August 1990): 154.

34. Sabin, 36-7.

35. Carole A. Shifrin, "Britain's Gulf Role Highlights Value Of Flexible Tactics, New Technology," *Aviation Week and Space Technology* (22 April 1991): 104.

36. Rodney A. Burden, Draper, Rough, Smith and Wilton, *Falklands: The Air War* (Dorset: Arms and Armour Press, 1987), 371.

37. Nick Cook, "RAF holds key to Hercules II," *Jane's Defence Weekly* (23 November 1991): 990.

38. Burden, et al., 405-9.

39. *Aerospace Daily*, 15 March 1991, 445.

40. "RAF still needs seven E-3Ds," *Jane's Defence Weekly* (12 May 1990): 893.

41. Sabin, 11.

42. Bridget Bloom, "Coyness Over Spinoff from Military Aid," *The Financial Times*, 1 September 1981, 6.

43. Roger Martin, "How British Policy Toward Africa is Shaped and Executed," *CSIS Africa Notes* 87 (27 July 1988): 2.

44. Bloom, 6.

45. James Blackwell, "British Security Assistance in Sub-Saharan Africa," *CSIS Interim Report, U.S. - Allied Cooperation in Africa*, Draft Report, Washington, D.C., 6 July 1989, MDA 903-89-C-0045, 46.

46. Roger Martin, 2.

47. Bloom, 6.

48. Blackwell, 48.

49. Major General K. Perkins, "Winning Friends: A Military Strategy in the Third World," *Royal United Service Institute for Defense Studies Journal*, 126, no. 2 (June 1981): 39.

50. Blackwell, 40.

51. Ministry of Defence, *British Defence Policy 1990-91*, London: Her Majesty's Stationery Office, April 1990, 15, and *Defending Our Future*, 52.

52. Roger Martin, 3.

53. Edmond Dantes, "British Industry Seeks Wider Customer Base in Asia," *Defense News*, 13 May 1991, 10.

54. US Arms Control and Disarmament Agency, *World Military Expenditures and Arms Transfers: 1989* (Washington, D.C.: U.S. Government Printing Office, October 1990), 131-2.

55. Ministry of Defence, *Statement on the Defence Estimates, Volume 2: 1991*, London: Her Majesty's Stationary Office, 1991, 13.

56. Roger Martin, 2.

57. Perkins, 39.

58. These countries include the Central African Republic, Benin, Liberia, Guinea-Bissau, Senegal, Rwanda, Angola and Zimbabwe.

59. Blackwell, 43.

60. Ibid., 44.

Chapter 8

1. Alastair Buchan, M.B.E, "Britain East of Suez: Part One - The Problem of Power," *RUSI* CXII (August 1967): 211.

2. Ministry of Defence, *Statement on Defence 1962: The Next Five Years*, London: Her Majesty's Stationery Office, February 1962, 4.

3. Ibid.

4. Ministry of Defence, *Statement on Defence 1965*, Her Majesty's Stationery Office, London: February 1965, 9.

5. Ministry of Defence, *Legal Obligations of Her Majesty's Government Arising out of the Simonstown Agreements*, Her Majesty's Stationary Office, London: February 1971, 2.

6. Colin Legum, "The African Continent," *RUSI* CVIII, no. 629 (London: February 1963): 14.

7. Ibid., 8.

8. Christopher Coker, "South Africa's Strategic Importance: a Re-assessment," *RUSI* 124, no. 4 (London: December 1979): 24.

9. Brian Lapping, *End of Empire* (New York: St. Martin's Press, 1985), 278.

10. Brigadier G.S. Heathcote, C.B.E., "Aden - A Reason Why," *RUSI* CXII, no. 650 (May 1968): 142.

11. Lapping, 298.

12. Ministry of Defence, *Statement on the Defence Estimates 1968*, London: Her Majesty's Stationery Office, February 1968, 14.

13. Ibid.

14. Ministry Of Defence, *Statement on the Defence Estimates: 1967*, London: Her Majesty's Stationery Office, February 1967, 8.

15. Ministry of Defence, *Agreement between the Government of the United Kingdom of Great Britain and Northern Ireland and the Government of Malta*, Treaty Series No. 44, London: Her Majesty's Stationary Office, 26 March 1972, 3.

16. Ibid.

17. Lapping, 311.

18. The Baghdad Pact was a mutual defense treaty signed on February 24, 1955, between Turkey and Iraq against Nasser's Egypt. Britain adhered two months later, while the United States, although in support of the idea, did not join. British membership to the Baghdad Pact inflamed Nasser's relations toward Britain and pro-western Iraq.

19. Ibid., 76.

20. Nigel West, *The Friends: Britain's Post-War Secret Intelligence Operations* (London: Weidenfeld and Nicolson, 1988), 77.

21. Tony Banks, "Cyprus: forward line for the Gulf," *Jane's Defence Weekly*, 19 October 1991, 714.

22. International Institute for Strategic Studies, *The Military Balance 1990-91* (London: Brassey's, 1990), 86.

23. Banks, 715.

24. Robert Boardman and A.J. Groom, *The Management of Britain's External Relations* (New York: Barnes and Noble Books, 1973), 3.

25. George Drower, *Britain and its Dependent Territories: The Decolonisation Experience 1968-82* (Ph.D. diss., London School of Economics, sine dato), 264.

26. "St. Helena: Ascension," *Africa South of the Sahara 1991, 20th ed.,* (London: Europa Publications Limited, 1990), 837.

27. Orlando Bonturi, *Brazil and the Vital South Atlantic* (Washington, D.C.: National Defense University, 1988), 34.

28. Squadron Leader J. Clementson, MA, "Diego Garcia," *RUSI* 126, no. 2 (London: June 1981): 33.

29. "Indian Ocean, Coral Bases," *The Economist*, 13 November 1965, 699.

30. Clementson, 33.

31. Indo-American Task Force on the Indian Ocean, *India, the United States and the Indian Ocean: report of the Indo-American task force on the Indian Ocean*, (Washington, D.C.: Carnegie Endowment for International Peace, 1985), 97.

32. The United States did not reduce its military facilities on Diego Garcia after the emergence of a new relationship between the superpowers in recent years. During the 1991 Gulf War, 28 B-52s were deployed at Diego Garcia, located about 3,200 from Iraq. These planes had to be situated far from the theater of operations due to the saturated landing space available in Saudi Arabia. As one defense analyst explained, "[t]he B-52 takes up an awful lot of strip space, especially when you consider all the maintenance and munitions people that go with it." "Air Force May Keep Out of Saudi Arabia," *Aerospace Daily*, 17 January 1991, 95.

33. *The Statesman's Year-Book: 1980-1981* (London: The Macmillan Press Ltd., 1980), 541.

34. IISS, 86.

35. Drower, 131.

36. Port Stanley is about one week's sailing time from South Africa. Drower, 108.

37. Ministry of Defence, *Statement on the Defence Estimates 1966, Part I: The Defence Review*, London: Her Majesty's Stationery Office, February 1966, 98.

38. IISS, 82.

Chapter 9

1. David Charters, *Armies in Low-Intensity Conflict* (London: Brassey's, 1989), 171; lists 84 operations for the period 1945-82; author's count for the period 1983-93.

2. Robert Conley, "Britain Bows to Kenya Somalis, Agrees to Regional Autonomy," *The New York Times*, 9 March 1963, 3.

3. "The Brushfire in East Africa," *Africa Report* 9, no. 2 (February 1964): 24.

4. "Zanzibar Long Divided by Arab-African Rivalry," *New York Times*, 13 January 1964, 9.

5. J.D. Duroselle, *Histoire Diplomatique de 1919 à nos jours* (Paris: Dalloz, 1978), 665.

6. On October 9,1962, the day of the Ugandan independence, 4 Battalion, King's African Rifles, became 1 Battalion, Uganda Rifles.

7. Ministry of Defence, *Statement on Defence 1962: The Next Five Years*, London: Her Majesty's Stationery Office, February 1962, 8.

8. Ibid.

9. Ibid.

10. "Tanganyika's Guardian: Julius Kambarage Nyerere," *New York Times*, 27 January, 1964, 2.

11. "The Brushfire in East Africa," 22.

12. Robert Conley, "British Put Down African Mutinies in Three Nations," *New York Times*, 26 January 1964, 1 and 3.

13. D.C. Watt, "The Role of the Aircraft Carrier in Some Recent British Military Operations," *RUSI* CXI (May 1966): 130.

14. "By Invitation Only," *The Economist*, 1 February 1964, 395.

15. Conley, "British Put Down African Mutinies in Three Nations," 1 and 3.

16. Ibid.

17. "By Invitation Only," 395.

18. "What the Communists Are Saying," *The Economist*, 1 February 1964, 397.

19. "The Brushfire in East Africa," 23.

20. "What East Africans Are Doing," *The Economist*, 1 February 1964, 396.

21. Conley, "British Put Down African Mutinies in Three Nations," 1 and 3.

22. George Weeks, "The Armies of Africa," *Africa Report* (January 1964): 12.

23. Former high ranking British official in Zimbabwe, interview by author, January 1990.

24. Harold Wilson, *A Personal Record: The Labour Government 1964-1970* (Boston: Little, Brown and Company, 1971), 180-1.

25. Roger Martin, interview by author, 1 July 1991, Washington, D.C.

26. Brian Lapping, *End of Empire* (New York: St. Martin's Press, 1985), 446.

27. Former high-ranking British official in Zimbabwe, interview by author, January 1990.

28. Jonathan Bloch and Patrick Fitzgerald, *British Intelligence and Covert Action: Africa, Middle East and Europe* (Dublin: Brandon, 1983), 25.

29. Ibid., 64.

30. Colin Legum, *The Battlefront of Southern Africa* (New York: Africana Publishing Company, 1988), 136-9.

31. Ibid., 141.

32. Ibid.

33. Lapping, 527.

34. J.D.B. Miller, *Survey of Commonwealth Affairs: Problems of Expansion and Attrition 1953-69* (London: Oxford University Press, 1974), 255.

35. John J. Stremlau, *The International Politics of the Nigerian Civil War: 1967-1970* (Princeton, NJ: Princeton University Press, 1977), 130.

36. Keith Somerville, *Foreign Military Intervention in Africa* (New York: St Martin's Press, 1990), 59.

37. Ibid, 59-60.

38. Ibid.

39. Ibid., 256.

40. Colonel R.S. Tailyour, "The Future of Amphibious Warfare," *RUSI Journal* 136, no. 1 (Spring 1991): 33.

41. "Gambia: Coup Plot Discovered," *Africa Research Bulletin* (15 March 1988): 8788.

42. François Soudan, "Sauvetage ou annexion?" *Jeune Afrique* (12 August 1981): 25.

43. Jack Halpern, "Botswana, Recent History" rev. by Richard Brown, *Africa South of the Sahara 1991*, (London: Europa Publications Limited, 1990), 271.

44. "Botswana-UK: Military Training," *Africa Research Bulletin* (15 March 1986): 7988.

45. Simon Barber, "Crocker sees UK assuming lead role in southern Africa," *Business Day*, 7 April 1989.

46. Ibid.

47. United Nations, *The Blue Helmets: A Review of United Nations Peace-Keeping* (New York: United Nations Department of Public Information, 1990), 354.

48. Ibid., 359.

49. Ibid., 364.

50. Thalif Deen, "Namibia's test of strength," *Jane's Defence Weekly* (21 July 1990): 85.

51. *Defending Our Future: Statement on the Defence Estimates 1993* (London: HMSO, July 1993), Cm 2270, 46.

52. Ibid., 125.

53. House of Commons, Defence Committee, *United Kingdom Peacekeeping and Intervention Forces* (London: HMSO, 9 June 1993), xxiii.

54. Ibid.

55. Ibid.

Chapter 10

1. CRISP, "Les Partis Politiques en Belgique," *Dossiers du CRISP* (November 1978): 32.

2. Ibid, 1-8.

3. Robert Senelle, "The Current Constitutional System," in Marina Boudart, Michel Boudart and René Bryssinck, *Modern Belgium* (Palo Alto, CA: The Society for the Promotion of Science and Scholarship, 1990), 174.

4. Xavier Mabille, "Political Decision-Making," in Boudart, Boudart and Bryssinck, 211.

5. Ibid., 215.

6. Although this is one single ministry encompassing Belgian foreign affairs, foreign trade, and development cooperation, there is a separate minister for each of the three areas.

7. "Zaire and Belgium: A Question of Upbringing," *The Economist*, 11 February 1989, 40.

8. Pierre Loppe, "Etienne Davignon ou l'Europe en Générale," *La Libre Belgique*, 12 July 1993, 2.

9. Barnabé Samuti, "Une ville sous le choc...mais qui cherche la vérité," *Le Soir*, 8 August 1990, 1; and Colette Braeckman, "Multipartisme et répression au Zaire," *Le Monde Diplomatique*, July 1990,, 5.

10. Canada sided with Belgium in protest against Mobutu's human rights record, and both countries lobbied successfully to move the next 1991 Francophone Summit, which was to be held in Kinshasa, to Paris.

11. Didier Grogna, "Kinshasa rabat les accords belgo-zaïrois," *L'Echo de la Bourse*, 23-25 June 1990, 1.

12. Mark Eyskens, departing minister of foreign affairs in "Une politique africaine indispensable," *La Libre Belgique*, 14-15 March 1992, 2.

13. Interview by Pierre Lefèvre and André Riche, "Claes: une fermeté mesurée," *Le Soir*, 5-6 February 1994, 8.

14. "La Belgique et l'Afrique," *Marchés Tropicaux*, 17 July 1992, 1881.

15. Institut National de Statistique, Brussels, December 1990; and François Misser, "Belgium Survey: Not just an old colonial power," *African Business* (September 1986): 75.

16. "La Belgique et l'Afrique," 1877.

17. Rapport d'activités, 1991-1992, Administration générale de la Coopération au Développement, Brussels, 14-15.

18. Eyskens, 2.

19. Braeckman, 5.

20. Lefèvre and Riche, 8.

21. "La Politique Africaine de la Belgique," *Ministère des Affaires Etrangères*, Annex No. 1 (Brussels: February 1983): 79. It is also for precisely the same reason that King Léopold I could secure a share of the African colonial pie despite French and British aspirations; Belgium did not represent any danger to these powers.

22. "Kolwezi: l'horreur et le gachis," *Pourquoi Pas?* 25-31 May 1978, 4.

23. "M. Bogaert Sentenced," *Africa Research Bulletin* (15 October 1985): 7805.

24. "Zaire and Belgium: A Question of Upbringing," 40.

25. Charles Perry, "Belgian Arms Sales and Security Assistance Programs and Policies," *CSIS Interim Report, U.S.-Allied Cooperation in Africa* [Draft] (Washington, D.C.: CSIS, 6 July 1989), 83, MDA 903-89-C-0045.

26. Thierry Fiorilli, "Les Belges défendent le droit d'ingérence," *Le Soir*, 5-6 February 1994, 1.

Chapter 11

1. The International Institute for Strategic Studies, *The Military Balance 1993-1994* (London: Brassey's, 1993), 38.

2. Professor Luc De Vos, *Ecole Royale Militaire* as quoted in: "Certains milieux vivent dans leurs rêves...," *La Libre Belgique*, 30-31 January 1993, 3.

3. "Government debt," *The Economist*, 5 February 1994, 119.

4. The Resources Strategy Project Team, Center for Strategic and International Studies, *Belgium Within the Alliance: The Present and the Future* (Washington, D.C.: CSIS, 2 March 1988), 44.

5. Theresa Hitchens, "Belgium Approves Limit on Procurement Programs," *Defense News*, 5-11 July 1993, 6.

6. General Jean Berhin, as quoted by Olivier Alsteens, "Armée: technologie hors de prix," *Le Soir*, 23 February 1993, 4.

7. Lieutenant General José Charlier, interview from: "Le général Charlier: 'maintenir la qualité,'" *La Libre Belgique*, 30-31 January 1993, 3.

8. IISS, *The Military Balance 1990-1991* (London: Brassey's, 1990), 59.

9. CSIS, 30.

10. François-Xavier de Donnéa, *Défense 2000* (Brussels: New Fashion Media s.a., 1988), 149.

11. Barbara Starr, "Cold War Battle Order Make Way for a New NATO Era," *Jane's Defence Weekly* (8 June 1991): 961.

12. "Un nouveau visage pour l'armée belge," *La Libre Belgique*, 30-31 January 1993, 3.

13. J.A.C. Lewis, "Belgian Corps to leave Germany," *Jane's Defence Weekly* (22 December 1990): 1266.

14. The Belgian airlift capability is insufficient to move troops, ammunition, light equipment and fuel for more than one battalion in one flight to central Africa. American planes and tankers have in several instances complemented the Belgian capability, except during the 1990 operation in Rwanda.

15. The official name of the country was changed from Congo to Zaire in October 1971.

16. "Law of 4 April 1972," *Moniteur Belge - Belgisch Staatsblad*, 28 March 1973, 3767-87.

17. Brent Fischmann, "Belgian Arms Sales and Security Assistance Policy Toward Africa," *CSIS Interim Report, U.S. - Allied Cooperation in Africa* [Draft] (Washington, D.C.: CSIS, 6 July 1989), 115, MDA 903-89-C-0045.

18. J. Brassine, "Douze années de coopération technique militaire belgo-zaïroise," *Etudes Africaines Du C.R.I.S.P.* (13 October 1972): 6.

19. Many Belgians came back as mercenaries for Tschombé.

20. These included ten C-47s, four C-130s, three B 26s, seven T 28s and six helicopters. Brassinne, 13-14.

21. Ibid., 17.

22. Ibid., 26.

23. The only units to be considered operational in Zaire are a Commando unit trained by the French and the presidential guard.

24. Charles Perry, "Belgian Arms Sales and Security Assistance Programs and Policies," *CSIS Interim Report, U.S. - Allied Cooperation in Africa* (Washington, D.C.: CSIS, 6 July 1989), 85, MDA 903-89-C-0045.

25. Ibid., 116.

26. Bernard Adam, "La Belgique, plaque tournante du trafic d'armes," *L'Europe des Armes, Trafics et exportations vers le tiers monde* (Brussels: GRIP, 1989), 35.

27. This includes countries like Sweden, Switzerland, and New Zealand.

28. Theresa Hitchens, "Budget Pinch, Competition Squeeze Belgium Defense Industry," *Defense News*, 3 December 1990, 38.

29. Bernard Adam, "La restructuration de la production d'armements en Belgique," in *L'Europe des Armes, Trafics et exportations vers le tiers monde* (Brussels: GRIP, 1989), 85.

30. Perry, 91.

31. Ibid., 97.

Chapter 12

1. J. Vanderlinden, *Du Congo au Zaire* (Brussels: CRISP, 1980), 1077.

2. Louis-François Vanderstraeten, *De La Force Publique à l'Armée Nationale Congolaise: Histoire d'une Mutinerie Juillet 1960* (Brussels: Palais des Académies, 1980), 255.

3. Ibid., 449.

4. R. Ernest and Trevor Dupuy, *The Encyclopedia of Military History* (New York: Harper & Row Publishers, 1986), 1321.

5. Vanderstraeten, 90.

6. Ibid., 57.

7. Ibid., 307.

8. Ibid., 395.

9. Etat-major général de la Force navale, sous-section information et relations publiques, *150 ans de marine militaire belge* (Brussels: Presses de l'imprimerie des Force armées belges, 1980).

10. Vanderstraeten, 418.

11. Ibid., 435.

12. Ibid., 447.

13. Ibid., 460.

14. Vanderlinden, 133.

15. Ibid.

16. Baron Patrick Nothomb, "Stanleyville août-novembre 1964," *Chronique de Politique Etrangère* (September-November 1965): 488.

17. Vanderlinden, 126.

18. United Nations, Security Council, S/5784, quoted in: Colonel Frédéric Vandewalle, *Odyssée et Reconquète de Stanleyville 1964, "L'Ommegang"* (Brussels: Collection Teimoignage Africain, 1970), 55.

19. Vanderlinden, 94.

20. David Reed, *111 Days in Stanleyville*, 173; in Vandewalle, 275.

21. Vandewalle, 356-7.

22. The number of Congolese casualties cannot be estimated because the bodies of many of the dead were never recovered. The total figure probably amounts to many thousands.

23. V. Galuszka, "Dragon Rouge, Dragon Noir," *Vox*, 30 November 1989, 4.

24. Vandewalle, 63-64.

25. Ernest and Dupuy, 1322.

26. Vandewalle, 147.

27. See "Un entretien avec le président Mobutu," by Philippe Decraene in *Le Monde* (Paris), 12-13 June 1977, where Mobutu brags about the severe beating inflicted on the invaders, in Romain Yakemtchouk, "Les Deux Guerres Du Shaba," *Studia Diplomatica* 41, no. 4-5-6 (Brussels: Institut Royal des Relations Internationales, 1988): 402.

28. Général Yves Gras, then colonel and commander of the French operation in Shaba, would later point out how this move might in fact well have been inspired by East German advisers in Angola.

29. Yakemtchouk, 493.

30. Samy Cohen, *La monarchie nucléaire* (Paris: Hachette, 1986), 184.

31. As reported by Foreign Minister Henri Simonet in his memoirs, *Je n'efface rien et je recommence* (Brussels: D. Hatier, 1986), 190, in Yakemtchouk, 514.

32. Général Yves Gras, "L'opération Kolwezi," *Mondes et Cultures (Paris)*, 8 November 1985, 694.

33. Ibid., 694.

34. Later the worst assumptions with regard to their fate was confirmed; the six men had been executed.

35. Yakemtchouk, 510.

36. Zaire is geographically the largest francophone country in the world. It is second largest in terms of population, with roughly 34 million inhabitants. For most Zairians, however, French is a second language. Some do not speak French at all.

37. Serge Brabant, "Aspects politiques et diplomatiques de l'intervention de Kolwezi en 1978: Realite - Information," *Toutes Armes* (Thesis 120e Promotion, Brussels Ecole Royale Militaire, 1983-4), 39.

38. The two routes were respectively 10,914 km and 11,753 km, compared to 7,287 km for the direct flight route with stopovers in Tunisia and Chad. This latter route includes an overflight of the Algerian-Libyan border, countries with little sympathy for a Belgian military operation. Toward the end of the Belgian intervention, a third route was opened which included only a single stopover in Luxor, Egypt, for a total of 8,426 km. "Opération 'Red Bean,'" *Wing pro Avia*, no.3 (September 1978): 4-5.

39. Brabant, 42.

40. Cohen, 184.

41. Ibid., 73.

42. Major Malherbe, "Un officier belge témoigne sur Kolwezi: 'Nous sommes fiers de nos hommes et de notre opération,'" *Vers l'Avenir*, 25 November 1978.

43. De Guiringaud, "A la une: les grands évènements du 20è siècle et les journaux," sine loco, sine dato, 119, in Brabant, 124-5.

44. Simonet, in Yakemtchouk, 538.

45. Yakemtchouk, 573.

46. Gras, 702.

47. Ibid.

48. Ambassador Rittweger de Moor, quoted in Brabant, 56.

49. Gras, 715.

50. Yakemtchouk, 581.

51. Gras, 702.

52. Yakemtchouk, 618.

53. Gras, 702.

54. Yakemtchouk, 516.

55. "Operation 'Red Bean,'" 5, 15, and 18-20.

56. "NATO Airlift Deficiencies Seen in Zaire Evacuation," *Aviation Week & Space Technology* (29 May 1978): 22.

57. Ibid.

58. Yakemtchouk, 534.

59. Ibid., 661.

60. "Belgian Troops Withdrawn," *Africa Research Bulletin* (March 1979): 5200.

61. "Belgium Sends Paratroops," *Africa Research Bulletin* (February 1979): 5166.

62. Chris Simpson, "The Boys from Brussels," *West Africa* (15-21 October 1990): 2653.

63. Actual figures were never made public. The refugees also received some local reinforcements once they entered Rwanda.

64. Colette Braeckman, "Les Tutsi veulent rentrer au pays par tous les moyens," *Le Soir*, 4 October 1990.

65. In fact, Belgium sped up the delivery of some back-orders from the Rwandan armed forces.

66. "Nos para-commandos en mission humanitaire au Rwanda," *Vox*, 9 October 1990, 16; and J. Reyniers, "Commandos et paras à Kigali," *Vox*, 23 October 1990, 6.

67. Marie-France Cros, "Une nuit de combats aux quatre coins de Kigali," *La Libre Belgique*, 6-7 October 1990, 2.

68. "Rwanda: 101 expatriés témoignent," *Le Soir*, 22 October 1990, 2.

69. "Evacués de force, les coopérants belges sont mécontents," *Le Soir*, 15 October 1990, 15.

70. "Cinq cents paras belges sont envoyés au Rwanda," *La Libre Belgique*, 5 October 1990, 1.

71. Reyniers, 7.

72. Clifford Krauss, "3-Nation Force Helps Rwanda Meet Tutsi Invaders," *New York Times*, 6 October 1990, 3.

73. Agence France Presse, quoted in "L'ancien chef de la sûreté de l'armée ougandaise à la tête du FPR," *Afrique Fax*, 5 November 1990, 1.

74. Thierry Evens, "Rwanda: Martens a repris la route de l'Afrique," *Le Soir*, 22 October 1990, 1.

75. Didier Grogna, "Quelle décision pour nos ressortissants au Rwanda," *L'Echo de la Bourse*, 13-15 October 1990, 3.

76. Agence France Presse, quoted in *Afrique Fax*, 30 October 1990, 2.

77. "Le Rwanda s'enlise dans les difficultés," *Le Quotidien de l'Economie et de la Finance*, 9 November 1990.

78. "Rwanda Battles Rebels to Control District Capital," *The New York Times*, 24 January 1991.

79. The rebel forces had increased to approximately 2,000, according to some rumors, due to an influx of Tutsi refugees in Rwanda.

80. François-Xavier Buissonnière, "Opération Baumier," *Terre Magazine* no. 29 (November 1991): 11.

81. Emmanuel Commissaire, "Opération Baumier," *Armées d'Aujourd'hui* (November 1991): 27.

82. H. Leclercq, "Blue Beam en chiffres," *Vox*, 19 November 1991, 20.

83. G. Borlée, "Le 15ème Wing se pose partout," *Vox*, 19 November 1991, 4.

84. "L'objectif de la mission: protéger l'évacuation," *Le Soir*, 25 September 1991, 1.

85. Buissonnière, 12.

86. Commissaire, 27.

87. Colette Braeckman, "Le mariage de déraison," *Le Soir*, 21 October 1991, 1.

88. "'Blue Beam' s'étend à tout le Zaïre," *Le Soir*, 27 September 1991, 7.

89. Pierre Haski, "Les troupes de la 'Paristroïka,'" *Libération*, 29 September 1991, 3.

90. Colette Braeckman, "Politique africaine: nuances entre Paris et Bruxelles," *Le Soir*, 26 September 1991, 6.

91. "Chronologie des événements," *Vox*, 19 November 1991, back cover.

92. Didier Grogna, "Les industriels belges au Zaïre se sentent seuls," *L'Echo de la Bourse*, 29 October 1991, 4.

93. "Premier retrait des paras," *Le Soir*, 4 October 1991, 3.

94. United States Congress, Senate, Testimony for Assistant Secretary of State for African Affairs, Herman J. Cohen, Hearing before the Foreign Relations Subcommittee on Africa (6 November 1991).

95. Stephen Smith, "Le président français sous pression," *Libération*, 29 October 1991, 18.

96. Julian Ozanne, "France sends troops to Zaire after army mutiny," *The Financial Times*, 30-31 January 1993, 1.

97. Eric de Bellefroid, "Les paras en attente sur l'autre rive," *La Libre Belgique*, 1 February 1993, 2.

98. Eric de Bellefroid, "Les paras belges de retour au Zaïre," *La Libre Belgique*, 30-31 January 1993, 1.

99. Eric de Bellefroid, "Les paras en attente sur l'autre rive."

100. "Zairian Asks West to Send Troops to Force Mobutu Out," *The Washington Post*, 5 February 1993, A30.

101. Colette Braeckman, "Nos paras étaient prêts pour Kin," *Le Soir*, 6-7 February 1993, 7.

102. "Quelles sanctions contre Mobutu?" *Le Soir*, 17 February 1993, 1.

103. Gérald Papy, "Mobutu veut chasser les Belges du Zaïre," *Le Soir*, 1 February 1993, 1.

104. Colette Braeckman, "Les Nations unies saisies du dossier Zaïre," *Le Soir*, 24-25 April 1993, 6.

105. "Plus de 350 soldats belges au Rwanda," *La Libre Belgique*, 12 November 1993, 4.

106. "Le FPR escorté vers Kigali," *Le Soir*, 29 December 1993, 6.

107. "La Politique Africaine de la Belgique," Annex No. 1.

Chapter 13

1. Edward N. Luttwak, *The Grand Strategy of the Roman Empire* (Baltimore: Johns Hopkins University Press, 1976), 5.

2. Stephen D. Krasner, *International Regimes* (Ithaca: Cornell University Press, 1983), 2.

3. Donald J. Puchala and Raymond F. Hopkins, "International Regimes: Lessons from Inductive Analysis," in Krasner, 69.

4. D.K. Fieldhouse, *The Colonial Empires* (London: Weidenfeld and Nicolson, 1966), 393.

5. Chester A. Crocker, "Military Dependence: the Colonial Legacy in Africa," *The Journal of Modern African Studies*, 12, 2, 1974, 268.

6. Pascal Bruckner, "Point de vue," *France Magazine*, Fall 1991, 8.

7. John Chipman, "French Military Policy and African Security," *Adelphi Papers*, No. 201, Summer 1985, 1-2.

8. Richard Joseph, *Gaullist Africa: Cameroon under Ahmadu Ahidjo* (New York: Fourth Dimension Publishers, 1978), 5.

9. Don Cook, "French Are Staying the Course in Africa," *International Herald Tribune*, 24 August 1983.

10. Chipman, 1-2.

11. A.F. Mullins, Jr., *Born Arming: Development and Military Power in New States* (Stanford CA: Stanford University Press, 1987), 29.

12. Tshiyembe Mwayila, "Théorie et pratique de la stratégie Est-Ouest en Afrique," *Le Mois en Afrique*, June-July 1986, 7.

13. Quoted by Jacques Attali, *Verbatim I, 1981-1986* (Paris: Fayard, 1993), 329.

14. James Mayall, "Britain, Africa and International Order," in *Africa and the Great Powers in the 1980s*, ed. by Olajide Aluko (Lanham, MD: University Press of America, 1987), 99.

15. Ibid., 108.

16. Ibid., 118.

17. Nicholas Mansergh, *The Commonwealth Experience* (London: Weidenfeld and Nicolson, 1969), 401-2.

18. Crocker, 284.

19. A French journalist reported during the crisis: "It would be hardly an exaggeration to say that the real 'strong man' of Zaire, today, is Henri Rethore, French ambassador in Kinshasa! It is he who is in communication with Mobutu, on board of his yacht, and urges him to make 'a credible political move' to defuse the crisis." Pierre Haski, *L'Evénement*, 29 September, 1991

20. Mayall, 100.

21. Donald George Morrison, et al, *Black Africa: A Comparative Handbook*, 2nd Edition, Macmillan Press Ltd., 1989, 243-4.

22. World Bank, *The World Bank Atlas*, World Bank, Washington, D.C., 1990, 6-7.

23. "Democracy in Africa: A lull in the wind," *The Economist*, 4 September 1993, 69.

24. Jean-Louis Triaud, "Le mouvement de démocratisation en Afrique," *Relations internationales et stratégiques*, Winter 1991, 88.

25. B. Haas, "Words can hurt you," in Krasner, 27-8.

26. Krasner, 5.

27. Two examples, from the American and French press, are illustrative. David Brooks, "A Kinder, Gentler Colonialism," *The Wall Street Journal*, 15 January 1993, A10; and François Soudan, "L'Afrique recolonisée... faute de mieux," *Jeune Afrique*, 10-16 December 1992, 16-8.

Selected Bibliography

Alexander, Major General H.T. *African Tightrope: My Two Years as Nkrumah's Chief of Staff*. London: Pall Mall Press, 1966.

Allen, Charles D., Jr. *The Uses of Navies in Peacetime*. Washington, D.C.: American Enterprise Institute for Public Policy Research, 1980.

Aluko, Olajide, ed. *Africa and the Great Powers in the 1980s*. Lanham, MD: University Press of America, 1987.

Arlinghaus, Bruce E. *Military Development in Africa: The Political and Economic Risks of Arms Transfers*. Boulder, CO: Westview Press, 1984.

Attali, Jacques. *Verbatim I, 1981-1986*. Paris: Fayard, 1993.

Bayart, Jean-François. *La politique africaine de François Mitterrand*. Paris: Karthala, 1984.

Baynham, Simon. *The Military Politics in Nkrumah's Ghana*. Boulder, CO: Westview Press, 1988.

_____. ed. *Military Power and Politics in Black Africa*. New York: St. Martin's Press, 1986.

Benchenene, Mustapha. *Les Armées Africaines*. Paris: Publisud, 1983.

_____. *Les coups d'état en Afrique*. Paris: Publisud, 1983.

Bender, Gerald J., James S. Coleman and Richard L. Skylar, eds. *African Crisis Areas and U.S. Foreign Policy*. Los Angeles: University of California Press, 1985.

Biarnes, Pierre. *L'Afrique aux Africains: 20 Ans d'Indépendance en Afrique Noire Francophone*. Paris: Armand Colin, 1980.

Biteghe, Moïse N'Solé. *Échec aux Militaires au Gabon*. Paris: Chaka, 1990.

Block, Jonathan and Patrick Fitzgerald. *British Intelligence and Covert Action: Africa, Middle East & Europe*. Dublin: Brandon, 1983.

Bonds, Ray, ed. *Combat Arms - Modern Carriers*. New York: Prentice Hall Press, 1988.

Boucheron, M. Jean-Michel. *Rapport fait au nom de la Commission de la Défense Nationale et des Forces Armées (1) sur le projet de loi de Programmation (n° 733) relatif à l'équipement militaire pour les années 1990-1993*. Assemblée Nationale, no. 897, Neuvième Legislature, Première session ordinaire, 2 October 1989.

Brabant, Serge. *Aspects politiques et diplomatiques de l'intervention de Kolwezi en 1978: Realite - Information*. Travail de fin d'études (diss.) 120e Promotion. Belgium, École Royale Militaire, 1983-4.

Braeckman, Colette. *Le dinosaure*. Paris: Fayard, 1992.

Brassinne, J. *Douze Années de Coopération Technique Militaire Belgo-Zaïroise*. Brussels: Centre de Recherche et d'Information Socio-Politiques, 1972.

Center for Strategic and International Studies (CSIS). *U.S.-Allied Cooperation in Security Assistance to Sub-saharan Africa*. Washington, D.C.: CSIS, 27 February 1991.

Centre des Hautes Etudes sur l'Afrique et l'Asie Modernes (CHEAM). *France Océan Indien Mer Rouge*. Paris: Fondation Pour les Études de Défense Nationale, 1986.

Centre de Recherche et d'Information Socio-Politiques (CRISP). *Congo 1959: Documents belges et africains*. 2d ed. Brussels: Centre de Recherche et d'Information Socio-Politique, 1961.

_____. *Congo 1964: Political Documents of a Developing Nation*. Princeton, NJ: Princeton University Press, 1966 and 1967.

Chaigneau, Pascal. *La politique militaire de la France*. Paris: Publications du CHEAM, 1984.

Chant, Christopher. *Warfare of the 20th Century: Armed Conflicts Outside of the Two World Wars*. Secaucus, NJ: Chartwell Books, Inc., 1988.

Chapman, Keith, ed. *Military Air Transport Operations*. Vol 6, *Brassey's Air Power: Aircraft, Weapons Systems & Technology Series*. London: Brassey's Defense Publishers Ltd, 1989.

Charters, David, and Maurice Tugwell, eds. *Armies in Low-Intensity Conflict: A Comparative Analysis*. London: Brassey's, 1989.

Chipman, John. *French Power in Africa*. Cambridge, MA: Basil Blackwell, 1989.

_____. *La Ve République et Défense de l'Afrique*. Paris: Bosquet, 1986.

Clayton, Anthony. "Foreign Intervention in Africa." Chap. in *Military Power and Politics in Black Africa*, ed. Simon Baynham. New York: St. Martin's Press, 1986.

Clementson, J, Squadron Leader, MA. "Diego Garcia" *RUSI Journal* 126, no. 2 (June 1981).

Coker, Christopher. *NATO, The Warsaw Pact and Africa*. New York: St. Martin's Press, 1985.

Coolsaet, Rik. *Histoire de la politique étrangère belge*. Brussels: Vie Ouvrière, 1988.

Copans, Jean, ed. *Le Tchad, Politique Africaine*. 16 Paris: Karthala, December 1984.

Cormevin, Robert. *Histoire du Zaïre: des origines à nos jours*, 4th ed. Brussels: Hayez, 1989.

Cot, Jean Pierre. *A l'épreuve du pouvoir: le tiers-mondisme, pour quoi faire?* Paris: Seuil, 1984.

Coutau-Bégarie, Hervé. *Le Problème du Porte-Avions*. Paris: Economica & CREST/École Polytechnique, 1990.

De Donnea, François-Xavier. *Défense 2000*. Brussels: New Fashion Media S.A., 1988.

De Masi, Paula and Lorie, Henri. "How Resilient Are Military Expenditures," in *IMF Staff Papers*. Washington, D.C. International Monetary Fund, 1988, Nr. 36.

De Raeymaeker, Omer. *Belgisch Buitenlands Beleid en Internationale Betrekkingen*. Leuven, Belgium: Leuven University Press, 1978.

Decalo, Samuel. *Coups and Army Rule in Africa: Studies in Military Style*. 1st ed. New Haven, CT: Yale University Press, 1976.

_____. *Coups and Army Rule in Africa: Studies in Military Style*. 2d ed. New Haven, CT: Yale University Press, 1990.

Deeb, Mary-Jane. *Libya's Foreign Policy in North Africa*. Boulder, CO: Westview Press, 1991.

Deng, Francis M. and I. William Zartman, eds. *Conflict Resolution in Africa*. Washington, D.C.: Brookings Institute, 1991.

Dia, Mamadou. *Mémoires d'un militant du tiers-monde*. Paris: Publisud, 1985.

Dodd, Norman L. "The Simonstown Agreement and the Cape Sea Route." *RUSI Journal* 120, no. 3 (September 1975).

Dunn, Lewis A. and James S. Tomashoff. *New Technologies and the Changing Dimensions of Third World Military Conflict* Vol. 2, no. 1. McLean, VA: Center for National Security Negotiations, 1990.

French, David. *The British Way in Warfare 1688-2000*. Boston: Unwin Hyman, 1990.

Galle, Hubert and Yannis Thanassekos. *Le Congo: de la découverte à l'indépendence*. Brussels: JM Collet, 1983.

Gerard-Libois, Jules and Jean Heinen. *Belgique Congo 1960*. Brussels: Massoz-CRISP, 1989.

Griffiths, Ieuan L.L. *An Atlas of African Affairs*. New York: Methuen & Co., 1985.

GRIP Informations, ed. *Congo-Zaïre: la colonization, l'indépendance, le régime Mobutu et demain?* Brussels: Group de Recherche et d'Information sur la Paix, 1989.

_____. *L'Europe des Armes, Trafics et Exportations vers le Tiers Monde*. Brussels: Group de Recherche et d'Information sur la Paix, 1989.

Grundy, Kenneth W. *Guerilla Struggle in Africa: An Analysis and Preview*. New York: Grossman Publisher, 1971.

Guisnel, Jean and Bernard Violet. *Services Secrets: le pouvoir et les services de renseignements sous François Mitterrand*. Paris: La Découverte, 1988.

Heathcote, Brigadier G.S., C.B.E. *Aden - A Reason Why*. London: Royal United Service Institute series CXII, no. 650, May 1968.

Hewitt, Daniel P. *Military Expenditure: International Comparison of Trends*, IMF Working Paper. Washington, D.C.: International Monetary Fund, May 1991.

Horne, Alistar. *Harold Macmillian Vol II: 1957-1986*. New York: Viking Press, 1989.

Howard, Michael. *The Causes of Wars and Other Essays*. Cambridge, MA: Harvard University Press, 1983.

Institut Africain d'Etudes Stratégiques. *Les Armées Africaines*. Paris: Economica, 1986.

_____. *La France et le Monde*. Paris: Economica, 1986.

Institut Royal des Relations Internationales. "Stanleyville: Août-Novembre 1964." *Chronique de Politique Etrangère* 18, no. 5-6 (September-November 1965).

Jaster, Robert S. *A Regional Security Role for Africa's Front Line States: Experience and Prospects.* Adelphi Papers, no. 180. London: International Institute for Strategic Studies, Spring 1983.

_____. *South Africa and its Neighbors: The Dynamics of Regional Conflict.* Adelphi Papers, no. 209. London: International Institute for Strategic Studies, Summer 1986.

Joseph, Richard, ed. *Gaullist Africa: Cameroon under Ahmadu Ahidjo.* Enugu, Nigeria: Fourth Dimension Publishers, 1978.

Kaké, Ibrahima Baba, ed. *Conflit Belgo-Zaïrois.* Paris: Présence Africaine, 1990.

Kennedy, Paul M. *The Rise and Fall of British Naval Mastery.* Atlantic Highlands, NJ: The Ashfield Press, 1989.

Ki-Zerbo, Joseph. *Histoire de l'Afrique Noire.* Paris: Hatier, 1978.

Kolodziej, Edward A. *Making and Marketing Arms: The French Experience and its Implications for the International System.* Princeton, NJ: Princeton University Press, 1987.

Krasner, Stephen D. *International Regimes.* Ithaca and London: Cornell University Press, 1983.

Labrousse. *Le Golfe et le Canal.* Paris: Presses Universitaires de France, 1973.

Laidi, Zaki. *The Superpowers and Africa: The Constraints of a Rivalry 1960-1990.* Chicago: University of Chicago Press, 1990.

Lapping, Brian. *End of Empire.* New York: St. Martin's Press, 1985.

Lavroff, D.G. *La Politique Africaine du Général de Gaulle 1958-1969.* Paris: A. Pedone, 1979.

Lebscqz, Albert. *Le Septennat.* Paris: France-Empire, 1980.

Le Bailly, C.B., O.B.E., Rear Admiral L.E.S.H. "The Role of Britain as a Sea Power." *RUSI Journal* CXIV, no. 654 (June 1969).

Lemarchand, René. *African Crisis Areas - The Crisis in Chad.* Los Angeles, CA: UCLA, 1985.

Luttwak, Edward N. *Coup d'État: A Practical Handbook.* Cambridge, MA: Harvard University Press, 1968.

_____. *The Political Uses of Sea Power - Studies in International Affairs.* no. 23, Washington Center of Foreign Policy Research. Baltimore: Johns Hopkins University Press, 1974.

Maluwa, Tiyanja. "The Peaceful Settlement of Disputes Among African States, 1963-1983: Some Conceptual Issues and Practical Trends." *International And Comparative Law Quarterly* 38, No. 2 (April 1989).

Manning, Patrick. *Francophone Sub-Saharan Africa, 1880-1985.* Cambridge, MA: Cambridge University Press, 1988.

Mansergh, Nicholas. *The Commonwealth Experience.* London: Weidenfeld and Nicolson, 1969.

Martin, L.W. *British Defense Policy: The Long Recessional.* Adelphi Papers, no. 61. London: Institute for Strategic Studies, 1969.

McNamara, Francis Terry. *France in Black Africa.* Washington, D.C.: National Defense University Press, 1989.

McNamara, Robert S. The Post-Cold War World: Implications for Military Expenditure in the Developing Countries, in *Proceedings of the World Bank Annual Conference on Development Economics 1991.* Washington, D.C.: International Bank for Reconstruction and Development, 1992.

M'Bokolo, Elikia. *L'Afrique au XX Siècle: Le Continent Convoité.* Paris: Seuil, 1985.

Michel, Albin. *Mobutu: Dignité pour l'Afrique: Entretiens avec Jean-Louis Remilleux.* Paris: Editions Albin Michel S.A., 1989.

Miller, J.D.B. *Survey of Commonwealth Affairs: Problems of Expansion and Attrition 1953-69.* London: Oxford University Press, 1974.

Morrison, Donald George. *Black Africa: A Comparative Handbook.* 2d ed. New York: Irvington Publishers, 1989.

_____. *Understanding Black Africa: Data and Analysis of Social Change and Nation Building.* New York: Paragon House and Irvington Publishers, Inc., 1989.

Mullins, A.F. Jr. *Born Arming: Development and Military Power in New States.* Stanford, CA: Stanford University Press, 1987.

Newitt, Malyn. *The Comoro Islands: Struggle Against Dependency in the Indian Ocean.* Boulder, CO: Westview Press, 1984.

Newhouse, John. *De Gaulle and the Anglo-Saxons.* New York: The Viking Press, 1970.

Nwokedi, Emeka. "Sub-Regional Security and Nigerian Foreign Policy." *Journal of African Affairs* 84, no. 335. Oxford: Royal African Society, Oxford University Press, April 1985.

O'Brien, William V. *Guidelines for Limited War,* "Military Review," February 1979.

Ockrent, Christine. *Dans le Secret des Princes.* Paris: Stock, 1986.

O'Toole, Thomas. *The Central African Republic: The Continent's Hidden Heart.* Boulder, CO: Westview Press, 1986.

Paschall, Rod. *LIC 2010: Special Operations and Unconventional Warfare in the Next Century.* Washington, D.C.: Brassey's, 1990.

Péan, Pierre. *L'Homme de l'Ombre.* Paris: Fayard, 1990.

Pannant-Rea, Ruppert. *The African Burden.* New York: Priority Press Publishers, 1986.

Prouteau, Jean Pierre. *Rapport Patronal 1988.* Paris: France-Afrique, 1987.

Rice, Edward E. *Wars of the Third Kind: Conflict in Underdeveloped Countries.* Los Angeles, CA: University of California Press, 1988.

Riley, Stephen P. *The Democratic Transition in Africa: An End to the One-Party State?* London: Research Institute for the Study of Conflict and Terrorism, October 1991.

Rodney, Walter. *How Europe Underdeveloped Africa.* Washington, D.C.: Howard University Press, 1982.

Rouvez, Alain. *Demobilization and Reintegration of Military Personnel in Sub-Saharan Africa.* Study prepared for the World Bank, Washington, D.C., 11 September 1992.

Rubin, Barry. *Modern Dictators: Third World Coup Makers, Strongmen and Populist Tyrants.* New York, NY: McGraw-Hill, 1987.

Samuels, Michael A., ed. *Africa and the West.* Boulder, CO: Westview Press, 1980.

Schifres, Michael and Michel Sarazin. *L'Elysée de Mitterrand: secrets de la maison du Prince.* Paris: Alain Moreau, 1985.

Shaw, Timothy M. and Sola OJO, eds. *Africa and the International Political System.* New York, NY: University Press of America, 1982.

Somerville, Keith. *Foreign Military Intervention in Africa.* New York: St. Martin's Press, 1990.

Thomas, Gerry S. *Mercenary Troops in Modern Africa.* Boulder, CO: Westview Press, 1984.

Thompson, W. Scott. *Ghana's Foreign Policy: 1957-1966.* Princeton, NJ: Princeton University Press, 1969.

Trefon, Theodore. *French Policy Toward Zaire during the Giscard d'Estaing Presidency.* Brussels: CEDAF/ASDOC, May 1989.

Tshiyembe, Mwayila and Mayele BUKASA. *L'Afrique face à ses problèmes de sécurité et de défense.* Paris: Présence Africaine, 1989.

United Nations. *The Blue Helmets: A Review of United Nations Peace-keeping.* 2d ed. New York: United Nations Department of Public Information, 1990.

_____. *Disarmament: Programme of Training on Conflict Resolution, Crisis Prevention and Management and Confidence-building among African States, Workshop for Senior African Military & Civilian Officials.* New York: United Nations, 1991.

United Nations Institute for Disarmament Research. *Africa, Disarmament and Security: Proceedings of the Conference of African Research Institutes (Algiers, 24-25 March 1990).* New York: United Nations, 1991.

U.S. Weapons: The Low Intensity Threat is not Necessarily a Low-Technology Threat. Washington, D.C.: GAO, 1990. GAO/PEMD-90-13.

Vanderlinden, J., ed. *Du Congo au Zaïre: 1960-1980.* Brussels: Centre de Recherche et d'Information Socio-Politiques, 1980.

Vanderstraeten, Louis-François. *De la Force Publique à l'Armée Nationale Congolaise: Histoire d'une Mutinerie Juillet 1960.* Brussels: Palais des Académies, 1985.

Vanderwalle, Colonel Frédéric. *L'Ommegang: Odyssée et Reconquête de Stanleyville 1964.* Brussels: Collection Témoignage Africain, 1970.

Viaud, Pierre and Jacques De Lestapis. *Afrique: Les Souverainetés en Armes.* Paris: Fondation pour les Études de Défense Nationale, 1987.

Walker, Air Vice Marshal J.R. *Air-to-Ground Operations.* Vol. 2, *Brassey's Air Power: Aircraft, Weapons Systems and Technology Series.* London: Brassey's Defence Publishers Ltd, 1987.

Watt, D.C., "The Role of the Aircraft Carrier in Some Recent British Military Operations." *RUSI Journal* CXI, no. 642 (May 1966).

West, Robert L. West. *The Cost of Armaments: Africa 1970-1985*, Paper for Presentation at the Conference of the Project on International Security in Africa, Tangier, Morocco, 2-7 July 1989.

_____. *Problems of Third World National Security Expenditures*, Paper prepared for presentation at the United States Institute of Peace Conference on Conflict Resolution in the Post-Cold War Third World, Washington, D.C., October 3-5, 1990.

Wilson, Harold. *Harold Wilson, A Personal Record: The Labour Government 1964-70*. Boston: Little Brown & Company, 1971.

Wright, John. *Libya, Chad and the Central Sahara*. Totowa, NJ: Barnes and Noble Books, 1989.

Yakemtchouk, Romain. "Les Deux Guerres Du Shaba." *Studia Diplomatica* 41, no. 4-6. Brussels: Institut Royal des Relations Internationales, 1988.

Yost, David S. *French Policy in Chad and the Libyan Challenge*. Orbis. Winter 1983.

Zartman, I. William. *Ripe for Resolution: Conflict and Intervention in Africa*. updated ed. New York: Oxford University Press, 1989.

Index

About the Author

Alain Rouvez is a consultant for the World Bank on issues of military demobilization in sub-Saharan Africa and for the European Union on defense conversion in the former Soviet Union. He was previously Executive Director of U.S.-CREST, a research center in the Washington, D.C. area which deals primarily with security issues affecting NATO allies. He has also worked in West Africa for the United Nations High Commissioner for Refugees.

He holds graduate degrees from Georgetown University in Washington, D.C. and the *Université Catholique de Louvain* in Belgium. He has also studied at the Moscow State University in Russia.

About the Assistants

Michael Coco holds a Master's Degree in International Affairs from Columbia University and a Bachelor's Degree from Georgetown University. Since graduating, he has been a researcher at U.S.-CREST while preparing this book.

Jean-Paul Paddack works for the U.S. Agency for International Development in Madagascar. He holds a Master's Degree from the School of Advanced International Studies/Johns Hopkins University and a Bachelor's Degree from Georgetown University.